PRECIOUS
IN HIS SIGHT

Books by Roy B. Zuck

A Biblical Theology of the New Testament (editor)
A Biblical Theology of the Old Testament (editor)
Adult Education in the Church (coeditor)
Basic Bible Interpretation
Barb, Please Wake Up!
The Bib Sac Reader (coeditor)
The Bible Knowledge Commentary (coeditor)
Biblical Archaeology Leader's Guide
Childhood Education in the Church (coeditor)
Christian Youth: An In-Depth Survey (coauthor)
Church History Leader's Guide
Creation: Evidence from Scripture and Science
Communism and Christianity Leader's Guide
Devotions for Kindred Spirits (editor)
How to Be a Youth Sponsor
Integrity of Heart, Skillfulness of Hands: Biblical and Leadership Studies in Honor of Donald K. Campbell (coeditor)
Job
Learning from the Sages: Selected Studies on the Book of Proverbs (editor)
Precious in His Sight
Readings in Biblical Hermeneutics (editor)
Reflecting with Solomon: Selected Studies on the Book of Ecclesiastes (editor)
Sitting with Job: Selected Studies on the Book of Job (editor)
Teaching as Jesus Taught
Teaching with Spiritual Power
The Life of Christ Commentary (coeditor)
Vital Apologetic Issues (editor)
Vital Biblical Issues (editor)
Vital Contemporary Issues (editor)
Vital Ministry Issues (editor)
Vital New Testament Issues (editor)
Vital Old Testament Issues (editor)
Vital Prophetic Issues (editor)
Vital Theological Issues (editor)
Youth and the Church (coeditor)
Youth Education in the Church (coeditor)

PRECIOUS IN HIS SIGHT

CHILDHOOD AND CHILDREN IN THE BIBLE

ROY B. ZUCK

Baker Books

A Division of Baker Book House Co
Grand Rapids, Michigan 49516

Published by Baker Books
a division of Baker Book House Company
PO Box 6287, Grand Rapids, MI 49516–6287

Printed in the United States of America

Library of Congress Catalogin-in-Publication Data

Zuck, Roy B.
    Precious in His sight : childhood and children in the Bible / Roy B. Zuck.
      p. cm.
    Includes bibliographical references.
    ISBN 0-8010-5715-9 (pbk.)
    1. Children in the Bible. 2. Children—Biblical teaching. 3. Children in the Bible—Biography. 4. Child rearing—Religious aspects—Christianity. 5. Parent and child—Religious aspects—Christianity. I. Title.
    BS576.Z83 1996
    220.8′30523—dc20   96-25788

For information about academic books, resources for Christian leaders, and all new releases available from Baker Book House, visit our web site:
http://www.bakerbooks.com/

Dedicated affectionately to my grandchildren
    Jason,
    Jennifer, and
    Allison,
    children of our daughter Barb Hanes and her husband Greg

    and
    Audrey,
    Ethan, and
    Alden,
    children of our son Ken and his wife Kim

with the prayer that each of them
will love and serve the Lord Jesus
with all their hearts all their lives.

    Grandpa

CONTENTS

LIST OF TABLES

1

"LET THE CHILDREN COME TO ME"

The Challenge of Children

"Children are a nuisance! I don't like to be around children because they are so demanding and annoying."

Do you react toward children this way? Do any of the following comments reflect your thinking?

"My wife and I don't plan to have children. We can't be tied down to parenting, which demands such time, energy, attention, and money."

"Kids are so boisterous and unruly. I could never teach a Sunday school class of children."

"I'm pregnant, but I don't want a baby. So I'll simply get an abortion."

"How can I have time for child-rearing when my career demands so much time?"

"Changing diapers, getting up in the night with a sick child, helping kids with homework are not for me. I'd rather be child-free."

"As a pastor, I leave children's work to women in the church because I don't have time for ministering to kids. What's more, children can't contribute money or leadership to the church."

Or do the following statements more closely reveal your opinions of childhood?

"Children are so much fun! They are full of life and energy, and are so eager to learn new things."

"I enjoy the way children respond so readily to love and attention."

"Raising kids is one of the greatest rewards in all of life."

"It's a delight to teach children. They are so open to spiritual truths."

"No thrill compares to leading children to Christ and watching them grow spiritually."

"As a pastor, I view children as an important segment of our church. We need to reach children in their formative years, helping offset the formidable pull of anti-Christian forces in our society."

Centuries ago a group of twelve men showed their disdain toward children. Parents had brought their young offspring to Jesus for him to place his hands on them and pray for them, but his disciples told the parents not to bring them to Jesus. The Twelve even "rebuked" those parents, a word meaning to reprove or censure in order to prevent an action.

Jesus' disciples may have thought that his praying for children was insignificant compared with his other important ministries such as teaching and healing, or that he was too busy or tired to be bothered with anyone other than adults. Or they may have supposed children were too young to benefit from his attention.

Their attitude contrasts sharply, however, with Jesus' approach to children. Rather than agreeing with the disciples and refusing to see the children, he was indignant with the disciples for their actions. Besides encouraging the children to come to him, he used them as an illustration of the childlike trust and ready acceptance of him required of anyone who desires salvation. Then Jesus revealed his love and affection for those children by taking them in his arms, placing his hands on them, and blessing them (Matt. 19:13–15; Mark 10:13–16; Luke 18:15–17).

On another occasion the Lord asked a little child to stand beside him and then he took him in his arms so he could point out two important truths to the disciples. First, they needed humility like that of a child; second, giving attention to children equals serving him (Matt. 18:1–5; Mark 9:33–37; Luke 9:46–48).

Jesus' deep interest in the young is also seen in his healing three sick children (two boys and a girl) and in bringing two children, a boy and a girl, back from death to life. The sick were an official's son (John 4:43–53), a Syrophoenician woman's demon-possessed daughter (Matt. 15:21–28; Mark 7:24–30), and an epileptic, demon-possessed boy (Matt. 17:14–21; Mark 9:14–29; Luke 9:37–43a). The two who were raised to life were the son of a widow of Nain (Luke 7:11–17) and Jairus's twelve-year-old daughter (Matt. 9:18–26; Mark 5:22–43; Luke 8:41–56).

Clearly Jesus did not neglect or despise children. He loved them, enjoyed being with them, ministered to them, and even used them to teach spiritual lessons to adults.

Parents, teachers, church leaders, and others who fail to focus adequately on children stand in opposition to Jesus' valuation of the young. On the other hand, those who give attention to children and their needs are following the example set by Jesus himself!

Several factors underscore the need to heed Jesus' interest in children. The following pages in this chapter and chapter 2 discuss six such elements.

1. The sizable number of biblical references to children
2. The striking physical and emotional needs of children
3. The significant impact of childhood years on adult life
4. The spiritual openness of children
5. The salient theological issues pertaining to children
6. The societal pressures on children

The Sizable Number of Biblical References to Children

We normally think of the Bible as a book about adults and for adults—and it is. However, the Bible includes hundreds, even thousands, of references to children and related subjects such as conception, childbirth, families, and descendants.

The frequency with which many family-related terms are used suggests the importance God places on children. In the New International Version the word "child" occurs 121 times, "children" occurs 448 times, and "childhood" 4 times. Not surprisingly "son" or "sons" occurs more than 2,700 times (not counting more than 200 references to Jesus as the Son of God). "Baby," "babies," "infant(s)," and "infancy" are found 24 times, and "firstborn" occurs over 100 times (excluding 6 references to Jesus Christ as the "Firstborn" and other references to the firstborn of animals).

Terms referring to infertility, pregnancy, and birth occur over 500 times. "Father(s)," is used more than 1,200 times (excluding 273 references to God as Father), and "mother(s)" almost 400 times.

To these terms may be added words for immediate and extended family members, including "brother(s)," "sister(s)," "mother-in-law," "grandfather(s)," "grandmother(s)," "grandparents," "grandchildren," "grandson(s)," "granddaughter(s)," "aunt(s)," "uncle(s)," "forefather(s)," and more general terms such as "home(s)," "family," "families," "offspring," "household(s)," "generation(s)," and "descendant(s)." These occurrences total more than 2,300. "Boy(s)" and "girl(s)" add another 196 occurrences, and "young," "younger," "youngest," and "youth" add 401 more. All together these child- and family-related words occur more than 8,000 times! Is there any doubt the Bible is family-centered and child-focused?

In addition, Bible narratives include the stories of dozens of children. Some were obedient to their parents, others were disobedient. Some were respectful, others were rebellious. Some, like Samuel, served the Lord faithfully. Others, like Samson, who had great promise, became adults who sinned against the Lord. Some had few or no siblings; others were born into large families. Some Bible children were born to wealthy parents such as Ishmael and Isaac, sons of Abraham. Others, such as the widow's son whom Elijah raised to life, lived in poverty. Some had godly parents, some had ungodly fathers and mothers, and some, like Timothy, were born in a home where one parent was a believer and the other was not. Some children were given unlikely names like Ichabod ("There is no glory"). Others received desirable names like Solomon, meaning "Peace," who was also named Jedidiah, meaning "Beloved of the Lord." Some children were born with physical ailments. Some children were murdered; others died of illnesses or from natural catastrophes. Some individuals were spared death in childhood by divine intervention such as Moses, Isaac, Joseph, the Israelites' firstborn in Egypt, Daniel's three friends, and Jesus.

"Miracle babies," those born to women previously barren, include Isaac, Jacob, Esau, Joseph, Samson, Samuel, and John the Baptist. And the most miraculous birth of all was that of Jesus, born to the Virgin Mary.

Of course, every adult began as a child, except Adam and Eve. But the Bible mentions the childhood of only a select number of those individuals. These include the following:

Cain
Abel
Isaac
Esau
Jacob
Jacob's twelve sons, including Joseph and Benjamin
Job's three named daughters: Jemimah, Keziah, and Keren-Happuch
Moses
Miriam
Jephthah's daughter
Samson
Samuel
Ichabod
Jonathan
A small boy with Jonathan
David
A son of David and Bathsheba
Absalom
Mephibosheth
Solomon
Son of the Zarephath widow
Son of the Shunamite woman

Naaman's servant girl
King Joash
King Manasseh
King Josiah
Isaiah's two sons, Shear-Jashub and Maher-Shalal-Hash-Baz
Daniel
Shadrach
Meshach
Abednego
Gomer's three children: Jezreel, Lo-Ruhamah, and Lo-Ammi
John the Baptist
Jesus
An official's son
A boy who gave food to Jesus for the five thousand
A Syrophoenician woman's daughter
An epileptic, demon-possessed boy
The son of the Nain widow
Jairus's daughter
A child whom Jesus took in His arms to teach the disciples
Rhoda, a servant girl
Timothy

Dozens more individuals are named in the Bible's genealogies, though not much more is said about most of them in narratives.

Groups of unnamed children include Job's first ten children, his second group of seven sons, the forty-two boys who jeered at Elisha, the children with the five thousand men who were fed by Jesus, the children with the four thousand men who were fed by Jesus, the children brought to Jesus for him to bless, children who shouted "Hosanna" to Jesus, and the children of the Philippian jailer.

Another aspect of the pervasive nature of Bible references to children is the almost numberless admonitions to parents to raise their children, the many admonitions of parents to their sons and daughters on how to live uprightly, and the admonitions to children on their relationships to their parents and others. The Book of Proverbs alone includes hundreds of instructions and exhortations by the writers to "my son(s)" on wise living. (The Bible's many God-given instructions to parents and to children are discussed in chapters 7, 8, 10.)

Truly the Bible is a book about children!

The Striking Physical and Emotional Needs of Children

A second reason for giving priority to children in our homes and churches is that children have many needs—needs that can be met only by adults.

At birth, human babies are more helpless than any other living creatures. Infants cannot feed or change themselves. They cannot bathe themselves. They cannot even lift up their heads or roll over in bed. It is months before they can sit up, crawl, stand, and then walk. And more than a year passes by before they can express themselves in sentences to make known their needs. When they hurt or are hungry or are uncomfortable, all they can do is cry.

Some infants born prematurely or with physical or other disabilities face a fierce battle for life right from the start. Only adults can help them in these battles.

Some are born into homes of poverty or to mothers whose husbands have deserted them. These environments give these children a less-than-desirable start in life. As preschoolers grow, they have much learning to do, learning that can be enhanced by wise adults. They learn to say the alphabet, to be toilet-trained, to color, to print, to ride a tricycle, to swim, to sense the consequences of obedience and disobedience. All these learning tasks require adult assistance and guidance. School-age children also need adult help in learning to read, write, do arithmetic, draw, ride a bicycle, skate, and get along with others.

The dependent, helpless nature of children is seen in their fears. Young children fear the dark, strangers, fierce animals, thunder, and mean people. Other fears include parents leaving them alone, parents dying, getting lost, dying, burglars, being rejected, being bullied, new environments, being abused, hospitals, and failure.[1] Caring adults are needed to help youngsters overcome these fears.

Emotional trauma is experienced by children whose parents divorce,[2] whose parents argue and physically abuse each other, and whose parents mistreat, neglect, or abandon them. When single unwed mothers or married mothers are employed outside the home, those children often sense a "loss" of their mother. "Clinging, whining, and downright panic become very common in such children."[3] Other emotional concerns are felt by children when they face disabilities, surgery, a prolonged illness, or death.[4]

Being a child is not easy. In light of childhood needs, both physical and emotional, we would do well to direct more love and ministry to those who are, as the children's chorus puts it, "precious in his sight."

1. Robert Schachter and Carole Spearin McCauley discuss these and other childhood fears in their book, *When Your Child Is Afraid* (New York: Simon and Schuster, 1988).
2. See chapter 2 for discussions on the effect of divorce on children, and on child abuse and other problems our society has brought to children in recent years.
3. Gerald E. Nelson, *The One-Minute Scolding* (New York: Random House, 1984), 65.
4. For ways on how churches can minister to children facing these and other crises, see chapters 6 and 14 in Andrew D. Lester, ed., *When Children Suffer: A Sourcebook for Ministry with Children in Crisis* (Philadelphia: Westminster Press, 1987).

The Significant Impact of Childhood Years on Adult Life

Because an individual's early experiences profoundly influence his or her entire life, concern for children is critical. Children readily pick up and copy the attitudes, interests, values, beliefs, and actions of adults around them. And many of those perspectives stay with them throughout their lives. What children hear from and see in adults, what children notice in others, they begin to copy and appropriate in their own lives. And many of those actions and attitudes stay with them permanently.

Dorothy Law Nolte has stated this principle in her well-known assertions in "Children Learn What They Live."

If a child lives with criticism, he learns to condemn.
If a child lives with hostility, he learns to fight.
If a child lives with ridicule, he learns to be shy.
If a child lives with shame, he learns to feel guilty.
If a child lives with tolerance, he learns to be patient.
If a child lives with encouragement, he learns confidence.
If a child lives with praise, he learns to appreciate.
If a child lives with fairness, he learns justice.
If a child lives with security, he learns to have faith.
If a child lives with approval, he learns to like himself.
If a child lives with acceptance and friendship, he learns to find love in the world.[5]

Christian psychiatrist Paul Meier observes that studies by psychiatrists reveal that approximately 85 percent of an adult's personality "is already formed by the time the individual is six years old."[6] How a young child is trained in those early, formative years will largely determine how that individual will react the rest of his or her life!

The character and actions—whether good or bad, strong or weak, godly or ungodly—of teens and adults result not only from their present environment but also to a great extent from childhood experiences. One way, then, to impact adults for Christ is to influence boys and girls toward godly living.

The Spiritual Openness of Children

Another reason for esteeming children and for elevating our ministries to them is their responsiveness to spiritual realities. Many adults, however, ques-

5. Dorothy Law Nolte, "Children Learn What They Live" (Los Angeles: American Institute of Family Relations, n.d.).
6. Paul D. Meier and Linda Burnett, *The Unwanted Generation* (Grand Rapids: Baker Book House, 1980), 68.

tion this assertion, contending that youngsters are incapable of accepting Christ and comprehending spiritual truths. Because of their immaturity, it is argued, children cannot understand the gospel. These adults say, "Don't try to win a child to Christ; wait till he is older and is more capable of making an intelligent decision."[7]

But children can grasp the meaning of the gospel. As Coleman asks, "Is not a child that is old enough knowingly to sin also old enough savingly to believe?"[8] Children can sense the guilt of sin. They can comprehend the fact that Jesus died for them, and that by believing in him as their Savior, they can be saved and go to heaven when they die. Coleman quotes Charles Spurgeon as saying, "A child of five, if properly instructed, can as truly believe and be regenerated as any adult."[9]

Questions children ask about God and heaven reveal their spiritual interests.

"Why did people kill Jesus?"
"Does Jesus love me even when I'm bad?"
"What is heaven like?"
"Will my dog be in heaven?"
"Is my mommy with Jesus in heaven?"
"Is the devil real?"
"Why did God let me get so sick?"
"Will Jesus always give me what I ask for in prayer?"

Most young children readily believe God exists.[10] Not needing arguments to prove his existence, they readily approach him in prayer.

Samuel stands as an impressive example of a young boy sensitive to the Lord (1 Sam. 3:1–20) and who ministered to the Lord (2:11; 3:1) at an early age. When Naaman's young captive servant girl encouraged him to go to Elisha for healing, she revealed her awareness of God and his servants (2 Kings 5:1–3).

Young King Joash was only seven years old when he was crowned king of Judah (2 Kings 11:21); yet he "did what was right in the eyes of the LORD" because of the spiritual instructions and guidance Jehoiada the priest gave him (12:2). Josiah began his reign at age eight, and like Joash, he too followed the Lord (22:1–2), and at age sixteen he began to "seek" God (2 Chron. 34:3). The commitment of the teenagers Joseph, David, Daniel, and Daniel's three friends, Shadrach, Meshach, and Abednego, to the Lord evidenced their upbringing by parents who taught them spiritual truths, no

7. Frank G. Coleman, *The Romance of Winning Children* (Cleveland: Union Gospel Press, 1967), 9–10.
8. Ibid., 10.
9. Ibid.
10. Donald M. Joy, "Why Teach Children?" in *Childhood Education in the Church*, ed. Robert E. Clark, Joanne Brubaker, and Roy B. Zuck, rev. ed. (Chicago: Moody Press, 1986), 12.

doubt at an early age. This was consistent with God's repeated commands to Israelite parents to instruct their children in the ways of God (e.g., Deut. 4:9–10; 6:4–9; 11:18–21; 31:12–13; 32:46). If children were not able to understand and respond to divine truths, why would God have given these commands to parents?

David wrote of his childhood ability to comprehend something of the things of God: "You made me trust in you even at my mother's breast. . . from my mother's womb you have been my God" (Ps. 22:9–10). Though writing with hyperboles, David was emphasizing that he trusted the Lord from an early age. An anonymous psalmist wrote along similar lines: "You have been my hope, O Sovereign LORD, my confidence since my youth. From birth I have relied on you [again, a hyperbole]. . . . Since my youth, O God, you have taught me" (Ps. 71:5–6, 17).

Jesus underscored the ability of children to comprehend spiritual matters when he praised God the Father for revealing such truths to "little children" (Matt. 11:25). Children were capable of praising Jesus, as seen in their shouting in the temple area, "Hosanna to the Son of David" (21:15). Jesus explained that this was in keeping with David's words that God ordained that children and infants praise him (21:16; cf. Ps. 8:2).

Though no doubt an exception, John the Baptist was filled with the Holy Spirit even from birth (Luke 1:15). Timothy is a New Testament example of a young child who knows the Scriptures. In fact, he knew them, Paul wrote, "from infancy" (2 Tim. 3:15). And Paul himself exemplified Jewish piety in his childhood (Acts 26:4).

Several surveys demonstrate that childhood is a ripe time for conversion. Children are more likely to become Christians than are teenagers or adults. Statistics reveal that 75 percent of saved people trusted Christ before age fourteen.[11] Dobbins reported in 1953 that of approximately one thousand representative Sunday school teachers at a conference center, 50 percent of them indicated they received Christ between the ages of nine and twelve, and 30 percent between the ages of thirteen and sixteen, whereas not one had been saved after age fifty.[12] A century ago Starbuck wrote, "One may say that if conversion has not occurred before [age] 20, the chances are small that it will ever be experienced."[13]

11. Fred Kraft and Vicki Kraft, "Can Children Receive Christ?" *Moody Magazine,* September 1982, 143.

12. Gaines S. Dobbins, *Winning the Children* (Nashville: Broadman Press, 1953), 2. Admittedly not many teachers past age fifty may have been attending that conference. Still this points up the receptivity of children to the gospel, and Dobbins reports that almost identical findings were noted at three such conferences of about one thousand attendees each.

13. Edwin Diller Starbuck, *The Psychology of Religion* (New York: Charles Scribner's Sons, 1899), 28.

Horatius Bonar, nineteenth-century Scottish preacher, asked 253 Christians at what ages they were converted. He found that 54 percent (138 out of 253) were saved before age twenty.[14]

Four decades ago a survey of five thousand Christian college students revealed that children ages eight through twelve from Christian homes and high school-age children from non-Christian homes respond more readily to the gospel than any other age groups.[15]

The fact that many Christian leaders throughout history were converted at an early age substantiates the value of leading children to Christ. Polycarp, saved at age nine, was martyred for Christ at age eighty-six. Count Zinzendorf, eighteenth-century Moravian founder of the modern missionary movement, came to Christ at age four. Matthew Henry was saved at age ten, Jonathan Edwards at age seven, Richard Baxter at six, and Charles Spurgeon at twelve.[16]

LeBar records a well-known incident in the ministry of evangelist D. L. Moody.

> Returning to his friend's home after conducting meetings in a town in England, D. L. Moody was asked by his host, "How many were converted tonight in the meeting?"
>
> "Two and a half," replied Moody.
>
> "What do you mean?" asked his friend. "Were there two adults and a child?"
>
> "No," said the evangelist, "it was two children and an adult. The children have given their lives to Christ in their youth, while the adult has come with half of his life."[17]

Emphasizing the same truth that children won to Christ have their entire lives before them in which to influence others for Christ, Gypsy Smith, evangelist, said, "Save a man and you save a unit; save a boy and you save a multiplication table."[18] Spurgeon commented on the same truth: "Capacity for believing lies more in the child than in the man. We grow less rather than more capable of faith: every year brings the unregenerate mind further away from God, and makes it less capable of receiving the things of God."[19]

14. Cited in Paul Lee Tan, *Encyclopedia of 7,700 Illustrations* (Rockville, Md.: Assurance Publishers, 1979), 1662.

15. J. Robertson McQuilkin, "Born of the Spirit," *Christian Life*, March 1954, 26.

16. Coleman, *The Romance of Winning Children*, 10. My own two children and three of my six grandchildren each received Christ at age four, and I was saved at age ten.

17. Lois E. LeBar, *Children in the Bible School* (Westwood, N.J.: Fleming H. Revell, 1962), 26–27.

18. Cited in ibid., 27.

19. Charles H. Spurgeon, *Come, Ye Children* (reprint, Warrenton, Mo.: Child Evangelism Fellowship, n.d.), 24–25.

Can little children come to Christ for salvation? Certainly! Does the Bible set an age limit when one may believe? Certainly not! For Jesus himself referred to "these little ones who believe in me" (Matt. 18:6). And these were young enough to be held in his arms (Mark 9:36). Because of Jesus' special concern for children, "child evangelism should remain a priority, especially in light of children's particular openness to the gospel."[20]

Why are children so equipped to respond to spiritual truths? One reason is their dependency and trust. As stated earlier, children are dependent on adults for many of their needs, and this makes them ready to trust others. Because of their built-in credulity, "children are capable of a childlike faith in the Lord Jesus Christ."[21] Another reason is their sensitivity to sin. "The heart of a child is exceedingly tender" and "is real to boys and girls of tender years."[22] Their tenderness makes many of them eager for forgiveness. Cavalletti's research with young children reveals their natural attraction to God[23] and what she calls the "spontaneous religiousness" in children.[24] A third reason is their loving nature. Sensing the love of Christ for them, they readily can respond in love to him. Two other characteristics are their insatiable curiosity[25] and their teachability.[26]

The spiritual openness of the young presents an imposing argument in support of children's ministries—a strong reason to value boys and girls as did the Savior.

The Salient Theological Issues Pertaining to Children

The idea of boys and girls becoming Christians and growing in Christ presents some intriguing theological questions. Are infants born with a sin nature? What is the so-called "age of accountability"? What should young children be taught before conversion? Will infants who die go to heaven? Should infant baptism be practiced? What can preschoolers and elementary school children know about God? Are children of Christian parents in a covenant relationship to God? Are childhood conversions genuine? Should children be confronted with the need for radical conversion, or should they be encouraged to grow up as Christians with no need for con-

20. Craig L. Blomberg, *Matthew,* New American Commentary (Nashville: Broadman Press, 1992), 295.
21. Perry G. Downs, "Child Evangelization," *Journal of Christian Education* 3 (1983): 11.
22. Ibid., 16.
23. Sofia Cavalletti, *The Religious Potential of the Child,* trans. Patricia M. Coulter and Julie M. Coulter (New York: Paulist Press, 1983), 30–46.
24. Ibid., 31.
25. Kraft and Kraft, "Can Children Receive Christ?" 143.
26. Robert E. Coleman and Lois Goff, "Winning the Children," *Asbury Seminarian* 26 (October 1972): 10.

version? Do children of believing parents differ in some way from children of unbelievers?[27]

Anyone concerned with theology—or with children—must interact with these issues. Without question, children's studies and theological studies intercept each other.

A sixth reason for valuing children as Jesus did is discussed in the next chapter. Incredible societal pressures on children in our culture call for the greatest possible diligence on behalf of today's boys and girls.

27. These questions are discussed in chapter 13.

2

"CHILDREN DOOMED TO MISFORTUNE"

Children Are in Trouble!

On several airline flights recently I have seen children escorted from the airplane by flight attendants. These children, usually of elementary school age, were being shuttled for weekend visits with their divorced parents. This common occurrence was unheard of a few years ago.

Television newscasts occasionally show a toddler who has been severely battered, scalded, or isolated by an angry adult who tried to make the child be quiet.

Radio broadcasts tell of teens—and even younger boys and girls—toting guns and knives to school.

Newspaper articles recount instances of child abuse in some day care centers. Magazine articles discuss the emotional trauma experienced by incest victims.

"Latchkey children," home alone after school before their parents (or parent) return from work, are babysat by hours of unmonitored television or they experiment with alcohol, drugs, or even sex.

A teenage girl gets pregnant, doesn't want the child, and so decides, without telling her parents, to end the pregnancy at an abortion clinic.

The societal problems bombarding our boys and girls manifest what William Bennett, former United States Secretary of Education, calls a major "shift in the public's beliefs, attitudes, and priorities,"[1] a "substantial social regression."[2]

---

1. William J. Bennett, *The Index of Leading Cultural Indicators* (Washington, D.C.: Heritage Foundation, 1993), 1:ii.
2. Ibid., i.

23

These forces of decline also include drug and alcohol abuse, violence on television and in movies, cohabitation without marriage, unmarried teenage mothers, teen gangs, runaway teens, homeless children, premarital sexual experimentation, childhood and teen crime, pedophiles, child pornography, child prostitution, children adopted by lesbian and gay couples, rock music on MTV, CDs, and audiotapes that encourage rebelling against authority, homosexuality, satanism, violence, self-focused pleasures, and even suicide. Without question, these many societal trends are having a pernicious, even devastating, influence on American families and children. These astonishing conditions prevail throughout our nation to an almost immeasurable and seemingly irreversible degree.

This chapter presents information from a variety of sources in support of the contention that many of our children are indeed in serious trouble morally and spiritually. These facts are troubling, for as former president Ronald Reagan remarked, "There is no more fundamental test of a society than how it treats its children."[3]

In early 1994 the world's population reached over 5.6 billion, with one-third of the population being children fourteen years of age or under, for a total of 1.87 billion.[4]

The U.S. population as of April 1994 included 57.4 million children fourteen years of age or under, more than one-fifth (22%) of the total population of 261 million.[5]

What do we know about the home situations of these millions of children? The following facts point out the changing nature of America's homes.

- *Of the 68.1 million households in 1993, less than half (33 million) had children under age eighteen living in the home.[6]*
- *The percentage of children living with both parents has decreased from 85.2 percent in 1970 to 70.5 percent in 1993.[7]*
- *The number of households headed by females with no husband present has doubled from 1970 to 1993—from 5.5 million to 11.9 million.[8]*

3. Ronald Reagan, quoted in Katie de Koster, ed., *Child Abuse: Opposing Viewpoints* (San Diego: Greenhaven Press, 1994), 12.

4. U.S. Bureau of the Census, *Statistical Abstract of the United States 1994* (Washington, D.C.: U.S. Department of Commerce, 1994), 850, 853. Also see *1994 World Population Data Sheet* (Washington, D.C.: Population Reference Bureau, 1994).

5. *1994 World Population Data Sheet.*

6. *The World Almanac and Book of Facts 1995* (Mahwah, N.J.: Funk & Wagnalls, 1994), 960. The figures documented by footnotes 4–11 and 13–16 are from the Bureau of the Census of the United States Department of Commerce.

7. John W. Wright, ed., *The Universal Almanac 1995* (Kansas City, Mo.: Andrews and McNeel, 1994), 307.

8. Ibid., 306. Also see Donald J. Hernandez, *America's Children* (New York: Russell Sage Foundation, 1993), 65.

- *The number of children in those mother-only homes was 7.5 million in 1970 and 15.6 million in 1993—an increase from 10.8 percent of the children under eighteen to 23.3 percent.[9] Add to that the 2.2 million children living with only their father and the total is 17.8 million (26.7%) boys and girls living in 1993 with single parents, compared with 7.2 million (11.9%) in 1970.[10] This 1993 figure is more than one out of four of all the nation's children.*
- *The increase in single parenting is largely due to the increase in divorces. Another factor is that many women who carry their children to birth are not married. An estimated 2.3 million couples married in 1993, but 1.2 million couples divorced. Thus for every two marriages, one ended in divorce. But in 1970 the ratio was one divorce for every three marriages.[11] As a result of the rise in the divorce rate, "one in every three children experiences a divorce over the course of his or her childhood."[12]*
- *In 1993, 5 percent of the nation's children—3.4 million—were living with their grandparents. This is up from 3.2 percent, or 2.2 million, in 1970.[13]*
- *Remarriages of divorcees or widowed adults have resulted in a greater number of blended families, with 9.8 million children in these stepfamilies in 1991.[14]*
- *About 26 percent of the 4 million births in the nation in 1993 were out of wedlock, compared with 11 percent in 1970.[15] Approximately one million illegitimate births means an infant is born to an unmarried mother every thirty seconds—and almost half of those mothers are teenagers.[16]*

The following illustrates some of these changes.

Children Living with Birth Parents
1970 58.9 million
1993 47.1 million

Children Living with One Parent
1970 7.2 million
1993 17.8 million

Children Living with Grandparents
1970 2.2 million
1993 3.4 million

9. Wright, *The Universal Almanac 1995*, 306.
10. Ibid., 307.
11. Ibid., 301.
12. Thomas A. Nazario, *In Defense of Children* (New York: Scribner's Sons, 1988), 181.
13. *The World Almanac and Book of Facts 1995*, 962.
14. Ibid.
15. Wright, *The Universal Almanac 1995*, 306.
16. The U.S. birth total of 4.1 million babies in 1994 compares with 139 million for the entire world, which is nine babies born every two seconds (ibid., 354).

Children Living in Blended Families
1993 9.8 million

Babies Born Out of Wedlock
1970 0.4 million
1993 1.0 million

What accounts for these changes, this social downslide? I believe four factors are impacting our children adversely.

Rejection of Moral Absolutes

Children today are being raised in a culture that has rejected standards of morality. Dobson says the effort to manipulate and control the hearts and minds of children has resulted in "a great Civil War of Values."[17] Humanism champions the viewpoint that morality is relevant, that education should be "value free," that human beings, like animals, have no moral accountability and are thus free to embrace promiscuous sex, abortion, and self-focused pleasure without restraint or concern for others.

Sexual experimentation, acceptability of homosexuality as a legitimate lifestyle, distribution of pornographic literature to children, freedom to terminate marriages by divorce, rejection and even mocking of anything religious—these symptoms demonstrate the alarming deterioration of spiritual values and ethical ideals in our nation. Walker Perry calls this moral downturn a social "decay,"[18] Alexander Solzhenitsyn cites the problem as an "erosion,"[19] and Karen and Michael Maudlin, commenting on a recent report by the Council on Families in America, state that "divorce and family breakdown are killing our culture."[20]

Changes in Family Patterns

Abandon moral absolutes and one of the first institutions to be affected is the home—and children in it.

1. Working mothers. About half of all children have mothers employed outside the home.[21] Mothers of preschoolers who work outside the home rose from 12 percent in 1950 to 56 percent in 1990.[22] Working mothers of chil-

17. James Dobson and Gary Bauer, *Children at Risk* (Dallas, Tex.: Word Publishers, 1990), 19.
18. Cited by Bennett, *The Index of Leading Cultural Indicators,* 1:ii.
19. Ibid.
20. Karen L. Maudlin and Michael G. Maudlin, "The Fall and Rise of Marriage," *Christianity Today,* May 15, 1995, 14.
21. Vance Packard, *Our Endangered Children* (Boston: Little, Brown, 1983), 111.
22. Rita Kramer, *In Defense of the Family* (New York: Basic Books, 1983), 22.

dren under eighteen increased from 30 percent in the 1960s to an amazing 64 percent in 1987.[23]

Who is caring for these children? Many youngsters (3 million in 1991) are cared for by another relative whereas others (2.2 million in 1991) are placed in child-care centers.[24] School-age children left unsupervised at home after school, "latchkey children," are twice as likely to abuse drugs, engage in sexual intercourse, join gangs, or be involved in violent crime.[25]

2. *Divorce*. As noted earlier, divorces in America have increased at an alarming rate so that millions of children are the innocent victims of parental breakup. Less than 60 percent of all children today are living with their biological, married parents.[26]

Judith Wallerstein's fifteen-year study shows that divorce has a damaging psychological effect on many children, including the experiencing of anxieties, fears, anger, and guilt.[27] Young divorce victims experience denial, silence, regression, hostility, bodily stress, panic, confusion, blame, guilt, and depression.[28] Packard reports that though many children, being resilient, can take a lot of turmoil, for others the emotional disturbance of divorce can be distressing. He quotes John McDermott, chairman of the Department of Psychiatry at the University of Hawaii, who said, "Divorce is now the single largest cause of childhood depression."[29] What is more, children of divorced parents are more likely to divorce their future spouses.[30]

The first two years after a family breakup are often the most difficult for adults and children, with the children experiencing shock, anxiety, and anger. Though the extent of trauma varies greatly from child to child, boys seem to evidence more difficulties than girls.[31]

23. *The World Almanac and Book of Facts 1995*, 961.

24. Sar A. Levitan, Richard S. Belous, and Frank Gallo, *What's Happening to the American Family?* (Baltimore: Johns Hopkins University Press, 1988), 89. In 1991 David P. Snyder, a consulting futurist, stated in a University of Maryland commencement address that in two-parent households, 70 percent of both parents work and that 80 to 85 percent of single parents are employed outside the home (David P. Snyder, "The Family in Trans-Industrial America" [Bethesda, Md.: Snyder Family Enterprise, 1991], 2).

25. Charlene Marmer Solomon, "Latch Kids," *Parents*, March 1994, 42–44.

26. Bennett, *The Index of Leading Cultural Indicators*, 15.

27. Judith S. Wallerstein and Sandra Blakeslee, *Second Chances: Men, Women, and Children a Decade after Divorce* (New York: Triknor and Fields, 1990).

28. Benjamin T. Griffin, "Children Whose Parents Are Divorcing," in *When Children Suffer*, ed. Andrew D. Lester (Philadelphia: Westminster Press, 1987), 73–74.

29. Packard, *Our Endangered Children*, 191.

30. Fred Moody, "Divorce Is Abnormal," in *The Family in America: Opposing Viewpoints*, ed. Viqi Wagner (San Diego: Greenhaven Press, 1992), 105.

31. Frank F. Furstenberg and Andrew J. Cherlin, "Children's Adjustment to Divorce," in *Family in Transition*, ed. Arlene S. Skolnick and Jerome H. Skolnick, 8th ed. (New York: HarperCollins College Publishers, 1994), 317–20.

3. Single parenting. As already stated, more than one in every four children live with only one parent, and nine out of every ten children in those single-parent homes live with their mothers. How do children fare in a fatherless or motherless home environment? Numerous studies show that compared to children living with both parents, children in single-parent households are more likely to fail in school, suffer poor physical and mental health, be involved in drug abuse or criminal acts, or even commit suicide.[32]

David Blankenhorn, president of the Institute for American Values, New York, reports that poverty, child abuse, drug use, school dropouts, and teenage pregnancies are all caused in part by kids being raised in single-mother households.[33] Father absence is linked to boys' increased aggressiveness on one hand and greater manifestations of effeminacy on the other, and to girls' earlier sexual activity and illegitimate births.[34]

Though many single-parented boys and girls do not drop out of school, the psychological and emotional losses for fatherless children sound an ominous alarm of concern for the future of this nation. Blankenhorn affirms that fatherlessness is "the leading cause of declining child well-being in our society," a problem that, regrettably, is frequently ignored or denied.[35]

4. Poverty. In 1993 one in five of the nation's children under eighteen years old (21.9%) were living in poverty, which is up from one in six (14.9%) in 1970. More than one in three of the 14.6 million children in poverty lived in female-headed families. As for race, 16.9 percent of the impoverished children were whites and 46.9 percent were blacks.[36]

32. Bryce C. Christensen, "Taking Stock: Assessing Twenty Years of 'No Fault' Divorce," in *The Family in America,* September 1991, 6. Similar findings were reported by Sara McLanahan on a public television broadcast, "Frontline: The Vanishing Father," aired on May 16, 1995. She pointed out that these problems prevail almost equally in one-parent households, regardless of race, income level, or the parents' or children's education or sex. Also see Sara McLanahan and Gary Sandefur, *Growing Up with a Single Parent* (Cambridge, Mass.: Harvard University Press, 1994).

33. David Blankenhorn, *Fatherless America: Confronting Our Most Urgent Problem* (New York: Basic Books, 1995), 25–48.

34. Dobson and Bauer, *Children at Risk,* 167–68. Also fatherlessness is a strong contributing factor in teen crime (Patrick F. Fagan, "The Real Root Causes of Violent Crime: The Breakdown of Marriage, Family, and Community," *Backgrounder,* March 17, 1995, 9). In addition, single mothers, particularly those who are poor, suffer emotionally, including depression and stress (Martha T. Mednick, "Single Mothers: A Review and Critique of Current Research," in *Family Transition,* 372).

35. Blankenhorn, *Fatherless America,* 1. The same concern is reported in *Marriage in America: A Report to the Nation* (New York: Institute for Family Values, 1995), 4, 7–10.

36. *Statistical Abstract of the United States 1994,* 476. Also see Allison Hall, "Nearly Half of Black Kids Mired in Poverty," *USA Today,* December 11, 1990, and Alice C. Andrew and James W. Fonseca, *The Atlas of American Society* (New York: New York University Press, 1995), 56.

Poverty, too, has grim effects on children, including poor nutrition, inadequate health care, low school achievement, drug abuse, teen pregnancies, and teen suicides.[37]

5. *Unmarried couples.* An increasing number of families are living together apart from marriage. In 1993, 3.5 million couples were cohabiting without wedlock, more than double the number of 1.6 million in 1980 and seven times the number of half a million in 1970. A third of the 3.5 million couples have children under fifteen years of age.[38] These couples are products of a society that champions freedom without commitment, promiscuity, and abandonment of lifelong marital fidelity.

6. *Premarital sex and out-of-wedlock births.* In America's "sexual revolution" the number of teen pregnancies and births involving unmarried girls and women continues to rise. The National Center for Health Statistics reports that 20 percent of 15-year-olds and 81 percent of 19-year-olds are sexually active.[39] Seven out of 10 young people have had premarital sex by age 18,[40] and a nationwide survey of 10,645 12- to 21-year-olds shows that about 9 percent of boys and 4 percent of girls have had sexual intercourse at or before age 12.[41] As a result of adolescent promiscuity, about 10 percent of all teenage girls, more than one million, get pregnant each year, and almost all those pregnancies were not intended. The number has doubled since 1972. Almost half of those pregnancies (over 400,000) are aborted, compared with 1 out of 5 in 1972; about half (490,000) are illegitimate births.[42] Another consequence of promiscuity is the distressing increase in venereal diseases, including syphilis, gonorrhea, genital herpes, and AIDS. As of 1992, a total of 4,030 cases of AIDS were reported in children 12 years of age or under, but the number increases to 51,337 when those aged 13 through 29 are included.[43]

7. *Stepfamilies.* Most of the divorced people who remarry already have children, thus creating problems of adjustment for youngsters who now have an acquired parent besides two real parents, some stepsiblings, a new set of

---

37. These effects were noted in a two-decade study of 1,700 children by Robert H. Haverman and Barbara Wolfe, as reported in their book *Succeeding Generations* (New York: Russell Sage Foundation, 1994).

38. *The World Almanac and Book of Facts 1995,* 962.

39. Dobson and Bauer, *Children at Risk,* 9.

40. "Sex Unplugged," ABC television program, aired on June 1, 1995. This figure of 70 percent is a significant increase over the figure in 1981 of approximately half the girls between the ages of fifteen and nineteen who have had premarital sex, according to David Elkind (*The Hurried Child* [Reading, Mass.: Addison-Wesley, 1981], 12).

41. *Family Research Report,* May–June 1995, reported in *American Family Association Journal,* September 1995, 9.

42. Bennett, *The Index of Leading Cultural Indicators,* 9. Cf. the discussion of nonmarital pregnancies in Richard P. Olson and Joe H. Leonard, Jr., *Ministry with Families in Flux* (Louisville: Westminster/John Knox Press, 1990), 86–88.

43. *Statistical Abstract of the United States 1994,* 139.

grandparents, possibly some half siblings if children are born to the new marriage, and additional aunts, uncles, and cousins. In these "melded" or "reconstituted" families, stress from the loss of a parent by divorce or death may make children afraid to love and trust a "new" adult, whose lifestyle and personality may differ from the real parent.[44] Jaworski reports researcher Patricia Papernow, who states it takes about seven years for a stepfamily to get used to living together.[45]

The almost 10 million "blended" children, however, may have some advantages, including "the availability of more adults, who may provide stability and new experiences for the children."[46]

8. Homosexual parents. Still another change in American culture that is affecting some children is the fact that gay couples are adopting children and lesbian couples are either adopting children or are giving birth to children who are fathered by men not present in the relationship. According to the National Center for Lesbian Rights, there are more than 2 million homosexual mothers and fathers. Most of their children are from earlier heterosexual relationships, but between five thousand and ten thousand lesbians have borne children in recent years.[47] Hayton says the impact of homosexual "parents" on children is like the impact of single parenting on children. Studies demonstrate, he reports, that "these children experience the same emotional and behavioral problems as children of divorce,"[48] for the "parents" have unstable relationships, children are deprived of the benefits of a father *and* a mother, children are given a woefully poor view of marriage, and children are trained in promiscuous behavior.[49]

9. Anonymous parenting. Another current phenomenon on the American scene is the conceiving of children through reproductive technology rather than by sexual intercourse between a married couple. In artificial insemination a wife whose husband is infertile receives implanted semen from an anonymous male donor, thus making her pregnant by another man. This procedure makes fatherhood anonymous and reduces fathering to a biological dimension. Some wives who are infertile and who desire a child arrange for their husband's sperm to be implanted in another woman's womb, who then as a surrogate carries the fetus and gives the new-

44. Delores Friesen and Al Dueck, "The Changing Family in Today's World," *Direction* 19 (Spring 1990): 17.

45. Margaret Jaworski, "Blended Is Splendid?" *Family Circle,* January 8, 1991, 7.

46. Friesen and Dueck, "The Changing Family in Today's World," 19–20. For a demographic survey of blended families, see Paul C. Glick, "Remarried Families, Stepfamilies, and Stepchildren: A Brief Demographic Profile," *Family Relations,* January 1989, 24–27.

47. Jean Seligmann, *Newsweek,* Special Issue, Winter–Spring 1990.

48. Bradley P. Hayton, "Homosexual Partners Are Undermining the Family," in *The Family in America: Opposing Viewpoints,* 69.

49. Ibid., 66–70.

born child to the parents. This raises the question of who is the child's mother; in addition it may place strain on the relationship between the surrogate mother and her husband.

Anonymous parenting poses threats for the stability of the family and raises the potential of children being emotionally disturbed by the confusing questions related to the identity of their parents.[50]

10. Child-free married couples. More married men and women are choosing to have children later in life or are deciding not to have babies at all. Childlessness by choice seems to be rising, for the percentage of families without children rose from 44.1 percent in 1970 to 51.2 percent in 1993.[51] Packard suggests that at least a fourth of all women presently in the childbearing age range may never have children, and that plans to remain childless are particularly evident among young college-trained career women.[52]

Why is this? Perhaps these couples are more consumed with their careers, with advancing themselves materially, with spending their leisure time on themselves rather than being "tied down" to children's demands. Others may be apprehensive about the fearsome responsibilities of child training. Does the now popular term "child-free" suggest a growing disdain toward children?

11. Marital violence. Many children are growing up in homes where they observe frequent conflict and physical violence between their parents. This results in many of those children developing external behavorial problems such as aggression and delinquency or internal problems such as withdrawal, anxiety, and psychosomatic problems. In a recent study of 185 children living with their mothers at shelters for battered women, the children's behavior was adversely affected by their having witnessed numerous episodes of violence, by high mother-child violence, and by frequent stresses in the children's lives. On the other hand, factors mitigating against the impact of marital violence on children's behavior were feelings of self-worth, high sociability, and a positive relationship with the mother.[53]

Increase in Abusive Conduct

Accompanying the rejection of moral absolutes and the sweeping changes in family patterns, abusive conduct in our society is also affecting children pro-

50. Donald De Marco, "Reproductive Technology Is Undermining the Family," in *The Family in America: Opposing Viewpoints,* 79–86. Also see J. Kerby Anderson, "Artificial Reproduction: A Biblical Appraisal," *Bibliotheca Sacra* 143 (January–March 1986): 61–67.
51. Wright, *The Universal Almanac,* 307.
52. Packard, *Our Endangered Children,* 21.
53. Maura O'Keefe, "Adjustment of Children from Maritally Violent Homes," *Families in Society* 75 (August 1994): 403–14.

foundly to the point that many of them are "children doomed to misfortune" (Isa. 65:23).

1. Child abuse. Sadly, violence against children is increasing right in their homes. Some are slapped, beaten, kicked, burned, or thrown down stairs. Others are threatened, isolated, starved, or abandoned. Still others are raped or sodomized. From others, love, affection, attention, and care are intentionally withheld. As a result of such physical, emotional, or sexual maltreatment many children are seriously injured or killed.

And such horrible acts against the helpless young have more than quadrupled in eighteen years! In 1976, 669,000 cases of child abuse or neglect were reported;[54] in 1993 the number was 1,018,692;[55] and in 1994 the number climbed to 3.1 million![56] Each day in 1993 more than 2,700 children were abused, and 1,028 of those abuse victims died.[57] About 51 percent of the victims of abuse in 1993 were seven years of age or younger.[58]

What causes such injustice? Parents who abuse their offspring usually have experienced abusive behavior from their own parents. Many parents lack parenting skills; or are immature or insecure; or are facing money-related, family-related, or work-related stress or conflict; or have deprived backgrounds; or are experiencing a drug or alcohol problem.[59] Researchers have discovered that in most cases of "father-daughter incest" the offender is a stepfather or live-in roommate of the mother.[60] Without question, child battering is "the cruelest crime," as Cheryl McCall calls it.[61]

Neglected and abused children tend to be more prone to depression and drug and alcohol problems,[62] and many more grow up to become criminals.[63]

---

54. *Current Trends in Child Abuse Reporting and Fatalities* (Chicago: National Committee to Prevent Child Abuse, 1995), 3.

55. U. S. Department of Health and Human Services, National Center on Child Abuse and Neglect, *Child Maltreatment 1993: Reports from the States to the National Center on Child Abuse and Neglect* (Washington, D.C.: U.S. Government Printing Office, 1995). Also see *The State of America's Children Yearbook 1995* (Washington, D.C.: Children's Defense Fund, 1995), 71–72.

56. *Current Trends in Child Abuse Reporting and Fatalities*, 15.

57. *Child Maltreatment 1993: Reports from the States to the National Center on Child Abuse and Neglect*, 3–11.

58. Ibid., 2.8–2.9.

59. Virginia D. Ratliff and J. Bill Ratliff, "Abused Children," in *When Children Suffer*, 126–27; and Elaine Landau, "Many Factors Contribute to Child Abuse," in *Child Abuse: Opposing Viewpoints*, 118–22.

60. Bryce J. Christensen, "Nontraditional Values Support Family Violence," in *Violence in America: Opposing Viewpoints*, ed. Janselle Rohr (San Diego: Greenhaven Press, 1990), 110. Also see Leslie Margolin, "Child Abuse by Mothers' Boyfriends: Why the Overrepresentation?" *Child Abuse and Neglect* 16 (July–August 1992): 545–46.

61. Cheryl McCall, "The Cruelest Crime," *Life*, December 1984, 58.

62. "Abuse Takes Toll," *USA Today*, February 18, 1991.

63. Anthony Brandt, "Permanent Damage," *Parenting*, November 1990, 78.

Alarmingly these are only reported cases; no doubt many more incidents have gone unnoticed and therefore were not reported.

2. *Drug abuse.* While drug use by young people is down from its peak in the early 1980s, an alarmingly high percentage (87%) of high school seniors reported in 1993 that they had used alcohol at some time, and more than a third (35.3%) had used marijuana. Marijuana was used in 1993 by 9 percent of eighth-graders and 19 percent of tenth-graders.[64] Packard cites a report of the National Institute on Alcohol Abuse and Alcoholism that 1.3 million young people between twelve and seventeen years of age have serious drinking problems.[65] Substance abuse takes its toll on the unborn whose mothers have used illegal drugs. The National Institute on Drug Abuse reports that one out of every four babies born in the United States each year has been exposed to illegal drugs, alcohol, or cigarettes before birth.[66] Even smoking by young people is increasing. According to the ABC "Evening News" television broadcast on July 20, 1995, one in five high school seniors smoke every day, and one in five eighth-graders smoke occasionally. These figures represent a 30 percent increase in teen smoking from 1991 to 1994.

3. *Media violence.* The impact of mass media—including magazines, movies, videos, and television—on children is enormous. "Researchers estimate that the average child between the ages of 6 and 18 will spend between 15,000 and 18,000 hours watching TV compared to 13,000 hours spent in school. Even children younger than 6 will have put in many hours of viewing."[67] That means four hours of television every day, although the average for all Americans was seven hours a day in 1992.[68]

More disturbing than the hours of television watched is the content of what is seen both on television and in the movies. According to Americans for Responsible Television, studies indicate that by the time they reach age sixteen, children will witness 33,000 televised murders and 200,000 acts of violence. On Saturday mornings young children see thirty-two acts of violence every hour—one such act every two minutes!

Hollywood movies depict numerous acts of violence, and rock music lyrics have increased their presentation of violent acts. Pornographic magazines and books also present an increasing number of violent antisocial themes, as reported by the National Coalition on TV Violence.[69]

64. *The World Almanac and Book of Facts 1995,* 963. The source of these figures is the University of Michigan Institute for Social Research. Also see *The State of America's Children Yearbook 1995,* 83–84.

65. Packard, *Our Endangered Children,* 16.

66. Reported in *Hope Health Letter,* April 1995, 8.

67. Dobson and Bauer, *Children at Risk,* 205.

68. Bennett, *The Index of Leading Cultural Indicators,* 21.

69. Thomas E. Radecki, "Television Promotes Teen Violence," in *Violence in America: Opposing Viewpoints,* 162.

The National Institute of Health has reported that more than three thousand studies prove that children who watch television violence are more prone to physical aggression than those who do not. That TV violence is a cause of children's violence is affirmed by the American Academy of Pediatrics, the American Medical Association, the American Psychological Association, and the National Institute of Mental Health.

In addition television reduces children's playtime, child-family interaction time, and time for children to read and to express their ideas verbally.[70] Repeatedly television (and especially MTV) bombards children with behavior, language, and concepts that deliberately oppose moral values, biblical truths, and Christian standards. This humanistic, antigodly assault on our children and young people is cause for deep concern. These degrading forces purposely seek to pull children away from ethical ideals and toward self-destructive and other destructive behavior.

4. Crime. A deep scar on America's face is the staggering increase in crime—especially the rise of criminal acts by children and young people. Murders, robberies, aggravated assaults, rapes, burglaries, car thefts, and larcenies are committed not only by adults, but also by a growing number of juveniles. For instance, half of all burglars arrested are youngsters under eighteen,[71] and one out of every five violent crimes is committed by young people seventeen years of age or younger.[72] Juveniles of ages eleven through seventeen arrested for violent crimes have more than doubled from 55,000 in 1970 to 118,000 in 1992.[73]

Teenage criminal behavior stems from parental neglect and abuse, fatherlessness, and deprivation of parental love and affection even in early infancy.[74]

Another disturbing fact about youth crime is that children are often victims of those offenses. Two-thirds of the victimizers of children twelve to nineteen are other juveniles.[75] According to the NBC television program, "Evening News," on December 6, 1995, twelve children in the United States are killed by gunfire every day, that is, one child every two hours. No wonder, as that same television program reported, one out of ten children of ages seven through ten worry about being shot at school.

70. Rita Kramer, *In Defense of the Family,* 96–97. For an excellent analysis of MTV's destructive influence see Bob DeMoss, "MTV: Do You Know What Your Kids Are Watching?" *Focus on the Family,* August 1994, 2–4. Of interest is the fact that a large majority of parents (77%) are concerned about the strong negative influence of violence in the media, as reported by Richard Lacayo, "Violent Reaction," *Time,* June 12, 1995, 26.

71. Packard, *Our Endangered Children,* 14.

72. Nazario, *In Defense of Children,* 318.

73. *Statistical Abstract of the United States 1994,* 205.

74. Fagan, "The Real Root Causes of Violent Crime: The Breakdown of Marriage, Family, and Community," 5–19. Also see Richard J. Gelles and Murray A. Straus, "The Impact of Intimate Violence," in *Family in Transition,* 329.

75. Jennifer Allen, "The Danger Years," *Life,* July 1995, 50.

Abduction and kidnapping of children and teens continue to alarm parents. Allen reports that between two hundred and three hundred children are kidnapped each year by strangers who hold them overnight or longer, and of that number, about one hundred are killed.[76] "Another 4,300 children a year, mostly teenage girls, are seized by strangers who molest and then release them, in what experts call 'short-term abductions.'"[77]

Nationwide attention is drawn to this problem by milk carton photos of missing children and mailings of cards with "Have you seen us?" captions and photos of abducted youngsters.

5. *Abortion.* As stated earlier, child abuse results in hundreds of deaths of defenseless children every year. Another form of death-inducing abuse is abortion—and it means not hundreds of deaths but 1.6 million deaths every year![78]

Since the Supreme Court's *Roe v. Wade* decision on January 22, 1973, more than 28 million unborn babies have been victimized by "our society's worship of choice and rampant individualism."[79]

Is this violent ending of the lives of unborn children in their mothers' wombs any less culpable than a parent's molesting of a young child physically or emotionally? Like a child battered by an outraged adult, the unborn infant has no means of protection and is given no rights. Both are victimized. Is it not strange that many people who are exercised over the injustice of child abuse have no qualms about murderously ending the lives of the unborn?

Like child abuse, abortion manifests a loss of respect for human life, a devaluation of children. Taking the lives of 1.6 million unborn babies every year is an outrageous atrocity, one of the most despicable forms of abusive conduct in our nation.[80]

Rise in Permissive Child Rearing

More than thirty years ago, Dreikurs and Saltz wrote, "On every side and in every gathering, children make themselves obtrusive and obnoxious." Because children are "noisy, inconsiderate, boisterous, and unmannerly" and even defiant and delinquent, many parents are "increasingly upset and bewildered," and therefore "*we don't know what to do with our children.*"[81]

---

76. Ibid., 44.
77. Ibid.
78. In 1992 abortions totaled 1,529,000 (*Statistical Abstract of the United States 1994,* 85).
79. Dobson and Bauer, *Children at Risk,* 3. Whereas 29 percent of all women's pregnancies are aborted, the percentages are higher among unmarried women (56%), teenagers (41%), and nonwhite women (39%), according to the Alan Guttmacher Institute, as reported by Kim Lawton, "20 Years after Roe . . . ," *Christianity Today,* January 11, 1993, 37.
80. See chapter 5 for a discussion of abortion and the Bible.
81. Rudolf Dreikurs with Vicki Saltz, *Children: The Challenge* (New York: Hawthorn Books, 1964), 3–6 (italics theirs).

Parents have always been frustrated with the responsibility of child rearing. Even the Greek philosopher Socrates said 2,400 years ago that "children are tyrants. They contradict their parents, gobble their food, and tyrannize their teachers." Even so, 88 percent of the adults surveyed in 1991 by the National Commission on Children said they believe that parenting is more difficult now than in the past.[82]

Why is that? According to an increasing number of sociologists and psychologists, many problems in child behavior stem from letting children have unrestricted freedom. Undisciplined children become maladjusted children. Allowed to do whatever they please, children soon have no respect for authority, insist on having their own way, and become uncontrollable. Left to their own wishes, without loving parental guidance and supervision, boys and girls acquire the secularist's attitude that "whatever feels good, whatever seems convenient, what everyone does" is their guide.[83] Such an approach to unrestrained living leads to unhappiness, disorder, and delinquency. To fail to direct and discipline children, to raise them in an atmosphere of unbridled permissiveness contributes to their rebellious behavior. No wonder our children are in trouble!

What Results Are We Reaping?

Rejection of moral absolutes
Drastic changes in family patterns
Increase in abusive conduct
Rise in permissive child rearing

These four elements in our nation's social upheaval reveal that America has "mismanaged" its children, as Dobson has put it.[84] Many national agencies have been established to protect and help children, and innumerable resources are available to adults on child-parent relations. Yet at the same time we have burgeoned into an "anti-child culture."[85] Not wanting children, neglecting children, abusing children, not disciplining children, victimizing children, kidnapping children, aborting children—these all point to a squandering of our greatest resource, our boys and girls.

Two results are apparent. One is children's self-destructive conduct, including, as noted, criminal involvement, substance abuse, illicit pregnancies, and abortions. Not surprisingly, many teens run away from home. About half

82. Viqi Wagner, ed., *The Family in America: Opposing Viewpoints*, 16. The Commission's report is called *Beyond Rhetoric: A New American Agenda for Children and Families* (Washington, D.C.: U.S. Government Printing Office, 1991).

83. Kramer, *In Defense of the Family*, 20.

84. James Dobson, Speech at the Dallas Seminary Presidential Inaugural Conference, Dallas, Tex., October 28, 1994.

85. Packard, *Our Endangered Children*, xx.

of them run away to escape the pain of child abuse.[86] More than half a million children are runaways each year,[87] with about half of them fleeing from group homes, foster homes, or correctional institutions.[88]

It comes as no surprise, then, that the teen suicide rate has increased. In 1993, 310 children through age 14 took their lives, and 4,960 teens and young adults aged 15 through 24 committed suicide,[89] a rate that for the latter group of people has tripled since 1950.[90] In addition, 400,000 unsuccessful suicide attempts are made each year by youth and young adults.[91] Suicide is the third leading cause of death for teens.

Again, this serious problem goes back to the family. As Strommen writes, suicide and attempted suicide culminate from "progressive family disorganization and social maladjustment."[92]

Another result of our moral malaise in reference to children is that they are often deprived of childhood. Authors refer to "vanishing childhood," "endangered" childhood, "children without childhood," the "disappearance of childhood," "hurried children," and "the unwanted generation."[93] This "hurrying" includes parents pushing their children to overachieve in studies or athletics, or the media urging children to fill consumer wants normally expected of adolescents or adults. In addition television introduces children to all forms of adult situations and conduct. In this "erosion" of childhood,[94] we are depriving boys and girls of what Bill Cosby calls "that sweet scene known as childhood."[95]

To overcome children's self-destructive behavior and to give back boys and girls their childhood years with its joys, we must correct our mismanagement of children. The means by which this should be done is the subject of the next chapter.

86. Nazario, *In Defense of Children*, 442.

87. "American's Children: How Are They Doing? Fact Sheet No. 8" (Englewood, Colo.: American Humane Association Children's Division, 1993), 2.

88. Valerie Bell, *Nobody's Children* (Dallas, Tex.: Word Publishing, 1989), 14.

89. *The World Almanac and Book of Facts 1995,* 960.

90. Wright, *The Universal Almanac 1995,* 221.

91. Nazairo, *In Defense of Children,* 397. For a recent discussion of the problem of teen suicides, see David Lester, *The Cruelest Death: The Enigma of Adolescent Suicide* (Philadelphia: Charles Press, 1993).

92. Merton P. Strommen, *Five Cries of Youth* (New York: Harper & Row, Publishers, 1974), 46.

93. Roger Clapp, "Vanishing Childhood," *Christianity Today,* May 18, 1994, 12–19, 32, 34, and June 15, 1994, 18–24; Packard, *Our Endangered Children;* Marie Winn, *Children without Childhood* (New York: Pantheon Books, 1983); Neil Postman, *The Disappearance of Childhood* (New York: Delacorte Press, 1982); David Elkind, *The Hurried Child* (Reading, Mass.: Addison-Wesley Publishing Co., 1981); and Paul D. Meier and Linda Burkett, *The Unwanted Generation* (Grand Rapids: Baker Book House, 1980).

94. Clapp, "Vanishing Childhood," June 15, 1986, 20.

95. Bill Cosby, *Childhood* (New York: G. P. Putnam's Sons, 1991), 28.

3

"TO WHOM SHOULD WE GO?"

Is There No Answer?

When I was a boy, my dad used to enjoy telling about Douglas Corrigan, a pilot who in 1937 flew his one-engine plane nicknamed "Lizzy" in a direction opposite of what people thought he was flying. Having flown from Los Angeles to Floyd Bennett Airport, Long Island, New York, Corrigan climbed back in his cockpit for what everyone thought was his return flight to California. But twenty-eight hours later he landed in Dublin, Ireland. As he disembarked, he jokingly remarked, "Why, I thought this was California." At first, people assumed he had flown in the wrong direction, so they nicknamed him "Wrong-way Corrigan."[1]

That's the way with much of our culture regarding our children. We are flying in the wrong direction—and it is no joke!

Concerned for advancing their careers, fathers are neglecting their children.

Desiring unrestrained personal freedom, couples are marrying with no thought of lifelong commitment.

Interested in satisfying physical pleasures, adults are molesting children sexually.

Wanting emotionally "high" experiences, children and youth are engaging in premarital sex and are using drugs and alcohol.

Devoted to being "entertained," adults are subjecting themselves and their children to the constant portrayal of violence in the media.

1. Douglas Corrigan, *That's My Story* (New York: E. P. Dutton & Co., 1938).

Wanting freedom from child rearing responsibilities and freedom of "choice," pregnant women are aborting their children.

In essence, the moral direction in which we have been flying is self-centered. Our compass needle is bent, pointing only to ourselves. And the consequences are devastating! Our society is paying a high price for its narcissistic conduct based on self-realization and individualism. Thinking we are finding fulfillment, our abandonment of moral values has resulted in just the opposite—self-destruction. Thinking we are finding liberation from restraint and enjoying freedom of personal choice, our perversion of values has resulted in our mistreating and maligning our children.

Is there no solution? Is there any way to realign our moral compass so that we are headed in the right direction? Is there any way to counter the destructive influences on our children so that we can pilot them toward meaningful destinations in their lives?

Is the Government Our Answer?

One arena where attempts have been made to put our children back on course is governmental programs that offer monetary support and social services for families, especially for "nonnuclear" families.[2] "In some cases these programs assist with functions that families are unable to perform adequately; in other cases, the functions are taken over, transforming them from family to public responsibilities."[3]

Numerous government programs that affect households have been instituted. In 1980, 270 different federal programs were in existence, administered by seventeen departments and agencies.[4] The Department of Health and Human Services spends more than a billion dollars every year on numerous social and welfare programs.[5] In the past three decades money spent on education increased dramatically, "with total expenditures on public elementary and secondary education more than doubling in inflation-adjusted dollars."[6]

Over the years a number of White House Conferences on children or families have been called by presidents of our nation. In 1919 President Woodrow Wilson called a conference to discuss child welfare standards. Presidents

2. David Popenoe, "The Family Is in Decline," in *The Family in America: Opposing Viewpoints,* ed. Viqi Wagner (San Diego: Greenhaven Press, 1992), 24.

3. Ibid.

4. Sar A. Levitan, Richard S. Belous, and Frank Gallo, *What's Happening to the American Family?* (Baltimore: Johns Hopkins University Press, 1988), 138.

5. James Dobson and Gary L. Bauer, *Children at Risk* (Dallas, Tex.: Word Publishing, 1990), 29.

6. *Marriage in America: A Report to the Nation* (New York: Institute for American Values, 1995), 5.

Herbert Hoover, Franklin D. Roosevelt, and Harry Truman convened conferences centering on children in 1929, 1940, and 1950, respectively. In 1960 the White House Conference sponsored by President Dwight D. Eisenhower was on children and youth. In 1970 the White House Conference called by Richard M. Nixon focused on children, and in 1980 President Ronald Reagan engaged a White House Conference on Families. Obviously these conclaves have been summoned because our national leaders have recognized the persistence of family problems in our nation.

With the extreme expenditures of government agencies on behalf of children, and with the ongoing federal studies of and conferences on children, are children better off? In answer to this question, Dobson and Bauer affirm that these grandiose programs have been national disasters.[7] If increased government spending is the way to enhance the quality of families' and children's lives, why are we worse off than before? In the face of more government expenditures, why do children's problems continue to grow?

Many leaders now believe more spending will not cure our national malaise. "Unless we slow down these social trends—out-of-wedlock births, crime, drugs, the breakdown of values—government money is not going to do much."[8]

However, is not our nation dedicated to the betterment of children? Many national societies focus on children's needs, including the American Association for Lost Children, the Association for Childhood Education International, the Association of Child Advocates, the Child Abuse Institute of Research, the Child Study Association of America, the Child Welfare League of America, the Children's Defense Fund, the Coalition for America's Children, the Foundation for Child Development, the National Center for Missing and Exploited Children, and the National Committee for Prevention of Child Abuse. In addition the national Department of Health, Education, and Welfare includes the Children's Bureau under the Office of Child Development.

Manufacturers and producers recognize the enormous financial benefits in developing child-focused products and programs. Children's toy stores, video games for children, television programs for children (such as Sesame Street, Barney, the Muppets, and Saturday morning cartoons), children's magazines and books—all these are products designed exclusively for the "children's market." Playgrounds and public parks provide play equipment for children.

---

7. Dobson and Bauer, *Children at Risk,* 29.

8. Gary L. Bauer, cited by Patricia Edmonds and Margaret L. Usdansky, " 'Children Get Poorer; Nation Gets Richer,'" *USA Today,* November 14, 1994, 5A. Also see John Hood, "Increased Spending on Education Would Not Help Children," in *America's Children: Opposing Viewpoints,* ed. Carol Wekesser (San Diego: Greenhaven Press, 1991), 25–32; and Richard Vedder and Lowell Gallaway, "Increased Government Spending Would Not Help Poor Children," in *America's Children: Opposing Viewpoints,* 129–34.

Even the ubiquitous McDonald's fast-food restaurants cater to children with their playgrounds.

State-regulated day care centers provide all day, long-term care for thousands of children, most of whose mothers are employed. This practice of "proxy parenting" signals "a profound change in human history,"[9] a change that research shows has a negative effect on children.[10] What would seem to be a beneficial service to children often has deleterious effects on their mental health and personalities.

In recent years day care centers sponsored by government agencies have sprung up across the nation. In 1991, 1.9 million children were being cared for in such centers.[11]

Because of children's special emotional and physical needs, the fields of medicine and psychology now include specialists such as child psychiatrists, pediatric ophthalmologists, children's orthodontists, and others.

All these programs, products, and personnel would suggest children are valued.

Another indication of national concern for children, some politicians and sociologists argue, is the Convention on the Rights of the Child, which was adopted by the United Nations on November 20, 1989. Already ratified by 175 nations around the world, the fifty-four provisions of this treaty-like document would become law if endorsed by the Senate. However, far from being beneficial to children and families, this Convention would further erode our morals, destroy the authority of American parents, and violate the sanctity of our families.[12] For example, Article 13 grants freedom of expression to children through media of their choice with parental supervision prohibited. Article 14 guarantees children freedom "of thought, conscience, and religion." Article 15 prohibits parents from forbidding their children to join any gang, cult, or other group they wish. Article 16 provides for "a child's right to privacy, including the right to abortion without notice to parents, the purchase and use of contraceptives, the right to have heterosexual or homosexual sex, and the right to possess pornographic or obscene materials."[13]

Other sections entrust to the mass media the responsibility of providing children with information for their "social, spiritual, and moral well-being and physical and mental health" (Article 17), which would promote state-sanctioned beliefs and values, grant children "the right to benefit from child care

9. Karl Zinsmeister, "Day Care Harms Children," in *America's Children: Opposing Viewpoints*, 226.

10. Ibid., 225–30.

11. U.S. Bureau of the Census, *Statistical Abstract of the United States 1994* (Washington, D.C.: U.S. Department of Commerce, 1994), 961.

12. "CWA Special Legislative Report" (Washington, D.C.: Concerned Women of America, March 1995).

13. Ibid.

services" (Article 18), which could lead to universal child care and state control and state-induced values on children, and provide for an international committee to oversee and monitor the rights of children.[14]

Can such a treaty be beneficial to children when it distances them from parental authority and grants them freedoms that are detrimental to their social and spiritual well-being? This Convention, if ratified by the United States, would have malevolent effects of catastrophic proportions!

Is our nation genuinely devoted to its children? This alleged national concern may well be "just a facade."[15] We are looking for solutions to our social and spiritual problems in the wrong place; we are "Wrong-way Corrigans."

While the government can take a number of steps to reform our educational and welfare systems, to remove barriers to adoption, to promote responsible fatherhood,[16] and to deal with other family-related concerns, ultimately the answer lies elsewhere.

Back to the Bible

Why is our society spiritually diseased? Why is our nation morally corrupt? Why are our children in trouble? Because we have abandoned the Bible's standards for the home! We have forsaken the Bible's principles for family living. We have disregarded the Bible's principles for child rearing. We have ignored the Bible's instructions on how to find personal fulfillment and meaning in our lives. We have neglected the Bible's precepts for and examples of godly home life.

As Popenoe has argued, we need to "seek to reinvigorate the cultural ideas of 'family,' 'parents,' and 'children,' " rather than relying on the government.[17] Those ideals are to be found only in the Bible. And encouragingly, in a *Parents* magazine poll of one thousand people, 78 percent of those interviewed expressed a desire to return to "traditional values and old-fashioned morality."[18]

Decrying the intrusion of professionals seeking to control parents and their children, Kramer writes that "it is time to return child care to the home, responsibility to the family, and authority to parents."[19] Rather than political advocates, children need "appropriate parenting in healthy families."[20] Even the 1980 White House Conference on Families admitted that parenting roles "cannot be successfully relegated to any outside the family without seriously

---

14. Ibid. Also see "Convention on the Rights of the Child," Resolution Adopted by the United Nations Assembly: A/RES 44/25, December 5, 1989.

15. Kenneth O. Gangel, "Little Children: Big Challenge," *Kindred Spirit*, August 1989, 4.

16. William J. Bennett, *The Index of Leading Cultural Indicators* (Washington, D.C.: Heritage Foundation, 1993), 1:ii–iii.

17. Popenoe, "The Family Is in Decline," 24.

18. Ingrid Groller, "The Future of the Family," *Parents*, January 16, 1990, 31.

19. Rita Kramer, *In Defense of the Family* (New York: Basic Books, 1983), 19.

20. Ibid., 27.

jeopardizing the future of the individual and society in general."[21] The Institute for Family Values, in addressing the serious deterioration of child well-being, has stated, "For unless we reverse the decline of marriage, no other achievements—no tax cut, no new government program, no new idea—will be powerful enough to reverse the trend of declining child well-being."[22]

True, many differences may be noted. Children in Bible times were raised in extended families, whereas most of today's children live in "nuclear" families without grandparents or other close relatives. Mothers' and fathers' roles in Bible times focused on training their children, whereas many fathers today have abandoned their leadership role. Few examples of divorce are recorded in the Bible. Desiring to be child-free was unheard of in Bible times. Few cases of child molestation are recorded. Most couples married at an early age, whereas many couples today are postponing marriage by several years. Today's urban and suburban societies differ significantly from the Bible's agricultural setting.

However, families in the Bible are similar to today's households. Children's need for salvation and spiritual training, children's need for fatherly concern and instruction, rivalry between siblings, children's rebellion against their parents, the ever-present temptations that confront children and youth regarding premarital sex—in these and other ways the environments of children in Bible times and today are similar.

Four facts call for a return to the Bible for help in guiding our children. First, the Bible tells us what God thinks of children. He gives them to parents, he values them, he loves them. Because they are precious to God, they should be precious to us.

Second, the Bible repeatedly gives specific instructions to parents on how to raise their children. The Bible is "an inexhaustible sourcebook for successful child training."[23] We neglect these God-given, time-honored guidelines to our own peril.

Third, the Scriptures demonstrate the consequences of both faithful child rearing and inadequate child training. These examples, both good and bad, provide strong reasons for following the Bible's directives for developing youngsters in the home.

Fourth, the Bible addresses many of the child-related problems confronting our society. These include infertility, abortion, infanticide, adoption, undisciplined children, stepfamilies, orphans, and absence of training in godliness.

Only by returning to the Bible's focus on children—and following its directives for children—can we escape our nation's moral morass and go in the right direction.

21. *The 1980 White House Conference on Families: A Research Project* (Beverly Hills, Calif.: Charles Ward, Publisher, 1981), 216.

22. *Marriage in America: A Report to the Nation*, 4.

23. Richard L. Strauss, *Confident Children and How They Grow* (Wheaton, Ill.: Tyndale House Publishers, 1975), 24.

4

"THE CHILDREN THE LORD HAS GIVEN ME"

Childbirth in Bible Times

Shear-Jashub.

Maher-Shalal-Hash-Baz.

What odd names to modern ears!

Yet these were the names God told the prophet Isaiah to give his two boys (Isa. 7:3–8:3). Their names summarized God's message to the nation of Judah through Isaiah.

Each time someone would hear or say the name Shear-Jashub, he would be reminded of its meaning, "A remnant will return." And whenever someone would hear or say the name Maher-Shalal-Hash-Baz, he would recall that that name means "Quick to the plunder, swift to the spoil."

God gave Isaiah these boys' names—but he also gave him these boys! Isaiah said, "Here am I, and the children the LORD has given me" (Isa. 8:18).

This attitude toward children prevailed throughout Israel's history. Children are given by God; they come from him. How unlike the views of an increasing number of parents today. They ask, "Should we have children or not?" "Should we abort this fetus?" "Should we put our newborn up for adoption?" "We have one child; we aren't sure we want another one."

Parents in Bible times *wanted* children. In fact, not to bear offspring was a disgrace. Children brought blessing and joy to a family because parents knew youngsters were God's special gifts to them.

Of interest is the fact that the Lord's first command to Adam and Eve, his very first words of instruction to the human race, were, "Be fruitful and in-

45

crease in number" (Gen. 1:28). Then after the flood, God repeated these words to Noah (9:1).

Writing of parents' attitudes toward children in the home, a psalmist affirmed, "Sons are a heritage from the LORD, children a reward from him" (Ps. 127:3). In the Hebrew this verse begins with the attention-grabbing word "Behold." The psalmist was saying, in essence, "Take note of this significant fact that children come from God." The word "heritage" suggests that children belong to him, and that he shares these precious possessions with parents. Since he assigns children to parents, "there is no such thing as an 'accidental birth' or a 'surprise pregnancy' from God's viewpoint."[1]

In Psalm 127:3 the word "children" is literally "fruit of the womb," picturesquely comparing a mother's offspring to a plant-bearing fruit. The word "reward" denotes "pleasure—something given as a tangible proof of appreciation . . . God's very personal trophy of his love."[2]

Like arrows in a "quiver" (Ps. 127:4–5) sons can help defend the family in warfare or in adjudicating court cases "in the gate," where legal disputes were heard.[3] In addition the psalmist wrote that the righteous man's wife will be like a fruitful vine and his sons "like olive shoots around [his] table" (128:3). The grapevine and olive tree, essential products of Israelite agriculture, were often mentioned together (e.g., Exod. 23:11; Deut. 6:11; 28:39–40; 1 Sam. 8:14; Neh. 5:11; Job 15:33; James 3:12). They provided grapes and olives for food, grape juice for a pleasing drink, and olive oil as a means of light (Exod. 25:6; 35:8; Matt. 25:3–4), a lubricant (2 Sam. 1:21), a symbol of dedication of leaders when poured on their heads (Exod. 29:7; 1 Sam. 10:1), a means of relaxation or healing when applied to the body (Ps. 23:5; Luke 10:34). Small wonder that flourishing vineyards and olive trees—both long-lasting and evergreen—became apt pictures of a family with several children.

In Israel, to have many children was an honor, a sign of God's blessing. He told Abram that his offspring would be countless like the stars of the sky (Gen. 15:5; 22:17), a promise he repeated to Isaac (26:4). Hagar too was told that her descendants would be without number (16:10). When Rebekah left her home to marry Isaac, her brother and mother said they wished she would "increase to thousands" (24:60), that is, have many descendants. When Boaz was preparing to marry Ruth, the city officials blessed him with the wish, "May the Lord make the woman who is coming into your home like Rachel and Leah" (Ruth 4:11).

1. Charles R. Swindoll, *Living Beyond the Daily Grind, Book II* (Dallas, Tex.: Word Publishing, 1988), 326.
2. Ibid.
3. Old Testament writers often spoke of the city gate as the "courtroom" where "elders" adjudicated disputes (Deut. 17:5; 21:19; 22:15, 24; 25:7; Ruth 4:1, 11; Job 29:7; Prov. 31:23; Lam. 5:14).

Even ancient Hittites considered childlessness an evil and a cause for unhappiness, which could not be offset even by much wealth.[4] In classical Greece the family *(oikos)* without children, Aristotle said, was not fully an *oikos*.[5]

"Give Me Children or I'll Die!"

Why do married couples want to have children? Why would barren Sarah refer to her having children as a "pleasure" (Gen. 18:12)? Why would Isaac pray that the Lord would make his barren wife pregnant (25:21)? Why would Jacob's wife Rachel, who was barren, feel that if she did not bear children, she would die (30:1)? Why did she feel that being childless was a "disgrace" (30:23)?[6] Why did Agur personify the barren womb as "never satisfied," as always longing for children (Prov. 30:15–16)?

One reason is the sheer joy of parenthood. What parent can deny the indescribable delight at first seeing his or her newborn children, their own flesh and blood, and then delighting in seeing them grow? In recounting his past blessings, Job spoke of his children being around him (Job 29:5), and the psalmist referred to the "happy mother of children" (Ps. 113:9). When Leah's servant Zilpah bore Jacob a second son, Asher, Leah rejoiced, "How happy I am!" (Gen. 30:13). Centuries later the prophet Jeremiah referred to the announcement made to his father Hilkiah (Jer. 1:1) that he had a son—news that "made him very glad" (20:15). Jesus spoke of a mother's joy at bringing a child into the world (John 16:21). In Hosea 9:16 the Lord spoke of the Israelites' children as their "cherished offspring." When Zechariah learned that his wife Elizabeth would bear a child in her old age, the angel said, "He will be a joy and a delight to you" (Luke 1:14), and when Elizabeth, his wife, gave birth to John her neighbors and relatives "shared her joy" (1:58).

When Abraham's descendants under Joshua conquered the land of Palestine, the nation enjoyed the land as an inheritance from God. God promised, "You will possess their land; I will give it to you as an inheritance" (Lev. 20:24). But that inheritance could not be continued if husbands and wives remained childless. Eventually the nation would be extinguished, and the land useless. Another reason for bearing children, then, was to perpetuate the nation. In addition, one's progeny would continue his own name and family line. Boaz announced that one reason he was marrying the widow Ruth was so that her dead husband Mahlon's name would "not disappear from among

4. Gary M. Beckman, *Hittite Birth Rituals,* 2d ed. (Weisbaden: Otto Harrassowitz, 1983), 2–3.

5. Aristotle *Politics* 1.2.1.

6. How remarkable that Sarah, Rebekah, and Rachel, the wives of Israel's three patriarchs, were all barren! This demonstrates that the very existence of the nation stems from God's miraculous work in enabling barren wives to become mothers. Without these three miracles the nation could not have been inaugurated through Abraham, as God had promised. His promise required three miracles!

his family" (Ruth 4:10). A widow from Tekoa went to King David, concerned that if her one remaining son were put to death for killing his brother, she would have no heir. "They would put out the only burning coal I have left, leaving my husband neither name nor descendant on the face of the earth" (2 Sam. 14:7). Absalom had a monument made in memory of himself—quite an expression of pride!—because he had no son "to carry on the memory of [his] name" (2 Sam. 18:18). Jeremiah wrote that if he had no offspring, his name would "be remembered no more" (Jer. 11:19).

A third reason Israelites wanted children was so the offspring could support their parents in their old age. When Ruth gave birth to Obed, women said to Naomi, the boy's grandmother, that he would "renew [her] life and sustain [her] in [her] old age" (Ruth 4:15). Joseph is one among many examples of sons who cared for their fathers in their older years (Gen. 47:11–12). "The Instruction of Ani," an ancient Egyptian text, refers to a son's obligation to care for his mother in her old age.[7]

Because of the deep desire to bear children, parents often prayed that God would grant them offspring. Concerned because he was childless in his older years, Abraham asked God how he could possibly be the progenitor of a great nation. "What can you give me since I remain childless?" he asked God (Gen. 15:2). He was concerned that his estate would be inherited not by a son but by his servant Eliezer (15:2–3).

Because Rebekah, Isaac's wife, was barren, the patriarch "prayed to the LORD on behalf of his wife" (25:21). Rachel, too, prayed to the Lord about her longing for children (30:6). So when she finally gave birth to Joseph, she said her pregnancy was because God "listened to her" (30:22), a prayer that she called "my plea." Leah bore Jacob a fifth son, Issachar, because God "listened" to her (30:17). At the tabernacle in Shiloh, barren Hannah "wept much and prayed to the LORD" that he would "give her a son" (1 Sam. 1:10–11). She named him Samuel as a reminder that she had asked the Lord for him (1:20).[8]

The childless couple Zechariah and Elizabeth, though old, apparently had been praying for a child, because an angel told Zechariah, "Your prayer has been heard" and Elizabeth would have a son (Luke 1:13).[9]

---

7. James B. Pritchard, ed., *Ancient Near Eastern Texts Relating to the Old Testament*, 3d ed. (Princeton, N.J.: Princeton University Press, 1969), 420–21.

8. The name "Samuel" may mean "heard of God," not "asked of God" (Eugene H. Merrill, "1 Samuel," in *The Bible Knowledge Commentary, Old Testament*, ed. John F. Walvoord and Roy B. Zuck [Wheaton, Ill.: Victor Books, 1985], 433).

9. Pamela J. Scalise calls attention to similar situations in the Ugaritic epic poems of KRT and Aqhat, "in which the leading characters are childless kings who appeal to El for help" ("'I Have Produced a Man with the Lord': God as Provider of Offspring in Old Testament Theology," *Review and Expositor* 91 [1994]: 580).

Precious Gifts from God

Because children come ultimately from God, not merely by "human decision" (John 1:13) or "unplanned," we should value them as gifts. This is what Leah, Jacob's first wife, said when she had borne her sixth son Zebulun: "God has presented me with a precious gift" (Gen. 30:20).

Godly parents recognized that conception and birth come about by divine aid. When the world's very first child was born, Eve said of Cain, "With the help of the LORD I have brought forth a man" (4:1). Then when her third boy Seth was born, she commented, "God has granted me another child in place of Abel" (4:25).

God's words to Abraham about barren Sarah having a son bespeak the divine origin of children: "I will bless her and will surely give you a son by her" (17:16). Rachel's maidservant Bilhah gave birth to a son Dan, and Rachel said, "God has . . . given me a son" (30:6).

After years of silent separation, the twin brothers Jacob and Esau finally met east of the Jordan River. After Esau embraced Jacob in an emotionally joyful reunion, the older twin asked about Jacob's wives and eleven children: "Who are these with you?" Jacob replied, "They are the children God has graciously given your servant" (33:5).

Another testimony to the Lord's involvement in conception is Ruth and Boaz's experience, in which "the LORD enabled her to conceive" (Ruth 4:13). The Bible refers to God's intervention in bringing about pregnancies as his "opening the womb" (Leah, Gen. 29:31; and Rachel, 30:22).

Childbirth as well as conception were God's doings. David wrote, "You brought me forth from my mother's womb" (Ps. 71:6). Through Isaiah God reassured his people that he, the promise-keeping God, completes what he begins: "Do I bring to the moment of birth and not give delivery?" (Isa. 66:9). Given the hazards of childbearing without the modern conveniences of medical science, it was not difficult for godly parents to acknowledge God's hand in "delivering" their babies to them.

To receive these precious gifts from God's hand is spoken of as being remembered by God (Rachel, Gen. 30:22; Hannah, 1 Sam. 1:11, 19), rewarded by God (Leah, Gen. 30:18), and being given "good fortune" (30:11).

To be "fruitful" with children was to be a recipient of God's blessing (Gen. 17:16; 28:3; 49:25; Exod. 23:25–26; Deut. 7:13–14; 28:11; 30:9; Job 5:25; Pss. 127:3–5; 128:3–4).

This does not mean, however, that godly Israelites thought of Yahweh as a "fertility deity." Unlike pagan worship of gods who supposedly made land, animals, and people fertile, worship of the true God did not involve sexual activity as a kind of "imitative magic." Also unlike pagan deities, Yahweh has no consort, is not subject to cycles of nature, and is holy and righteous.[10]

---

10. Ibid., 577–78.

"The Lord Has Taken Away My Disgrace"

Barrenness was an embarrassment to Israelite wives. More than that, it was a social disgrace for it posed a threat, though a limited one, to the perpetuation of the nation. Since childbearing signified God's favor, the absence of children in a marriage caused the spouses to wonder if God was displeased with them or if they were guilty of some sin. Though delay in becoming pregnant meant God's timing differed from a couple's desires, occasionally childlessness was the result of sin. For example, the Lord "closed up every womb in Abimelech's household" because he had almost committed adultery with Sarah, Abraham's wife (Gen. 20:18). Michal's deep-seated jealousy and disrespectful chiding of David resulted in her having no children (2 Sam. 6:20–23), and thus being deprived of any opportunity to become the mother of the successor to the throne.[11] Eliphaz, one of Job's friends, spoke of the godless being barren (Job 15:34).

Since childlessness was a punishment for adultery (Lev. 20:20–21; Num. 5:20–22, 31), a childless wife "not only ran the risk of being disdained, or worse, repudiated by her husband and in-laws, she also incurred the suspicion of indecent behavior."[12] Not surprisingly, then, the wife without offspring was "spiritually ruined, socially disgraced, and psychologically defeated."[13]

However, sin was often not the reason for barrenness. Sarah acknowledged that "the LORD has kept me from having children" (Gen. 16:2), and Jacob pointed up the same truth when he angrily said to his barren wife Rachel, "Am I in the place of God, who has kept you from having children?" (30:2). Zechariah and Elizabeth's sterility did not result from sin, for they were "upright in the sight of God, observing all the Lord's commandments and regulations blamelessly" (Luke 1:6).

Barren wives considered their condition a "misery" (Leah, Gen. 29:32; Hannah, 1 Sam. 1:11) and a "disgrace" (Rachel, Gen. 30:23; Elizabeth, Luke 1:25). The Greek word for "disgrace" in Luke 1:25, *oneidos*, used only here in the New Testament, is related to the verb *oneidizō*, "to reproach, insult, revile." This verb is used of the robbers who were crucified with Jesus who "heaped insults on him" (Matt. 27:44), obviously an expression of strong derision.

Hannah illustrates the strong emotional tension of a barren wife. Being harassed by her husband's other wife Peninnah only intensified Hannah's deep disappointment at being unable to get pregnant. Her longing is expressed in words of intense pathos: "downhearted," "bitterness," "misery," "deeply

---

11. John Mauchline, *1 and 2 Samuel* (London: Oliphants, 1971), 226.
12. Karel van der Toorn, *From Her Cradle to Her Grave: The Role of Religion in the Life of the Israelite and the Babylonian Woman*, trans. Sara J. Denning-Bolle (Sheffield: JSOT Press, 1994), 79.
13. James I. Packer, Merrill C. Tenney, and William White, Jr., *The Bible Almanac* (Nashville: Thomas Nelson Publishers, 1980), 441.

troubled," "anguish," "grief," and "downcast" (1 Sam. 1:8, 10, 11, 15, 16, 18). This resulted in her tears—which her husband Elkanah could not understand (1:8)!—and loss of appetite (1:7).

Besides prayer, four other means were used by some Old Testament women to seek to provide children for their husbands. One was giving their maidservants to their husbands to bear children for them. At Sarah's suggestion, her servant Hagar bore Ishmael to Abraham (Gen. 16:1–3, 15). Rachel gave Bilhah her maidservant to Jacob, by whom was borne Dan and Naphtali (30:3–8), and Leah's maidservant Zilpah gave birth to Gad and Asher (30:9–13). These four children became the sons of Rachel and Leah, respectively, not of the maidservants (30:6, 10). Other ancient Near Eastern cultures carried out a similar practice. In the Code of Hammurabi, the king of Babylon about the time of Joseph, a man could have children by means of his wife's slave,[14] and in an Old Assyrian text from Anatolia, if a wife did not provide her husband with offspring within two years after the marriage, she could purchase a slave woman by whom her husband could father a child. He could then dispose of the slave by sale or send her away.[15]

A second means used in an attempt to overcome barrenness was the eating of mandrakes. These were vegetables of the nightshade family, whose roots have sometimes been considered valuable for medicine. Because the forked roots resemble the lower parts of a human body, some people superstitiously thought that eating mandrake roots was aphrodisiacal (Song of Songs 7:13) or induced pregnancy.[16] The mandrake, common in Palestine, ripens in the time of wheat harvest (Gen. 30:14). Childless Rachel asked her sister Leah for her mandrakes apparently to induce pregnancy, but obviously this manipulation was unsuccessful, for not until later did the Lord cause her to become pregnant (30:22–23). Was she superstitious because of her Aramean (northern Mesopotamian) background (25:20)?

Some women used a third—and more upright—means of inducing fertility, namely, making a vow to God. Hannah promised the Lord that if he would give her a son, she would dedicate him to the Lord for all his life (1 Sam. 1:11). The only other instance in the Bible of vow-taking for the sake of overcoming sterility is the mother of Lemuel, who referred to her child as the "son of my vows" (Prov. 31:2).

The Mosaic law provided a fourth means by which an infertile wife could have offspring. This legal provision, known as the levirate marriage and prescribed in Deuteronomy 25:5–10, enabled a childless widow to bear offspring

14. Tikva Frymer-Kensky, "Patriarchal Family Relationships and Near Eastern Law," *Biblical Archeologist* 44 (Fall 1981): 211.

15. Ibid., 211–12, citing J. Lewy, "On Some Institutions of the Old Assyrian Empire," *Hebrew Union College Annual* 27 (1956): 1–79.

16. *The NIV Study Bible* (Grand Rapids: Zondervan Publishing House, 1985), 51.

by marrying her husband's brother. ("Levirate" comes from the Latin *levir*, meaning "husband's brother.") The Old Testament records only two examples of such benefit to a widow: Genesis 38 and the Book of Ruth. A man could marry his sister-in-law (normally forbidden, Lev. 18:16) only if the brothers had been living together, having inherited their father's property jointly,[17] and the deceased brother had died without leaving a male heir (Deut. 25:5). The purpose was so that the son born to this relationship could "carry on the name of the dead brother" (25:6). Perpetuating one's name through male descendants was extremely important to Israel (2 Sam. 14:7; 18:18; Ps. 45:16–17; Jer. 11:19). In addition the levirate involvement enabled the deceased man's property to be kept in his family line (Num. 27:1–11; Ruth 4:10).

In some cases the brother of the deceased did not want to marry his widowed sister-in-law. In that case the widow could initiate a ceremony before the city elders in which she would publicly repudiate her brother-in-law for his refusal, thus making it a matter of public record that the guilt lay with him, not her (Deut. 25:7–10).

Genesis 38 relates a case in which a living brother refused to take up his levirate responsibility. Er, Judah's first of three sons by Shua, married Tamar. A wicked man, Er died at the Lord's hand. Therefore, Judah told Onan, his second son, to raise offspring for his brother Er by fulfilling "your duty to her as a brother-in-law" (v. 8). Realizing that children born to him and Tamar would not be his but would instead perpetuate his dead brother's name, Onan refused. While seeking sexual gratification with Tamar, he refused the levirate responsibility (v. 9). Tamar then deceptively arranged to have relations with her father-in-law Judah to gain offspring, and she gave birth to twins Zerah and Perez (vv. 11–30).

The other instance of levirate marriage is the story of Ruth. Boaz loved the young Moabite widow, but he knew there was a closer relative who had prior claim to her and the property of her father-in-law Elimelech. The closer relative refused to marry her and buy the property (Ruth 4:5–6), so Boaz, though not obligated by law to carry out the levirate marriage, did so because of his love for Ruth. In acquiring her and the family estate he helped "maintain the name of the dead with his property" (4:10). Thus widowed, childless Ruth was able to give birth to a boy Obed, whose grandson was David and whose later descendant was Jesus Christ himself! The levirate marriage law, carried out by Boaz and Ruth, thus served to perpetuate Elimelech's line down to the birth of the Messiah.

Some irregularities can be noted in this levirate case, however. Boaz was not a close relative of Elimelech; and he should have married Naomi,

---

17. Jack S. Deere, "Deuteronomy," in *The Bible Knowledge Commentary, Old Testament*, 306.

Elimelech's widow and property holder.[18] Naomi, however, was past child-bearing age.

The New Testament includes one reference to the levirate relationship. The Sadducees challenged Jesus about the resurrection (which they did not believe in) by asking how Moses' instructions about levirate marriage would apply to a woman who married seven brothers, each of whom died childless (Luke 20:28).

Patai suggests that the levirate provision existed in the ancient Near Eastern cultures including the Sumerians, the Assyrians, and the Hittites.[19] However, Leggett discusses a number of alleged parallels and concludes that this practice was probably not carried out in Babylonia or Assyria, but may have existed among the Hittites and in Ugarit.[20]

"Knit Together in My Mother's Womb"

Modern science has revealed some remarkable facts about the developing baby in the mother's womb. For instance, within twenty-four hours after fertilization of an ovum by a sperm the first cell division takes place. Three weeks after conception the first nerve cells of the embryo have formed. In four weeks the developing child is about one-fourth inch long and the heart is pumping. After five and a half weeks, when the embryo is only one-third of an inch long, the eyes, nose, and mouth are evident, and at six weeks the baby's heart is beating about 140 times a minute, twice the rate of the mother's heart. At eight weeks the embryo is one inch long. When ten or eleven weeks old, the fetus's body moves, the developing baby hiccups, and it flexes its arms and legs.[21]

How all this occurs, with the mother unaware of these complex developments of a new life within her body, staggers the imagination and causes parents to experience a deep sense of amazement and awe. Though people in Bible times bore children without being aware of these and other intricacies of the baby's development in its mother's womb, they, too, were struck by the amazing fact of fetal development. Like today, people then knew it happened but they did not know how. "As you do not know . . . how the body

18. Edith Deen, *Family Living in the Bible* (New York: Harper & Row, Publishers, 1963), 16; and David R. Mace, *Hebrew Marriage* (London: Epworth Press, 1953), 97–99.

19. Raphael Patai, *Family, Love and the Bible* (London: MacGibbon and Kee, 1960), 86.

20. Donald A. Leggett, *The Levirate and Goel Institutions in the Old Testament with Special Attention to the Book of Ruth* (Cherry Hill, N.J.: Mack Publishing Co., 1974), 10–27. The Hittite law reads, "If a man has a wife, and the man dies, his brother shall take his wife, then his father should take her. If also his father dies, his brother shall take his wife (and also) the son of his brother shall (take her). There shall be no punishment" (E. Neufeld, *The Hittite Laws* [London: Luzac, 1951], 55).

21. Lennart Nilsson and Lars Hamberger, *A Child Is Born*, trans. Clare James (New York: Delacorte Press, 1990), 39, 78, 83, 85, 108.

is formed in a mother's womb, so you cannot understand the work of God" (Eccles. 11:5).

In one of the Bible's earliest references to pregnancy,[22] Job recalled the careful, detailed way in which God had formed him in the womb: "Did you not pour me out like milk and curdle me like cheese, clothe me with skin and flesh and knit me together with bones and sinews?" (Job 10:10–11). The farmer's cheese-making and the seamstress's knitting provide striking metaphors of prenatal growth.

David, too, employed the figure of a seamstress to depict this work of God. "You knit me together in my mother's womb. . . . I was woven together" (lit., "embroidered"; Ps. 139:13, 15). Such knowledge led to spontaneous worship: "I praise you because I am fearfully and wonderfully made" (139:14). Verbs Bible writers used to describe God's forming of the human baby include "shaped" (Job 10:8), "molded" (Job 10:9), "made" (Job 10:8; 31:15; Ps. 139:14–15; Isa. 44:2), "formed" (Ps. 103:14; Eccles. 11:5; Isa. 29:16; 44:2, 24; 49:5; Jer. 1:5), and "created" (Ps. 139:13). The unborn consists of "skin and flesh" and "bones and sinews" (Job 10:10–11), which David called "my frame" and "my unformed [i.e., not fully developed] body" (Ps. 139:16).

Job spoke of God's molding him "like clay" (Job. 10:9), and Elihu said he too was "taken from clay," literally "nipped" like a potter fingering a small portion of clay (33:6). And David wrote that God "knows how we are formed, he remembers that we are dust" (Ps. 103:14). These statements recall the Lord's forming the first man, Adam, "from the dust of the ground" (Gen. 2:7), and Isaiah's comparing God's creation of the human race to the work of a potter in making pots out of clay (Isa. 29:16; 41:25; 45:9; 64:8; cf. Jer. 18:6; Rom. 9:21). The Hebrew word for man *('adām)* is related to the word for ground *('ădāmāh)*.

In anguish over the sudden catastrophic loss of his wealth and his ten children, Job said he came naked from his mother's womb and would return there naked (Job 1:21), that is, he would die without taking anything with him. But why did he say, literally, "naked I will return there"? Obviously he meant he would be buried in the ground, and not return to his mother's womb. But the womb was a poetic way of referring to the earth because of the similarities between the two. People are born of woman and are made of dust; the woman's offspring are like crops from the ground. This helps explain why David wrote about his prenatal growth, "I was woven together in the depths of the earth" (Ps. 139:15).

Today we know the human body consists of numerous chemical elements such as hydrogen, oxygen, carbon, nitrogen, iron, calcium, and phosphorus,

---

22. For reasons the Book of Job may be the first Bible book written, see my *Job*, Everyman's Bible Commentary (Chicago: Moody Press, 1978), 8–11; and Robert L. Alden, *Job*, New American Commentary (Nashville: Broadman Press, 1993), 25–29.

elements also found in the earth. How appropriate, then, that the biblical writers said the human body is made from clay or dust. But the human body is not just dirt! Man "became a living being" (lit., "a living soul") because God "breathed into his nostrils the breath of life" (Gen. 2:7). Man became a spiritual being, not just an animal. Animals also were "formed out of the ground" (2:19) but were not made spiritual creatures.

While a human baby is growing in the womb, God is not only forming the physical body in all its complex intricacies; he is also forming the human spirit. Zechariah affirmed this truth by writing that the Lord "forms the spirit of man within him" (Zech. 12:1), and Job, commenting on his own embryonic maturation, added, "You gave me life . . . and in your providence watched over my spirit" (Job 10:12). David wrote of the Lord's creating his "inmost being . . . in the secret place" (Ps. 139:13, 15) of the womb of his mother. We can all agree with David that such work is "wonderful" (139:14)!

The Bible mentions the experiences of several women in their pregnancies. Rebekah, puzzled by the extensive movements in her womb, was told by the Lord that she was carrying twins (Gen. 25:22–23), and Hosea added that in her womb Jacob grasped Esau's heel (Hos. 12:3). Manoah's wife, pregnant with Samson, was told by the angel of the Lord that she was to refrain from fermented drinks or ceremonially unclean foods during her nine-month waiting period (Judg. 13:4–5, 7). These were some of the same restrictions required of a person taking a Nazirite vow, which was to be true of Samson (13:5, 7; Num. 6:2–6). For the first five months of her pregnancy, Elizabeth "remained in seclusion" at home while awaiting the birth of John the Baptist (Luke 1:24). Reasons given for this confinement vary. Some say she may had thought she was "unsightly," but this seems unlikely "since pregnancy is *least* detectable during the early months."[23] Elizabeth may have wanted to be alone to meditate on the wonder of her pregnancy in her old age, or she may have wanted to avoid the gossip of village women, or she may have felt "unsociable" because of "morning sickness," typical of the first months of pregnancy—or perhaps she experienced all three!

In her sixth month, when Elizabeth was visited by Mary, "the baby leaped in her womb" (Luke 1:41; cf. v. 44). While every expectant mother begins to feel this kind of stirring in her womb on or before the sixth month, this movement was apparently divinely timed. Mary, pregnant and nearing the birth date, made a seventy-five-mile journey from Nazareth to Bethlehem, where her baby, the Lord Jesus, was born (Luke 2:1–7) in less than desirable surroundings.

The vulnerability of pregnant women in warfare is seen in the Ammonites unjustly ripping open the pregnant women of Gilead simply to extend the

23. Watson E. Mills, "Childbearing in Ancient Times," *Biblical Illustrator* 13 (Fall 1986): 55 (italics his).

borders of their land (Amos 1:13), and the Arameans under Hazael ripping open Israelite pregnant women (2 Kings 8:12). Menahem, the third from the last king of Israel (752–742 B.C.), "ripped open all the pregnant women" of the town of Tiphsah (15:16). The Assyrians committed this same terrible crime when they defeated the northern kingdom of Israel (Hos. 13:16). In this way soldiers sought to end the perpetuation of the peoples being conquered.

Instructing his disciples about the coming worldwide tribulation that will precede his millennial reign on earth, Jesus said the suffering will be so dreadful that it will be especially difficult "for pregnant women and nursing mothers" (Matt. 24:19; Luke 21:23).

"Wombs That Miscarry"

Miscarriages were feared in Bible times just as they are today. Carrying a baby to "full term" indicated God's blessing on faithful parents: "Worship the Lord your God . . . and none will miscarry" (Exod. 23:25–26). Hosea warned that one form of God's punishment on Israel's wickedness would be "wombs that miscarry" (Hos. 9:14).[24]

Sometimes a miscarriage was caused by accident, as explained in the Mosaic instruction in Exodus 21:22–23. If two men in a brawl happened to hit a pregnant woman, she might have a miscarriage or premature birth. If neither the baby nor the mother were injured, the guilty man was to pay a fine. However, if there was death or serious injury to either the fetus or the mother, then the penalty was to be in proportion to the nature of the injury. Interestingly, the unborn fetus was considered a human being for whom compensation was required just as much as for the mother.

A stillbirth refers to a full-term or near full-term baby who arrives from the womb dead. What an emotionally disheartening experience to anticipate with joy the arrival of a newborn and then have that excitement shattered by death at the time of birth! In an imprecation against the wicked, David asked God to destroy them by making them "like a stillborn child" (Ps. 58:8). And yet being unable to enjoy one's prosperity was worse than being a stillborn child (Eccles. 6:3). When Aaron expressed concern that his sister Miriam be healed from leprosy, he said he did not want her to become "like a stillborn infant" (Num. 12:10–12).

Both Job and Jeremiah bemoaned their condition to the extent that they said they wished they had been stillborns. "Why was I not hidden in the ground like a stillborn child, like an infant who never saw the light of day?"

---

24. We know today that miscarriages sometimes occur naturally because of faulty development in the fertilized ovum or because of some defect in the chromosomal development of the sperm (Nilsson and Hamberger, *A Child Is Born*, 69).

(Job 3:16). Job felt that having been born dead and then buried ("hidden in the ground") would have been preferable to his intense physical pain and emotional turmoil.

Jeremiah's wish that he would have never "come out of the womb" (Jer. 20:18) was so strong that he cursed his birthday (20:14–15), wishing that the Lord had killed him in the womb "with my mother as my grave" (20:17).

Childbirth, as now, was a dangerous experience in Bible times. Having a difficult delivery, Rachel died when her second son Benjamin, Jacob's twelfth son, was born (Gen. 35:16–18). Eli's daughter-in-law, the wife of Phinehas, heard that the ark of God was captured and that her father-in-law Eli and her husband had died. This tragic news caused her to go into labor. As she was dying in childbirth, she named her newborn Ichabod, "no glory," for God's glory had departed from the nation with the capture of the ark (1 Sam. 4:19–22).

"With Pain You Will Give Birth"

When Adam and Eve sinned, God told her one of the punishments for their sin would be increased "pains in childbearing; with pain you will give birth to children" (Gen. 3:16). Every woman who has borne children knows the excruciating pain that accompanies childbirth. While today various means of alleviating labor pains are available, no such means were accessible to women in the ancient world.

Because of the common experience of delivery pain, the Bible speaks of it often. "Overcome by her labor pains," Eli's daughter-in-law died in childbirth (1 Sam. 4:19). A woman who experienced great labor pains named her boy Jabez because she said, "I gave birth to him in pain" (1 Chron. 4:9).

The pain of childbirth became an apt metaphor of any kind of suffering or anguish. Enemies attacking Jerusalem would experience labor-like pain as they fled in defeat (Ps. 48:6). Other enemies of God's people, including Babylon (Isa. 13:8; Jer. 50:43), Tyre (Isa. 23:4), Edom (Jer. 49:22), Moab (48:41), and Damascus (49:24), will anguish in pain like a childbearing mother. Jerusalem would also suffer similar painful terror (Isa. 26:17–18; 66:7; Jer. 4:31; 6:24; 13:21; 22:23; Micah 4:9–10), as well as the northern kingdom of Israel (Hos. 13:13). A vision of enemy attacks on Judah brought similar anguish to Isaiah (Isa. 21:3).

Jeremiah predicted that in the terrible tribulation, the "time of trouble for Jacob" (Jer. 30:7), normally strong men will be so weakened by the terror of God's judgments that they will have their hands on their stomachs "like a woman in labor" (30:6). Paul, too, wrote that people in the tribulation will experience intense suffering like the "labor pains of a pregnant woman" (1 Thess. 5:3). Yet when God restores Israel to her land, those who will come "from the ends of the earth" will even include expectant mothers and women in labor (Jer. 31:8), so anxious will they be to return to their homeland.

Paul likened the hardships and groanings of the physical creation to the pains of childbirth (Rom. 8:22). He even compared his own suffering on behalf of his converts in Galatia to delivery pains (Gal. 4:19).[25]

The woman envisioned by John in Revelation 12, who probably depicts Israel,[26] gave birth to her child, probably a reference to Christ,[27] in great pain that caused her to cry out (Rev. 12:2).

Women in labor are said to experience pangs (Isa. 21:3), to writhe and cry out in pain (26:17), to gasp and pant (42:14), to groan (Jer. 4:31), and to experience panic and anguish (49:24).

However, even with all the pain, when a woman's baby is born, as Jesus said, she "forgets the anguish because of her joy" in bearing a child (John 16:21).

In ancient Near Eastern cultures, rituals were performed and incantations were recited to seek to keep mother and baby alive and free from harm or defect. The Babylonians, the Hittites, and people at Ugarit believed seven goddesses oversaw childbirth and celebrated a successful delivery.[28] Van der Toorn cites two Mesopotamian prayers to the god Marduk, who allegedly aided in a less painful delivery.[29] Mills observes that in Roman times, pregnant women made offerings to gods or goddesses to insure an easy birth.[30] Of course, Bible mothers who believed in Yahweh did not cite such prayers to a false god. They may have prayed to the Lord for an easy and safe delivery, though the Bible records no such prayers.

"Naked I Came from My Mother's Womb"

Today parents send birth announcements to relatives and friends to share the exciting news of the arrival. In Bible times God himself announced several births, but he did so long *before* the events. These included five announcements: Ishmael (Gen. 16:11), Isaac (18:10), Immanuel (Isa. 7:14), John the Baptist (Luke 1:13), and Jesus (Luke 1:31).

When the time of delivery came, several parents acknowledged God's help: Eve (Gen. 4:1), David (Ps. 22:9), and an anonymous psalmist (Ps. 71:6).

Presumably women bore their babies in their homes or tents, though one verse refers to birth occurring in open air under an apple tree: "Under the

25. For more on this subject, see Conrad Gempf, "The Imagery of Birth Pangs in the New Testament," *Tyndale Bulletin* 45 (1994): 119–35.

26. John F. Walvoord, "Revelation," in *The Bible Knowledge Commentary, New Testament*, ed. John F. Walvoord and Roy B. Zuck (Wheaton, Ill.: Victor Books, 1983), 957.

27. Ibid., 958.

28. Scalise, "I Have Produced a Man with the Lord," 584. Cf. Beckman, *Hittite Birth Rituals*, 250.

29. Van der Toorn, *From Her Cradle to Her Grave*, 89.

30. Mills, "Childbearing in Ancient Times," 56.

apple tree [sometimes a symbol of love] I roused you; there your mother conceived you, there she who was in labor gave you birth" (Song of Songs 8:5).

Exodus 1:16 mentions a "delivery stool" (lit., "two stones") used in childbirth by Hebrew women in Egypt. Presumably the woman in labor knelt on these stones for support while in a crouched position. Today the birthing position most women favor is to recline in a semi-sitting position. However, occasionally some prefer to kneel, perhaps similar to the Hebrew practice mentioned in Exodus 1:16.[31] Bearing children in a kneeling position is also referred to in Genesis 30:3 (cf. NASB), where Rachel asked Jacob to, literally, "give birth on her knees," and in Job 3:12, where Job asked, "Why were there knees to receive me and breasts that I might be nursed?"[32] Hittite literature mentions two stools on which the woman knelt while in labor,[33] and the midwife was called a "woman of the birth-stool."[34] The Mishnah, which records Jewish oral traditions, refers to a woman at childbirth being settled into a reclining "travail chair,"[35] with other women grasping her under her arms in her labor.[36] Apparently this was also the practice in the Roman Empire. A terracotta sculpture, housed in the Archaeological Museum of Ostia, near Rome, shows a woman in labor seated in a chair, while one midwife supports her from behind and another midwife is squatting, preparing to receive the child, presumably on her knees.[37] Some say the knees in Job 3:12 refer to the baby being received on the knees of the midwife seated in front of the birthing woman who was sitting, while supported from behind by another woman against whom she was leaning. Or the mother's squatting position may suggest her own knees.[38] On the other hand, when Joseph's great-grandchildren (Manasseh's grandchildren) were placed on Joseph's knees (Gen. 50:23), it may have been an act of grandfatherly affection or a gesture in which the offspring were acknowledged publicly as legally belonging to Joseph's family line.

31. For illustrations of this kneeling position in older times and today, see Nilsson and Hamberger, *A Child Is Born*, 133, 164.

32. This differs from the practice of placing a newborn on the knees of the father or grandfather as a gesture signifying the child belonged to him by legal adoption (Gen. 48:12; 50:23).

33. Beckman, *Hittite Birth Rituals*, 250.

34. Ibid., 233.

35. *M. Kelim* 23.4; *M. Arahin* 1.4.

36. *M. Oholoth* 7.4. Cf. S. Safrai and M. Stern, *The Jewish People in the First Century*, 2 vols. (Assen: Van Gorcum, 1976), 2:765.

37. This terra cotta is depicted in Paul Veyne, ed. *From Pagan Rome to Byzantium*, trans. Arthur Goldhammer (Cambridge, Mass.: Belknap Press, 1987), 10.

38. An Egyptian hieroglyphic sign depicts the concept of Egyptian women squatting on their knees during labor, and a Bronze Age clay statue from first millennium B.C. Cyprus shows a woman assisted by two midwives (see Gaalyahu Cornfield, ed., *Pictorial Bible Encyclopedia* [New York: Macmillan Co., 1964], 318 for the hieroglyphics and a picture of the statue; cf. Lawrence O. Richards, ed., *Revell Bible Dictionary* [Old Tappan, N.J.: Fleming H. Revell Co., 1990], 206).

Not too many decades ago fathers were excluded from the hospital delivery room but today fathers are welcomed because of the help and encouragement they can give to their wives. The absent father goes back to Bible times. Jeremiah, bemoaning the opposition he faced from his own people, wished he had never been born. In strong language he said he wished a messenger had never "brought my father the news" of his birth (Jer. 20:15). Job referred to the announcement made at his birth, "A boy is born!" (Job 3:3), perhaps words spoken to a father waiting at a distance.

A midwife encouraged Rachel in her difficult child labor, announcing to Rachel that her newborn was another son (Gen. 35:17). A midwife was present when Tamar's twins, Zerah and Perez, were born. The midwife identified the firstborn by tying a scarlet thread on his wrist (Gen. 38:27–30).

The only midwives in the Bible whose names we know were Shiprah and Puah, Egyptian women who feared the Hebrew God and who helped Hebrew women in childbirth (Exod. 1:16). They told Pharaoh that Hebrew women were more vigorous than Egyptian women so that their babies came before the midwives could arrive at the Hebrew homes (1:19). Were they stretching the truth to excuse themselves for disobeying Pharaoh's order to kill all Hebrew baby boys at birth, or were the Hebrew women actually having quick deliveries?

Sometimes other women were present (Ruth 4:14). Our Lord, however, was born to Mary without the help of anyone other than Joseph.

Midwifery was no doubt practiced throughout the ancient Near East. Mesopotamian literature refers to the Akkadian "birth goddesses" (*šassūrātu*) who were said to assist the mother goddess Belet-ili at the time of birth. Egyptians believed Isis protected women in their pregnancies, presided over their childbearing, and nurtured infants.[39] Hittite rites following a birth honored the goddess Ishtar.[40] In Ugarit, the birth goddesses were the Kotharot, daughters of Hilal, the new-moon god.[41] Presumably midwives represented these goddesses.

In the Roman Empire mothers believed that Juno Lucino was a goddess who assisted women in childbirth, and Picunnus and Pilumnus were "the gods of infants," who, in the *lustratio,* a ceremony following birth, were called on to drive off evil spirits.[42]

Two verses, both in the Bible's wisdom literature, refer to the baby being naked at the time of birth (Job 1:21; Eccles. 5:15).

39. Sharon Kelley Heyob, *The Cult of Isis among Women in the Graeco-Roman World* (Leiden: E. J. Brill, 1975), 50, 70–73, 80.
40. Beckman, *Hittite Birth Rituals,* 251.
41. Van der Toorn, *From Her Cradle to Her Grave,* 86–87.
42. Beryl Rawson, "Adult-Child Relationships in Roman Society," in *Marriage, Divorce, and Children in Ancient Rome,* ed. Beryl Rawson (Oxford: Clarendon Press, 1991), 13–14.

When the child was born, the midwife cut the umbilical cord, washed the baby, rubbed it with salt, and wrapped it in cloth (Ezek. 16:4). Rubbing the baby's body with salt water to get rid of mucus[43] is still practiced by Middle Eastern peoples including Syrians, Yemenites, and Arabs.[44] The midwife or the mother wrapped the baby tightly in strips of cloth, usually four or five inches wide and five or six yards long,[45] with the baby's arms at its sides. People believed that this practice, which was normally continued for at least forty days,[46] would help the infant's limbs grow straight and would firm up the body. The cloths "were loosened several times a day and the skin was rubbed with olive oil and dusted with myrtle leaves."[47]

Mary wrapped the baby Jesus in strips of cloth (Luke 2:7), in what the King James Version calls "swaddling clothes." This is not unlike the present-day practice of parents wrapping their newborn tightly in a blanket to give the infant a sense of security.

Jewish mothers nursed their babies (Gen. 21:7; 1 Sam. 1:21–23; 1 Kings 3:21) by breast-feeding (Gen. 49:25; Job 3:12; Isa. 28:9; 49:15). The natural, strong desire of a baby for milk provides a picture of believers yearning for the spiritual nourishment of God's Word (1 Peter 2:2). The peace the Lord will give the nation Israel in the millennium is likened to the peaceful scene of a mother nursing, carrying, playing with, and comforting her young (Isa. 66:11–13).

Sometimes a wet nurse was used. Rebekah had a nurse named Deborah (Gen. 35:8); Pharaoh's daughter hired a wet nurse to feed Moses, and the nurse turned out to be Moses' own mother (Exod. 2:9). When a nurse fled with five-year-old Mephibosheth, Jonathan's son, he fell and became crippled (2 Sam. 4:4). Young Joash was hidden by Jehosheba with Joash's nurse in the temple for six years to keep him safe from queen Athaliah, who intended to kill all the royal family in order to free her reign from opposition (2 Kings 11:1–3).

---

43. Soranus, a second-century A.D. Greek physician, referred to this practice (*Gynaecia* 2.12).

44. Patai, *Family, Love and the Bible*, 169–70.

45. Ralph Gower, *The New Manners and Customs of Bible Times* (Chicago: Moody Press, 1987), 62.

46. Packer, Tenney, and White, *The Bible Almanac*, 445. Soranus wrote that some parents removed the swaddling clothes around the fortieth day and most around the sixtieth day, but that it was to be gradual, with first one hand removed, then the other hand a few days later, then the feet (*Gynaecia* 2.42).

47. *The Lion Encyclopedia of the Bible*, rev. ed. (Batavia, Ill.: Lion Publishing Corp., 1986), 164. For pictures of what a baby in swaddling clothes may have looked like, see Hugo Blümner, *The Home Life of the Ancient Greeks*, trans. Alice Zimmern (New York: Cooper Square Publishers, 1966), 72, 83, and Robert Etienne, "Ancient Medical Conscience and the Life of Children," *Journal of Psychohistory* 4 (1976):144–45.

In the Roman Empire many women in wealthy families employed a wet nurse to breast-feed their children, and those nurses "continued to function as nannies to children they had previously nursed."[48]

When a young child was weaned in Bible times, the parents celebrated with a feast (Gen. 21:8). When Hannah weaned Samuel, she took him to Shiloh and left him there with Eli to serve the Lord in the tabernacle (1 Sam. 1:21–28). Since the apocryphal 2 Maccabees 7:27 refers to weaning when a young child is three years old, and since this custom was also followed in ancient Babylonia,[49] Samuel may have been three at the time of his weaning and dedication. According to the Talmud, however, children were weaned between the eighteenth and twenty-fourth months (*m. Git.* 7.6).

In Psalm 131:2 David likened his spiritual comfort and contentedness in the Lord to that of a weaned child, content with no longer needing its mother's milk, which previously was indispensable.

After Gomer had weaned her daughter Lo-Ruhamah, she had another son (Hos. 1:8). This point, along with the fact that Hannah had other children (three sons and two daughters) only after she weaned Samuel (1 Sam. 2:21), may reflect the fact that prolonged lactation may have temporarily led to the inability to conceive.

Like today, some babies born in Bible times had physical defects. Jesus healed a man born blind (John 9:1–7), which condition the Pharisees wrongly asserted was because of sin ("you were steeped in sin at birth," 9:34). The Lord used Peter and John to heal a beggar crippled from birth (Acts 3:1–10), the first miracle after the beginning of the church on the day of Pentecost. Another man lame from birth was healed by Paul when the apostle was in Lystra (Acts 14:8–10). Obviously the parents of these blind and lame babies allowed them to live. The parents did not abandon them or put them to death because of their infirmities.

In ancient Israel, childbirth made a woman ceremonially unclean. She was unclean for forty days if a boy were born, or eighty days following the birth of a girl (Lev. 12:1–8).[50] In this time period she was not to touch anything sacred, a regulation similar to her monthly period. Did this ceremonial impurity mean the child resulted from the parents' sin? Did it mean that sexual acts and childbirth were somehow sinful? Did it in some way serve to protect the mother?[51] None of these questions should be answered affirmatively, for the waiting period is related

48. Keith R. Bradley, *Discovering the Roman Family* (New York: Oxford University Press, 1991), 20, 27; cf. Suzanne Dixon, *The Roman Family* (Baltimore: Johns Hopkins University Press, 1992), 131, 178, plate 18.

49. Roland de Vaux, *Ancient Israel: Its Life and Institutions,* trans. John McHugh (New York: McGraw-Hill Book Co., 1961), 43; and Cornfield, *Pictorial Bible Encyclopedia,* 318. Also lengthy weaning periods are followed among Arab women today (Patai, *Family, Love and the Bible,* 174–75).

50. Van der Toorn points out similar rules obtained in ancient Mesopotamia (*From Her Cradle to Her Grave,* 92).

51. Packer, Tenney, and White, *The Bible Almanac,* 448.

to the mother's "bleeding" (Lev. 12:4) and "her flow of blood" (12:7). Undoubtedly, this refers to the fact that, as is known today in obstetrics, the stretched uterus bleeds for a few weeks after birth, much as in menstruation.[52] In the Mosaic code the bleeding may have suggested the body lacked wholeness[53] or that the discharge contained dead matter.[54] The sin offering and burnt offering to be presented to the priest was to be a lamb, or if the mother could not afford that, two doves or two young pigeons could be presented (Lev. 12:8). Interestingly, Mary, Jesus' mother, could afford only two birds (Luke 2:22–24).

"Give Him the Name. . . ."

Choosing a name for a child today can be difficult. Parents wonder whether to name the child after a relative or whether to choose a name that "sounds good." In biblical times, however, parents chose names more deliberately and purposefully, and seldom was a baby named after a grandparent or other close relative.[55]

In the Old Testament babies were named at the time of birth (e.g., Gen. 29:32; 35:18; 1 Sam. 1:20), but in New Testament times John the Baptist and Jesus were named at the time of their circumcision, when they were eight days old (Luke 1:59; 2:21).

On some occasions angels informed one or both of the parents what the child should be named. These included Ishmael (Gen. 16:11), John the Baptist (Luke 1:13), and Jesus (Luke 1:26–31). Other times God told the parent or parents what to name their children (e.g., the Virgin Mary was to name her child Immanuel, "God with us," Isa. 7:14; Matt. 1:23). And God instructed Hosea's wife Gomer to give her children names that were indicative of the nation Israel (Hos. 1:4–10): Jezreel ("God sows"), Lo-Ruhamah ("not loved"), and Lo-Ammi ("not my people").

Usually the mother chose the baby's name, but occasionally the father or both parents did. In the Bible, twenty-two children are said to be named by their mothers, twelve times the fathers did the naming, and in the case of four children both parents were involved.[56]

---

52. Nilsson and Hamberger, *A Child Is Born,* 172.

53. Gordon J. Wenham, *The Book of Leviticus,* New International Commentary on the Old Testament (Grand Rapids: Wm. B. Eerdmans Publishing Co., 1979), 188.

54. R. K. Harrison, *Leviticus: An Introduction and Commentary* (Downers Grove, Ill.: InterVarsity Press, 1980), 161.

55. One near exception is when John the Baptist was named. Neighbors and relatives of his parents thought he should be given the name of his father Zechariah (Luke 1:57–65).

56. Mothers who chose their babies' names were Eve (Gen. 4:25), Lot's two daughters (19:37–38), Jacob's two wives Leah and Rachel and his two concubines Bilhah and Zilpah (29:31–30:24), Judah's wife Shua (38:3–5), Manoah's wife (Judg. 13:24), Hannah (1 Sam. 1:20), Phinehas's wife (4:21), Jabez's mother (1 Chron. 4:9), and Maacah (1 Chron. 7:16).

On one occasion (Gen. 35:18) the mother (Rachel) gave the boy a name (Ben-Oni), but the father chose a different name (Benjamin). Apparently Jacob felt free to do this since Rachel was dying, and he may have preferred to call his boy Benjamin, "son of my right hand," rather than be reminded the rest of his life that this last son of his was "a son of my trouble," the meaning of Ben-Oni.

Moses is one child who was named by an adult other than a parent. Pharaoh's daughter gave him the name Moses (Exod. 2:10).

Some children's names included "el," part of the word "Elohim," meaning God, or "iah" (or "jah" or "jih"), part of "Yahweh," the name of the true God. These names clearly reflected the parents' piety before the Lord. For example, Azariah means "helped by Yahweh," Eli means "God is mine," Elijah is "my God is Yahweh," Isaiah means "salvation of Yahweh," and Obadiah is "servant of Yahweh." The names Daniel, Hananiah, Mishael, and Azariah each include the "el" or "iah" ending. How remarkable that their parents' godliness was known in this way when the nation of Judah was so debased spiritually.

Also the name Jesus is the Aramaic form of the Hebrew word for Joshua, which means "Yahweh saves," certainly an appropriate name for our Savior (Matt. 1:21)!

Other parents gave their children names for a variety of reasons. Often the name related in some way to the circumstances surrounding the mother's pregnancy or the baby's birth, with the name being a wordplay on those circumstances. Eve named her first son, the first baby born into the human race, Cain *(qayin)* because she had brought forth *(qānāh)* a man (Gen. 4:1). Cain, meaning "brought forth," was a fitting name for the firstborn of Eve, whom Adam said "would become the mother of all living" (3:20).[57] Every mother thereafter has "brought forth" offspring. Isaac, which means "he laughs," recalls Abraham's and Sarah's laughter at the prediction that they would have a son in their old age (17:17; 18:12–13; 21:3). When Jacob was born, he grabbed the heel *(ᶜāqēb)* of his twin Esau, and so he was given a name *(yaᶜāqōb)* that sounds like heel (25:26). Each of Jacob's twelve sons' names were wordplays on the birthing circumstances,[58] except, Rachel's first child, whose

---

The fathers were Cain (Gen. 4:17), Seth (4:26), Lamech (4:19–22), Jacob (35:18), Joseph (41:51–52), Moses (Exod. 2:22), Gideon (Judg. 8:29–32), Ephraim (1 Chron. 7:20–24), and Job (Job 42:14).

The pairs of parents who together decided on their son's names were Adam and Eve in naming Seth (Gen. 4:25; 5:3), Isaac and Rebekah in naming Esau and Jacob (25:25–26), and David and Bathsheba in naming Solomon (2 Sam. 12:24). Most often the Bible says a child "was named" or "was called," without specifying the one who selected the names.

57. Interestingly, Adam is the only husband in the Bible who named his wife.

58. For the meanings of these names see Allen P. Ross, "Genesis," in *The Bible Knowledge Commentary, Old Testament,* 76–77. Also see Allen P. Ross, "Paranomasia and Popular Etymology in the Naming Narratives of the Old Testament" (Ph.D. diss., Cambridge University, 1981), 83–180.

name signified a request. Because she said, "May the Lord add to me another son," she called him Joseph, which means "May he add" (30:24).

Tamar called the first of her twin boys Zerah, meaning "scarlet," redolent of the scarlet thread the midwife tied on his wrist, and the second she named Perez, "breaking out," because he came out of her womb first when Zerah drew back his hand (38:27–30).

Ephraim named one of his sons Beriah, meaning "misfortune," because of Ephraim's loss of sons and livestock (1 Chron. 7:21–23).

Pharaoh's daughter gave Moses that name because, she said, "I drew him out of the water" (Exod. 2:10). The Hebrew name *mōšeh* is a pun on the verb *māšāh*, "to draw out," which recalled her taking him out of the basket in which he was floating along the bank of the Nile River (2:5–6). The name may also have been a wordplay on the Egyptian word *mōse* meaning "son."[59]

As explained earlier, Samuel's name was a wordplay on Hannah's prayer request for a boy.

Joseph named his two boys Manasseh, which sounds like the verb "to forget," because God helped Joseph forget his many troubles, and Ephraim, similar in sound to "twice fruitful," "because God had made [Joseph] fruitful" (Gen. 41:51–52).

As she was dying in childbirth, Phinehas's wife named her boy Ichabod, "no glory," out of her concern that God's glory had departed from the nation (1 Sam. 4:21–22).

An Old Testament mother whose childbirth was extremely painful named her boy Jabez *(ya'bēṣ)*, which is an intriguing wordplay on the Hebrew word for pain (*'āṣeb;* 1 Chron. 4:9–10), in which the consonants *b* and *ṣ* are reversed.

Other times parents gave their children names based on appearance or traits already exhibited.[60] Esau's body had a lot of hair when he was born, and Esau means hairy (Gen. 25:25). Job's three daughters born to him after his wealth was restored were very beautiful, and so Job named them Jemimah, "dove"; Keziah, "perfume"; and Keren-Happuch, "horn of [eye] paint" (Job 42:14–15). Some names anticipated the individual's characteristic, such as Solomon (2 Sam. 12:24), whose name means peace and whose reign over Israel was a reign of national peace.

Some children were named after animals. Rachel means "sheep," not surprising because she and her parents were sheepherders (Gen. 29:9–10). Deb-

---

59. J. K. Hoffmeier, "Moses," in *International Standard Bible Encyclopedia*, 3 (1986):417.

60. This and other occasions of naming do not support the notion that naming someone or something is an act of control or domination. George W. Ramsey argues well against this common idea that naming involves controlling ("Is Name-Giving an Act of Domination in Genesis 2:23 and Elsewhere?" *Catholic Biblical Quarterly* 50 [1988]: 24–35).

orah means "bee" (does this mean she was active like a bee?); Caleb means "dog"; and Shaphan, Josiah's secretary (2 Kings 22:3), means "rabbit."

It comes as a surprise to learn that some parents gave rather despicable names to their children, such as Nabal, meaning "fool," who lived up to his name for he was "surly and mean in his dealings" with David and others (1 Sam. 25:3–11). Even his wife Abigail admitted that "he is just like his name—his name is Fool, and folly goes with him" (25:25). Strangely, Saul named one of his sons Ish-Bosheth (2 Sam. 2:8), which means "man of shame."

In New Testament times, sons' names were sometimes connected with their fathers' names, probably to distinguish two or more individuals with the same name. For example, James, son of Zebedee (Matt. 4:21), is distinguished from James, son of Alphaeus (Mark 3:18). And Simon, son of Jonah (Matt. 16:17), was different from Simon the Zealot (Mark 3:18), and Simon the Leper (Mark 14:3).

God changed a number of individuals' birth names when they became adults. He changed Abram ("exalted father") to Abraham ("father of many," Gen. 17:5), an ironic name because he was then ninety-nine years old (17:1) and had no children of his own. God renamed Sarai "Sarah" ("princess," 17:15), an honorable name since she would become the ancestress of many people including kings (17:16). Later the Lord changed Jacob's name to Israel (32:28), "he struggled with God," which recalls his wrestling with the Lord at the Jabbok River (32:22–30; cf. 35:10). So these names reflected divine predictions or circumstances in which God was involved.

Foreigners sometimes changed individual Israelites' names. Pharaoh gave Joseph an Egyptian name, Zaphenath-Paneah (41:45), whose meaning is unknown; and Nebuchadnezzar gave four of his Jewish captives, whose names denoted the true God, names that honored Babylonian gods.[61] Pharaoh Neco changed Eliakim's name to Jehoiakim (2 Kings 23:34), an act that depicted Pharaoh's control over this vassal king of Judah. Similarly Nebuchadnezzar changed Mattaniah to Zedekiah, appointing him as vassal under Babylonian rule (24:17).

Jesus gave Simon the name Peter ("rock," Mark 3:16), indicative of his sturdy, rock-like character (Matt. 16:18). Joseph from Cyprus was so encouraging to others that the apostles mirrored that quality of his by renaming him Barnabas, "son of [one noted for] encouragement" (Acts 4:36). Naming a child, or renaming an adult, took on significance.

In Athens the *amphidromia* ceremony took place on the tenth day after birth. In this ceremony the father "carried the child around the household hearth; women purified themselves; friends and relations sent traditional gifts,

---

61. For explanations of their Jewish and Babylonian names, see J. Dwight Pentecost, "Daniel," in *The Bible Knowledge Commentary, Old Testament,* 1330.

octupuses and cuttle fish, but did not attend unless they had been present at the birth."[62]

Romans named their boys on the ninth day after birth and the girls on the eighth day in a ceremony called the *lustratio* ("purification"[63]) a time of ritual purification and supposed warding off of evil spirits.

"Circumcised on the Eighth Day"

When the apostle Paul told the Philippian believers why he could have boasted about his Jewish heritage, the first thing he listed was that he was "circumcised on the eighth day" (Phil. 3:5). But why was that significant? The practice of Hebrew male infants being circumcised when they were only eight days old goes back to Abraham.

Surely Abraham and other Hebrews were unaware of the hygienic value of that timing. But many male boys in America today are circumcised on day eight because on that day the body contains ten percent more Vitamin K than normal, which helps cause the blood to coagulate.

God told Abraham to circumcise every male in his household as "the sign of the covenant" between God and the patriarch (Gen. 17:10–14), the covenant God had already inaugurated (15:4–21). This covenant was God's assurance to Abraham that he would be the progenitor of many nations and kings (17:5–6) and that "the whole land of Canaan" would belong to him and his descendants (17:8; cf. 15:21). This unilateral covenant—which guarantees the existence of Israel as a nation and the possession of the land by the nation—is an "everlasting" (i.e., ongoing and irrevocable) covenant, a fact God affirmed to Abraham four times (17:7, 8, 13, 19; cf. 48:4; Ps. 105:8–11). Appropriately Stephen called it "the covenant of circumcision" (Acts 7:8).

Circumcision, then, was unique to the nation Israel; it served as an indicator of the special spiritual relationship between the nation and God. Abraham obeyed God that very day (Gen. 17:23) by circumcising every male in his household, including thirteen-year-old Ishmael and all the male slaves (17:23–27). Also Abraham, then ninety-nine, had himself circumcised, though the Bible does not state who did it. Thereafter, starting with Isaac, Hebrew baby boys have been circumcised when eight days old (21:4; Acts 7:8), as God instructed Abraham (Gen. 17:12). Moses included this directive in the Law (Lev. 12:3), and John the Baptist and Jesus were both circumcised on the eighth day (Luke 1:59; 2:21).

---

62. Mark Golden, *Children and Childhood in Classical Athens* (Baltimore: Johns Hopkins University Press, 1990), 23. Demosthenes 39.22, 40.28 refers to this practice.

63. Rawson, *Marriage, Divorce, and Children in Ancient Rome,* 14. Dixon calls this the *dies lustricus,* "day of ritual purification" (Dixon, *The Roman Family,* 134; cf. Suzanne Dixon, *The Roman Mother* [Norman, Okla.: Oklahoma University Press, 1988], 239–40).

However, circumcision was practiced in the ancient world by other peoples including Egyptians,[64] Edomites, Ammonites, Moabites, and Arabs (Jer. 9:25). Phoenicians and Syrians also practiced circumcision,[65] but the Philistines, originally from Crete and the Aegean Sea islands, did not practice it (Judg. 14:3; 15:18; 1 Sam. 14:6; 17:26, 36; 18:25, 27; 31:4; 2 Sam. 1:20; 3:14; 1 Chron. 10:4). This was a custom, then, of western Semites, but not of eastern Semites of Mesopotamia. This explains why Abraham, having come as an adult from Mesopotamia, had not been circumcised. Also the uncircumcised Shechemites seemed to be a pocket of people in Canaan, so that it would have been a disgrace for an Israelite girl to marry a Shechemite unless he underwent circumcision (Gen. 34:13–31).

Though practiced by other nations, circumcision was distinctive for Israel in two ways. First, as stated, this practice took on significance for the nation as a physical sign or symbol of a spiritual covenantal relationship the people enjoyed with God. The separation of the foreskin symbolized separation from sin,[66] and also was "a self-maledictory oath. . . . 'If I am not loyal . . . to the Lord, may the sword cut off me and my offspring (see 17:14) as I have cut off my foreskin.'"[67] Second, the Hebrews were the only people to practice this rite in infancy, whereas surrounding Semite nations circumcised their young men at puberty or just before marriage.[68]

Circumcision was required for participating in the Passover, including foreigners living with the Jews (Exod. 12:48–49). In Jesus' day if the eighth day came on a Sabbath, circumcision was still to be done (John 7:22–23). For some unknown reason (perhaps spiritual indifference[69]) the custom was neglected in the wilderness wanderings, but after the Israelites crossed the Jordan River the males were circumcised near Gilgal at a place called Gibeath Haaraloth, "hill of the foreskins" (Josh. 5:5–9). In a wordplay on the name of the town Gilgal, which sounds like the Hebrew word "to roll," Joshua said this act "rolled away the reproach of Egypt" (5:9). This possibly refers to the fact that "the rite symbolically rolled away the reproach of their slavery in Egypt."[70]

64. "In Egypt, bar-reliefs bear witness to the custom from the third millennium B.C., [Egyptian] texts speak of it, [and] Herodutus speaks of it. . . ." (de Vaux, *Ancient Israel,* 46).

65. Ibid., 47.

66. Donald K. Campbell, "Joshua," in *The Bible Knowledge Commentary, Old Testament,* 337.

67. *NIV Study Bible,* 31.

68. Male Arab Muslims are circumcised at age thirteen, because their ancester Ishmael was circumcised at that age (*Baker Encyclopedia of the Bible,* 2 vols. [Grand Rapids: Baker Book House, 1988], 1:462).

69. Another suggested but unlikely reason is that the wilderness journey would have made circumcision hazardous (*Encyclopaedia Judaica,* 1972 ed., 5:568).

70. John Bright, "The Books of Joshua: Introduction and Exegesis," in *The Interpreter's Bible,* ed. George Arthur Buttrick, 12 vols. (Nashville: Abingdon Press, 1953), 2:575. The view that this is the reproach the Egyptians "would have cast upon Israel and her God if Israel had perished in the desert" (*NIV Study Bible,* 297) seems unlikely since that would be only a potential reproach, not an actual one.

The father normally performed circumcision (Gen. 17:23; 21:4; Acts 7:8), using a flint knife (Exod. 4:25; Josh. 5:2–3). By New Testament times this was done by someone outside the family (1 Macc. 1:61).[71] On one occasion the mother did the circumcising; this was Moses' wife Zipporah, who circumcised their son because Moses had neglected to do so (perhaps out of regard for Zipporah, a Midianite). Just as the Lord was about to take Moses' life for this violation, she prevented his death by carrying out the act (Exod. 4:24–26).[72]

Circumcision was to depict the inward condition of the heart, in which individuals were to be separated or cut off from sin (Deut. 10:16; 30:6; Jer. 4:4). Being disobedient to God was like being uncircumcised in heart (Jer. 9:25) or ear (in Jer. 6:10 the Hebrew speaks figuratively of ears being uncircumcised), or lips (Exod. 6:30).

Paul wrote that circumcision was meaningless for Jews if it was not accompanied with the circumcision of the heart (Rom. 2:28–29), that is, genuine conversion (Gal. 6:15; Col. 2:11, 13). At the Jerusalem Council the early church concluded that Gentile believers need not be circumcised to be saved (Acts 15:5–29; cf. Gal. 6:12). Faith in Christ is essential for salvation, whether a person is circumcised or not (Rom. 4:9–11; 1 Cor. 7:19). Being in Christ obliterates the national distinction between Jew (circumcised) and Gentile (uncircumcised; Col. 3:11).

A puzzling verse in relation to childbearing is 1 Timothy 2:15, "But women will be saved through childbearing—if they continue in faith, love and holiness with propriety." Commentators have proposed a number of views. (1) Women will be saved physically through the difficult process of childbirth.[73] However, many women have died in childbirth. (2) Women will be saved spiritually through the childbearing of the Messiah.[74] This view overlooks the fact that the verse refers to women, not just one woman, Mary. (3) Women will be saved spiritually even though they must bear children. In other words, childbearing does not preclude the possibility of salvation.[75] Against this view is the fact that the proposition *dia*, "through," rarely means

---

71. Packer, Tenney, and White, *The Bible Almanac*, 448.

72. Ronald B. Allen presents the intriguing view that Zipporah tossed the foreskin not at Moses' feet but at the feet of the Lord (" 'The Bloody Bridegroom' in Exodus 4:24–26," *Bibliotheca Sacra* 153 [July–September 1996]: 264–65). When Zipporah called God (not Moses) her "bridegroom of blood," she may have meant that God, like a father-in-law, was requiring circumcision. This is because the Hebrew word for bridegroom is the word for father-in-law, which is related to the Arabic noun, "a circumciser." In Arab cultures fathers-in-law performed circumcision on their future sons-in-law just before marriage (ibid., 282, n. 25).

73. H. A. Ironside, *Addresses on the First and Second Epistles of Timothy* (New York: Loizeaux Brothers, 1947), 72; and E. K. Simpson, *The Pastoral Epistles* (Grand Rapids: Wm. B. Eerdmans Publishing Co., 1954), 24.

74. Homer A. Kent, Jr., *The Pastoral Epistles*, rev. ed. (Chicago: Moody Press, 1982), 114–17; and Walter Lock, *A Critical and Exegetical Commentary on the Pastoral Epistles* (Edinburgh: T. & T. Clark, 1924), 32.

75. E. F. Scott, *The Pastoral Epistles* (London: Hodder & Stoughton, 1936), 28.

"even though." (4) Women will be saved spiritually through being faithful to their role as Christian women.[76] This view, however, wrongly broadens the meaning of childbearing to refer to activities of Christian women. (5) Women will be saved spiritually through performing their duties as mothers.[77] This incorrectly bases salvation on a work rather than on faith. (6) Women will be kept safe from the sinful influence of society by being at home raising children.[78] This view broadens the meaning of *teknogonia,* "childbearing," to child rearing, which is a possible meaning. (7) Women will be kept safe from Eve's error of usurping the husband's leadership role by being a godly mother.[79] This view has the advantage of relating closely to the immediately preceding verses on womanly submission and Eve's sin (1 Tim. 2:11–14).

While it is difficult to say with certainty what this verse means, the seventh view certainly seems plausible because of the context of 1 Timothy 2. In addition, this view seems to relate well to the last part of verse 15: Women are kept safe from following Eve's ways by exhibiting faith, love, holiness, and discretion as godly women.

Conclusion

This chapter has shown that God is especially concerned about children.

He enables women to conceive.

He forms children in the womb.

He helps bring them into the world.

He gives them "on loan" to parents.

He loves them and cares for them.

Parents today do well to acknowledge the Lord's hand in all these aspects of childhood including conception, pregnancy, delivery, and loving care.

76. Ann L. Bowman, "Women in Ministry: An Exegetical Study of 1 Timothy 2:11–15," *Bibliotheca Sacra* 149 (April–June 1992): 210; Douglas J. Moo, "1 Timothy 2:11–15: Meaning and Significance," *Trinity Journal* n.s. 1 (1980): 72; and Thomas D. Lea and Hayne P. Grifin, Jr., *1, 2 Timothy, Titus,* New American Commentary (Nashville: Broadman Press, 1992), 102.

77. Robinson, cited in Albert Barnes, *Barnes' Notes on the New Testament* (Grand Rapids: Kregel Publications, 1962), 1137.

78. Barnes cites Wetstein as holding this view (ibid.).

79. S. Jebb, "A Suggested Interpretation of 1 Ti[m.] 2:15," *Expository Times* 81 (1969–70): 221–22.

5

"You Shall Not Murder"

America's National Crime against the Unborn

"Keep abortion legal!" "Stop abortion now!"
"Abortion is a woman's right." "Abortion is murder."
"Not all pregnancies are wanted." "Every abortion stops a beating heart."
"Pro-choice is constitutional." "It's not a choice; it's a baby."

These and other slogans attest to the heated polarization that characterizes the debate about abortion. "Pro-life" proponents argue that life begins at conception and that, therefore, terminating a pregnancy ends a human life and is morally wrong. "Pro-choice" advocates, on the other hand, maintain that the fetus is not a person and that, therefore, a woman has a legal and moral right to end a pregnancy if she so chooses.

Demonstrations in front of abortion clinics and rallies in front of the White House evidence the feverish pitch of this debate. Most states had made laws that declared abortions illegal, but those were overturned when the United States Supreme Court decided on January 22, 1973 that women have the legal right to terminate their pregnancies. The Court ruled that states could not forbid abortions in the first three months of pregnancy, and that states could allow abortions at any time before birth if the woman's health were endangered.

Since this *Roe v. Wade* landmark decision, more than 28 million fetuses have been aborted. As pointed out in chapter 2, each year 1.6 million abortions are being induced. This is far more in one year than the 1.2 million United States soldiers killed in our nation's nine major wars in 198 years from the Revolutionary War through the Vietnam War (1775–1973)![1]

---

1. *World Book Encyclopedia*, 1992 ed., 21:25.

Because this book addresses the subject of childbirth and childhood, it is important to consider here the subject of abortion. Does the Bible discuss this subject? What theological and other arguments favor or oppose abortion? Was abortion practiced in ancient cultures? What does the Bible say about the related subject of infanticide?

Is the Abortion Debate New?

Abortions have been carried out by ancient and modern societies, by tribal and urbanized groups around the world.[2] Ancient Assyrians, for example, considered abortion a serious crime, for which the woman was impaled and her body left unburied.[3] Even if she died in the aborting process, her corpse was to be impaled. The person who caused the abortion was to pay for it by his own life.[4] The Sumerians and the Hittites fined a person who caused an abortion by a blow to the mother,[5] as did the Babylonians (according to the Code of Hammurabi).[6]

In classical Greece, Plato (427–347 B.C.) and Aristotle (384–322 B.C.) believed the fetus is a living being, but they allowed for abortions in order to control the population or to eliminate infants who by their deformities would be detrimental to the state.[7]

In the Roman Empire abortion was considered wrong, according to Cicero (106–43 B.C.) and Musonius Rufus, first-century Stoic, not because it was viewed as a crime, but because the abortive act deprived the father of an heir to continue his family line.[8] Seneca, a Roman statesman of the first century A.D., wrote that abortions were performed for reasons of "poverty, sensuality,

2. Charles P. Cozic and Stacey L. Tipp, eds., *Abortion: Opposing Viewpoints* (San Diego: Greenhaven Press, 1991), 13.
3. Middle Assyrian Laws, Tablet A, law 53; Godfrey Ralles Driver and John C. Miles, *The Assyrian Laws* (Darmstadt: Scientia Verlag Aalen, 1975), 115–17.
4. James B. Pritchard, ed., *Ancient Near Eastern Texts Relating to the Old Testament*, 3d ed. (Princeton, N.J.: Princeton University Press, 1969), 184.
5. *Encyclopaedia Judaica*, 1971 ed., 2:100; Gary M. Beckman, *Hittite Birth Rituals*, 2d ed. (Weisbaden: Otto Harrassowitz, 1983), 10.
6. Pritchard, *Ancient Near Eastern Texts Relating to the Old Testament*, 175.
7. Plato *Republic* 5.9, and Aristotle *Politics* 7.14.10. Cf. John A. Rasmussen, "Abortion: Historical and Biblical Perspective," *Concordia Theological Quarterly* 43 (January 1979): 19. According to Aristotle, abortion was permissible only if the fetus was not "animated," which for boys was the fortieth day after conception and for girls the ninetieth day (*Historia animalium* 7.3).
8. Cicero *Pro Cluentro* 11.32, and Musonius Rufus *Discourse* 15. Cf. Keith R. Bradley, *Discovering the Roman Family* (New York: Oxford University Press, 1991), 140; Edyth Binkowski and Beryl Rawson, "Sources for the Study of the Roman Family," in *The Family in Ancient Rome: New Perspectives,* ed. Beryl Rawson (Ithaca, N.Y.: Cornell University Press, 1986), 251; and Michael J. Gorman, *Abortion and the Early Church* (Downers Grove, Ill.: InterVarsity Press, 1982), 26, 30. Beryl Rawson points out elsewhere that this practice in Rome is known from medical, legal, and literary sources ("Adult-Child Relationships in Roman Society," in *Marriage, Divorce, and Children in Ancient Rome*, ed. Beryl Rawson [Oxford: Clarendon Press, 1991], 9).

or luxury."[9] That is, either the parents felt they could not afford another child, or a pregnancy resulting from wanton conduct was unwanted, or the rich did not want to be bothered with the responsibility of another child. These reasons sound stunningly contemporary.

Philo, Hellenistic Jewish philosopher of Alexandria, Egypt (25 B.C.–A.D. 41), distinguished between an unformed and a formed fetus (the latter having been shaped and having all its limbs), but he held that a person who harmed the formed fetus "is guilty of the murder of a human being and is thus deserving of death."[10] Gorman cites the Sentences of Pseudo-Phocylides 184–85 and the Sibylline Oracles 2.339–42, first-century B.C. writings, both of which opposed abortion.[11]

Josephus, Jewish historian of the first century, wrote against abortion: "The [Mosaic] Law has commanded to raise all the children and prohibited women from aborting or destroying seed; a woman who does so shall be judged a murderess of children for she has caused a soul to be lost and the family of man to be diminished."[12] A number of various botanical, chemical, and mechanical means of abortion were used in ancient Greece and Rome.[13] In ancient Greece women ate seeds of various plants to prevent and terminate pregnancies. These contraceptives and abortifacients included silphium, asafoetida, Queen Anne's Lace, pennyroyal, artemisia, myrrh, and rue.[14]

The early church opposed abortion, as summarized in these words from the Epistle of Barnabas, written in the first or second century A.D.: "You shall not murder a child by abortion nor shall you kill a newborn."[15] Clement of Alexandria (ca. 150–ca. 220) quoted the apocryphal Apocalypse of Peter, noting that parents who abort their children "will suffer punishment for their sins."[16] Clement also quoted an anonymous writer who argued that the fetus has a soul. Clement's contemporary, Tertullian (ca. 160–230), said destroying a fetus in the womb is murder: "To hinder a birth is merely a speedier man-killing; nor does it matter whether you take away a life that is born, or

9. Seneca *Digesta* 25.3.4. Soranus, a second-century A.D. Greek physician, proposed about sixty abortive methods for women who were "determined to abort" (Soranus *Gynaecia* 1.65; cf. Robert Etienne, "Ancient Medical Conscience and the Life of Children," *Journal of Psychohistory* 4 [1976]:134).
10. Philo *Special Laws* 3.108–9.
11. Gorman, *Abortion and the Early Church,* 37.
12. Josephus *Apion* 2.202.
13. Gorman, *Abortion and the Early Church,* 15–18.
14. John M. Riddle, J. Worth Estes, and Josiah C. Russell, "Ever Since Eve . . . Birth Control in the Ancient World," *Archaeology* 47 (March/April 1994): 29–31, 34–35. Also see John M. Riddle, *Contraception and Abortion from the Ancient World to the Renaissance* (Cambridge, Mass.: Harvard University Press, 1992).
15. *Epistle of Barnabas* 19.5. The *Didache,* a document summarizing early church beliefs and written about the same time as the *Epistle of Barnabas,* has similar wording: "Do not murder a child by abortion or kill a newborn infant" (*Didache* 2.2).
16. Clement of Alexandria *Prophetic Eclogues* 41, 48–49.

destroy one that is coming to the birth. That is a man which is going to be one; you have the fruit already in the seed."[17] In opposition to Roman law which said that a fetus is not a person,[18] Tertullian asserted that the fetus, while not a fully developed human, is nevertheless a person.[19]

In the reign of the Roman emperor Lucius Septimius Severus (A.D. 193–211) a law was passed against abortion, which prescribed temporary exile for any woman who got an abortion against the will of her husband. Such action was "violence to her womb,"[20] and deprived her husband of possible posterity.

In the Talmud, writings that record Jewish traditions following the Babylonian exile, abortion was not considered wrong if it were performed before the fetus was viable (i.e., was capable of living outside the womb if birth occurred), nor was abortion wrong if it became necessary to save the mother's life.[21] And yet the Zohar prohibited abortion because "a person who kills the foetus [sic] in his wife's womb desecrates that which was built by the Holy One and his craftsmanship."[22]

Does the Bible Discuss Abortion?

Some people argue for abortion by saying the Bible is silent on the subject. While it is true that the Bible does not explicitly state, "You shall not have an abortion," it does address the subject in a number of ways. Ward argues, however, that since the Bible condemns sinful practices of other nations such as idol worship and religious prostitution but does not condemn abortion, it therefore implies that abortion is acceptable.[23] But such an act was so unthinkable in Israelite society that there was no need to mention this in the Mosaic law.[24] Abortion in Israel was unthinkable because, as discussed in chapter 4, children were considered a gift from God, and childlessness was a despicable condition (Gen. 30:1; 1 Sam. 1:11; Job 15:34; Prov. 30:16).

Six truths from the Scriptures argue convincingly against abortion.

God's Forming of the Unborn in the Womb

God is actively involved in the marvelous development of the unborn in their mother's womb. Bible authors employed striking words to depict this

17. Tertullian *Apology* 9.6.
18. Justinian *Digest* 35.2.9.1; 25.4.1.1.
19. Tertullian *De Anima* 37.2. For further discussion of these quotations documented by notes 16, 17, and 19 see Gorman, *Abortion and the Early Church,* 52, 55, 58.
20. Justinian *Digest* 47.11.4; 48.8.8. Cf. Sheila K. Dickison, "Abortion in Antiquity," *Arethusa* 6 (1973): 161.
21. *Encyclopaedia Judaica,* 2:100.
22. Ibid.
23. Roy Bowen Ward, "Is the Fetus a Person—According to the Bible?" *Mission Journal* 19 (January 1986): 7.
24. Meredith G. Kline, "Lex Talionis and the Human Fetus," *Journal of the Evangelical Theological Society* 20 (September 1977): 193.

process. Job said God "shaped *ʿāṣab*, 'to cut, fashion, shape or carve,' as in making a vessel] me and made me" (Job 10:8), and "molded [lit., 'made'] me like clay" used by a potter (10:9). Seven times in 10:8–11 the patriarch used the word "me" in reference to God's developing him in the womb. This conveyed the idea that he existed in the womb as himself, as a prenatal human. He did not refer to "my mother's nonhuman tissue," nor did he speak of his "prehuman condition."

In Psalm 139:13–16 David said God "created" (*qānāh*, "to acquire or form") his "inmost being," "made" him "wonderfully," and "in the secret place" (his mother's womb) wove him together. God saw his "frame"(*ʿeṣem*, "skeleton") and his "unformed body" (*gōlem*, "embryo"). In speaking in these verses of his embryonic formation, David used personal pronouns eight times ("my" four times, "I" three times, and "me" once). To say "You knit *me*," "*I* was made," and You "saw *my* embryo" points to the psalmist's existence as a person having his beginning in the womb. An anonymous psalmist wrote along a similar line: "Your hands made *me* and formed [*kûn*, 'to establish'] *me*" (Ps. 119:73).

Isaiah too said that God "formed *me* in the womb" (Isa. 49:5), and God told Jeremiah, "I formed *you* in the womb" (Jer. 1:5). The word "formed" (*yāṣar*) in these two verses is also used of God's creation of Adam (Gen. 2:7–8), forming him like a potter forms a pot from clay. Jeremiah also wrote that God "did not kill *me* in the womb," and "Why did *I* even come out of the womb?" (Jer. 20:17–18). Had he died in the womb, "his death would have been the death of God's prophet, not a nonperson."[25]

When Job expressed his desire to die, he exclaimed, "Why did I not perish at birth, and die as I came from the womb?" (Job 3:11). Even before he was born, he spoke of himself as a person, as "I." In 3:16 he asked, "Why was I not . . . like a stillborn child, like an infant who never saw the light of day?" Here too he used the personal pronoun "I" in referring to himself before birth. He did not say, "Why was my mother's fetus not stillborn?"

Clearly these writers recognized their existence as persons in the womb. For them, human life did not begin at birth; it began in their prenatal condition, in the embryo, in which God was actively and directly involved. An abortion, then, deliberately destroys life which God has begun and is in the process of fashioning.

God's Calling of Individuals in the Womb

Isaiah and Jeremiah both wrote of God ordaining them before birth to serve him. "Before I was born the Lord called me" (Isa. 49:1). "The word of the Lord came to me, saying, 'Before you were born I set you apart' " (Jer. 1:5). Again the personal pronouns "I" and "You" demonstrate the existence of these prophets as

25. Richard Mayhue, "The Abortion Atrocity," *Spire* (Summer 1987): 7.

individuals, not as mere prenatal tissue, before birth. God had his hand on them in the womb, not only in their fetal development, but also in his plan to use them as his prophets. He consecrated them as persons, not as nonpersons.

God's Equating the Child in the Womb with the Child after Birth

The Bible does not distinguish between a child in the womb and a child after birth, as if the one is a nonperson and the other a person. When Rebekah asked about the jostling in her womb, the Genesis record refers to them as babies (Gen. 25:22). The Hebrew *bānín* is the word for boys, a word most often used of male offspring after birth. Yet Genesis 25:22 used that same word of Rebekah's unborn twins. Before birth, Jacob and Esau were "boys," not mere nonpersonal fetuses.

The word used of John the Baptist in Elizabeth's womb is the Greek *brephos* (Luke 1:41, 44), the same word used of babies after their birth (Luke 2:12, 16; Acts 7:19; 2 Tim. 3:15). In 1 Samuel 15:3 the word for children in the New International Version is the same word for infant used by Job of his unborn condition as "an infant who never saw the light of day" (Job 3:16). The ones in the womb were individuals with personhood as much as those after birth.

God's Transmitting Depravity in Conception

In acknowledging his sinful bent toward evil, David wrote in his psalm of confession, "Surely I was sinful at birth, sinful from the time my mother conceived me" (Ps. 51:5). This verse does not suggest that copulation of husband and wife is sinful, nor that conception or childbirth are in some way immoral. Rather, David was affirming his sinfulness from the very beginning of his existence.

He was saying that the sin nature is present from conception onwards. The Amplified Bible clarifies this thought by paraphrasing this verse this way: "Behold, I was brought forth in [a state of] iniquity; my mother was sinful who conceived me [and I, too, am sinful]." Therefore, since only human beings possess a sin nature, the one conceived in the womb is a human being.

God's Demanding of Adult Life for Fetal Life

The Mosaic code includes this regulation: "If men who are fighting hit a pregnant woman and she gives birth prematurely but there is no serious injury, the offender must be fined whatever the woman's husband demands and the court allows. But if there is serious injury, you are to take life for life, eye for eye, tooth for tooth, hand for hand, foot for foot, burn for burn, wound for wound, bruise for bruise" (Exod. 21:22–25). The point of this instruction is that a fetus is viewed as equal in value to its mother. If either the expectant mother or the child is injured unintentionally, "the assailant was to be penalized in proportion to the nature of severity of the injury."[26] While the passage

26. John D. Hannah, "Exodus," in *The Bible Knowledge Commentary, Old Testament*, ed. John F. Walvoord and Roy B. Zuck (Wheaton, Ill.: Victor Books, 1985), 141.

does not specify whether the "serious injury" is to the child or to the mother, it seems best to take it as referring to either.[27]

Some argue that this law addresses the problem of an accidentally caused miscarriage, not an aborting of a live infant. Based on this approach, they say that abortions are not being prohibited. However, the Hebrew speaks of the mother giving birth, literally, if "her child comes out [yāsaʾ]." This verb normally refers to live births (Gen. 25:26; 38:28–30; Job 3:11; 10:18; Jer. 1:5; 20:18). If a miscarriage were being referred to, the verb šākal, "to miscarry," would be expected (Gen. 31:38; Exod. 23:26; Job 21:10; Hos. 9:14).

Exodus 21:22, then, refers not to an accidental miscarriage, but to a premature birth.[28] If a child is born by an accident, a fine is to be paid (presumably because of the physical danger to which the mother and child are exposed[29]). But if there is some injury to the mother or the child, then the law of retaliation (*lex talionis*) is to be enacted. If the injury results in death, the guilty man is to pay with his life. Obviously God places a high value on the human fetus. Requiring the death penalty for a dead fetus shows that God considers the fetus a human.[30] Since he levied such a high penalty on an accidentally induced birth, what must God think of today's millions of *intentionally* caused fetal deaths by abortion?

God's Becoming Incarnate in Christ

If the fetus is not a person, then Jesus Christ, when he was in Mary's womb, was not a person. Such an idea, of course, is unthinkable. In the incarnation Christ took on a human nature (Gal. 4:4; Heb. 2:17), and since he was a person in the womb, it follows that all humans have personhood in their prenatal state.[31]

---

27. One reason for including the mother as one possibly injured is that the retaliation in verse 24 includes "tooth for tooth," an injury obviously not possible for a fetus.

28. J. Carl Laney, "The Abortion Epidemic: America's Silent Holocaust," *Bibliotheca Sacra* 139 (October–December 1982): 347.

29. Ibid.

30. For more on this passage see Francis J. Beckwith, "A Critical Appraisal of Theological Arguments for Abortion Rights," *Bibliotheca Sacra* 140 (July–September 1991): 343–46; Umberto Cassuto, *Commentary of the Book of Exodus*, trans. Israel Abrahams (Jerusalem: Magnes Press, 1967), 275–77; Jack W. Cottrell, "Abortion and the Mosaic Law," *Christianity Today*, March 16, 1973, 6–9; John I. Durham, *Exodus*, Word Biblical Commentary (Waco, Tex.: Word Books, 1987), 323–24; Ron du Perez, "The Fetus in Biblical Law," *Ministry*, September 1992, 11–14; Richard A. Fowler and H. Wayne House, *Civilization in Crisis*, 2d ed. (Grand Rapids: Baker Book House, 1988), 83–87; H. Wayne House, "Miscarriage or Premature Birth: Additional Thoughts on Exodus 21:22–25," *Westminster Theological Journal* 41 (1978): 108–23; and Bernard S. Jackson, "The Problem of Exod. XXI 22–25 (Ius Talionis)," *Vetus Testamentum* 23 (1973): 273–304.

31. Though the Bible makes it clear that human life begins at conception (fertilization of the ovum by a sperm), people's opinions on when life begins have varied over the centuries. Aristotle, for example, believed that life began for boys forty days after conception and for girls eighty days after conception. The Stoics believed life began when the fully formed fetus was born and took its first breath. In Europe in the seventeenth century many believed life began at "quickening," when the women felt the fetus move (which is normally several months into the pregnancy), and that abortion was wrong after the quickening but was acceptable before it.

Are Pro-Abortion Arguments Valid?

In spite of the strong biblical evidence in support of the pro-life position, those who favor abortion set forth several arguments to favor their view.

First, some argue that because Adam became "a living being" when God "breathed into his nostrils the breath of life" (Gen. 2:7), a child becomes a living being when at birth he or she begins to breathe.[32] However, while the fetus does not breathe in the normal sense, it does have *"respiration* in the more technical biological sense of the transfer of oxygen" from the mother's blood.[33] Also the creation of the first man, Adam, differs from the birth of a child, so that Genesis 2:7 does not apply to babies in their mothers' wombs.

Second, abortion advocates argue that personhood begins at birth, because, though the fetus appears human, it is not a human being for it lacks consciousness.[34] Therefore, since the fetus is not a person, abortion is justifiable.[35] However, if consciousness determines personhood, then an individual who is unconscious because of a head injury is not a person.

Opponents point out that abortion procedures cause pain to the fetus. Prochoice defenders, on the other hand, contend that "the fact that the fetus can feel pain is not an argument for the fetus's personness."[36] They maintain that many organisms feel pain, and that pain simply indicates the presence of a nervous system.[37] The fetus's response to pain is no different, they say, from the response of an earthworm to a needle prick. However, the anti-abortionists' point is that pain proves aliveness, not personhood. The existence of a nervous system demonstrates that the fetus is alive; it is a living organism. This fact argues against abortion, not in favor of it.

The fetus's pain felt in the abortive process is far more profound than the response of an earthworm's nervous system. Abortion procedures include suction aspiration (in which a strong suction force tears the baby to pieces), saline injection (which kills the unborn by salt poisoning), and prostaglandin (hormones injected into the womb to induce labor prematurely).[38]

Abortions often endanger the life of the mother, lead to complications in future pregnancies, or, as numerous studies have shown, result in high inci-

32. Ward, "Is the Fetus a Person—According to the Bible?" 7–9.

33. John Jefferson Davis, *Abortion and the Christian* (Phillipsburg, N.J.: Presbyterian and Reformed Publishing Co., 1984), 101 (italics his).

34. Michael Bettencourt, "Case for Fetal Personhood a Dubious Conception," *In These Times,* September 20–26, 1989, 17.

35. Augustine (A.D. 354–430) advocated this view, saying he did not consider abortion homicide because the fetus, being unformed and "not endowed with its senses," was not yet a living soul. Gregory of Nyssa (330–395) expressed the same view (John M. Riddle, "From Plato to Pius: The Ethics of Birth Control," *Archaeology* 34 [March/April 1994]: 33).

36. Bettencourt, "Case for Fetal Personhood a Dubious Conception," 17.

37. Ibid.

38. For more on these procedures, see John Lippis, *The Challenge to Be "Pro-Life,"* rev. ed. (Santa Barbara, Calif.: Santa Barbara Pro-Life Education, 1982), 7–8.

dences of guilt, depression, stress, and suicidal feelings.[39] Abortionists, however, seldom call attention to these disturbing facts.

Third, pro-choice promoters say that the fetus tissue is part of the pregnant woman and, therefore, is not a separate person. To them, this means that a woman has a right to do with her body what she wishes. Related to this is the argument that the being in the womb is only a potential person. Schwarz answers this in these words: "It is not so that there is something in the womb— 'a blob of tissue' or a mere biological organism—that turns into a child. The child is already there, the same child, the same person all the way through."[40] He adds that the being in the womb is "a fully real person, the same person he will later be. He is only smaller, less developed, in a different environment, and more dependent, in comparison to a born baby."[41] It is not that he is a potential person, but that he is a *person* who *has* potential.

According to Daniel Callahan, director of the Institute of Society, Ethics, and the Life Sciences, "Genetically, hormonally and in all organic respects, save for the source of its nourishment, a fetus and even an embryo is separate from the woman."[42] Abortionists seek to justify their practice by ignoring the clear scientific fact that the embryo is the product of forty-six chromosomes combined to make "a distinct entity" at the time an egg is fertilized by a sperm.[43] The fetus is not simply a mass of tissue, a growth of the mother's cells. Fetal tissue is different from that of the mother. "Its chromosome composition, or genetic makeup . . . is a biological blend of both parents and therefore distinct from either."[44] The fertilized egg contains the complete "blueprint" of the new individual. Within twenty-four hours after the fusion of ovum and sperm, the first cell division takes place in the woman's Fallopian tube, where it is free-floating for several days as it journeys toward the uterus to implant itself in the endometrium, the uterine lining. This is a separate new life within the mother's body, not simply a mass of the mother's tissue.[45] A woman, then, who "chooses" an abortion is destroying a new life.

Fourth, abortion advocates state that abortions are a way of avoiding the bearing of unwanted children. It is argued that unplanned offspring force

39. Vincent M. Rue, "The Psychological Realities of Induced Abortion," *Post-Abortion Aftermath: A Comprehensive Consideration*, ed. Michael T. Munnion (London: Sheed & Ward, 1994), 5–43. Also see R. Jay Sappington, "Abortion: A Non-Controversial Approach," *Trinity Journal* n.s. 14 (1993): 183–99; and Lippis, *The Challenge to Be "Pro-Life,"* 9–17.

40. Stephen Schwarz, "The Fetus Is a Person," in *Abortion: Opposing Viewpoints*, 33.

41. Ibid., 34.

42. Quoted by Landrum B. Shettles with David Rorvik, *Rites of Life* (Grand Rapids: Zondervan Publishing House, 1983), 52.

43. Ibid.

44. "Abortion," *Christopher News Notes*, March 1971, 2.

45. For a graphic presentation of this marvelous process see the photographs in Lennart Nilsson and Lars Hamberger, *A Child Is Born*, trans. Clare James (New York: Delacorte Press, 1990), 38–64.

many individuals into parenthood long before they are prepared for it, and thus those children and parents are at a serious disadvantage. Also, they contend that unwanted children are more likely to suffer child abuse, and terminating "accidental" pregnancies is a form of controlling world population growth.[46] In addition, congenital disorders, according to abortion protagonists, justify feticide. Why burden parents with a disabled or retarded child, they say, when it can be avoided?

In response to this question of bringing unwanted children into the world, Roper says, "Unwanted to whom? I know many couples who desperately want children and who would accept them and love them if given the chance. How about placing unwanted children in wanting families."[47] To those who argue that birthing mentally or physically handicapped babies is cruel, Roper says,

> Cruel to whom? I personally have not found that handicapped people are unhappy. Have you? Furthermore, from a Biblical perspective, handicaps are often the means God uses to perfect and beautify character. Besides, aren't we all handicapped in some way? Who will decide which handicaps make one less than human?[48]

The view that allowing abortions would decrease child abuse against unwanted children is not correct. Child abuse has risen dramatically in countries that have permissive abortion laws. In the United States child abuse has nearly tripled, and in Great Britain it has increased twofold.[49]

Others say that rape justifies abortion, that a pregnancy resulting from rape should be terminated. However, why kill a blameless baby? "If anyone should get capital punishment, it is the rapist, not his child."[50] Also such cases are extremely rare. A ten-year study in Minnesota revealed that *no* pregnancies resulted from 3,500 rape cases.[51] This probing question should be considered: "If you found out today that you were the product of a rape, would you wish that your mother had aborted you?"[52]

Practically all children aborted "are killed for reasons of convenience; not incest, not rape, not the physical condition of the unborn, and not the threatened health of the mother (according to data from the Alan Guttmacher Institute, the research arm of Planned Parenthood)."[53] C. Everett Koop, former

46. K. B. Welton, *Abortion Is Not a Sin* (Costa Mesa, Calif.: Pandit Press, 1987).
47. David H. Roper, *The Abortion Question* (Palo Alto, Calif.: Discovery Publishing, 1983), 20.
48. Ibid., 19.
49. Lippis, *The Challenge to Be "Pro-Life,"* 17.
50. Mary Monica, "Abortion in Case of Rape?" *Fidelity,* March 1989, cited in *Abortion: Opposing Viewpoints,* 160.
51. Laney, "The Abortion Epidemic: America's Silent Holocaust," 351.
52. Ibid.
53. Charles R. Swindoll, "Why I Stand for Life," *Focus on the Family,* August 1990, 19.

Surgeon General of the United States, and a renowned pediatric surgeon, has noted that in his practice he has not known of one instance where the child had to be aborted to save the mother's life.[54] Tertullian pointed out that if doctors killed an unborn child to save the mother's life, they, as pagans, must have believed the fetus was alive in order to be able to "kill" it.[55]

Is it not strange that physicians who practice abortion are in direct violation of the Hippocratic Oath, which graduating medical students take. That Oath includes the statement, "I will not give to a woman an abortive remedy."[56]

With 1.6 million babies aborted annually, is it any wonder William J. Bennett, former United States Secretary of Education, has called abortion "a national disaster"?[57]

What Does the Bible Say about Infanticide?

C. Everett Koop says the public's openness to infanticide results from abortion.[58] The so-called right to abort an unborn baby has led to the view that parents have a right to terminate a live baby. However, if abortion is abhorrent, certainly infanticide, taking the life of a born child, is even more so.[59]

A well-known contemporary case of infanticide in the United States is that of Baby Doe. He was born with Down's Syndrome on April 9, 1982 in Bloomington, Indiana. In addition he had a small hole between his esophagus and his trachea, which meant he had to be fed intravenously. Some medical specialists said the esophageal-tracheal problem was correctable. However, a judge ruled that the parents had the right to let the baby die by withholding

54. C. Everett Koop, "Abortion: Deception-on-Demand," *Moody Magazine,* May 1980, 26.

55. Tertullian *De Anima* 25.2. Cf. W. J. Walts, "Ovid, the Law and Roman Society on Abortion," *Acta Classica* 16 (1973): 99.

56. *The Hippocratic Oath,* trans. Ludwig Edelstein, No. 1 of the *Supplements to the Bulletin of the History of Medicine* (Baltimore: Johns Hopkins University Press, 1943). The Oath of Hippocrates (460–357 B.C.) was cited by Plato (*Republic* 5.9) and Aristotle (*Politics* 7.14.10). Apparently, however, Hippocrates did allow for abortions of "unanimated" fetuses, that is, of embryos up to one month old (Hippocrates *On Diseases of Women* 1.72, 78; cf. Etienne, "Ancient Medical Conscience and the Life of Children," 141–42).

For more answers to the pro-abortionists' answers see Francis J. Beckwith, "A Critical Appraisal of Theological Arguments for Abortion Rights," *Bibliotheca Sacra* 148 (July–September 1991): 337–55; Francis J. Beckwith and Norman L. Geisler, *Matters of Life and Death* (Grand Rapids: Baker Book House, 1991); and Francis J. Beckwith, *Politically Correct Death: Answering Arguments for Abortion Rights* (Grand Rapids: Baker Book House, 1993).

57. Peter Ross Range, "MM Interview: William J. Bennett," *Modern Maturity,* March–April 1995, 30.

58. Koop, "Abortion: Deception-on-Demand," 29. Also see C. Horn III, "Abortion," in *Evangelical Dictionary of Theology,* ed. Walter A. Elwell (Grand Rapids: Baker Book House, 1984), 5.

59. China's policy of one child per family has resulted in countless abortions and cases of infanticide in that nation. For a moving story of a female obstetrician who was forced against her will to carry out a hospital-sanctioned infanticide, see Yin Wong, "A Question of Duty," *Reader's Digest,* September 1955, 65–70.

food and water. Rather than viewing the parents as being guilty of neglect, the Indiana Supreme Court, to which the case was appealed, confirmed the view that the parents were legally inculpable, for they were simply exercising their freedom of choice. Baby Doe starved to death, dying on his sixth day. No instances exactly like that of Infant Doe are recorded in the Bible. But three forms of infanticide did exist in Bible times: killing infants and children of the enemy in warfare, offering children in the fire in sacrifice to gods, and child cannibalism in times of siege and famine.

Infanticide in the Bible

Unfortunate victims of warfare, infants and children were often killed mercilessly by enemy armies. Elisha said the Arameans would dash Israelite infants to pieces (2 Kings 8:12). The Medes would do this to the infants of Babylon (Isa. 13:16, 18) as God's judgment on the Babylonians who had killed Jewish infants the same way (Ps. 137:9). Earlier, in its conquest of Samaria, Assyria dashed little ones to the ground, as Hosea prophesied (Hos. 10:14; 13:16). In turn, Assyria would experience the same fate (Nahum 3:10). The Jews underwent the same warfare atrocities when the Romans destroyed Jerusalem (Luke 19:44) in A.D. 70.

It is repulsive to think of young children suffering a painful death by having their heads beat against rocks and their skulls cracked open.

Equally repugnant was the unbelievable practice of the Ammonites, descendants of Lot, who sacrificed their *own* children in worship to their god Molech, whom the writer of 1 Kings called a "detestable god" (1 Kings 11:5, 7). Knowing of the danger of being engaged in this practice, God specifically forbade it, for he said it would profane his name and defile his sanctuary (Lev. 18:21; 20:3), and the penalty would be death by stoning for any parent who so abused his child (Lev. 20:2–5). In offering their children to the gods, the pagans burned them in the fire (Deut. 12:31) and so God commanded Israel not to do the same (Deut. 18:10). The fact that this prohibition was recorded by Moses indicates that as early as 1400 B.C. the Ammonites were guilty of this repulsive crime.

The Moabites, also descendants of Lot (Gen. 19:36–38), apparently engaged in the same revolting kind of worship, for their king offered his firstborn son, presumably to win the favor of his god and thus to repel the Israelites who had been successful in battle (2 Kings 3:26–27). The people of the northern kingdom of Israel became so engrossed in the sins of their neighboring nations that they too sacrificed their sons and daughters in the fire (17:17), and this was one of the sins that led to the nation's exile to Assyria (17:6–7).

When the Assyrians took the Israelites of the northern kingdom into exile in 722 B.C., they transferred some of their own people to Israel. Those replaced peoples set up idols of their Assyrian gods right in the land of Israel.

One group, known as the Sepharvites, burned their children in the fire as sacrifices to their gods Adrammelech and Anammelech (17:31).[60]

In spite of God's warnings to his people against child sacrifice, Judah too became engrossed in it in the reigns of Ahaz (16:2–3; 2 Chron. 28:3) and his grandson Manasseh (2 Kings 21:1, 6; 2 Chron. 33:6). Both these evil kings offered several of their sons in the fire: Ahaz during the Syro-Ephraimite War, and Manasseh when threatened by the Assyrians. Ahaz was reigning in the south in Judah when Assyria invaded Israel in the north, and Manasseh reigned after that conquest. Perhaps then, these two spiritually weak kings were influenced by the Assyrians toward this practice of religious infanticide.

The prophet Jeremiah pronounced stinging denunciations against the many sins of Judah in its final decades before it was exiled. In his day[61] parents in Judah were sacrificing their children to Molech, the Ammonite god,[62] and to Baal, the Canaanite god (Jer. 7:31; 19:6; 32:35), on high places of Topheth in the Valley of Ben Hinnom. The word "Topheth" probably comes from a word for fireplace or incinerator.[63] It included a fire pit (Isa. 30:33) where children were thrown and allowed to burn to death. In the Valley of Ben Hinnom (also called simply the Valley of Hinnom), located southwest of Jerusalem, the city's refuse was dumped and burned. The city dump became the ghastly place where, unbelievably, babies were burned with the garbage![64]

Ezekiel too denounced this horrific practice, referring to the sacrifice of Judah's firstborn (Ezek. 20:26) and of their sons and daughters as "food to the idols" (16:20–21; 23:37) and "gifts" to the idols (20:26, 31). He condemned the hypocrisy of their sacrificing their children and then the same day entering the temple (23:39).

The thought of offering their firstborn to God to atone for their sins was repugnant, Micah said (Micah 6:7). It would be as useless and senseless as offering him thousands of rams or ten thousand rivers of oil. None of those so-called sacrifices could replace the need for a pure heart of justice, mercy, and humility (6:8).

---

60. These gods probably refer to Adad the Babylonian storm god and Anu the god of the heavens (J. M. Wiebe, "Sepharvites," in *International Standard Bible Encyclopedia*, 4 [1988]: 399), or they may be the names of deities of Syria or Canaan (William S. LaSor, "Adrammelech," in *International Standard Bible Encyclopedia*, 1 [1979]: 120).

61. Jeremiah prophesied from about 627 B.C. to the fall of Judah to Babylon in 586 B.C. and beyond, in the reigns of Judah's last five kings: Josiah, Jehoahaz, Jehoiakim, Jehoiachin, and Zedekiah.

62. Amazingly after eight hundred years—from Moses' time to Jeremiah's—Molech the Ammonite god was still being worshiped!

63. De Vaux explains that the "incinerator" is justified by the Aramaic and Syriac (Roland de Vaux, *Studies in Old Testament Sacrifice* [Cardiff: University of Wales Press, 1964], 74, n. 81).

64. From the Hebrew *gē'-hinnōm* the Greek *Gehenna*, the valley where garbage was kept burning, became a picture of the fire of eternal hell (Matt. 5:22, 29–30; 10:28; 18:9; 23:15, 33; James 3:6).

Another form of infanticide was evident in battle sieges, when the parents, starving because they were unable to get out of their walled cities to get food, ate their own children. This happened in Samaria, when the city was besieged by the Arameans (2 Kings 6:24–29) and in Jerusalem when it was surrounded by the Babylonians for two and a half years and was finally defeated and burned in August 586 B.C. (2 Kings 25:1–21). Women in Jerusalem, normally compassionate toward their offspring, cooked them and ate them to stave off their own hunger (Lam. 2:20; 4:10), as Ezekiel had predicted they would do (Ezek. 5:10).

About eight hundred years earlier, Moses had warned the people twice that their disobedience would result in this grisly form of cannibalism (Lev. 26:27–29; Deut. 28:53–57), in which "the most gentle and sensitive" men and women would consume the very "fruit of their womb."

In Egypt the pharaoh[65] ordered the Hebrew midwives to kill Hebrew baby boys at the moment of birth. But when that order was not carried out, he decreed that every baby boy be killed by being thrown into the river (Exod. 1:15–22; Acts 7:19). Obviously this form of infanticide was designed to reduce the growing Israelite population, and it was a satanic plan (unknown to the pharaoh) to keep Moses from growing up to lead the Israelites out of Egypt.

Haman's plan to kill all Jews in March 473 B.C.—"young and old, women and little children" (Esth. 3:13)—was thwarted by Esther (7:1–10).

In a similar move, no doubt instigated by Satan, Herod the Great sought to kill baby Jesus by ordering all the boys in and around Bethlehem who were two years old and under to be killed (Matt. 2:16).[66] This act of terrorism resulted from his having been "outwitted by the Magi," who did not report Jesus' whereabouts to Herod so he could kill him. Herod was also outwitted by Joseph and Mary taking Jesus to Egypt, where they stayed until Herod died (Matt. 2:13–19). The death of many baby boys in Bethlehem, a terrible, futile waste of lives, was so horrible that Matthew likened it to Jewish mothers weeping for their children (2:18) who had been taken into exile by the Assyrians seven centuries earlier. Matthew quoted Jeremiah 31:15, where the prophet referred to Rachel weeping for her children. Perhaps "Rachel" was used as a synonym for Israel since Rachel's son Joseph was the father of

---

65. Assuming the exodus occurred in 1446 B.C. when Moses was eighty years old (Exod. 7:7), Moses was born in 1526. This pharaoh was either Amenhotep I (1545–1526) or Thutmose I (1526–1512).

66. Herod's action is not surprising for "he put to death several of his own children and some of his wives whom he thought were plotting against him. Emperor Augustus reportedly said it was better to be Herod's sow [*huos* in Greek] than his son [*huios*] for his sow had a better chance of surviving" (Louis A. Barbieri, "Matthew," in *The Bible Knowledge Commentary, New Testament*, ed. John F. Walvoord and Roy B. Zuck [Wheaton, Ill.: Victor Books, 1983], 23). On Herod's family intrigues and violence see Josephus *The Antiquities of the Jews* and *The Jewish Wars*. On Augustus's statement about the pig and the son, see Macrobius *Saturnalia* 2.4.11.

Ephraim and Manasseh, from whom descended the two major tribes of the ten-tribe northern kingdom.

An Old Testament judge named Jephthah may have been involved in a form of child sacrifice. In this strange case, he rashly vowed that if God gave him victory over the Ammonites, he would sacrifice as a burnt offering "whatever comes out of the door of my house to meet me when I return in triumph" (Judg. 11:30–31). To his surprise and great consternation, when he returned from battle, his daughter, his only child, was the first to meet him.

Scholars differ on whether the words, "he did to her as he had vowed" (11:39), mean he killed her as a sacrifice or whether she remained a virgin the rest of her life. Arguments favoring the latter view include the observations that (a) it would seem unlikely for Jephthah to have been included among the heroes of faith in Hebrews 11:32 if he had killed his daughter, (b) it would seem strange for his daughter to spend two months in the mountains with her friends (Judg. 11:38) rather than with her father if she were to die, (c) it seems unusual for her to encourage her father to keep a vow resulting in her death (11:30), (d) it seems unexpected for Israel to celebrate her death rather than her virginity (11:38), and (e) it seems reasonable to expect Jephthah to be aware of the prohibition in the Law against human sacrifice (Lev. 18:21; 20:2–5; Deut. 12:31; 18:10).

On the other hand, several arguments point toward his actual sacrifice of his daughter. First, the Hebrew word for burnt offering in Judges 11:31 is the normal word for burnt sacrifices, and is the word God used when he spoke to Abraham about the sacrifice of Isaac (Gen. 22:2). Second, it is not surprising that Jephthah would carry through on his vow, since vows to the Lord were not to be broken (Judg. 11:35; Num. 30:2). Third, Jephthah's distress over his vow (Judg. 11:35) shows he was concerned about her death. Fourth, his daughter's two months of wailing because she would never marry implies that because of her impending death Jephthah would have no further offspring. Fifth, his rash vow may be partially explainable by the fact that his mother was a prostitute (11:1) and he had lived outside Israel in the land of Tob (11:3).[67]

Abraham's willingness to sacrifice his son Isaac (Gen. 22) reflects not a pagan custom of child sacrifice, but a desire to obey God whatever the cost. This act was a test of the patriarch's faith. Would he trust God to keep his promise to make him the ancestor of many people (17:4–7)? "God's intervention—so dramatic and instructive—showed that he never intended Abraham

---

67. Leon Wood argues for her perpetual virginity (*Distressing Days of the Judges* [Grand Rapids: Zondervan Publishing House, 1975], 288–95), whereas several argue for her sacrificial death, including Arthur E. Cundall (*Judges: An Introduction and Commentary*, Tyndale Old Testament Commentaries [Downers Grove, Ill.: InterVarsity Press, 1968], 146–47); Dale Ralph Davis (*Such a Great Salvation* [Grand Rapids: Baker Book House, 1990], 146–50); and Walter C. Kaiser, Jr. (*Hard Sayings of the Old Testament* [Downers Grove, Ill.: InverVarsity Press, 1988], 101–5).

to go through with the sacrifice (child sacrifice was not to be practiced in Israel) but that it indeed was a test."[68] Abraham's obedience showed he truly feared God and trusted him completely.

Why Did God Command the Slaughtering of Children?

Was God being unduly harsh against children when he commanded the Israelites to destroy all the inhabitants of Jericho—"men and women, young and old" (Josh. 6:21)? Is this not merciless cruelty against innocent children? How can a loving God approve—even command—the genocide of the entire population of a town, which surely included young children and babies? The conquest of other cities too involved the slaughter of young ones, including Ai (Josh. 8:26), Makedah (10:28), Lachish (10:32), Eglon (10:35), Debir (10:39), towns of the Negev and the foothills (10:40), and several towns of the north including Hazor (11:11). Many of these towns were under God's *ḥerem*, a word that means "curse," "what stood under God's ban," or "what was devoted to destruction." Centuries earlier God told Abram that the sin of the Amorites (Canaanites) had "not yet reached its full measure" (Gen. 15:16). He waited patiently for more than four hundred years to see if they would repent. He was "not wanting anyone to perish" (2 Peter 3:9). But because they failed to repent, God ordered that they be exterminated because of their "wickedness" (Deut. 9:4–5). Centuries earlier God had annihilated the entire human race, except for eight people, by the flood because he "saw how great man's wickedness on the earth had become" (Gen. 6:5). And Sodom and Gomorrah were destroyed by fire because their sin was "so grievous" (18:20).

God also told Saul to destroy all the Amalekites (1 Sam. 15:2–3), nomads in southern Canaan who had attacked the Israelites in the wilderness (Exod. 17:8; Deut. 25:17–18). God ordered Saul to "put to death men and women, children and infants" (1 Sam. 15:3).

The slaughter of adults in these Canaanite cities is understandable when we realize that these people had engaged for centuries in vile idolatry, licentious religious practices (Jer. 7:9; Hos. 4:10–14; Amos 2:7), and child sacrifice (Jer. 19:5; 32:35).

If they were allowed to coexist in Canaan with the Israelites, those indescribably sinful people would become a "snare" to Israel (Exod. 23:33), and like thorns in their sides (Num. 33:55; cf. Josh. 23:13; Judg. 2:3), influencing them "to serve other gods" (Deut. 7:4; cf. Exod. 34:16), to "eat their sacrifices" (Exod. 34:15), and "to follow all the detestable things they do in worshiping their gods" (Deut. 20:18). Therefore, we can understand why God ordered the destruction of these wicked, pagan adults.

---

68. Ross, "Genesis," 65.

But why should Canaanite children and infants be slaughtered? Let's suppose God had ordered Joshua and Saul to spare the children. Who would care for them? Obviously, Israelite families would be obligated to adopt them, and in a few years Israelites would undoubtedly intermarry with those grown-up Canaanites. The blood line of Israel would be polluted irreversibly! Furthermore, Canaanite children had surely seen their own parents and other adults engage in sexually oriented idol worship. It would be difficult for those youngsters to erase those impressions from their minds. Their minds and hearts were indelibly tainted with evil thoughts and ideas. In addition, many of them would be sacrificed by their own parents in their vile pagan worship. Was death by the sword at the hands of the Israelites any worse than a slow death by burning?

True, some innocent children were no doubt included in these wartime slaughters. However, "just as a surgeon does not hesitate to amputate a gangrenous limb, even if he cannot help cutting off some healthy flesh, so God must do the same."[69]

Infanticide in Other Nations

Infanticide has been carried out by other nations as well, in both the ancient and the modern world. For some people, infanticide is a form of limiting family size; for others it is a way of ridding the population of unwanted children because of illegitimacy or deformity, or children who may be born into families of poverty. Appeasing the gods in times of national calamity comprises another reason for infanticide. This was especially evident among the Phoenicians. The Greek historian Diodorus Siculus wrote that when a disaster was threatening Carthage in 310 B.C., parents from the noblest families offered their children in sacrifice to the god Kronos.[70] Diodorus told of the Tyrian god Melkart at Carthage, "whose statue received the children who then passed down into a furnace."[71] Diodorus wrote, "There was in their city a bronze image . . . extending its hands, palms up and sloping toward the ground, so that each of the children when placed thereon rolled down and fell into a sort of gaping pit filled with fire."[72] The parents who sacrificed their

69. Kaiser, *Hard Sayings of the Old Testament*, 108. Also see Gleason L. Archer, *Encyclopedia of Bible Difficulties* (Grand Rapids: Zondervan Publishing House, 1982), 157–59.

70. Roland de Vaux, *Ancient Israel: Its Life and Institutions*, trans. John McHugh (New York: McGraw-Hill Book Co., 1961), 445. "Thousands of bones of sacrificed children have been dug up by archeologists, often with inscriptions identifying the victims as first-born sons of noble families, reaching in time all the way back to the Jericho of 7,000 B.C." (Lloyd de Mause, "The Evolution of Childhood," in *The History of Childhood*, ed. Lloyd de Mause [New York: Psychohistory Press, 1974], 27).

71. Johannes Pedersen, *Israel: Its Life and Culture*, 2 vols. (Atlanta: Scholars Press, 1991), 2:698.

72. Gilbert Charles-Picard, "The World of Hannibal," in *Greece and Rome: Builders of Our World*, ed. Merle Severy (Washington, D.C.: National Geographic Society, 1968), 284.

young in this way believed they would be favored with bountiful harvests and that the little victim would live forever in the god's palace.[73] "Porphyry (*De abstm.* II 56) says that the Phoenician history written by Sanchuniaton and translated by Philo of Byblos was full of stories about child sacrifices offered to Kronos in times of calamity."[74]

The Roman statesmen Cicero (106–43 B.C.) and Seneca (d. A.D. 65) wrote of deformed children in Rome being exposed to the elements or killed outright, and Plutarch, first-century Greek biographer, pointed out that poverty was often an inducement to infanticide. Tacitus and Juvenal, first-century Roman historian and poet, respectively, mentioned exposure as the more common form of family limitation.[75] Pliny the Elder (A.D. 23–79), Roman scholar, defended exposure as a means of regulating the population.

Some Greek and Roman art and literature express parents' loving sentiments toward their young.[76] But if the austere, military-minded Spartans discovered a mental or physical infirmity in a newborn, they would toss the infant over a cliff of Mount Taygetus to an untimely death.[77] In the Greco-Roman world, girls apparently were more often the victims of infanticide and exposure than boys.[78] The Twelve Tables, the earliest Roman law code (ca. 450 B.C.), allowed a father to expose a female infant or any deformed baby of either sex.[79]

Exposure of unwanted babies was conveyed in myths. Oedipus, for example, was exposed on a mountainside as an infant, but a shepherd found him, he was raised by the king of Corinth, and when he grew up he unknowingly murdered his father and married his mother. Euripedes' tragedy *Ion* portrays an abandoned infant who was found and brought up as a servant boy in the temple of Apollo at Delphi.

When children were exposed, they died of starvation or were eaten by wild animals or birds of prey, or were found and the girls were raised as prostitutes and boys were raised to become slaves or gladiators. Some deliberately maimed the abandoned children they found and used them to beg for food or money for their "owners."[80] "The kindest fate was when an abandoned

---

73. Ibid., 285. Diggers in Tunis have uncovered thousands of urns each with the ashes of a young child (ibid., 286).

74. De Vaux, *Ancient Israel,* 445.

75. Cicero *De legibus* 3.19; Seneca *De ira* 1.15; Plutarch *Moralia* 8E, 497E; Tacitus *Germania* 19; and Juvenal 6.603.

76. Ian Jenkins, *Greek and Roman Life* (London: Trustees of the British Museum, 1986), 30, 32.

77. Ibid., 32. See Plutarch *Lycurgus* 16.1ff.

78. De Mause, "The Evolution of Childhood," 26; William L. Langer, "Infanticide: A Historical Survey," *History of Childhood Quarterly* 2 (1974): 354; and Ross S. Kraemer, "Jewish Mothers and Daughters in the Greco-Roman World," in *The Jewish Family in Antiquity,* ed. Shaye J. D. Cohen (Atlanta: Scholars Press, 1993), 107–8.

79. Gorman, *Abortion and the Early Church,* 25.

80. William Barclay, *Educational Ideals in the Ancient World* (reprint, Grand Rapids: Baker Book House, 1974), 265.

child was collected by some mother, who was either unable to have a child of her own or unwilling to face the processes of childbirth. Chrysostom said he knew that free women often substituted a child of another when they themselves could not conceive (*Orations* 15, p. 447)."[81]

Laws against exposure were not established in the Roman Empire until the fourth century,[82] but their confirmation in 529 by the Roman Byzantine emperor Justinian (483–505) "shows the persistence of the economic pressures and social assumptions behind the practice."[83]

Killing legitimate children was only slowly reduced during the Middle Ages.[84] With the advances of medical technology in recent years, the lives of many babies born prematurely can now be saved. And many children's diseases have been virtually wiped out, thus saving many more children from death. Is it not ironic, however, that with these scientific capabilities to save young lives, the destroying of unborn lives is practiced so widely as an acceptable procedure? And is the taking of a human life in the womb any different from infanticide? Are not these practices essentially the same—willfully taking the lives of young, helpless human beings? Since God so emphatically condemned infanticide in the biblical world, can we expect him to have any less harsh attitude toward abortion, which is destroying far more lives?

81. Ibid.
82. Justinian refers to a law established in A.D. 374, banning exposure of children (cf. Jane F. Gardner, *Women in Roman Law and Society* [Bloomington, Ill.: Indiana University Press, 1986], 161). "It is not just a person who smothers a child who is held to kill it, but also the person who abandons it, denies it food, or puts it on show in public places to excite pity which he himself does not have" (Justinian *Digest* 25.3.4).
83. Suzanne Dixon, *The Roman Family* (Baltimore: Johns Hopkins University Press, 1992), 122.
84. De Mause, "The Evolution of Childhood," 26. For infanticide in Europe in the Middle Ages and through the nineteenth century, see Langer, "Infanticide: A Historical Survey," 355–64.

"A Full Quiver"

Size and Membership in Bible Families

How do you define a family?

In the past almost no one would disagree with the answer that a family consists of a father, mother, and children, and perhaps some close, live-in relatives like a widowed grandparent.

Today, however, a family may consist of a divorced or never-married mother and her child or children. Or some say an unmarried couple living together, with or without children, is a family. Or what about households with adopted children? Or a grandmother and her grandchild? Are they to be considered families? Even homosexual couples are demanding that they be treated like married couples, viewed legally as families.

How do these trends compare with families in the Bible? What constituted a family in biblical times? Who were included in those families? How large were Old Testament and New Testament families?

Family Membership and Size

Most biblical families were large. They included the father, mother (or mothers in a polygamous marriage), and a "full quiver" (Ps. 127:5) of sons and daughters. Other members in some families included grandparents, in-laws, and servants. Several men also had concubines, slave girls who were considered part of the family because of their role in bearing children.

The number of children in these households differed from family to family; quivers differed in size! The number ranged from 88 children born to Rehoboam, Solomon's son and king of Judah, borne to him by 18 wives and 60 concubines (2 Chron. 11:21). Table 1 shows the number of sons and daughters born to a selected list of fathers, as recorded in the Scriptures. Of these 51 fathers, 17 had 7 children or more. The average number of children per biblical household was 10.4. However, if the children born by concubines to Abraham and Nahor are excluded and if all the children born to Jair, Ibzan, Abdon, Rehoboam, and Abijah are excluded (since we do not know how many children their wives bore and how many their concubines bore), the average number of children per family was 6.1.[1] (The median number—the point with an equal number of children above and below it—is 5.) Interestingly, the average of 6 children per family is almost twice the average number of children in each household in the United States, which was 3.17 in 1993.[2] This number has declined from 3.58 in 1970.[3] Having large families in Bible times gave fathers help in their farming or other occupations and also contributed to a greater extension of their family names through their progeny. Having many children was seen as a blessing from God, for when Eliphaz encouraged Job to repent, he assured Job that his restored blessings would include having many children (Job 5:25).

Table 1
Number of Sons and Daughters Born to a
Selected Number of Fathers in the Bible

Fathers	Number of Sons	Number of Daughters
Adam	3	0[4]
Lamech	4	0
Job	7 (+7 later)	3 (+3 later)
Noah	3	0
Japheth	7	
Ham	4	
Cush (Ham's son)		5
Shem	5	
Aram (Shem's son)		4
Joktan (great-great grandson of Shem)		13
Abraham	8[5]	

1. One must keep in mind that these numbers are based on a relatively small number of families. If other families are included, the averages may differ, though the averages cited above do help indicate that Bible families, particularly those in the Old Testament, were fairly large.

2. John W. Wright, ed., *The Universal Almanac 1995* (Kansas City, Mo.: Andrews and McMeel, 1994), 307.

3. Ibid. In 1970, 20.4 percent of the households had three or more children. In 1993 the percentage had dropped to 9.9.

4. Note: If it is known that no sons (or daughters) were born to the family, then zero is noted. If the Scriptures say nothing about either sons or daughters one way or the other, the space is left blank.

5. Ishmael was born by his maidservant Hagar, Isaac was born by his wife Sarah, and six sons were born by his concubine Keturah.

Nahor (Abraham's uncle)[6]	12	
Lot	0	2
Isaac	2	0
Ishmael	12	1
Jacob[7]	12	1
Esau	5	
Eliphaz (Esau's son)	6	
Reuel (Esau's son)	4	
Judah	3	
Simeon	5	
Shimei (Simeon's grandson)	16	6
Reuben	4	
Levi	3	
Issachar	4	
Benjamin	10	
Naphtali	4	
Manasseh (Joseph's son)	3	
Ephraim	4	
Asher	4	1
Dan	1 (plus others?)	
Zebulun	3	
Gad	7	
Amram (father of Moses)	2	1
Aaron	4	
Moses	2	
Elkanah (Samuel's father)	4	2
Eli	2	
Jair	30	
Ibzan	30	30
Abdon	40	
Saul	22	
Jesse	8	
David[8]	19	
Rehoboam[9]+	28	60
Abijah[10]	22	16
Isaiah	20	
Hosea	21	
Joseph[11] (married to Mary, Jesus' mother)	4	(several; number unknown)
John (brother of Peter and Andrew)	2 (plus others?)	
Zebedee (father of James and John)	2 (plus others?)	

6. Eight sons were born by his wife, and four sons were born by a concubine.

7. Six sons and one daughter were born by his wife Leah, two sons by his wife Rachel, and two sons each by his maidservants, Bilhah and Zilpah.

8. Nineteen sons were by David's wives, and an undesignated number of sons were born by his concubines.

9. Rehoboam had eighteen wives and sixty concubines.

10. Abijah had fourteen wives.

11. After Jesus was born, Mary gave birth (presumably through Joseph) to four other sons, Jesus' stepbrothers, and several daughters (Matt. 13:55–56).

Having seven children was considered an ideal number, apparently a token of ample blessing from God. When Obed was born to Ruth, women said to Naomi that having Ruth was better than having seven sons (Ruth 4:15). After Hannah gave birth to Samuel, she exclaimed in poetic hyperbole in her praise to God, "She who was barren has borne seven children" (1 Sam. 2:5). Job's seven sons (along with three daughters) born to him before his calamities (Job 1:4), and another seven sons (and three daughters) born after his calamities (42:13), picture an ideal family. Speaking of God's forthcoming destruction of Judah by enemy armies, Jeremiah wrote, "The mother of seven will grow faint and breathe her last" (Jer. 15:9).

Other large numbers of children are referred to. Elkanah, seeking to console his barren wife Hannah and not understanding her tears and loss of appetite, asked her, "Don't I mean more to you than ten sons?" (1 Sam. 1:8). Apparently he felt her sorrowful longing for a child meant she had little regard for him. Solomon wrote that if a man had one hundred children but could not enjoy them, he may as well not have lived (Eccles. 6:3).

To have only one child and to lose him or her was a tragedy, as in the case of the two prostitutes who brought a son to Solomon (1 Kings 3:16–28), the widow of Zarephath whose son died but was restored to life by Elijah (17:7–24), the widow with two sons whose oil was multiplied (2 Kings 4:1–7), the Shunamite's son who died and was restored by Elijah (4:8–37), the synagogue ruler whose only daughter Jesus raised to life (Luke 8:40–42, 49–56), and the widow of Nain whose son Jesus restored to life from his coffin in the funeral procession to the graveyard (7:11–17).

The New Testament makes relatively few comments about the number of children in families. Peter and Andrew, two of Jesus' disciples, were brothers, and two other disciples of his, James and John, were brothers. Whether these four had other siblings is unknown; their parents may or may not have had more than two sons each.

Roman families varied in size too. In studying the archaeological ruins of Pompeii and Herculaneum, Wallace-Hadrill estimated that the average household size in those towns may have been between 7.7 and 8.3 persons.[12] However, as he acknowledges, in a population of an estimated 10,000, it is extremely difficult to know if the 1,200 or 1,300 habitable units, each represents a separate family and how many slaves may have been included. If both parents were still living in each of those households, the average number of children and slaves per family would be between 5.7 and 6.3. The number of slaves in Roman households varied greatly, depending

---

12. Andrew Wallace-Hadrill, "Houses and Households: Sampling Pompeii and Herculaneum," in *Marriage, Divorce, and Children in Ancient Rome,* ed. Beryl Rawson (Oxford: Clarendon Press, 1991), 204.

on the wealth of the families. Most modest households, Rawson observes, might have had one or two slaves.[13]

"Extended" Families

Some Bible households may have included other relatives besides the "immediate" family members, such as in-laws or grandparents. If grandparents did not live with their sons or daughters and grandchildren, they no doubt often lived nearby (e.g., Laban's children, Gen. 31:28; Jacob's grandchildren, 46:7; Abdon's thirty grandsons, Judg. 12:14). Naomi lived near Ruth, her daughter-in-law, when Ruth gave birth to Obed (Ruth 4:13–16). Apparently Timothy's grandmother Lois lived with or near Timothy for she modeled the Christian faith to her grandson (2 Tim. 1:5). Paul instructed children and grandchildren to care for their widowed mothers and grandmothers (1 Tim. 5:4).

Rebekah spoke of the irritation of her daughters-in-law, Esau's wives, who were Hittites (Gen. 27:46). Naomi is probably the best-known Old Testament mother-in-law (Ruth 1:3–19) and Peter's mother-in-law was living with him (Luke 4:38–39). The best-known Old Testament father-in-law is Jethro, father of Zipporah, Moses' wife (Exod. 18).

The word "household" sometimes refers to one's immediate family (e.g., Exod. 12:3–4) but more often it included slaves and hired servants (e.g., 2 Sam. 12:17; 1 Kings 5:9). Abram had 318 trained men born in his household (Gen. 14:14), and foreigners whom he purchased as slaves were part of his "household" (17:27). Job had many servants to care for his extensive livestock and those servants were part of his household (Job. 1:10; cf. 1:15–17), whom he treated fairly (31:13–15, 31).

Sarah had an Egyptian maidservant, Hagar (Gen. 16:1), and Rebekah had maids (24:61). Slaves were to observe the Sabbath along with the other family members (Exod. 20:10; 23:12) and to share in taking offerings to the tabernacle (Deut. 12:11–12, 18). If a man purchased slaves who then married and had children, those children became part of his household as well (Exod. 23:12; Lev. 22:11; Eccles. 2:7).

Though polygamy enabled a husband to have more children and though a number of Old Testament men had more than one wife, God never approved of it. Marriage, which God established with Adam and Eve, is to consist of one man and one woman (Gen. 2:24). With two wives, Lamech was the first polygamous man recorded in the Bible (4:19). Jacob had two wives, Leah and Rachel; the judges Gideon, Jair, Ibzan, and Abdon, each with their many sons, had several wives (Judg. 8:30; 10:4; 12:9, 14). David had eight wives, Solomon had seven hundred (1 Kings 11:3), and his son Rehoboam had

13. Beryl Rawson, "The Roman Family," in *The Family in Ancient Rome,* ed. Beryl Rawson (Ithaca, N.Y.: Cornell University Press, 1986), 12.

eighteen (2 Chron. 11:21). Polygamy makes for friction and jealousy in the home, as in the case of Elkanah's wives, Peninnah and Hannah (1 Sam. 1:1–2, 4–7).

Men who had children by concubines included Abraham (Gen. 16; 25:6; 1 Chron. 1:32), Jacob (Gen. 30:3–12), Gideon (Judg. 8:31), Saul (2 Sam. 3:7), David (2 Sam. 5:13; 15:16; 19:5; 1 Chron. 3:9), Solomon (1 Kings 11:3), and Rehoboam (2 Chron. 11:21).[14] The New Testament makes no mention of concubines. In inheritance rights sons of concubines were considered equal to sons of wives. Perhaps these semi-siblings experienced strife and disharmony as well. This may be part of the cause of the strife between Joseph and his ten older brothers.

Adoption

Today many married couples face the problem of infertility.[15] Wanting to have children, they choose to adopt a child, usually one who has resulted from an unwanted pregnancy of an unmarried mother, or a child who is orphaned. The adoption thus benefits the parents, giving them the joy of parenthood and provision for them in their old age, and also the child, giving him or her a secure home. The adopted child has legal rights as if he or she were born naturally into the family.

In the ancient Near East adoption was well known, but the purpose was primarily to provide an heir who could carry on the parents' name. The Code of Hammurabi, developed by the king of Babylonia who ruled from 1850 to 1750 B.C., includes several regulations pertaining to adoption.[16] Also the Nuzi tablets, discovered between 1925 and 1931 east of the Tigris River in present-day Iraq, specify Mesopotamian adoption procedures.[17] Even in classical Greece, a few hundred years before Christ, a father who had no sons could adopt a relative such as a son-in-law, grandson, or nephew to have someone with the status of a son to inherit the father's property.[18]

Scholars differ on whether adoption existed in Bible times. No alleged instances in the Bible reflect the strict meaning of adoption, in which parents

14. Difference of opinion exists on whether maidservants, such as Abraham's Hagar and Jacob's Bilhah and Zilpah, are to be considered concubines. Hagar was never called a concubine, whereas Abraham's Keturah was.

15. Lippis points out that "in one recent year, there were 800,000 couples in the U.S. cleared and waiting to adopt, but only 100,000 babies to be placed" (John Lippis, *The Challenge to Be "Pro-Life,"* rev. ed. [Santa Barbara, Calif.: Santa Barbara Pro-Life Education, 1982], 15). As of 1991, more than one million children were in adoptive families (*The World Almanac and Book of Facts 1995* [Mahwah, N.J.: Funk & Wagnalls, 1994], 962).

16. James B. Pritchard, ed., *Ancient Near Eastern Texts Pertaining to the Old Testament,* 3d ed. (Princeton, N.J.: Princeton University Press, 1969), 173–75, pars. 170–71, 185–93.

17. Ibid., 219–20.

18. W. K. Lacey, *The Family in Classical Greece* (Ithaca, N.Y.: Cornell University Press, 1968), 145.

accept a child born to a mother outside their home, who becomes an heir (the present-day practice). However, biblical adoption can include cases of adopting a relative, such as a grandchild, a cousin, an illegitimate son, or even a slave. The fact that the Mosaic law includes no adoption laws suggests that parents in Israel were concerned about providing heirs primarily through blood lines, such as through a levirate marriage arrangement (in which a brother married his widowed, childless sister-in-law) or through polygamy.[19]

Concerned that he was childless, Abram anticipated adopting his servant Eliezer to be the recipient of his estate (Gen. 15:2–3). This seems to be a clear case of anticipated adoption of an adult as the adopter's legal heir. Childless couples adopting adult slaves for this purpose was well known in the ancient Near East.

Sarah, Rachel, and Leah each gave a female maidservant to her husband to bear a child (Gen. 16:1–4; 30:1–13). The children born to Hagar, Bilhah, and Zilpah need not be thought of as being adopted because they were the legitimate, blood offspring of Abram and Jacob. Abram called Ishmael "my son" (21:11); and Jacob referred to those born to his two wives and their maidservants as "the children" God graciously gave him (33:5).

Some suggest that Ephraim and Manasseh were adopted by their grandfather Jacob, when he said to Joseph, "Your two sons born to you in Egypt . . . will be reckoned as mine" (48:5). But what Jacob did "was simply to 'step up' their status by one generation, treating them as his sons instead of his grandsons."[20] His words did not make them legal heirs of his estate.

When Joseph's great-grandchildren, the children of Makir, son of Manasseh, "were placed at birth on Joseph's knees" (50:23), this act was not adoption (Joseph did not raise them as his own children in his home), but was an act of welcoming them into his family line, that is, recognizing them as his legitimate descendants.[21]

Opinions differ on whether Moses was legitimately adopted by Pharaoh's daughter or whether this was a case of his being a foster child. Several facts point to this as a genuine case of adoption (though in Egypt, not Israel). First, Exodus 2:10 states "he became her son," and Stephen said that she "brought him up as her own son" (Acts 7:21). Second, he was brought up as an Egyptian, being "educated in all the wisdom of the Egyptians" (7:22). Third, payment to Moses' natural mother to nurse him (Exod. 2:9) "echoes identical arrangements in Mesopotamian adoption contracts."[22]

19. For discussion of the levirate marriage, see chapter 4. On adoption, see Gaalyahu Cornfeld, *Pictorial Bible Encyclopedia* (New York: Macmillan Co., 1964), 319; and J. H. Tigay, "Adoption," in *Encyclopaedia Judaica*, 1972 ed., 2:298.

20. David R. Mace, *Hebrew Marriage: A Sociological Study* (London: Epworth Press, 1953), 212.

21. Frederick W. Knobloch, "Adoption," in *Anchor Bible Dictionary*, 1992 ed., 1:78.

22. Ibid.

Also in Egypt was the adoption of Genubath, who was born to Hadad, an Edomite, and a sister of the Egyptian Queen Tahpenes, and who was "brought up in the royal palace" by Tahpenes (1 Kings 11:19–20).

Another alleged case of adoption is that of Naomi, when she laid her grandson Obed "in her lap and cared for him" (Ruth 4:16), and women there commented, "Naomi has a son" (4:17). However, this can hardly be a case of adoption, for her daughter-in-law Ruth had married Boaz in a levirate marriage to perpetuate the name of her former husband Mahlon. Surely Ruth and Boaz raised Obed as their own naturally born son. The women's words simply indicate that Obed was legally Naomi's grandson.

Jarha, an Egyptian servant, was a slave of Sheshan, who, because he had no sons, made Jarha, the servant, his son-in-law (1 Chron. 2:34–35). This was a legal adoption because if Jarha had not been adopted by his master, his descendants through his son Attai would not have been listed in the genealogy of Judah.[23]

After Esther's parents died, her cousin Mordecai supported her "as his own daughter" (Esther 2:7; cf. v. 15). This may be a case of fosterage or guardianship, rather than legal adoption, since nothing in the story suggests that Mordecai made legal arrangements for her as an heir. Foster children obeyed their parents as if they were their natural parents (2:20).

Perhaps, then, the only legitimate cases of adoption in the Old Testament were those of Moses and Genubath—but both of them were by Egyptian, not Israelite, parents—and Abram's plan to adopt his slave Eliezer as his heir, and Sheshan's adoption of his son-in-law. In no case was an unrelated newborn adopted by childless Israelite parents as their heir, as in the practice of adoption today.

During Paul's day, Greeks and Romans practiced adoption. In Greece, a man might adopt a male citizen or designate the adoption, by will, to take effect after the adopter's death.

> Men who had no children or whose children failed to live to adulthood sometimes compensated for this by adopting a son from another family to continue the family. . . . Most of the adoptive sons whom we know were already adult at the time of adoption: by then, chances of survival were greater and the adopting father could see what he was getting as a son and heir.[24]

Adoption most often was of a close relative such as a nephew or a grandson. Marcus Aurelius, for example, when he lost his father, was adopted by his paternal grandfather, Antoninus Pius, who later became a Roman emperor, and

---

23. Cornfeld, *Pictorial Bible Encyclopedia*, 319.
24. Rawson, "The Roman Family," 12. Adoptive sons differed from foster children, as Rawson explains ("Children in the Roman *Familia*," in *The Family in Ancient Rome*, 170–200).

was raised by him.[25] And Pliny the Younger was adopted by his maternal uncle. A brother or cousin could give a son to a man who had none.[26] The most striking example of Roman adoption was that of Octavian, who was adopted by Julius Caesar and became Octavius Augustus, the first Roman emperor.[27] The Roman adoption of a son-in-law by a father-in-law recalls Sheshan's adopting of his slave Jarha as his son-in-law (1 Chron. 2:34–35). While most adoptees were adult males, for the purpose of continuing the family name, occasionally boys or girls were adopted.[28]

Five times Paul referred to adoption as a picture of spiritual truths. The word *huiothesia* (lit., "placing as a son") is used in reference to God's election of Israel as his sons (Rom. 9:4), to believers who are redeemed from spiritual slavery by the Spirit of adoption (8:15) "to be adopted as his sons through Jesus Christ" (Eph. 1:5). Redeemed or freed from any obligation to keep the Mosaic law, believers now enjoy "the full rights of sons" (*tēn huiothesian*, "the adoption," Gal. 4:5).[29] Yet they will experience adoption in an even more complete and final sense when they are in heaven and their bodies are fully "redeemed"; therefore, now they "wait eagerly for [their] adoption as sons" (*huiothesian*, Rom. 8:23).

Being adopted into God's family at salvation beautifully depicts God's love for us, his choosing us, his purchasing and freeing us from the authority and domination of sin and the Law, his making us his sons (Gal. 4:7) and his children (1 John 3:2), and his giving us an "eternal inheritance" (Heb. 9:15) in heaven (1 Peter 1:4) as his heirs and co-heirs with Christ (Rom. 8:17).

Firstborn

Do you remember the excitement of being a parent for the first time? You experienced such joy in having your very own! Being your firstborn, your young child got all kinds of attention. You were always taking photos of your child; you noticed every little indication of growth; you were amazed at how smart your young one was!

In contrast to later-borns, firstborns "are 'first come,' and they are 'first served' by eager parents who want to do this job of parenting" well.[30] First-

25. Mireille Corbier, "Divorce and Adoption as Roman Familial Strategies," in *Marriage, Divorce, and Children in Ancient Rome,* ed. Beryl Rawson (Oxford: Clarendon Press, 1991), 68.

26. Ibid.

27. Paul Veyne, ed., *From Pagan Rome to Byzantium,* trans. Arthur Goldhammer (Cambridge, Mass.: Belknap Press, 1987), 17.

28. Suzanne Dixon, *The Roman Family* (Baltimore: Johns Hopkins University Press, 1992), 112, 219, n. 69.

29. The relationship of redemption to adoption is based on the Roman practice in which an adoptive father bought the adoptee out from the authority of his natural father (Thomas Rees, "Adoption," in *International Standard Bible Encyclopedia,* 1 [1979]:54), or it may picture buying a slave and adopting him as a son, a less common practice among the Romans.

30. Kevin Leman, *The Birth Order Book* (Old Tappan, N.J.: Fleming H. Revell Co., 1985), 48.

borns do not have to share the attention of their parents with siblings; they are the sole focus of mom and dad's affection and training. However, being in the spotlight usually means firstborns face more pressure—pressure to obey, to grow up fast, to excel, to be the family's standard-bearer. Firstborns are often conscientious, aggressive, perfectionistic, serious, and responsible.[31]

The Bible focuses on a number of children who were firstborns. Jesus Christ was Mary's firstborn (Luke 2:7). As with parents today, Bible-time fathers and mothers highly esteemed their firstborn children, especially sons, and took great delight in them (see, e.g., Gen. 4:1; 21:6; 29:32; 30:6, 23; Luke 1:57–58). Firstborn sons felt greater responsibility (e.g., Reuben, Gen. 37:22), received preferential treatment (43:33), and were blessed by their father when he was dying (27:1–4, 35–37). As the principal heir and successor of his father, the firstborn received a double portion of the estate when his father died (Deut. 21:17). Thus if there were two sons, the property would be divided three ways and the eldest would receive two-thirds. If there were three sons, the inheritance would be divided into four parts, with the eldest son receiving half.[32] When Elisha prayed for a double portion of Elijah's spirit (2 Kings 2:9), he was not asking for twice as much spiritual power or the ability to perform twice as many miracles as Elijah. Instead Elisha was asking to be like Elijah's firstborn, that is, to be his successor.

Sometimes an older man, being a morally upright person and blessed materially by the Lord, would leave an inheritance not only to his sons, but also to his grandchildren (Prov. 13:22a). Normally daughters were excluded from inheriting their father's property, since they would be cared for materially by marriage. But if there were no male heirs, the daughters gained the inheritance, as in the case of Zelophehad's daughters (Num. 27:1–8; cf. 1 Chron. 1:15). An exception was Job's three daughters, to whom he granted a portion of the inheritance along with their seven brothers (Job 42:13–15). Perhaps this exception was because Job lived outside Israel, in the land of Uz (1:1). An old Babylonian text from Nippur, a Sumerian city fifty miles southeast of Babylon, reads, "If a man dies and he has no sons, his unmarried daughters shall become his heirs."[33] A Nuzi text of about 1300 B.C. records that a father gave his daughter the status of a son for inheritance purposes.[34] According to the law of Moses, if a man in Israel died childless, his estate went to his brothers, his father's brothers, or another near relative (Num. 27:8–11).

31. Ibid., 44, 48–49.

32. This and similar privileges were also granted to the firstborn in Mesopotamia, as revealed by documents discovered at Mari and Nuzi (Matitiahu Tsevat, "$b^e k\hat{o}r$," in *Theological Dictionary of the Old Testament*, 2 [1975]: 123–24).

33. Zafrira Ben-Barak, "Inheritance by Daughters in the Ancient Near East," *Journal of Semitic Studies* 25 (Spring 1980): 23.

34. Jonathan Paradise, "A Daughter and Her Father's Property at Nuzi," *Journal of Cuneiform Studies* 32 (October 1980): 189.

Sons of a man's concubines were not eligible to receive any of his inheritance. For this reason Abraham gave the sons of his concubines gifts and sent them away (Gen. 25:5–6). However, Ishmael, born to Hagar, Sarah's maidservant, would have been Abraham's primary heir if he had no biological sons by Sarah, or if Sarah elevated Ishmael as her legal son, or if after Sarah's death Abraham did not marry another chief wife and have sons.[35] But Hagar's hopes for her and her son were dashed when she learned, to everyone's surprise, that Sarah was pregnant.[36]

An Old Assyrian marriage contract that predates Abraham shows that a wife had control over her slave-wife and her offspring and could sell the slave-wife even if the slave-wife had borne a child.[37] Apparently Sarah was sending Hagar and Ishmael away (Gen. 21:8–13), rather than taking the more harsh action of selling her.[38] As a result, Ishmael could not share the inheritance with Isaac.

The double portion allotted to the firstborn son was not unique to Israel, for a similar arrangement was provided for in the Middle Assyrian Laws,[39] and the laws at Mari and Nuzi.[40] However, in ancient Babylon, firstborns were sometimes given a special gift though all sons received equal shares of the estate.

The firstborn could sell his inheritance right, his "birthright" (as Esau did, Gen. 25:31–34, and as specified in Old Babylonian and Nuzi laws[41]). Other times the primogeniture was forfeited by wrong conduct, as in Reuben's case by incest (35:22; 49:3–4; 1 Chron. 5:1–2). Strikingly, the world's first firstborn, Cain, became a murderer (Gen. 4:1–8), perhaps driven by a strong desire to be accepted by God and to be given preferential treatment.

Several times the Lord favored a younger son over the eldest, thereby showing that as Lord he "transcends cultural norms."[42] These choices include

35. James R. Baker, *Women's Rights in Old Testament Times* (Salt Lake City: Signature Books, 1992), 88.

36. Ibid., 89. The Code of Hammurabi provided that if a slave girl bore children and the father accepted them as his own, they were to share his inheritance with the children of the man's wife, if she had any (Pritchard, *Ancient Near Eastern Texts Relating to the Old Testament*, 173, par. 170). But apparently Abraham had not legally acknowledged Ishmael as his son, no doubt because of God's promise that he would give the patriarch a son by Sarah (17:15–16, 19).

37. Julius Lewy, "On Some Institutions of the Old Assyrian Empire," *Hebrew Union College Annual* 27 (1956): 9–10; Tikva Frymer-Kensky, "Patriarchal Family Relationships and Near Eastern Law," *Biblical Archeologist* 44 (Fall 1981): 212; and A. K. Grayson and J. Van Seeters, "The Childless Wife in Assyria and the Stories of Genesis," *Orientalia* 44 (1975): 485–86.

38. Baker, *Women's Rights in Old Testament Times*, 96.

39. Ibid., 185; and Roland de Vaux, *The Early History of Israel*, trans. David Smith (Philadelphia: Westminster Press, 1978), 251.

40. Baker, *Women's Rights in Old Testament Times*, 220. Also see I. Mendolsohn, "On the Preferential Status of the Eldest Son," *Bulletin of the American Schools of Oriental Research* no. 156 (December 1959): 38–40; and Barry J. Beitzel, "The Right of the Firstborn (Pî Šnayim) in the Old Testament (Deut. 21:15–17)," in *A Tribute to Gleason Archer*, ed. Walter C. Kaiser, Jr. and Ronald E. Youngblood (Chicago: Moody Press, 1986), 179–90.

41. Tsevant, "*bᵉkôr*," 2:126. Cf. E. M. Cassin, *L'adoption à Nuzi* (Paris: Adrien-Maison Neuve, 1938), 230–33.

42. John S. Oswalt, "*bᵉkôr*," in *Theological Wordbook of the Old Testament*, 1:109.

Jacob over Esau (27:21–37), Joseph over Reuben (48:22; 1 Chron. 5:1–2), Ephraim over Manasseh (Gen. 48:17–20), Moses over Aaron, and David over his brothers (1 Sam. 16:6–13). Also, the father apparently had the right to designate as the "firstborn" a son who was not born first, as in Jacob designating Joseph, his eleventh son, as the "firstborn" (Gen. 48:22), or Hosah the Merarite appointing Shimri as his "first" (1 Chron. 26:10).

One of the firstborn's responsibilities was to care economically for his mother[43] and for his unwed sisters till they were married.[44] The fact that Laban gave his sisters Leah and Rachel in marriage to Jacob (Gen. 29) may suggest that their father had died.

Firstborn sons, as well as the firstborn in livestock, were special to the Lord (Exod. 13:2; 22:29b; 34:19; Num. 18:15; Neh. 10:36). Because the firstborn in Israelite families were not killed in the tenth plague on Egypt, when all the Egyptians' firstborn had died, all Israel's firstborn sons belonged to the Lord. He had saved them in the Passover (he had "passed over" those families), and, therefore, they were consecrated to him. However, the fathers were to buy back ("redeem") their firstborn from the Lord by paying the priest five silver shekels when the boy was a month old (Num. 18:16). This act was a reminder of the Lord's having redeemed his people from Egypt (Exod. 13:13–16). In place of all the firstborn serving the Lord, he designated the Levites as his servants (Num. 3:12, 45; 8:15–18).

As a nation, Israel was the Lord's firstborn (Exod. 4:22; Jer. 31:9), chosen by him to be in a privileged relationship, the recipients of his blessings and his inheritance (Deut. 9:26, 29; Ps. 28:9; Jer. 12:7). Christ is God the Father's "firstborn" (Heb. 1:6) in the sense of his being preeminent over all believers, who are God's children (Rom. 8:29). As "the firstborn of all creation" (Col. 1:15), Christ is the sovereign Creator, the one by whom "all things were created" (1:16). And as "the firstborn from the dead" (Rev. 1:5), he is the first to have received a glorified, resurrected body.

As God's children, believers are heirs of his blessings (Rom. 8:17; Gal. 4:1, 7). Those who believe in Christ in this Church Age are "the church of the firstborn" (Heb. 12:23), in the sense that they belong to him. Believers receive spiritual blessings as an "inheritance" from the Lord (Acts 20:32; Eph. 1:14, 18; Col. 1:12; 3:24; Heb. 9:15; 1 Peter 1:4).

Grandparents in Bible Families

Most adults are delighted to become grandparents. They thrill at the thought of their own children having children. What grandfather or grand-

43. Godfrey Ralles Driver and John C. Miles, *The Babylonian Laws*, 2 vols. (Oxford: Clarendon Press, 1955), 1:334–35.
44. M. Cohen, "Primogeniture," in *Universal Jewish Encyclopedia*, 8:644.

mother does not enjoy seeing their children's children come into the world and grow?

To live long enough to see one's grandchildren ("your children's children") signified the Lord's blessing (Ps. 128:5–6). They are "a crown to the aged" (Prov. 17:6) in the sense that they, like a crown on the head, are cause for joy and pride. As someone has quipped, "Grandchildren are God's compensation for our growing old."

After Job recovered from his calamities and God blessed him with double his livestock and ten more children, he lived 140 years (perhaps he was about 200 years old when he died). He saw his descendants to the fourth generation (Job 42:16), that is, his great-great-grandchildren.[45]

David wrote that people who fear the Lord, that is, who trust, obey, worship, and serve him, experience the Lord's love not only for themselves, but also for their children's children (Ps. 103:17). The locust plague in Joel's day was such an awesome judgment from God that grandchildren were to be told about it (Joel 1:3). Asaph wrote that teaching God's commands was not to end with one's children, because his laws are to be taught in such a way that the children, when they become parents, teach *their* children also (Ps. 78:5–6). Godly grandparents, in other words, can have a salutary influence on their grandchildren. Teaching the young God's ways is a responsibility assigned not only to parents, but also to grandparents: "Teach them to your children and to their children after them" (Deut. 4:9).

Only a few individuals in the Bible are referred to as grandparents or grandchildren. Laban complained that his son-in-law (and nephew) Jacob had left Haran without letting Laban kiss his grandchildren goodbye (Gen. 31:28). When blind Jacob was dying, he blessed his grandsons Manasseh and Ephraim, kissing and embracing them and placing them on his knees—a typical gesture for a loving grandfather (48:8–12).

Joseph lived in Egypt to the age of 110, seeing, like Job, his great-great-grandchildren (50:22–23). Joseph's grandchildren through his son Manasseh included Makir, and Makir had four children (Peresh, Sherech, Gilead, and Hammoleketh), who were Joseph's great-grandchildren. Sheresh's two sons, Ulam and Rakem, were Joseph's great-great-grandchildren (1 Chron. 7:14–18)—seven descendants through Manasseh. Joseph's grandchildren through his son Ephraim included Shuthelah, Ezer, Elead, Beriah, and Rephah. Great-grandchildren included Bered, son of Shuthelah, and Resheph, son of Rephah. Great-great-grandchildren were Tahath, Bered's son, and Telah,

---

45. That this phrase "his children and their children to the fourth generation" means great-great-grandchildren is verified by God's word, to Jehu, that his descendants would be kings over Israel "to the fourth generation" (2 Kings 10:30; 15:12), and they included his son Jehoahaz, his grandson Jehoash, his great-grandson Jeroboam II, and his great-great-grandson Zechariah (13:1–15:12).

Resheph's son (1 Chron. 7:20–25)—nine descendants through Ephraim, and Joseph lived to see them all.

Grandson Obed, born to Ruth, would so delight grandmother Naomi that he would "renew" her life (Ruth 4:15). Her affection for the child, who would now continue her line, is seen in her placing him in her lap and caring for him (4:16). Many adults, on the birth of their first grandchild, could testify with Naomi that their new offspring has perked them up emotionally and spiritually!

As discussed in chapter 7, some godly grandparents who were kings in Judah may have had a favorable influence on their grandchildren. On the other hand, some ungodly kings, no doubt, influenced their children's children toward evil. Assyrians who were transferred to live in Israel so influenced their grandchildren that their offspring continued in the same evil, idolatrous practices (2 Kings 17:41).

In the New Testament, Timothy's grandmother Lois helped guide him into spiritual interests (2 Tim. 1:5), perhaps helping compensate for the lack of belief in the Lord on the part of Timothy's Greek father (Acts 16:1). Paul wrote that an important way adult grandchildren can live out their faith in Christ is by caring for their widowed grandmothers. Such acts of kindness do not go unnoticed by the Lord; in fact they are "pleasing to God" (1 Tim. 5:4).

God's tender interest in children and grandchildren is seen in his prophetic words to Ezekiel that when Israel is in the land during the millennium, "they and their children and their children's children will live there forever" (Ezek. 37:25).

7

"Bringing Up Children"

Parental Responsibilities in Bible Families

Childless parents and parentless children—these two family situations stand as contemporary problems almost unheard of in Bible times.

Most husbands and wives in the Old and New Testaments wanted children, were expected to have them, and were delighted when the children were born. To be childless, as discussed in chapter 4, was a social and spiritual disgrace.

Also, for children to be without parents was an unusual circumstance, which called for special attention on the part of society to those children without fathers (the fatherless) or both parents (the orphans).

By contrast, in present-day American society parents without children and children without parents have become commonplace. More married couples are opting not to bear children, to be, as they call it, "child-free."[1] And an alarming number of children live without one or both parents—either for part of the day, as "latchkey children," or permanently with an unmarried mother, or with a divorced "single mom" or "single dad."

The biblical portrait of the family consists of father, mother, and children, each with special responsibilities and concerns for the other. God's very first command to the first married couple, Adam and Eve, was to bear children.

---

1. For a thorough study of voluntary childlessness, see J. E. Veevers, "Voluntary Childlessness: A Review of Issues and Evidence," *Marriage and Family Review* 2 (Summer 1979): 1, 3–24.

As in Bible times, children today need parents. Many children who are raised without one or both of their parents are affected adversely, often being emotionally scarred and socially disadvantaged.

In addition, many fathers have abandoned their child-rearing responsibilities, leaving the task of "raising the kids" to their wives. The pull of heavy job obligations, the need to travel extensively in one's employment, ignorance of how to train and discipline their children, the desire to spend time away from home in pleasurable pursuits, or fathering children illegitimately—these and other factors have made many boys and girls virtually "fatherless." This tragic scene carries forboding consequences for our society. Well-known anthropologist Bronislaw Malinowski put it this way: "In all human societies the father is regarded by tradition as indispensable . . . no child should be brought into the world without a man—and one man at that—assuming the role of sociological father, that is, guardian and protector, the male link between the child and the rest of the community."[2]

Even when fathers are home, many of them spend little time with their youngsters. Many parents spend only a few minutes each day with their children.[3]

Mothers employed outside the home end up with less time with their children. Working parents place their preschoolers in day care centers or with relatives, thus reducing the extent of important mother-child relations. Of course, some mothers find it necessary to have outside-the-home employment. But having "absent mothers," like "absent fathers," makes it difficult for young boys and girls.

Without parents, young children go hungry and are not cared for (unless other adults assume those responsibilities). Without parents, children left to themselves are undisciplined, lack self-control, and get into trouble. Some become involved in delinquent conduct and serious crime.

Clearly God placed children in families, to be raised under the influence and guidance of wise parents. He assigned certain duties to the parents in relation to the children, and certain obligations to the boys and girls. This chapter and the next examine what the Bible says about these parent-child relations in an effort to help mothers and fathers—and children—more effectively carry out those obligations in the arena in which God placed them, namely, the home, the world's oldest human institution.

When you bring your newborn home from the hospital, you are filled with inexpressible joy at this beautiful little bundle of life and you marvel that this cuddly, but helpless, infant is *yours*, a "miracle" you helped "create."

---

2. Quoted in Daniel Patrick Moynihan, *Family and Nation* (San Diego: Harcourt Brace & Co., 1986), 169–70.

3. Vance Packard, *Our Endangered Children* (Boston: Brown, Little & Co., 1983), 71.

Now what? Sleepless nights, diaper changing, frequent feedings—these and other demanding, tiring tasks are only the beginning. As your infant becomes a toddler, and then as he or she grows into a preschooler, a school-age child, and, eventually, a teenager, what will parenting involve?

What does God expect of parents? Is it enough simply to procreate offspring and provide their material needs? Most parents agree that fathering and mothering demands far more. But what are those responsibilities? How can parents best fulfill their task of bringing up mature, responsible children?

The best answer is to look to God's directives for parents given in the Bible, his timeless handbook on child rearing. Since God places children in the hands of parents, it makes sense to follow the instructions he gave in his Word for parenting. Billy Graham said it well: "For best results in marriage and in rearing children and building a stable home, follow the instructions of the one who performed the first wedding in the Garden of Eden."[4]

The Bible includes a number of direct commands to parents on how to carry out their job. The Scriptures also present biographical portraits of families—profiles that show parenting in action. The successes and failures of those fathers and mothers draw crucial lessons for us today.

These biblical precepts and profiles point up eleven tasks every parent today should follow: to lead, pray, dedicate, provide, love, enjoy, model, worship, discipline, encourage, and teach.

Lead

The father in Bible families was considered the leader of the home. As the head of his wife (Eph. 5:23) and children (Gen. 18:19; Num. 1:4), he was responsible for their physical and spiritual welfare. No godly father abdicated his responsibilities to his wife. And yet, mothers were actively engaged in child rearing, along with their husbands.

While wives are to be submissive to their husbands (Eph. 5:22; Col. 3:18), they are not inferior. Submission does not mean inferiority, but responding to her husband as the head of the home without usurping his authority to herself. They are partners, "heirs . . . of the gracious gift of life" (1 Peter 3:7). Both fathers and mothers are challenged to manage their families. As a qualification for leadership and service in the local church, elders and deacons are to lead or direct their families and children ("manage" in 1 Tim. 3:4–5; v. 12 translates *proistēmi*, "to be at the head"). And young mothers are to bear children and to "manage their homes" (*oikadespoteō*, "to head up a home," 1 Tim. 5:14).

4. Billy Graham, *Unto the Hills* (Bloomington, Minn.: Garborg's Heart 'n Home, 1995), page for March 1.

In Bible times family solidarity existed because of the central father figure. How different from so many families today in which fathers neglect their wives and children or even abandon them for other women. One of the major reasons for the moral malady and spiritual sickness of our nation is the decline in strong fatherly leadership. Children are destitute because fathers are deserting their roles! We need to return to the biblical patterns of loving, patriarchal headship.

Pray

One of the greatest benefits parents can give their children is to pray for them. Many adults, looking back on their childhood, have expressed keen appreciation for their parents' prayers for them. The Bible records a few examples of praying parents. Job regularly offered a burnt offering for each of his ten children, out of concern that they might have sinned in their hearts (Job 1:5). Abraham prayed for Ishmael (Gen. 17:18), and Hannah prayed that the Lord would give her a son (1 Sam. 1:11, 27). When David and Bathsheba's illegitimate son was ill, David prayed for the child's healing (2 Sam. 12:16). Later, as David prepared the people for his son Solomon's installment as king, David prayed publicly for his son: "Give my son Solomon the wholehearted devotion to keep your commands, requirements and decrees" (1 Chron. 29:19). What a marvelous prayer for parents to voice on behalf of their sons and daughters!

When Ezra returned from Babylon to Jerusalem, he and others prayed for a safe trip for themselves and their children (Ezra 8:21). Obviously, parents today would do well to emulate that prayer for their children's physical safety.

Dedicate

Many Christian parents dedicate their children to the Lord in a "baby dedication" as part of a church service. This is a wonderful opportunity for parents to commit themselves to teaching their children God's ways and for the congregation to covenant to help train and nurture the child. This heartwarming practice has biblical precedence in that Mary and Joseph took Jesus to the temple in Jerusalem "to present him to the Lord" (Luke 2:22). This was done when Jesus was still an infant, only forty days old.[5]

Because the angel of the Lord told Manoah to "set apart to God from birth" the child to be born to his wife, who had been sterile up to that time (Judg. 13:2, 5), the parents dedicated the boy Samson as a Nazirite, one specially separated to God (Num. 6:1–21).

---

5. Following the birth of a boy, Israelite women were involved in a ritual purification for forty days, after which the baby was to be taken to the priest (Lev. 12:1–8).

Barren Hannah vowed to give her son back to the Lord if the Lord would enable her to conceive a boy (1 Sam. 1:11). Then when Samuel was three years old, she took him "to the house of the Lord at Shiloh" and gave him to the Lord "for his whole life" (1:24, 28).

Three Bible authors noted that God had set them apart to his service even before they were born: Isaiah (Isa. 49:1), Jeremiah (Jer. 1:5), and Paul (Gal. 1:15).

Parents genuinely interested in their children's spiritual well-being do well to dedicate their infants publicly to the Lord and to pray for and dedicate them to the Lord even before they are born. The nine-month pregnancy can be an excellent time for husband and wife consciously to pray about and commit their unborn child to the Lord.

Provide

Since children are incapable of providing food, clothing, shelter, and other material needs for themselves, it is imperative that parents do so. The apostle Paul spoke bluntly when he wrote that if a parent fails to provide for his family, he contradicts his profession of faith. In fact, he is worse, Paul stated, than an unbeliever (1 Tim. 5:8) "since even many non-Christians understand and fulfill their familial responsibilities."[6] Parents need to care not only for their youngsters' present needs, but also their future needs (2 Cor. 12:14).

Wise parents are also careful what they give their children. Loving fathers, Jesus said, don't feed them harmful things, such as snakes or scorpions (Luke 11:11–12); they give them edible, wholesome foods such as fish and eggs.

The wife and mother "of noble character" (Prov. 31:10) demonstrates the love, commitment, and diligence mothers should have for the sake of their children. She provides food, clothing, and bed coverings for her family, and "watches" over or supervises the affairs of her household (31:15, 22, 27).[7]

Another example of the concern of a mother for her child's physical needs is the widow of Zarephath, who was concerned that she had only a little flour and oil left to feed herself and her son (1 Kings 17:10–12).

In the Bible a number of parents were concerned about the health of their children. As stated earlier, David was so burdened about his sick infant that he wept and refused to eat (2 Sam. 12:15–16, 21). When Abijah, the son of Jeroboam, king of Judah, became ill, Jeroboam's wife went to Ahijah the

6. A. Duane Litfin, "1 Timothy," in *The Bible Knowledge Commentary, New Testament*, ed. John F. Walvoord and Roy B. Zuck (Wheaton, Ill.: Victor Books, 1983), 743.

7. For a discussion of the character of this wife and mother in Proverbs 31:10–31 and the view that she is an actual woman and the epitome of wise living (and not merely a personification of wisdom), see Roy B. Zuck, "A Theology of the Wisdom Books and the Song of Songs," in *A Biblical Theology of the Old Testament* (Chicago: Moody Press, 1991), 237–38; and Tom R. Hawkins, "The Wife of Noble Character in Proverbs 31:10–31," *Bibliotheca Sacra* 153 (January–March 1996): 12–23.

prophet to ask him what would happen to the boy (1 Kings 14:1–2). When the widow of Zarephath met Elijah, she felt she was on her last meal (17:10–12). Later the boy became ill and when he died, she approached Elijah (17:17–24).

The son of the wealthy Shunammite suffered an apparent sunstroke, and while she was holding him in her lap, he died. In her desperation ("bitter distress") she rode on a donkey to get Elisha to come see about him (2 Kings 4:8–37).

A royal official of Capernaum, whose son was deathly ill with a bad fever, went to Jesus and begged him to heal his son (John 4:46–54). Jairus, a synagogue ruler, asked Jesus to heal his twelve-year-old daughter who was dying (Luke 8:40–42, 49–56). The father of an epileptic, demon-possessed boy approached Jesus and begged him to heal his son (Matt. 17:14–18). On several occasions people brought sick relatives and friends to Jesus for him to heal them (Matt. 4:24; 8:16; 12:15; 14:14, 35; Mark 1:32; 6:55–56; Luke 5:17; John 6:2), and they probably included children.

Remarkably, in each case the parents went to a man of God or to the Lord Jesus himself for healing. These were cases where the illness was beyond the limits of medical help. Parents today whose children have become seriously ill can appreciate the desperation of these Bible fathers and mothers and their gratitude at having their sons or daughters healed, and in some cases even brought back to life. Concerned parents, then and now, want to help provide for their children's health.

Love

Far more important than food and health is the provision of parental love. Without love from their parents, boys and girls starve emotionally. To give children material things without genuinely loving them is to fail as a parent. Nothing substitutes for love. As one girl complained, "The one thing parents don't give is love, understanding, and acceptance of you as a person."[8] Unfortunately, many families do not place a high value on loving their children unconditionally.[9]

The Bible gives us a number of examples of fathers who loved their children. God spoke to Abraham about his son "whom you love" (Gen. 22:2). Isaac loved Esau, the firstborn of his twin boys (25:28). Laban's love for his grown daughters, Rachel and Leah, is seen in his desire to kiss them

8. David Elkind, *The Hurried Child* (Reading, Mass.: Addison-Wesley Publishing Co., 1981), 19.

9. "Perhaps the most serious problem is a weakening in many families of the fundamental assumption that children are to be loved and valued at the highest level of priority" (David Popenoe, "The Family in Decline," in *The Family in America: Opposing Viewpoints*, ed. Viqi Wagner [San Diego: Greenhaven Press, 1992], 22).

good-by when they left with Jacob (31:28). Of his twelve sons, Jacob loved Joseph more (37:3), and Joseph's brothers knew it (37:4). Joseph's ten older brothers also knew of their father's love for his youngest son, Benjamin (44:20).

David had a special place in his heart for his son Absalom.[10] After Absalom murdered his brother Amnon and fled to his maternal grandfather Talmai, with whom Absalom stayed for three years, David mourned for his son and longed to see him (2 Sam. 13:37–14:1). When Absalom was finally persuaded by Joab to see his father, David kissed him (14:33).

A father's affectionately carrying his little boy dramatically pictures God's love for the nation Israel (Isa. 46:3).

Interestingly, in Jesus' ministry three fathers—not mothers—went to Jesus on behalf of their sick children (the royal official for his son, John 4:46–49; Jairus, a synagogue ruler, for his daughter, Luke 8:41–42; and the father of the demon-possessed boy, Matt. 17:14–15). The eagerness of these fathers to ask Jesus to heal their children revealed their love for them.

Another evidence of a father's love for his son is his disciplining him when necessary (Prov. 3:12; 13:24).

The natural love of a father for his son was mentioned by Jesus in his parable of the tenants. The owner of the vineyard, whose servants were mistreated by the tenants when they were sent to gather some grapes from the vineyard, decided to send his son, "whom I love" (Luke 20:13). And in Jesus' parable of the prodigal son, the father's compassion for his wayward son is seen in his running to meet his son, throwing his arms around him, kissing him, and then celebrating with a feast (Luke 15:20–24).

Surprisingly, Jesus stated that a parent who loves his or her son or daughter more than him "cannot be my disciple" (Luke 14:26). He even said that a person wanting to follow him must hate his family members, as well as his own life. But how could Jesus encourage anyone to hate his parents, spouse, children, or sibling? To do so literally would have violated the Law. Therefore, he seems to have been emphasizing the priority of love: love for one's family should not be greater than his or her love for the Lord. (This matter of love's priority, rather than literal hatred, is seen in the parallel passage, Matt. 10:37, in which Matthew wrote that Jesus said, "Anyone who loves his son or daughter more than me is not worthy of me.")

Remarkably, the Old Testament closes with a reference to fathers and their children (Mal. 4:5–6). Before the Lord returns to earth to establish his millennial reign, an Elijah-like prophet will lead both fathers and children to re-

10. Second Samuel 13:28–33 records Absalom's revengeful murder of his brother Amnon, but the Bible says nothing about Kileab except to record his birth to Abigail (2 Sam. 3:3).

pent, thus uniting their hearts together.[11] Even today when both parents and children in a family know the Lord, they experience a kind of spiritual unity, in which their hearts are turned toward each other. As might be expected, the Bible refers also to the love of mothers for their children. God asked, "Can a mother forget the baby at her breast and have no compassion on the child she has borne?" (Isa. 49:15). And he compared his comfort for Jerusalem to that of "a mother [who] comforts her child" (66:13). Paul wrote that his tender, gentle affection for his converts in Thessalonica was "like a mother [*trophos*, 'a nursing mother'] caring for [*thalpō*, 'to keep warm, to comfort'] her little children [*tekna*, 'born ones']" (1 Thess. 2:7). Younger women, Paul wrote to Titus, should be trained by older women "to love their husbands and children" (Titus 2:4).

Biblical examples of mothers' love include Rebekah's love for Jacob (Gen. 25:28); Jochebed's love for Moses, seen in her hiding him in a carefully made basket in the Nile River (Exod. 2:3) and in nursing him (2:9); Hannah's love for Samuel in making him a robe each year and taking it to him (1 Sam. 2:19); a prostitute's love for her infant son, seen in her not wanting him to be cut in two by Solomon (1 Kings 3:16–28); and Mary, who searched with Joseph for twelve-year-old Jesus for three days (Luke 2:41–50).

Expressions of parents' grief for their children demonstrate their love for them. When Hagar's son Ishmael was dying of thirst and hunger in the desert, her heart was torn as she sobbed and said to herself, "I cannot watch the boy die" (Gen. 21:15–16). Thinking Joseph had been killed by a wild animal, Jacob "mourned for his son many days," weeping and refusing to be comforted by his other children (37:31–35). Later he refused at first to let Benjamin go to Egypt, lest he too be harmed. Jacob said Benjamin's death would cause him to die "in sorrow" and "in misery" (42:38; 44:29, 31, 34). His brothers knew of their father's love for Benjamin, for they said, "The boy cannot leave his father; if he leaves him, his father will die" (44:22). They were well aware, as Judah explained, that their father Jacob's "life [was] closely bound up with the boy's life" (44:30), because Benjamin was "born to him in his old age" (44:20).[12]

David's fatherly love is unmistakably apparent in his fasting, lying on the ground at night, and praying for his and Bathsheba's young son (2 Sam. 12:15–17), and his weeping over the death of his firstborn Amnon (13:36).

---

11. For discussions on whether John the Baptist fulfilled this prophecy about Elijah, see Craig A. Blaising, "Malachi," in *The Bible Knowledge Commentary, Old Testament*, ed. John F. Walvoord and Roy B. Zuck (Wheaton, Ill.: Victor Books, 1985), 1587–88, and Craig L. Blomberg, *Matthew*, New American Commentary (Nashville: Broadman Press, 1992), 188.

12. Benjamin would have been born when Jacob was near or older than one hundred years. When Jacob went to Egypt, he was one hundred thirty years old (Gen. 47:9) and Joseph was thirty-nine, making Jacob ninety-one when Joseph was born. Sometime after that, Benjamin was born, which means Jacob was approaching or older than one hundred. Thus Benjamin, the youngest of two boys born to Jacob by his favorite wife Rachel, would have been especially dear to this man.

And what can be more heartrending than David's poignant wail in grieving for his murdered son: "O my son Absalom! My son, my son Absalom! If only I had died instead of you—O Absalom, my son, my son!" (18:33). Any parent who has lost a child in death can readily identify with David's grief. A parent's heart of love is deeply and inexplicably moved by the loss of a dear child.

Love of parents for their children pictures in a small way the even deeper love of God for his own spiritual "children." The Lord loves his people Israel (Deut. 23:5; 2 Chron. 2:11; Hos. 3:1; 11:1), the just and righteous (Pss. 37:28; 146:8), and all who belong to him (Prov. 3:12; Heb. 12:6). His compassionate love for those who fear him (the verb "to have compassion" is a tender word for parental affection) compares to the tender love of a father for his children (Ps. 103:13). Those who believe in Jesus Christ become God's sons, whom he loves (John 13:34; 16:27; Gal. 2:20; Eph. 2:4; 5:1–2; 2 Thess. 2:13, 16; 1 John 3:1; 4:9–11, 16, 19; Jude 1; Rev. 1:5; 3:9).[13]

Enjoy

Bringing children into the world is one of the greatest joys we can experience. Not surprisingly, Leah gave the names Gad and Asher to the two boys borne to her by her maidservant Zilpah (Gen. 30:9–13). Gad means "good fortune," and Asher means "happy." In their growing-up years children can also bring great delight to parents. Isaiah wrote of parents carrying "sons in their arms" and "daughters on their shoulders" (Isa. 49:22), a picture of the closeness of parents to their children. And in the millennium the Lord will so bless and enjoy Jerusalem that it will be like a mother jostling her infant "on her knees" (66:12). What parent has not been delighted at seeing his child take his first steps, and then helping him or her learn to walk. In a similar way the Lord delighted in Ephraim, helping them learn to walk by "taking them by the arms" (Hos. 11:3), that is, guiding the nation in his ways by his love.

One of life's blessings Job experienced before his calamities came on him was that "my children were around me" (Job 29:5). Apparently, sometimes children slept in the same bed with their parents. This is mentioned by Jesus in his parable of the man at midnight who refused to get up to give a neighbor some food for a traveling friend because "the door is already locked, and my children are with me in bed" (Luke 11:7; cf. 1 Kings 3:20).

What is it about children that brings happiness to parents? According to Proverbs, two characteristics in a son's life that bring joy to fathers and mothers are wisdom and godliness (Prov. 10:1; 13:1; 15:20; 17:21; 22:15; 23:15, 24–25; 27:11; 29:3, 17).

13. Also noteworthy is the love of God the Father for his Son, Jesus Christ (Matt. 3:17; 12:18; 17:5; Mark 1:11; 9:7; Luke 3:22; John 3:35; 5:20; 10:17; 15:9; 17:26; Eph. 1:6; Col. 1:13; 2 Peter 1:17).

Every Christian parent can testify with the apostle John that the greatest source of joy is knowing that their "children are walking in the truth" (2 John 4). While John was, no doubt, writing of his spiritual "children," that is, his converts, the point is certainly applicable to one's physical offspring.

The tender love of God-fearing parents in the Bible contrasts notably with the brutality of some pagan parents in the Roman Empire toward their children, as discussed in chapter 5.[14]

Worship

A major responsibility of parents in the Old Testament was to lead their children to love and worship the Lord. In early biblical history, fathers served as the priests of the home, offering sacrifices to the Lord on behalf of their children. Noah, Jacob, and Job stand as leading examples of their exemplary spiritual leadership (Gen. 8:20; 31:54; Job 1:5). Seeing their father offer sacrifices to the Lord would have made a lasting impression on the offspring of these patriarchs.

As places of worship, altars built by Noah and Isaac served as excellent visual reminders to all family members of God's faithfulness (Gen. 8:20; 26:25). The memorial stones Joshua had the tribes place on the west side of the Jordan River recalled God's miraculous work in dividing the river and evinced questions from children about their meaning (Josh. 4:1–7). Think too of the impression at seeing the altar Joshua built on Mount Ebal and having the law of Moses read by Joshua to the assembly of all Israelite adults and children (8:30–35).

The observance of the Sabbath as a religious holiday and a day of rest, no doubt, affected the children in every Israelite home in a positive way. This weekly observance would repeatedly call the children's attention to God's creative power and his rest, which the Sabbath commemorated (Exod. 20:8–11; 31:13–17; Jer. 17:21–22; Ezek. 20:20).

Imagine the deep impression made on children when they would see their parents take an animal or cooking material to the priest of the tabernacle or temple for a burnt, grain, fellowship, sin, or guilt offering (Lev. 1–7). Preparing for, observing, and participating in the Passover as a family every year in the spring would also have profoundly affected the children, impressing on their minds the fact of God's miraculous deliverance of the Israelites out of Egypt (12:1–11, 14). The Passover ceremony in the home would arouse the children's curiosity, leading them to ask its meaning and giving parents a great teaching opportunity (12:26–27). Immediately following the Passover was

14. "Ancient attitudes toward children are singularly paradoxical. Parents in classical antiquity undoubtedly loved their children. . . . And yet the treatment accorded children in ancient society was often severe, even brutal" (David Herlihy, *Medieval Households* [Cambridge, Mass.: Harvard University Press, 1985], 23).

the week-long Feast of Unleavened Bread (Exod. 12:14–20; Lev. 23:6–8), also a commemoration of their escape from Egyptian bondage (Exod. 12:17).

Think too of the deep impact made on children when families observed the other annual feasts: Firstfruits and Pentecost in the spring, and the Day of Trumpets, the Day of Atonement, and the seven-day Tabernacles in the fall (Lev. 23:9–36).[15]

Christian parents, of course, do not observe the Sabbath and these feasts, for those festivals were part of the Mosaic law which has been abolished by the cross (Col. 2:14). However, God expects parents today to lead their children in worshiping him. This can be done in the home through reading the Bible together; praying together; reading Bible storybooks; discussing answers to prayers; encouraging children to read Christian books; attending church and Sunday school together regularly; displaying Bible verses in wall plaques; encouraging children to become involved in children's activities in the church, such as children's choirs, camps, weekday programs, and Bible memory programs; and viewing Christian videos together.

It is not enough for parents to assume their children will somehow know the Bible and follow biblical standards—especially in our day of declining morals and anti-Christian sentiment. It is imperative to provide every means possible to impart God's truth and to encourage boys and girls to love and worship the Lord.

Model

"Do as I say, not as I do." Unfortunately, this idea is often conveyed to children, if not in our words, then in our actions. But encouraging children to heed what we tell them without accompanying those words with consistent living is confusing and hypocritical. Do you want your children to love, obey, trust, and follow the Lord? Then *you* must do the same. Boys and girls seldom live up to standards they do not see exemplified in their fathers and mothers.

Before parents can teach their children to love the Lord and know the Word (Deut. 6:7; 11:19), they themselves need to set the example by loving him and having his Word in their hearts (6:5–6; 11:18; 32:46).

If you fear the Lord, then this will be evident to your children and it will provide security for them as if they were safe in a fortress or refuge (Prov.

---

15. The two-day Feast of Purim was established in Esther's day (ca. 473 B.C.) to celebrate God's protection of his people from Haman's attempted execution of the Jews in Persia (Esth. 9:25–28), and the eight-day Feast of Hannukah or Dedication began in the intertestamental period in remembrance of the reconsecrating of the temple by Judas Maccabeus in 165 B.C. after it had been desecrated by Antiochus IV (Epiphanes). On this latter feast, also called the Feast of Lights, see Jerry R. Lancaster and Larry R. Overstreet, "Jesus' Celebration of Hanukkah in John 10," *Bibliotheca Sacra* 152 (July–September 1995): 318–33.

14:26). If you lead a righteous, blameless life, your children, Solomon wrote, will be blessed after you (Prov. 20:7).

Joshua exemplifies parents who model the truth for their families, for in challenging the Israelites to decide whether to follow the Lord, he affirmed, "But as for me and my household, we will serve the Lord" (Josh. 24:15).

Some parents have a bad influence on their children by their ungodly or inconsistent living. For example, Abraham was deceptive about Sarah when he met with Abimelech in Gerar (Gen. 20:1–17), and later Isaac, his son, did the same thing in Gerar (26:1–11). Isaac favored one of his sons over the other (25:28), and later Jacob followed this negative example in favoring Joseph over his other brothers (37:3–4). Jacob had two concubines, Bilhah and Zilpah, and Reuben, Jacob's son, slept with Zilpah (35:22). The sin of the father was repeated by the son.

David's polygamous marriages included eight wives and at least ten concubines (2 Sam. 3:2–5; 5:13–16; 15:16; 20:3; 1 Chron. 3:1–9). It comes as no surprise to read that his son Absalom slept with those concubines (2 Sam. 16:21), and that David's son Solomon had seven hundred wives and three hundred concubines (1 Kings 11:3). Rehoboam, in turn, followed Solomon's sinful example, by having eighteen wives and sixty concubines (2 Chron. 11:21).

Gideon, too, had a concubine (Judg. 8:31), to whom was born Abimelech. The son, Abimelech, influenced wrongly by his father's conduct, murdered his seventy half brothers (9:5). Athaliah, the daughter of Ahab and Jezebel, was a wicked person like her parents. She married Jehoram, king of Judah, and when their son Ahaziah was made king, she "encouraged him in doing wrong" (2 Chron. 22:1–3).[16] Here was evil influence penetrating through four generations: from Omri to Ahab, his son (who married Jezebel), to his daughter Athaliah, and to her son, Ahaziah. Wicked Jezebel's bad influence on her daughter, Athaliah, illustrates the proverb, "Like mother, like daughter" (Ezek. 16:44).

Is it possible that one reason for Absalom's rebellious spirit was that his mother Maacah was a pagan? Maacah, David's fourth wife, was the daughter of Talmai, king of Geshur (2 Sam. 3:3), an area in Aramea northeast of Israel (15:8). This shows the influence of a grandfather on his daughter, and through her on her son. One wonders, too, how much evil influence Talmai had on his grandson when Absalom fled from David to stay with Talmai for three years (13:37–38). David's poor decision to marry a pagan wife, no

16. Why would Jehoram, king of Judah, have married Athaliah, daughter of wicked Ahab and Jezebel? One reason may be that Jehoram's father, Jehoshaphat, had unwisely allied with Ahab in war against Aram, against which Micaiah, the prophet, had warned Jehoshaphat (1 Kings 21). This association, no doubt, made it possible for Jehoshaphat's son to be interested in Ahab's daughter. The unwise action on Jehoshaphat's part influenced his son adversely.

doubt, contributed to Absalom's rebellious spirit and thus to David's grief over his son's premature death. Often the sins of parents are not only copied by their offspring, but are carried out more intensively. David's marrying eight wives (two of whom were non-Israelites—Bathsheba, a Hittite, and Maacah, an Aramean) eventuated in his son Solomon marrying seven hundred wives, including foreigners who were Moabites, Ammonites, Edomites, Sidonians, and Hittites (1 Kings 11:1).

Jeroboam stands as a striking example of a king's negative influence in leading a nation into sin for many generations. Leading a rebellion against Solomon's son, Rehoboam, Jeroboam was made king over the ten northern tribes of Israel (1 Kings 12:20). As a wicked leader, he encouraged the people to worship two golden calves he made, built shrines on high places, and installed men as priests who were not of the tribe of Levi, all of which provoked God to anger (12:26–33; 14:9). God's immediate judgment on Jeroboam included the death of his boy, Abijah (14:1–5, 17–18).

The amazing, alarming consequence of Jeroboam's wickedness ("You have done more evil than all who lived before you," God's prophet Ahijah told him, 14:9) is that every one of the nineteen kings of the northern kingdom of Israel was evil. In fact, the summaries of almost all those kings' reigns state that they did evil, just as Jeroboam did! Fifteen of the eighteen kings after Jeroboam walked in his ways and did evil just as he did (1 Kings 15:26, 34; 16:19, 26, 31; 22:52; 2 Kings 3:3; 10:29, 31; 13:2, 11; 14:24; 15:9, 18, 24, 28).[17]

The sins of one man, Jeroboam, influenced his son Nadab, his grandson Baasha, and his great-grandson Elah—as well as all the other kings of Israel—to sin against the Lord. One man's bad influence caused an entire nation to be caught in an irretractable downward spiral for 209 years (from 931 B.C. to Israel's fall to Assyria in 722 B.C.)!

In the southern kingdom of Judah, twelve of her twenty kings were evil. Only eight "did right in the eyes of the Lord": Asa (1 Kings 15:11), Jehoshaphat (22:43), Joash (2 Kings 12:2), Amaziah (14:3), Azariah, also known as Uzziah (15:3), Jotham (15:34), Hezekiah (18:3), and Josiah (22:2).[18]

The accounts of all but three of Judah's kings make mention of their mothers (whereas this is seldom said of the kings of the north). Why is this?

17. These fifteen kings are Nadab, Baasha, Zimri, Omri, Ahab, Ahaziah, Joram, Jehu, Jehoahaz, Jehoash, Jeroboam II, Zechariah, Menahem, Pekahiah, and Pekah. The three of whom no statement is made about their following Jeroboam's ways are Elah, who reigned only two years, Shallum, who reigned only one month, and Menahem, the last of the nineteen kings, who did "evil in the eyes of the LORD, but not like the kings of Israel who preceded him" (2 Kings 17:2).

18. Of interest is the fact that three of these eight good kings were crowned when they were boys. Joash was seven years old (2 Kings 11:21), Uzziah was sixteen (14:21), and Josiah was eight (22:1). Another boy king, Manasseh, who had a wicked reign, began at age twelve (21:1).

Possibly the purpose is to hint at the influence—either for good or bad—of the mothers on their sons' political leadership. Table 2 lists these kings and their mothers.

Several bad kings—Solomon, Rehoboam, Abijah, Ahaziah, Amon, Jehoiakim, Jehoiachin, and Zedekiah—had wicked fathers or mothers. Jehoahaz may be another example if his mother Hamutal was evil. Being from Libnah, a former Canaanite city conquered by Joshua (Josh. 12:8, 15) and which later revolted against Judah (2 Kings 8:22), she may or may not have been a pagan (or perhaps she was of pagan ancestry).[19]

Table 2

Mothers of the Kings of Judah				
Kings	Character of the Kings' Reign	Mothers of the Kings	Facts about the Mothers	References
1. Solomon	Bad	Bathsheba	A Hittite	2 Sam. 11:3; 12:24
2. Rehoboam	Bad	Naamah	An Ammonite	1 Kings 14:21, 31
3. Abijah	Bad	Maacah	Made an Asherah pole	1 Kings 15:2, 13
4. Asa	Good			
5. Jehoshaphat	Good	Azubah	Daughter of Shilhi	1 Kings 22:42
6. Jehoram	Bad			
7. Ahaziah	Bad	Athaliah	Daughter of Ahab and Jezebel	2 Kings 8:26; 2 Chron. 22:2
8. Joash	Good	Zibiah	From Beersheba	2 Kings 12:1
9. Amaziah	Good	Jehoaddin	From Jerusalem	2 Kings 14:2
10. Azariah (Uzziah)	Good	Jecoliah	From Jerusalem	2 Kings 15:1-2
11. Jotham	Good	Jerusha	Daughter of Zadok	2 Kings 15:33
12. Ahaz	Bad			

19. This may also account for Amon's wicked two-year rule, for his mother was from Jotbah. If this town is the same as Jotbathah, though that is in no way certain, then Amon's mother Meshullemeth was possibly a Midianite, for Jotbathah was in the Sinai Peninsula near Elath (Num. 33:33–34; Deut. 10:7).

13. Hezekiah	Good	Abijah	Daughter of Zechariah	2 Kings 18:2
14. Manasseh	Bad	Hephzibah		2 Kings 21:1
15. Amon	Bad	Meshullemeth	Daughter of Haruz, from Jotbah	2 Kings 21:19
16. Josiah	Good	Jedidah	Daughter of Adaiah, from Bozkath	2 Kings 22:1
17. Jehoahaz	Bad	Hamutal	Daughter of Jeremiah, from Libnah	2 Kings 23:31
18. Jehoiakim	Bad	Zebidah	Daughter of Pedaiah, from Rumah	2 Kings 23:36
19. Jehoiachin	Bad	Nehushta	Daughter of Elnathan, from Jerusalem	2 Kings 24:8
20. Zedekiah	Bad	Hamutal	Daughter of Jeremiah, from Libnah	2 Kings 24:18

Yet some good kings—Asa, Jehoshaphat, Josiah, Hezekiah, and Josiah—had bad fathers or mothers. The Bible does not explain why this is so. But Josiah demonstrates how other people can compensate for one's poor parental guidance. His evil father was Ahaziah, son of the wicked Ahab and Jezebel, and his grandmother was wicked Athaliah who made herself queen for six years (2 Kings 11:3). When Josiah was about one year old, his great-aunt Jehosheba, Athaliah's sister, stole him to the temple (to keep him from being killed by Athaliah, his own grandmother!), where he was hidden by the priest Jehoiada for six years till Athaliah died and Joash was crowned king at the age of seven (11:1–4, 21).

Living in the temple with a godly priest for six of his first seven years must have profoundly influenced young Joash's tender heart toward spiritual things! Another favorable factor was Jehoiada's making a covenant between the Lord and the people (including the new boy king) that they would serve the Lord (11:4, 17). Still another influence on the young king was Jehoiada's teaching and guiding Joash (12:2), no doubt in his boyhood and teenage years. Jehoiada ranks as one of the Lord's great, but little-known, unsung heroes. His impact on Joash proves that even today children from non-Christian homes can be encouraged and guided by concerned Christian adults to follow the Lord. And there are countless young Joashs today waiting to be brought into a favorable environment and to be led in paths of godly living.

Why Manasseh was a bad king when he had a godly father, Hezekiah, we do not know. However, when Manasseh was a captive of the Assyrians (2 Chron. 33:11), he repented of his sins (33:12–13, 18–19). When he was released and returned to Judah, he abolished many of the idols to foreign gods (33:15–16). Is it possible that when Manasseh returned, he realized his bad influence on his own son Amon was irreversible, and so he sought to influence his grandson Josiah toward godly standards? Josiah began reigning in 640 B.C. at the age of eight, so he was born in 648. That year was six years before Manasseh died in 642. Also in 648, Manasseh's son Amon was sixteen years old. (Since Amon began reigning in 642 at the age of twenty-two, he was sixteen in 648.) Whether Manasseh favorably influenced his grandson is conjecture, but it may help explain how Josiah became a godly ruler.

While little is known about the mothers of Judah's kings, one cannot help wonder why God included their names. Were the human authors of Kings and Chronicles "trying to stress that a nation's rise or fall may be determined by its mothers?" Does this say that "if you would sway the world in the direction of good, you must begin with its mothers?"[20]

Still another case of poor fatherly influence is the priest Eli, whose sons Hophni and Phinehas, though serving as priests with their father, "were wicked men" (1 Sam. 2:12). They were ungodly ("they had no regard for the LORD," 2:12), greedy (2:13–16), disrespectful of spiritual things (2:17), and adulterous (2:22). Why did Eli falter and fail as a father? Though he did rebuke his sons for their sins (2:25), three facts may account for their refusal to heed his reproach. First, he rebuked them when they were adults. Perhaps this reprimand came too late. Had he not corrected them in their growing-up years? Second, he was involved in their sins of greed and gluttony (2:29). As Swindoll put it, "he bought into their lifestyle."[21] His chiding, therefore, would have been hypocritical and would have fallen on deaf ears. Third, perhaps, though 1 Samuel does not say this, he was so busy serving in the tabernacle that he gave little attention to his boys. Unfortunately, this same pattern has been repeated many times since. How easy it is for pastors and other Christian leaders to become so engaged in their ministries that they neglect to nurture their own children spiritually. This is tragic. As David O. MacKay observed, "No success can compensate for failure in the home."

Mention should be made of two other godly mothers: Hannah, whose spiritual depth and concern for her son Samuel has been discussed earlier, and Eunice, mother of Timothy, who, with Timothy's grandmother Lois, trained him in the Scriptures when he was very young (2 Tim. 1:5; 3:15).

What the Scriptures report by way of parental influence—for good or bad—demonstrates that the way parents relate or do not relate to God has "a profound influence on the value systems and ethical standards of their children."[22]

20. Edith Deen, *Family Living in the Bible* (New York: Harper & Row, Publishers, 1963), 80.

21. Charles R. Swindoll, *Growing Wise in Family Life* (Portland, Oreg.: Multnomah Press, 1988), 32.

22. Kenneth O. Gangel, "Toward a Biblical Theology of Marriage and Family; Part One: Pentateuch and Historical Books," *Journal of Psychology and Theology* 5 (1977): 64.

This raises the question, Were children punished along with, or instead of, guilty parents, and if so, is this fair? Exodus 20:5 and Deuteronomy 5:9 seem to suggest an affirmative answer: "I, the Lord your God, am a jealous God, punishing the children for the sin of the fathers to the third and fourth generation of those who hate me." Exodus 34:7 and Numbers 14:18 also seem to point to an affirmative answer: God "punishes the children and their children for the sin of the fathers to the third and fourth generation." Two answers help explain this apparent dilemma. First, the words "those who hate me" (Exod. 20:5; Deut. 5:9) indicate that God's punishment was on children of the third and fourth generations, who *themselves* hated the Lord. And they hated the Lord because their progenitors did so. "Rebellious, God-hating parents often produce children [and grandchildren and great-grandchildren] who also hate the Lord."[23] Second, other Old Testament verses clearly show that each person is punished for his own sin, not that of an ancestor. "Fathers shall not be put to death for their children, nor children put to death for their fathers; each is to die for his own sin" (Deut. 24:16). The idea that children pay for the guilt of their fathers became a proverb in Judah's last days: "The fathers eat sour grapes, and the children's teeth are set on edge" (Jer. 31:29; Ezek. 18:2). But the prophets announced that this was wrong because "everyone will die for his own sin; whoever eats sour grapes—his own teeth will be set on edge" (Jer. 31:30), and "the soul who sins is the one who will die" (Ezek. 18:4). Therefore, verses referring to divine judgment on future generations are addressing the matter of parental influence. This is sobering to think that how we live today may have a propitious or adverse effect, either directly or indirectly, not only on our children, but also on our grandchildren and great-grandchildren.[24]

Discipline

Is your child unruly or rowdy? Does he intentionally disobey what you tell him to do or not to do? Does he delay following through on what he knows needs to be done? Does he get into mischief or even into serious trouble?

How should you discipline children so that they obey more willingly and readily? How can you channel them into meaningful, rather than disruptive or mischievous, conduct?

Many parents readily admit that disciplining children is one of the most formidable tasks of parenting. As a result, many mothers and fathers feel frus-

23. Jack S. Deere, "Deuteronomy," in *The Bible Knowledge Commentary, Old Testament,* 272. In Leviticus 26:39, God said Israelites would be punished because of their sins and "also because of their fathers' sins," who apparently influenced their children wrongly (cf. Jer. 32:18).

24. For practical suggestions on how Christian parents can be effective models for their children, see chapter 10, "How to Be a Good Model," in Kathi Hudson, *Raising Kids God's Way* (Wheaton, Ill.: Crossway Books, 1995), 113–28.

trated, confused, bewildered, even distraught. Some even neglect to correct their children, leaving their youngsters instead to do as they wish. This, however, only compounds the problem, for unless a boy or girl receives discipline from others he finds it difficult to exercise self-discipline. An undisciplined child becomes an undisciplined adult.

The Book of Proverbs, with its father-to-son instructions on how to be wise, frequently touches on this subject. Every child possesses an inclination toward misconduct, acquired at birth. As Solomon wrote, "Folly is bound up in the heart of a child" (Prov. 22:15). Children do not readily welcome discipline or correction, but to reject it is a sign of folly. "Fools despise wisdom and discipline" (1:7b); "A fool spurns his father's discipline" (15:5a); "He who ignores discipline despises himself" (15:32a); and "He who hates correction is stupid" (12:1b).

An undisciplined child experiences serious consequences, including poverty and shame (13:18a), leading others astray by the influence of his bad conduct (10:17b), disgrace to his mother (29:15), and even death (5:23; 15:10b; 19:18b; 23:14).

On the other hand, a disciplined person experiences a full life (6:23), leads others to experience life (10:17), is honored (13:18b), and shows he is prudent (15:5b), knowledgeable (15:32b), and wise (29:15a). Therefore, a child ought not spurn his father's discipline (15:5a) or ignore it (15:32a).

Parental discipline, while unpleasant to administer, reveals love for the child (3:12; 13:24), gives hope to both the child and the parents (19:18a), and brings peace and delight to the parents (29:17). Therefore, it ought not be withheld (23:13a). Punishment will not kill the child (23:13b), but failure to punish him will lead to his death (23:14). Death here may refer to loss of enjoyment of life in its fullness as God intended it, or it may even suggest an occasional physical loss of life. To withhold punishment when it is due indicates that the parent does not really love the child ("He who spares the rod [when it is deserved] hates his son," 13:24a), and the child who ignores what discipline can do for him shows he does not like himself (15:32a).

No wonder Meier and Burnett wrote, "Our children *need* to be corrected."[25] It is a serious mistake to withhold correction and let a child always have his own way because "a child left to himself" is a "disgrace" to his or her parents (29:15).

Five verses from Proverbs referred to in the preceding paragraphs mention the rod (13:24; 22:15; 23:13–14; 29:15). In addition, the rod is mentioned in three other verses in Proverbs in relation to discipline: "A rod is for the back

25. Paul D. Meier and Linda Burnett, *The Unwanted Generation* (Grand Rapids: Baker Book House, 1980), 63 (italics theirs).

of him who lacks judgment" (10:13b). "A fool's talk brings a rod to his back" (14:3a). "A whip for the horse, a halter for the donkey, and a rod for the backs of fools" (26:3). Also, Proverbs 19:29 says, "Penalties are prepared for mockers, and beatings for the backs of fools."

These suggestions to use the rod indicate that the Bible approves of physical punishment. However, these verses in no way justify harsh, extreme, or unreasonable physical punishment of a child. The discipline should be carefully suited to the misbehavior, and should be given in love, not hate. In fact, discipline is to stem from a parent's heart of love (Prov. 3:12; Heb. 12:7), thus distinguishing discipline from abuse.[26]

The rod is to be applied because of the child's folly or foolishness (Prov. 10:13b; 14:3a; 19:29; 22:15b; 26:3). However, folly in the Bible does not mean silliness or lightheartedness. Instead, it connotes a wicked, sinful heart, or the opposite of godliness. "Fools despise wisdom and discipline" (1:7b), "fools detest turning from evil" (13:19), and "fools mock at making amends for sin" (14:9). Therefore, physical punishment is to be limited to children's persistence in sinful, God-defying actions. "Folly brings punishment to fools" (16:22b).

Foolish (that is, wicked) children need to be punished, because without it they bring grief, bitterness, and disgrace to their mothers and fathers (10:1b; 17:21, 25; 19:13a).

The "rod," on the other hand, "may also be used figuratively for any form of discipline,"[27] including verbal correction or rebuke. When a child willingly accepts a verbal rebuke for a wrongdoing, he shows he is wise. "He who listens to a life-giving rebuke will be at home among the wise" (Prov. 15:31). "A rebuke impresses a man of discernment" (17:10a). Conversely, "a mocker does not listen to rebuke" (13:1b). Rebuking a person who is wise enables him to gain even more knowledge (19:25b), and in that way rebukes are beneficial and valuable (25:12). Wise parents encourage their children to respond to their verbal corrections, and to do so willingly.

As stated earlier, Eli's inept parental discipline resulted in recalcitrant sons. How sad to read that "he failed to restrain him" (1 Sam. 3:13). The loss of their lives to the Philistines demonstrates the truth of Proverbs 15:10: "He who hates correction will die."

David too was guilty of not exercising adequate discipline over his sons. When Amnon raped his sister Tamar, David "was furious" at his son (2 Sam. 13:21), but presumably did nothing more to Amnon than to be angry. And when David's fourth son Adonijah tried to usurp the throne, David "never in-

26. Swindoll points out seven helpful contrasts between child abuse and child discipline (*Growing Wise in Family Living*, 113–14).
27. Sid S. Buzzell, "Proverbs," in *The Bible Knowledge Commentary, Old Testament*, 956.

terfered with him by asking, 'Why do you behave as you do?' " (1 Kings 1:6). Isaac and Jacob had their failings as fathers too.[28]

As fathers discipline their children, doing so in love, they depict the Lord's loving discipline of his children when they sin. "As a man disciplines his son, so the Lord your God disciplines you" (Deut. 8:5).[29] His discipline of believers evidences the fact that they are his sons and that he loves them (Heb. 12:6–8). While neither human nor divine discipline is pleasant at the time and is even painful (12:11), we are grateful for it later (12:9) as we realize its benefits of righteousness and peace (12:10–11). Therefore, believers should endure God's discipline (12:7), being submissive to God when he brings it into our lives (12:9). We should not be discouraged (12:5) or make light of or resent his disciplinary corrections in our lives[30] (12:5; cf. Job 5:17; Prov. 3:11). To be disciplined by the Lord is to be blessed by him (Ps. 94:12).

Encourage

While children often need verbal correction and punishment, they just as often—or more often—need encouragement. Growing up can be a difficult, frustrating time of life, as children struggle to learn how to get along with others and to learn various skills. Therefore, one of the greatest benefits parents can give their children is to encourage them and to build them up by commending them often.

We ought to commend more than we correct. We ought to encourage more than we discipline. We ought to help build their self-esteem by applauding good conduct. Parents who never praise their children when they do something well do them a great disservice. On the other hand, being complimented for a job well done, for a task completed on time, for desirable behavior—these parental responses reinforce those good traits and prod children to repeat them. Positive appreciation can also encourage boys and girls to be appreciative of others.

The apostle Paul wrote that believers are to "encourage each other" (1 Thess. 4:18; 5:11) and "build each other up" (5:11), and the writer of the Epistle to the Hebrews said believers should "encourage one another *daily*" (Heb. 3:13; cf. 10:25). If believers are to lift each other up by words of encouragement, should not parents do the same with their children? Perhaps

28. Helpful books by James Dobson on child discipline include *The Strong-Willed Child* (Wheaton, Ill.: Tyndale Publishers, 1992); *Parenting Isn't for Cowards* (Waco, Tex.: Word Books Publisher, 1987); and *The New Dare to Discipline* (Wheaton, Ill.: Tyndale House Publishers, 1992). Also see chapter 18, "Discipline: Beyond Punishment," in Hudson, *Raising Kids God's Way*, 205–18, and chapter 9, "Use Appropriate Discipline," in Kent R. and Barbara Hughes, *Common Sense Parenting* (Wheaton, Ill.: Tyndale House Publishers, 1995), 125–37.

29. The Bible comments a number of times on God's discipline of his people, that is, his correcting them or punishing them because of their sin (Deut. 4:36; 11:2; Ps. 39:11; Isa. 26:16; Jer. 17:23; 30:11; 31:18; 32:33; 46:28; Hos. 5:2; 1 Cor. 11:32; Rev. 3:19).

30. The word *holigōreō*, appearing only here in the New Testament, means "to regard as a small matter or a trivial thing."

more parents need to ask themselves what they can do *each day* to commend, encourage, and compliment each of their children. What a different atmosphere such expressions of love can bring into the home! Constant yelling, correcting, and punishing can be greatly reduced by our appreciating, thanking, affirming, and commending our children.

When parents do not affirm and build up their children, those youngsters grow up with low self-esteem. Emotionally damaged, they have a low view of themselves, which, in turn, leads to other psychological problems. On the other hand, building a child's self-esteem is one of the greatest contributions parents can make to their children's well-being and their future success.[31]

To encourage is one of the responsibilities not just of mothers, but especially of fathers. When Paul recalled how he had ministered to the Thessalonian believers, he wrote that he dealt with them individually "as a father deals with his own children, encouraging, comforting, and urging" (1 Thess. 2:11–12). If Timothy's ministry to believers in the church should include encouraging, along with correcting and rebuking "with great patience and careful instruction" (2 Tim. 4:2), then surely, parents too should see that encouragement accompanies correction.[32]

Constant corrections—without commendations—can greatly discourage children, as Paul indicated in Ephesians 6:4, "Fathers, do no exasperate your children," and Colossians 3:21, "Fathers, do not embitter your children, or they will become discouraged." The Greek word rendered "exasperate" is *parorgizō*, meaning "to provoke to anger." A father's unreasonable demands, petty rules, or unjust treatment,[33] can lead children to be angry, which is an undesirable trait. "Embitter" translates *erethizō*, meaning "to be aroused or provoked." Such agitation by constant criticism and unreasonableness can readily lead boys and girls to be discouraged (*athymeō*, used only here in the Greek New Testament, means "to lose heart" or "to be without enthusiasm"[34]).

---

31. Two excellent books on building a child's self-esteem are Dorothy C. Briggs, *Your Child's Self-Esteem* (Garden City, N.Y.: Doubleday & Co., 1970), and James Dobson, *Hide or Seek* (Old Tappan, N.J.: Fleming H. Revell Co., 1974). Chapter 16, "The Art of Encouragement" in Hudson, *Raising Kids God's Way,* 181–96 offers specific ideas on ways parents can encourage their children. Also see chapter 8, "Install Healthy Self-Regard," in Hughes and Hughes, *Common Sense Parenting,* 105–22.

32. Parents would do well to follow Gerald E. Nelson's approach to discipline, presented in *The One-Minute Scolding* (New York: Random House, 1984). He suggests that thirty-second corrections of children and teens always be followed by thirty seconds of reassuring the child of the parent's love. This is an excellent approach to giving children encouragement.

33. Inchley lists pettiness or overcorrection as one of several ways parents hinder the spiritual development of their children. The other obstacles include hypocrisy, anxiety, parental rudeness, lack of discipline and authority, overindulgence, immaturity, lack of instruction, no time for the children, lack of security, wrong motives, and boasting (John Inchley, *Kids and the Kingdom* [Wheaton, Ill.: Tyndale House Publishers, 1976], 95–105).

34. Applied to children, this word *athymeō* means "to go about their task in a listless, moody, sullen frame of mind" (J. B. Lightfoot, *Saint Paul's Epistles to the Colossians and to Philemon* [London: Macmillan & Co., 1879; reprint, Grand Rapids: Zondervan Publishing House, 1959], 227).

Hendriksen discusses six errors parents make in bringing up their children: (a) overprotection; (b) favoritism; (c) discouragement; (d) failure to make allowance for the fact that the child is growing up, has a right to have ideas of his own, and need not be an exact copy of his father to be a success; (e) neglect; and (f) bitter words and outright physical cruelty.[35]

On faultfinding, Jack Graham makes an excellent point. "Are you a good 'finder' with your kids? Some parents are constantly finding fault: Do this, do that, stop that. When was the last time you went looking to find something good in your child? We need to affirm and encourage children, rather than always provoking, pressuring, and prodding them."[36]

Do you want your children to respond to you without bitterness, irritation, anger, or discouragement? Then be careful your corrections are not unduly rash—and find ways each day to commend and encourage them.

Teach

Another positive aspect of parental responsibilities is teaching and training children. Throughout the Bible, fathers and mothers are challenged to teach their young the things of God, to nurture them spiritually, to "bring them up in the training and instruction of the Lord" (Eph. 6:4).

This includes their participating in and observing religious activities, giving them specific instruction in the Scriptures, pointing out how God is working in your family and in the lives of others, and reminding them of what God has done and will do for them. God challenges parents to be teachers, to be engaged in communicating God's ways and desires informally as well as formally, in conversation as well as visually (Deut. 6:4–9; 11:18–20).

Since the Bible says so much about the teaching part of parenting, the next chapter is devoted to this subject, along with a discussion of the education of children both in the home and in schools in Israel and in other ancient Near Eastern cultures and the Greco-Roman world.

All parents do well to echo the prayer of Manoah, Samson's father: "Teach us how to bring up the boy who is to be born" (Judg. 13:8).

---

35. William Hendriksen, *Exposition of Ephesians*, New Testament Commentary (Grand Rapids: Baker Book House, 1967), 261–62.

36. Jack Graham, "Give Your Children Constant Affirmation," *Dallas/Fort Worth Heritage*, July 1995, S3.

"In the Way He Should Go"

Educating Children in Bible Times

"I hope my kids turn out right."

Every forward-looking parent expresses the sentiment of that sentence. In the daily grind of baby feeding, diaper changing, arithmetic helping, piano practice encouraging, our thoughts occasionally fly ahead to the time when our children will be grown.

Off to college. College graduation. A full-time job. The wedding ceremony. These are events in our children's lives which come with their growth. We are told, "They don't stay young forever." "Enjoy them while they are young." "They grow up fast."

But when they leave the nest and enter into adulthood, will they have "turned out okay"? And what does that mean? For some parents it means their children are sharp intellectually, popular socially, or well-off financially. Is that what the Bible says is the goal of child rearing? To have children who excel academically, have lots of friends, and have no financial needs? Hardly.

The Bible tells us that helping our youngsters turn out right means we are concerned for their character. Besides their having clean rooms, we want them to have clean hearts. Besides their acquiring good manners, we want them to become people of quality. Besides their knowing how to read, write, and do arithmetic, we want our children to know and love the Lord and to serve and worship him. Besides their obeying us as parents, we want them to obey the Lord.

Parents Are Teachers

God placed this responsibility of developing godly character in our children squarely on the shoulders of parents. The Bible views fathers and mothers as teachers—those who instruct their own in the ways of God. Sometimes sons of kings were under the care of a tutor (2 Kings 10:1, 5; 1 Chron. 27:32), and only occasionally were teachers referred to other than one's parents (Ps. 119:99; Prov. 5:13). Ur, Abraham's birthplace, was in Sumer, where the world's oldest schools existed. The curriculum included mathematics, language, geography, history, drawing,[1] and writing.[2] These schools focused on the training of scribes.[3]

As a boy Moses was taught by teachers in Egypt (he was "educated in all the wisdom of the Egyptians," Acts 7:22),[4] and adolescent Daniel and his captive friends from Judah were taught "the language and literature of the Babylonians" (Dan. 1:4), which may have called for their learning agriculture, architecture, astronomy, law, mathematics, and the difficult Akkadian language. But Moses and Daniel received these educational experiences while out of the land of Israel. Schools as such did not exist in Israel in their day.

Religious instruction—teaching that was directed toward the spiritual development of the child—was given by each child's parents. This does not mean that Christian parents should neglect enlisting the help of others in training their children in spiritual matters. Just the opposite! Parents wisely place their children under the tutelage of dedicated Sunday school teachers, club leaders, camp counselors, Christian school teachers, and others. Consistent teaching from every possible source is needed to help offset the godless environment in which children today are so easily engulfed. However, parents should never think these other Christian teachers can take their own place in the home. They are to be thought of as partners, not substitutes.

In Bible times religious instruction of children in the home was to be given primarily by fathers. But mothers were also teachers. "Do not forsake your mother's teaching" (Prov. 1:8; 6:20), Solomon wrote. King Lemuel's

1. Ralph Gower, *The New Manners and Customs of Bible Times* (Chicago: Moody Press, 1987), 76.
2. "In Sumerian city-states writing was taught in schools as early as the third millennium B.C." (Joseph Blenkinsopp, *Wisdom and Law in the Old Testament* [New York: Oxford University Press, 1983], 12).
3. C. J. Gadd, *Teachers and Students in the Oldest Schools* (London: School of Oriental and African Studies, 1956); Barry D. Halvorsen, "Scribes and Scribal Schools in the Ancient Near East: A Historical Survey" (Th.M. thesis, Grace Theological Seminary, 1981); Samuel Noah Kramer, "Schooldays: A Sumerian Composition Relating to the Education of a Scribe," *Journal of the American Oriental Society* 69 (1949): 199–215; idem, *The Sumerians* (Chicago: University of Chicago Press, 1963), 229–48; and William A. Smith, *Ancient Education* (New York: Philosophical Library, 1955), 34–41.
4. In his Egyptian schooling Moses probably learned reading, writing, mathematics, astronomy, and music.

mother taught him (31:1), the wife of noble character taught her children (31:26), and Timothy learned the Scriptures from his mother Eunice (2 Tim. 1:5; 3:14–15). Because fathers and mothers are mentioned together in Proverbs 1:8 and 6:20, "father" was not a term for a schoolteacher or other authoritative adult.[5] In Mesopotamia mothers, along with fathers, were teachers in the home, but this may not have been the case in Egypt.[6] The father and mother word pair in numerous proverbs (10:1; 15:20; 20:20; 23:22, 25; 28:24; 30:11, 17) verifies the role of both parents in raising and teaching their children. Still, the father is the one who addressed his son(s) in Proverbs (1:8, 10, 15; 2:1; 3:1, 11, 21; 4:1, 10, 20; 5:1, 7, 20; 6:1, 3, 20; 7:1, 24; 8:32; 19:27; 23:15, 19, 26; 24:13, 21; 27:11). And in the New Testament Paul addressed fathers about child rearing (Eph. 6:4; Col. 3:21; cf. 1 Thess. 2:11–12).

What Are Parents to Teach Their Children?

Teaching is the eleventh responsibility God has given parents regarding their children. (See the previous chapter for the other ten responsibilities.) God made it clear to Abraham that he was to serve as the spiritual teacher and leader of his children: "For I have chosen him [Abraham], so that he will direct his children and his household after him to keep the way of the Lord by doing what is right and just, so that the Lord will bring about for Abraham what he has promised him" (Gen. 18:19). The Hebrew word rendered "direct" (sāwah) means "to appoint, command, commission, order, or direct." Jesse directed or commanded his son David to take food to his brothers in battle (1 Sam. 17:20) and Boaz ordered his workers to help Ruth (Ruth 2:9). Moses used the same word when he told the people "to command" their "children to obey carefully all the words" of the law (Deut. 32:46).

By giving specific direction and commands to his children, Abraham was assuming parental leadership. By directing his children "after him," Abraham was setting the example for them to follow. By urging them "to keep the way of the Lord," the patriarch was underscoring his goal for his children. By urging them to do "what is right and just," Abraham emphasized the means by which his children would be keeping the way of the Lord. What is "right" (ṣᵉdāqāh) connotes conformity to an ethical or moral standard,[7] and "just" (mišpoṭ) points to the attribute of justice or fairness.[8] These embrace the two

5. In ancient Mesopotamia and Egypt, however, "father" and "son" became technical terms for "teacher" and "pupil" (Hans-Peter Rüger, "Oral Tradition in the Old Testament," in *Jesus and the Oral Gospel Tradition*, ed. Henry Wansborough [Sheffield: JSOT Press, 1991], 112; and Philip Nel, "The Concept of 'Father' in the Wisdom Literature of the Ancient Near East," *Journal of Northwest Semitic Languages* 5 [1973]: 53–66).

6. Stuart Weeks, *Early Israelite Wisdom* (Oxford: Clarendon Press, 1994), 15, ns. 21, 22.

7. Harald G. Stigers, "ṣādēq," in *Theological Wordbook of the Old Testament*, 2:792.

8. Robert D. Culver, "šāphaṭ," in *Theological Wordbook of the Old Testament*, 1:947.

essential qualities of morality in relationship to God and fairness in relationship to others. The result of Abraham's wise parenting was God blessing the
patriarch's life. God's directive to Abraham to lead his children so that they
"keep the way of the Lord" is another way of saying they were to obey the
Lord. In this context, "keep" means "to give careful attention to," and, therefore, heeding God's path involves following his commands.

Other Bible verses make more explicit what parents are to teach their children in the spiritual realm.

God's Actions

God's plagues on Egypt constituted a remarkable demonstration of his
awesome power. These miraculous deeds were to be told by parents to their
children and grandchildren (Exod. 10:1–2). God's sparing the lives of Israel's
firstborn children in the tenth plague, when all the Egyptian firstborn were
killed, was another momentous occasion in Israel's early history. Celebrating
this event annually in Israelite homes led children to ask the meaning of the
"Passover"—a "teachable moment" in which parents could share with their
children the fact of God's miraculous care for and deliverance of his people
(Exod. 12:25–27).

The Passover was to be followed immediately by a week-long celebration
known as the Feast of Unleavened Bread. This was another occasion for
teaching children the significance of God's power in delivering the nation
out of Egyptian bondage. This festival recalled the Israelites' Passover meal
when no leaven was to be in their homes. Children were to see this as an
occasion for parental gratitude: "I do this because of what the Lord did for
me" (Exod. 13:8).

Every firstborn male child born to Israelite parents and all the firstborn
males of their livestock were to be consecrated to the Lord as a reminder that
God spared all their firstborn in Egypt. Also, the firstborn were to be redeemed (see discussion on this in chap. 4). That is, since the firstborn belonged to the Lord, they could be redeemed (bought back) by a payment to
the priests. This too would elicit childhood curiosity: "What does this mean?"
Some children may have asked the typical, parent-exhausting, childhood
question "Why?" "Why give our very best baby goat to the Lord?" "Why did
Uncle Micah take his first son, my cousin, to the priest and then pay money
to get him back?" Again, curiosity would evoke an answer from the parents:
"This is why . . ." (Exod. 13:1–2, 11–16).

After the Exodus, the generation that wandered in the Sinai Peninsula wilderness experienced God's loving care for forty years. As they were nearing
the time to enter and conquer the Promised Land, God told Moses to write
the Book of Deuteronomy. One of the reasons for this book was to encourage
the people to savor what God had done for them in the wilderness. Sixteen
times in Deuteronomy God told them to "remember," and nine times he

said, "don't forget." If they were not careful, as time passed, these events would not be so fresh in their minds and their memory of them would slip. That is why Moses said, "Do not forget the things your eyes have seen" (Deut. 4:9), and he added, "Teach them to your children and to their children after them" (4:9b).

Another question-and-answer text is Deuteronomy 6:20, but this time the child's question would pertain to God's many commands and laws. And parents were to point out God's miracles, to mention the fulfillment of his plans to give them the land, and to explain that God gave the decrees so they would "fear the Lord our God, so that we might always prosper and be kept alive" (Deut. 6:24). Then when the nation was in Gilgal, just inside the land, Joshua had a cairn constructed of twelve stones. This too would lead boys and girls to ask, "What do these stones mean?" and parents could answer by explaining the nation's miraculous crossing of the Jordan River (Josh. 4:4–7, 19–23), which exhibited God's power and would lead others to fear him (4:24). Years later an anonymous psalmist wrote that his readers' fathers explained to them that God had enabled Joshua to conquer the inhabitants of the land of Canaan (Ps. 44:1–4).

The facts of biblical history—God's miracles on behalf of the nation Israel—were to be taught by parents to their children. Since there were no schools, as such, in Israel, these Bible history events were to be communicated from parent to child. "Our fathers have told us what you [God] did in their days, in days long ago," days in which he "drove out the nations" (44:1–2).

The Passover, the safety of the firstborn, the escape from Egypt, God's provisions in the wilderness, his drying of the Jordan River, and his helping Israel defeat the land's inhabitants—these were six of the Lord's actions to be taught to children in the home.

For parents today the point is this: Teach your children Bible history! Help them learn how great is God's power.

God's Commands

Besides teaching boys and girls God's actions in the past, Old Testament parents were to teach their youngsters God's commands and laws. These included his command to love him (Deut. 6:5–7), his "words" (i.e., his commands given by Moses) which the parents were to "teach" to their children (11:18–19), the "words of this law" (31:12; 32:46), and "statutes" and the law "which he commanded our forefathers to teach their children" who "in turn would tell their children" (Ps. 78:5–6).[9]

9. Josephus, Jewish historian, wrote, "Let the children also learn the laws, as the first thing they are taught, which will be the best thing they can be taught, and will be the cause of their future felicity" (*The Antiquities of the Jews* 4.8.12).

Timothy's godly mother, Eunice, and grandmother, Lois, taught Timothy "the holy Scriptures" (2 Tim. 3:15). Of course, believers today are not under the Mosaic law, but the principle is the same: Parents are to teach their children God's Word, helping them learn his standards and requirements.

God's Character

An elderly psalmist (Ps. 71:5–6, 9) wrote of his intense desire to declare "[God's] power to the next generation" and his "might to all who are to come" (71:18). Along a similar line, Asaph wrote that they would "tell the next generation" what he and others had heard from their ancestors (Ps. 78:3–4). These things included "the praiseworthy deeds of the LORD, his power, and the wonders he has done" (78:4b). As a result, children are encouraged to trust in the Lord and to obey his commands (78:7).

When Hezekiah recovered from his near-death illness, he praised the Lord, acknowledging that he had restored him. Hezekiah affirmed that those who are alive can praise the Lord, including fathers who "tell their children about your faithfulness" (Isa. 38:19).

Fearing God

God's power, might, and faithfulness are only some of his marvelous attributes which parents should tell their children. Bible history (what God has done in the past), God's Word (what God requires of us today), and his character (what he was and always will be)—these are important elements in a Christian's home curriculum.

But why teach these facts? There is a purpose behind it all, as God told Moses: "so that you, your children, and their children after them may fear the LORD your God as long as you live by keeping all his decrees and commands" (Deut. 6:2). When Moses assembled the people so he could read the Law to them, he did it so that they would learn to fear the Lord "and may teach them to their children" (4:10). In the sabbatical year, that is, every seventh year, the Israelites were to assemble with their children to hear the Law read audibly so they would "learn to fear the LORD your God" (31:12). This would help reinforce parental instruction in the Mosaic law so that "their children" would "hear it and learn to fear the LORD your God" (31:13). David too wrote of teaching his children "the fear of the Lord"[10] (Ps. 34:11).

What does fearing the Lord mean? Are children to be taught to be afraid of God? No. The "fear of the Lord" is associated with obeying him, as seen in God's words to Abraham after the patriarch obeyed his orders to sacrifice his son: "Now I know that you fear God" (Gen. 22:12). Fearing God is also associated with trusting him. When the Israelites were brought across the Red Sea on dry ground, safe from the Egyptian soldiers, they "feared the LORD and put

10. "Children" here might be David's affectionate term for the Israelites.

their trust in him" (Exod. 14:31). In Deuteronomy, fearing God was often associated with obeying the Law (5:29; 6:2, 24; 8:6; 13:4; 17:19; 28:58; 31:12–13), or with serving him (6:13; 10:12, 20), or loving him (10:12).

Fearing God means acknowledging his character and responding in awe, humility, worship, love, trust, service, and obedience. Here, then, is the goal of parenting: to teach children God's actions, standards, and character so that in humility before God they worship, love, trust, serve, and obey him. Parents, is this your goal for your children? Anything less than this is an inadequate goal! Leading your youngsters to Christ and then helping them fear him is the greatest privilege—and responsibility—in the world.

Do you want your children to be wise? Then teach them to fear the Lord, because "the fear of the Lord—that is wisdom" (Job 28:28). Solomon put it this way: "The fear of the Lord teaches a man wisdom" (Prov. 15:33). In the Old Testament the word "wisdom" (*ḥokmāh*) refers to skills in relation to the working of crafts, giving advice or counsel, managing people, being sharp mentally, and being rightly related to God. A person with *ḥokmāh* was skillful or successful.[11] And only by fearing the LORD can individuals, including boys and girls, be skillful in coping with life's problems. Only by fearing the Lord can a person be successful or have expertise in life, or be effective in the true, biblical sense. "The fear of the Lord," Solomon affirmed, "is the beginning of knowledge" (Prov. 1:7). As wisdom's "beginning" (cf. 9:10; Ps. 111:10), fearing the Lord is the starting point of wisdom. (You want to be wise? Then *start* by fearing God.) Fearing the Lord is also the "essence and heart" of wisdom.[12] (You want to be wise? Then the very *essence* of wisdom is fearing God.) To state it differently, if an adult or child does not know the Lord, he is not wise in God's sight, no matter how much knowledge he may have. To give our children a good education and yet not lead them to fear God—to know, worship, love, trust, serve, and obey him—is to fail miserably as parents.

Solomon stated that the Book of Proverbs, with all its practical tips, instructions, and guidelines, was for that single, overriding purpose: to get his son and others to live skillfully and successfully. He spelled this out in a summary statement at the beginning of Proverbs: "for attaining wisdom [*ḥokmāh*, 'expertise in godly living'] and discipline [*mûsār*, 'moral discipline or correction']" (Prov. 1:2). Elaborating on this overriding purpose in verses 3–5, Solomon said that this kind of quality life involves discipline, prudence,[13] high moral standards ("doing what is right and just and fair"; cf. Gen. 18:19; Prov.

11. For more on wisdom in the Old Testament, see Roy B. Zuck, "A Theology of the Wisdom Books and the Song of Songs," in *A Biblical Theology of the Old Testament*, ed. Roy B. Zuck (Chicago: Moody Press, 1991), 209–19.

12. Walter C. Kaiser, Jr., "Wisdom Theology and the Centre of Old Testament Theology," *Evangelical Quarterly* 50 (1978):138.

13. "Prudent life" in Proverbs 1:3 translates *śēkel*, "sensibleness or discretion," and "prudence" in 1:4 renders *ʿormāh*, "shrewdness or cleverness" in a good sense.

2:9), knowledge, discretion (i.e., wise planning; cf. Prov. 2:11; 3:21; 5:2; 8:12), and guidance.[14]

Nothing is said here about the goal of being physically attractive, financially independent, or having a high IQ. Solomon's goals for his son and other sons relate exclusively to producing people of quality.[15] And these inner characteristics of discipline, morality, and discretion can be attained only as a person fears the Lord. Parents, ask yourself: What am I doing to help my children acquire these traits? How am I helping them develop these wise, God-pleasing characteristics?

Godly Conduct

Numerous verses in the Book of Proverbs spell out the qualities introduced in 1:2–7. Those thumbnail portraits of life address, among others, the subjects of work, diligence, self-control, faithfulness, honesty, fairness, truth, honor, humility, purity, encouragement, peace, love, mercy, generosity, joy, hope, friendliness, virtue, soberness, trust, quietness, contentment, and teachableness. These traits characterize the "wise" person in opposition to the foolish person. In fact, in Proverbs the wise and foolish are synonyms of the godly and ungodly. These qualities, then, describe the godly individual. The son who fears the Lord and develops these qualities is noted for godly conduct.

One of the better known Old Testament verses on rearing children in godly living is Proverbs 22:6, "Train a child in the way he should go, and when he is old he will not turn from it." This verse gives many Christian parents great comfort as they rest on the affirmation that if they train their children properly, they will grow up to honor the Lord. But what about those children raised in Christian homes who repudiate their upbringing? Many parents respond with guilt, assuming they failed as parents.

Is this verse an inviolable promise? Will parents who teach their children standards of godliness find that those youngsters always adhere to those principles? Or is the verse saying something else?

How are we to understand this verse? What does "train" mean? Who is the "child"? What does the phrase "in the way he should go" mean? What is the point of the second part of the verse?

The word "train" (or "train up," NASB) renders the verb ḥānak, which occurs only four other times in the Old Testament. A number of writers assume this verb stems from the Hebrew word for palate or mouth (ḥek), and they refer to the Arabic practice of a mother rubbing date jam on a newborn baby's

---

14. The word for guidance is taḥbūlôt, literally "steering" (like the tackle for directing a ship), suggesting moving one's life in the right direction through difficulties (Sid S. Buzzell, "Proverbs," in *The Bible Knowledge Commentary, Old Testament*, ed. John F. Walvoord and Roy B. Zuck [Wheaton, Ill.: Victor Books, 1985], 907).

15. Wes Haystead, *The 3,000-Year-Old Guide to Parenting: Wisdom from Proverbs for Today's Parents* (Ventura, Calif.: Regal Books, 1991), 33.

palate to stimulate its appetite. This, in turn, supposedly suggests that parents should stimulate the desire of their children for spiritual truth.

However, the other occurrences of the verb *ḥānak* have nothing to do with the palate. The verb refers to dedicating a house (Deut. 20:5), Solomon's temple (1 Kings 8:63; 2 Chron. 7:5), and Nebuchadnezzar's gold image (Dan. 3:2). The related noun *ḥănukkāh*, used twelve times in the Old Testament, refers to the dedication of the altar of burnt offering (Num. 7:10) and of Jerusalem's rebuilt wall (Neh. 12:27). In the case of the house, the temple, and the image, the idea of narrowing or specifying its use seems to be present, more than the idea of dedication. Archer points out that the related Egyptian verb *ḥnk* means "give to the gods," or "set up something for divine service."[16] Its use was narrowed. These observations suggest that in Proverbs 22:6, *ḥānak* means to limit, narrow, focus, or "hedge in" the child's conduct in godly directions. To *ḥānak* a structure was to limit, narrow, or specify its use. Every child is to be started in the right direction morally, an idea conveyed by the Revised English Bible, "Start a child on the right road."

The word for "child" in this verse is *naʿar*, a word which, as discussed in chapter 9, ranges in meaning from the unborn to a young man. Here it probably refers to a young child because of the narrowing or limiting of one's conduct, which should be started at a very early age.[17]

Many understand the phrase "in the way he should go" to mean that the training should be according to the child's unique personality or natural bent,[18] or in accord with his level of understanding at any given stage in his development.[19] However, "in the Book of Proverbs there are only two 'ways' a child can go, the way of the wise and the righteous or the way of the fool and the wicked."[20] The child's "way," then, means " 'his proper way' in the

16. Gleason L. Archer, *Encyclopedia of Bible Difficulties* (Grand Rapids: Zondervan Publishing House, 1982), 252.

17. Hildebrandt argues that *naʿar* in Proverbs 22:6 means a young man who was an attendant of a person of status, a royal squire who, as a late adolescent or young adult, was being apprenticed in wisdom for assuming royal responsibilities (Ted Hildebrandt, "Proverbs 22:6a: Train Up a Child?" *Grace Theological Journal* 9 [1988]: 10–14). However, this seems to ignore the broad age range suggested by the usage of *naʿar* and its relationship to early training in Proverbs 22:6. As Ross observes, "The 'child' (*naʿar*) presumably is in the youngest years" (Allen P. Ross, "Proverbs," in *The Expositor's Bible Commentary*, 12 vols. [Grand Rapids: Zondervan Publishing House, 1979–1992], 5:1061).

18. Derek Kidner, *Proverbs: An Introduction and Commentary*, Tyndale Old Testament Commentaries (Downers Grove, Ill.: InterVarsity Press, 1964), 147; and Charles G. Martin, "Proverbs," in *The New Layman's Bible Commentary*, ed. G. L. D. Howley, F. F. Bruce, and H. L. E. Ellison (Grand Rapids: Zondervan Publishing House, 1979), 728.

19. A. Cohen, *Proverbs* (London: Soncino Press, 1946), 146; and Edgar Jones, *Proverbs and Ecclesiastes*, Touch Bible Commentaries (London: SCM Press, 1961), 183–84. A variation of this is Hildebrandt's view that "according to his way" means "according to the office that he will occupy" as a high-born squire, that is, "according to the standard of who he is and what he is to become" (Hildebrandt, "Proverbs 22:6a: Train Up a Child?" 18).

20. Ross, "Proverbs," 1061.

light of the goals and standards set forth in verse 4," namely, humility and the fear of the Lord. This view finds support in the fact that the second half of the verse states that later the child will not depart from "it." "It" can hardly refer to his personality or state of development.

The way of wisdom propounded in Proverbs is the path toward which each child's conduct should be influenced and into which his or her life should be narrowed. Parents are responsible to set the child "undeviatingly on the right road by disciplining his habits and enlightening his attitudes."[21]

Will a child trained in godliness never veer from it when he is old, that is, when he is grown? Experience points to some exceptions, and this accords with the general nature of proverbs. Many of them are observations of what is generally true; they "are not absolute guarantees for they express truths that are necessarily conditioned by prevailing circumstances. For example, verses 3–4, 9, 11, 16, and 29 do not express promises that are *always* binding."[22] Furthermore, the child must take responsibility for his own actions without all the blame being borne by the parents. As verse 15a indicates, some children, in spite of sound parental guidance, choose to continue in the way of folly instead of the way of wisdom, and for that they are personally accountable to God. Even so, Christian parents who faithfully follow the command in the first part of verse 6 can take comfort in the fact that the observation stated in the second part of the verse *is* usually true. "Even though he may stray during his young adulthood [this individual] will never be able to get away completely from his parental training and from the example of a God-fearing home."[23]

In Proverbs, Solomon often held up his words of instruction as teachings his son(s) was to accept and apply. Table 3 lists the many ways Solomon referred to his teachings and how his son(s) was to respond to them. It is appropriate to note these terms since Proverbs is "a work of instruction" and "a book of education."[24]

Table 3
Commands in Proverbs from Solomon
to His Son(s) Regarding Parental Instruction

1. Listen to	"your father's instruction" (1:8; 4:1)[25]
	"what I say" (4:10)
	"my words" (4:20)

21. William McKane, *Proverbs: A New Approach* (Philadelphia: Westminster Press, 1970), 564.

22. Buzzell, "Proverbs," 953 (italics his). "The recognition that the proverbs have limitations does not nullify the fact that some proverbs may always be true. Frequently these are connected to an attribute or action of God (11:1; 12:22; 15:3; 16:2, 33; 22:2)." Greg W. Parsons, "Guidelines for Understanding and Proclaiming the Book of Proverbs," *Bibliotheca Sacra* 150 (April–June 1993): 161; reprinted in Roy B. Zuck, ed., *Learning from the Sages: Selected Studies on the Book of Proverbs* (Grand Rapids: Baker Book House, 1995).

23. Archer, *Encyclopedia of Bible Difficulties*, 253.

24. Duane H. Garrett, *Proverbs, Ecclesiastes, Song of Songs* (Nashville: Broadman Press, 1993), 57.

25. This word for "instruction" in 1:8; 4:1, 13; 8:33; 13:1; 16:20; 19:20; and 23:12 is *mûsār*, "moral discipline."

	"my words of insight" (5:1)
	"me" (5:7; 7:24; 8:32)
	"my instructions" (8:33)
	"advice" (19:20)
	"the sayings of the wise" (22:17)
	"your father" (23:22)
2. Pay attention to	"what I say" (4:20; 7:24)
	"my wisdom" (5:1)
	"the sayings of the wise" (22:17)
3. Do not turn aside	"from what I say" (5:7)
4. Do not forget	"my teaching" (3:1)[26]
5. Do not swerve	"from [my words]" (4:5)
6. Do not forsake	"your mother's teaching" (1:8; 6:20)
	"my teaching" (4:2)
7. Accept	"my words" (2:1)
	"what I say" (4:10)
	"commands" (10:8)
	"instruction" (19:20)
8. Lay hold of	"my words" (4:4)
9. Hold on to	"instruction" (4:13)
10. Guard	"instruction" (4:13)
	"my teachings" (7:2)
11. Heed	"father's instruction" (13:1)
	"instruction" (16:20)
12. Keep	"my commands" (3:1; 4:4; 7:2)
13. Store up	"my commands" (2:1; 7:1)
14. Apply your heart to	"instruction" (23:12)
15. Apply your ears to	"words of knowledge" (23:12)

The New Testament counterpart of child-rearing verses in Proverbs is the brief command in Ephesians 6:4: "Fathers, do not exasperate your children; instead, bring them up in the training and instruction of the Lord." (See chapter 7 for discussion of the negative "do not exasperate your children.")

The command "bring up" *(ektrepbō)* means "to nourish, to provide for with tender care,"[27] no doubt here denoting both physical and spiritual provisions. The word occurs in the New Testament only in Ephesians 5:29. The New International Version renders it "feeds," but it means "nourish."

"Training" ("nurture," KJV) occurs six times in the New Testament, with four of those references speaking of discipline or correction (Heb. 12:5, 7–8, 11). The other usage is in the phrase "training in righteousness" in 2 Timothy 3:16. This word *paideia*, related to *pais*, "child," and *paidion*, "young child," indicates child education, and all that it involves in directing and correcting.

---

26. The word "teaching" or "teachings" in 1:8; 3:1; 4:2; 6:20 and 7:2 is *tôrāh* (always in the singular in the Hebrew). It may be related to the verb *yārāh* "to point or direct" so that the idea of teaching is "pointing the student in the right direction" (Ross, "Proverbs," 175). The wife of noble character speaks with wisdom, and instruction *(tôrāh)* is on her tongue, that is, she readily directs others to God's ways (Prov. 31:26).

27. William Hendriksen suggests the translation "to rear tenderly" (*Exposition of Ephesians* [Grand Rapids: Baker Book House, 1967], 262).

Paul wrote of "instruction" (*nouthesia*, "admonition," KJV) three times. In 1 Corinthians 10:1 and Titus 3:10 it conveys the idea of a warning, but in Ephesians 6:4 it communicates both positive and negative ideas: a word of encouragement, or reproof where that is needed.[28] Hendriksen suggests *paideia* is what is done to the child and *nouthesia* is what is said to the child.[29] This, however, may be too tight a distinction since *paideia*, no doubt, includes verbal instruction.

Children are to obey their parents "in the Lord" (Eph. 6:1), and parents are to educate their children "in the Lord" (6:4). That God is to be the focus of their learning and teaching echoes the same God-centered home education of the Old Testament.

Ephesians 6:4b could be paraphrased: Nourish your children physically and spiritually by educating, encouraging, and, as necessary, warning them, directing their focus to the Lord.

How Are Parents to Teach Their Children?

The previous pages presented the content parents are to teach their children. But how should they do it? The Bible suggests a number of ways by which parents should impart a God-centered education to their boys and girls.

Gain Attention

As Table 3 shows, one of the first things parents need to do in instructing their children is to get their attention, to capture their interest, helping them focus on what is to be learned. Haystead gives several ideas on how to do this: Start with the child's name, get close to the child, establish eye contact, gain a verbal response, and respect the child.[30]

Communicate Verbally

Several verbs in Hebrew point to this process of parents telling their children: *ʾāmar*, "to say" (Exod. 12:27; 13:14; Deut. 6:21; 32:7; Josh. 4:7); *dābar*, "to talk about" (Deut. 6:7; 11:19); *yādaʿ*, "to teach" (Deut. 4:9, 10; 11:19; Josh. 4:22; Ps. 78:5, 56; Isa. 38:19);[31] *nāqad*, "to explain" (Exod. 13:8; Deut. 32:7); *sāphar*, "to tell or recount" (Exod. 10:2; Pss. 44:1; 48:13; 78:3–4, 6).[32]

28. R. C. Trench, *Synonyms of the New Testament* (reprint, Grand Rapids: Wm. B. Eerdmans Publishing Co., 1953), 112. Paul's eightfold use of the related verb *noutheteō* always conveys the negative thought "to warn or admonish."

29. Hendriksen, *Exposition of Ephesians*, 262.

30. Haystead, *The 3,000-Year-Old Guide to Parenting*, 110–11.

31. In Psalm 78:56 the NIV renders this verb "keep," and in Isaiah 38:19 the NIV translates this verb "talk" but in each case the verse has the word "to teach."

32. For more on the transmission of God's truths orally, see Rüger, "Oral Tradition in the Old Testament," 107–20. For more on the Hebrew and Greek words for teach and learn, see Lawrence O. Richards, *Expository Dictionary of Bible Words* (Grand Rapids: Zondervan Publishing House, 1985), 588–92; Roy B. Zuck, "Hebrew Words for 'Teach,'" *Bibliotheca Sacra* 121 (July–September 1964): 228–35; and idem, "Greek Words for 'Teach,'" *Bibliotheca Sacra* 122 (April–June 1965): 158–68.

Moses used an interesting word when he told parents to "impress" *(šānan)* God's commandments on their children (Deut. 6:7). Occurring only nine times in the Old Testament, *šānan* means "to sharpen a tool or whet a knife." Used in an intensive form in this verse, the word means "to teach incisively" or "to inculcate." This suggests teaching with diligence, communicating God's truth persistently, consistently, and intensely so that God's Word is applied to children's hearts and made a part of their lives.[33]

One effective way to communicate God's ways to children in the home is by informal conversation. Moses wrote, "Talk about them when you sit at home and when you walk along the road, when you lie down and when you get up" (6:7). Moses approached this subject a second time: "Teach them to your children, talking about them when you sit at home and when you walk along the road, when you lie down and when you get up" (11:19). In this verse the word "teach" is a causal form of *lāmad,* "to learn"; therefore, it literally means "to cause to learn." When we are relaxing or sitting together at the dinner table, when we are on the go (taking a walk or going for a ride), when we are putting our children to bed, or when they are getting up—in these informal times we should converse with our children about spiritual values. Carefully guided, but natural conversations at the dinner table can be unusually effective for instilling biblical concepts and strong moral values. As Moses said, God's Word is "to be on your lips" (Exod. 13:9).

Bedtime with younger children is a great time for reading Bible stories, praying, talking about the events of the day, letting the child express his or her concerns, and reflecting on issues from God's perspective.[34]

Visualize God's Truths

Twice in Deuteronomy Moses told the people to visualize what they talk about in the home: "Write them on the doorframes of your houses and on your gates" (6:9; 11:20). By having God's commands in written form in various places in the home, parents reach their children through the "eye gate," in addition to their receiving verbal communication through the "ear gate." The atmosphere of the house should make it obvious that the home is a place where God is honored.[35] Wall plaques with Bible verses, an open Bible on a table, Bible storybooks, framed pictures of Bible scenes, and Sunday school handiwork displayed on the refrigerator door—these and other means can help carry out this principle of visualizing God's truth.

33. Zuck, "Hebrew Words for 'Teach,'" 234.

34. Wesley R. Willis, "Child-Rearing and Angelology," in *Basic Theology: Applied,* ed. Wesley and Elaine Willis and John and Janet Master (Wheaton, Ill.: Victor Books, 1995), 72.

35. Ibid., 73.

Arouse Curiosity

As indicated earlier, certain religious functions in Israelite homes led children to inquire about their meaning. This gave parents ideal opportunities for instructing their children. If children today hesitate to ask similar questions, parents can help arouse youngsters' curiosity by asking questions such as these: "Do you know why we celebrate Good Friday?" "What is Ascension Sunday?" "What do you think is the reason Jews celebrate Passover each year?" Or parents can raise questions about doctrine for discussion with their children. "Why did God allow our dog to get run over?" "Does God love us even when we disobey?" "Will people go to heaven if they refuse to believe in Christ?" "What difference does it make that the Holy Spirit lives in us?" "What do you think the world will be like when Jesus comes back?"

Bible quiz books, Bible puzzles, Bible coloring books, Bible crossword puzzles, and other Bible-related games can help foster a continued interest in and curiosity about the Scriptures. Another helpful activity is to discuss the meaning of Bible verses being memorized. Another way to help children relate Scripture to life is to ask something like, "Did you see anyone at school today who was obviously disobeying God's standards? What happened as a result?"

Give Reasons for Your Rules

"You don't need to know why; just do it." Parents often take this approach with children, insisting that they follow parental orders without explanations. While young children may not be able to comprehend reasons behind certain regulations, we should seek to give explanations where possible. This helps children be better motivated to follow through. "Do it because I said so" often comes across as an authoritative, "I-don't-care-what-you-think" approach—an approach that often builds walls rather than burns them between parents and their young.

The Book of Proverbs, a parental guidebook par excellence, often gives reasons with its rules, motivations with its messages. Many of its proverbs include motive clauses. Stating the consequences, both positive and negative, of certain actions serves to motivate the child to be wise and to avoid being foolish. For example, a number of proverbs appeal to basic human-avoidance motives, including the desire to avoid hunger (10:3a; 13:25; 15:15b, 17a), harm (10:7b, 15b, 16b, 29b, 31b), and death (10:21b, 27b; 11:3b, 19b; 13:9b).[36] Nelson points out that good child rearing "includes pointing out to [the child or young person] the consequences of his misbehavior."[37]

36. Ted Hildebrandt, "Motivation and Antithetic Parallelism in Proverbs 10–15," *Journal of the Evangelical Theological Society* 35 (December 1992): 439. This article is reprinted in Zuck, ed., *Learning from the Sages*, 253–65.
37. Gerald E. Nelson, *The One-Minute Scolding* (New York: Random House, 1984), 118.

Positive motivational incentives in Proverbs include the drives for friendships, success, honor, love, joy, blessing, self-control, concern for others, fellowship with God, and others. Table 4 lists verses from Proverbs 1–9 that include commands with the corresponding reasons or motives. Reading these verses helps reveal the frequency of motive clauses in this section of Proverbs.

Table 4
Commands in Proverbs 1–9

Command	Reasons/Motives
1:8	1:9
1:15	1:16
1:25	1:26
1:30	1:31
2:1–4	2:5
3:1	3:2
3:3	3:4
3:5–6a	3:6b
3:7	3:8
3:9	3:10
3:11	3:12
3:21	3:22–24
4:6a	4:6a
4:6b	4:6b
4:8a	4:8a
4:8b	4:8b
4:10a	4:10b
4:20	4:22
4:23a	4:23b
5:1	5:2
5:7–8	5:9–14
6:9–10	6:11
6:12–14	6:15
6:20–21	6:22–24
6:25	6:26–29
6:32a	6:32b–35
7:1–4	7:5
7:24–25	7:26–27
8:10	8:11
8:34	8:35–36
9:8a	9:8a
9:8b	9:8b

Want an interesting study? As you read Proverbs 10–31, jot down what kind of motivation—negative or positive—is suggested by each verse. Not all verses include a motive clause, but those that do are revealing. This can help you use explanations and reasons in seeking to motivate children to action.

Another approach is to list the characteristic or conduct and the accompanying consequence in various verses in Proverbs. For example, the characteristic in Proverbs 10:1a is a wise son and the consequence is joy to his father. Or in 10:8b the characteristic is a chattering fool and the consequence is ruin.

Where Are Parents to Teach Their Children?

After the Israelites conquered Canaan, Joshua allotted eleven of the tribes to their territories. Those of the tribe of Levi, however, were not given a separate land allotment but were assigned to various cities throughout the other tribes (Num. 35:11–15; Josh. 21:1–42). One of the purposes of this arrangement was so the Levites would be present among the people to teach them God's law (Deut. 17:11; 33:8, 10; 2 Chron. 15:3; 17:7–9; 35:3). However, their teaching responsibilities in no way eliminated the need for fathers and mothers to teach their children in the home.

No formal schools, to which children were sent each day to be taught by professional educators, existed before the Hellenistic period.[38] "Beyond their primary role as nurturers in their offspring's early years, [parents]—along with others—instructed children by word and example in the technical skills and behavioral modes essential to household life."[39] The role of parents, then, was highly significant, "in ways more comprehensive than we can fathom easily, accustomed as we are to having specialists take on the lion's share of teaching our children beginning at even earlier ages."[40] While the Bible does not stipulate the locus of child education for modern cultures, a precedent for the present growing trend of home schooling is seen in the Old Testament.[41] The Israelite home was indeed an educational institution—a place of parental teaching and of child learning. Parents who neglect to teach their children the Bible and biblical standards of living—leaving it entirely in the hands of others or in no one's hands—are deviating far from God's design for the teaching and learning of children.

38. James L. Crenshaw, "Education in Ancient Israel," *Journal of Biblical Literature* 104 (1985): 601–15. Some writers, on the other hand, suggest that because of Solomon's contact with Egypt through his marrying Pharaoh's daughter (1 Kings 9:17; 11:1), he may have established schools in Israel similar to those in Egypt for training royal scribes (R. Alan Culpepper, "Education," in *International Standard Bible Encyclopedia*, 2 [1982]:33; Tryggve N. D. Mettinger, *Solomon's State Officials* [Lund: G. W. K. Gleerup, 1971], 143–57; and André Lemaire, "Education [Israel]," in *Anchor Bible Dictionary*, 2 [1992]: 308). However, this is an assumption lacking specific evidence. Also, some writers suggest that several short, fragmentary inscriptions such as the Gezer Calendar are school exercises of pupils. But, again, this is conjecture, for these fragments, as Weeks correctly points out, do not demand the existence of schools (*Early Israelite Wisdom*, 152–53, 156).

39. Carol Meyers, *Discovering Eve: Ancient Israelite Women in Context* (New York: Oxford University Press, 1988), 194.

40. Ibid.

41. On trends in the significant home schooling movement, see John W. Kennedy, "Home Schooling Grows Up," *Christianity Today*, July 17, 1995, 50–52. Also see Ray E. Ballmann, *The How & Why of Home Schooling* (Wheaton, Ill.: Crossway Books, 1995).

However, when the Jews were captives in Babylon (605–536 B.C.), they, of course, were without their central place of worship, the temple. Many believe this loss of temple worship and the disruption of normal social life by captivity in a foreign country led the Jews to establish synagogues as places of worship and instruction. Perhaps the death of Jewish fathers and young men in defending their country against Babylonian attacks left many widowed mothers in need of help in teaching their young. Though the origin of synagogues is obscure, they may have arisen during the exile or soon thereafter under Ezra's leadership. For several hundred years before Christ, during his life on earth, and in the days of the early church, synagogues enabled Jews in most cities in Palestine, and elsewhere where Jews were dispersed, to meet to study the Law.[42] The weekly worship services included reading portions of the Old Testament, explanations and applications of the Scriptures, and reciting psalms and prayers of praise and petition. The synagogue was used for community gatherings, but "above all the facilities of the synagogue were used for the education of children."[43] As Culpepper suggests, "emphasis in the synagogues on the study of the Torah gave them much of the character of a school."[44] As children attended synagogue services with their parents, they learned the Old Testament. Therefore, the synagogue continued the teaching that boys and girls received at home. The synagogues did not replace family instruction; they supplemented it. The Gospels frequently refer to Jesus' teaching in the synagogues (Matt. 4:23; Mark 1:21; 6:2; Luke 4:15; 6:6; 13:10; John 6:59; 18:20), and Paul preached the gospel to Jewish audiences in synagogues in Antioch of Pisidia (Acts 13:14), Iconium (14:1), Thessalonica (17:1–2), Berea (17:10), Athens (17:17), Corinth (18:4), and Ephesus (18:19; 19:8). No doubt children attending those services heard Jesus or the apostle teaching.

In addition to the learning received from an early age at home and weekly in the synagogues, children were taught in Jewish elementary schools. The Palestinian Talmud says that Simon ben Shetah (ca. 100 B.C.) ordered that children were to attend elementary school. This means that such schools were then in existence. Rabbi Joshua ben Gamala (high priest about A.D. 63–65) decreed that teachers of children be appointed in every district and town.[45] The elementary school, where children were to begin attending at age six or

42. The oldest dated evidence of a synagogue is in Schedia near Alexandria, Egypt and is dated in the third century B.C. (R. P. Jean-Baptiste Frey, ed., *Corpus Inscriptionum Judiacarum* 2 [1952]: 1440).

43. *Encyclopaedia Britannica*, 1963 ed., 21:704A.

44. Culpepper, "Education," 25. Also see Wolfgang Schrage, "*synagōgē*," in *Theologoical Dictionary of the New Testament*, 7 (1971): 824–25 on the educational purposes of the synagogue.

45. William Barclay, *Educational Ideals in the Ancient World* (1959; reprint, Grand Rapids: Baker Book House, 1974), 33–34.

seven (according to Joshua ben Gamala), was known as the *Beth Ha-Sepher* ("House of the Book") because its primary purpose was to teach children the Torah. Like the home, the school was an institution of religious learning. Some schools were held in special buildings, others were in the teachers' homes, but usually the schools were in annexes of the synagogues.[46] Studying the Law in school meant that the children's learning was both factual and practical, because the Law had to be studied and then put into practice. This differed from the Greeks, whose consuming passion in learning was theory and ideas, not practice, as Josephus observed.[47]

Students were taught by repetition and memorization. Barclay quotes Rabbi Akiba as saying, "The teacher should strive to make the lesson agreeable to the pupils by clear reasons, as well as by frequent repetitions, until they thoroughly understood the matter, and are able to recite it with great fluency."[48] Boys were taught to read so that as adults they could read the Torah in the synagogue. Students were to memorize the *Shema* (Num. 15:37–41; Deut. 6:4–9; 11:13–21), the Hallel psalms (Pss. 113–118), Genesis 1–5, and Leviticus 1–8.

According to Rabbi Jehuda ben Tema (*Aboth* 5.21), children ten years of age were to begin studying the Mishnah (oral law), and at age fifteen, the Talmud (Mishnah with commentary).[49]

Secondary schools known as *Beth Ha-Midrash* ("House of Study") were developed in Judaism for older boys. Emphasis was placed on reading, meditating on, and discussing the Law.[50] If Christian parents today are to follow this general pattern of education, they should seriously consider enrolling their children in Christian elementary schools or at least be sure the public schools their children attend are not contradicting and opposing the godly standards and Christian values the parents are seeking to instill at home.

As in Jewish families, children in Greek and Roman homes were taught by parents until they were six or seven years old. Then if a child in a Christian home received a formal education, he did so only in pagan schools.[51] Education was not compulsory, and, generally, girls did not attend school. Elementary-age Greek and Roman children were taught reading, writing, and arithmetic by a *litterator*, and in secondary education the *grammaticus* taught

46. Ibid., 37.

47. Josephus *Against Apion* 2.17.

48. Barclay, *Educational Ideals in the Ancient World*, 40–41.

49. Alfred Edersheim, *Sketches of Jewish Social Life in the Days of Christ* (reprint, Grand Rapids: Wm. B. Eerdmans Publishing Co., 1976), 105. Another source (*Ketubot* 50a) states the child was ready to study the Scriptures at age six and the Mishnah at age twelve. (O. Larry Yarbrough, "Parents and Children in the Jewish Family of Antiquity," in *The Jewish Family in Antiquity*, ed. Shaye J. D. Cohen (Atlanta: Scholars Press, 1993), 44.

50. Isaac Levy, *The Synagogue: Its History and Function* (London: Vallentine, Mitchell, and Co., 1963), 19.

51. Tertullian *De Idololatria* 10. See Culpepper, "Education," 27.

young people (between the ages of twelve and fifteen) Greek literature (mainly Homer's writings), grammar, writing, mathematics, science,[52] geography, physical training, and music.[53] In an advanced level of education a few Roman young men between the ages of sixteen and eighteen or twenty studied under the *rhetor*. In this college-level equivalent the young men studied rhetoric, which included the "trivium"—grammar, logic, and rhetoric—all of which emphasized literary pursuits and the art of discourse or oratorical speech.[54] The apostle Paul may have received some training in rhetoric under Gamaliel at Tarsus, in addition to his schooling in Judaism (Acts 22:3).

In wealthy families an interesting aspect of Greek education, which the Romans assimilated from the Greeks, was the use of a pedagogue (*paidagōgos*, lit., "child leader"). Usually a slave, the man took the child or youth to school, sat in on his classes, and escorted him back home.[55] Besides protecting the child from harm (including homosexual harassment), the pedagogue helped the child with his lessons, taught him manners (especially table manners) and morals, and disciplined him when necessary. The pedagogue usually began these duties when the child started school at age six or seven, and he continued until the student was a late adolescent.[56] Often a close bond of friendship developed between a child and his pedagogue. The adult was to be a role

52. Ibid.

53. Mark Golden, *Children and Childhood in Classical Athens* (Baltimore: Johns Hopkins University Press, 1990), 62.

54. Donald Lemen Clark, *Rhetoric in Greco-Roman Education* (New York: Columbia University Press, 1957), 64–65. Whereas Greek schooling emphasized philosophy, the Roman stressed rhetoric, which they believed to be more useful (Edwin Yamauchi, *Harper's World of the New Testament* [San Francisco: Harper & Row, Publishers, 1981], 100). For more on Greek and Roman education see Barclay, *Educational Ideals in the Ancient World*, 49–191; Hugo Blümner, *The Home Life of the Ancient Greeks*, trans. Alice Zimmern (New York: Cooper Square Publishers, 1966), 99–132; Stanley F. Bonner, *Education in Ancient Rome* (Berkeley, Calif.: University of California Press, 1977), 10–75; Jerome Carcopino, *Daily Life in Ancient Rome* (New Haven, Conn.: Yale University Press, 1960), 104–13; M. L. Clarke, *Higher Education in the Ancient World* (London: Routledge & Kegan Paul, 1971), 11–108; Frederik Eby and Charles Finn Arrowood, *The History and Philosophy of Education Ancient and Medieval* (New York: Prentice-Hall, 1940), 219–86, 515–77; H. I. Marrou, *A History of Education in Antiquity* (New York: Sheed and Ward, 1956), 21–49, 63–94, 147–418; James E. Reed and Ronnie Prevost, *A History of Christian Education* (Nashville: Broadman and Holman Publishers, 1993), 25–52; William A. Smith, *Ancient Education* (New York: Philosophical Library, 1955), 125–49, 183–96; John T. Townsend, "Ancient Education in the Time of the Early Roman Empire," in *The Catacombs and the Coliseum*, ed. S. Benko and J. J. O'Rourke (Valley Forge, Penn.: Judson Press, 1971), 139–63; idem, "Education," in *Anchor Bible Dictionary*, 2 (1992): 301–17; and Paul Veyne, ed., *From Pagan Rome to Byzantium*, trans. Arthur Goldhammer (Cambridge, Mass.: Belknap Press, 1987), 18–22.

55. Plato *Lysis* 208C; idem *Laws* 808C; Plutarch *De Moralia* 439–40; idem *On the Education of Children* 7.

56. For more details on the pedagogue's role, see Barclay, *Educational Ideals in the Ancient World*, 96–100; Bonner, *Education in Ancient Rome*, 37–45; Keith R. Bradley, *Discovering the Roman Family* (New York: Oxford University Press, 1991), 49–56; Marrou, *A History of Education in Antiquity*, 201, 206, 301, 360–61; and Norman H. Young, "Paidagogues: The Social Setting of a Pauline Metaphor," *Novum Testamentum* (April 1987): 150–76. For illustrations of some Roman pedagogues with their children, see Bonner, *Education in Ancient Rome*, 24–26.

model and an authority to be obeyed. He was usually an old and trusted slave, no longer able to work for the family in manual labor. In Galatians 3:24 Paul compared the Mosaic law to the pedagogue (not "schoolmaster" as in the KJV). "Was put in charge" is the NIV's loose rendering of this noun. The Law served a disciplinary, protective, tutoring kind of relationship to the nation Israel, leading them eventually to Christ. When Christ came, the Law was no longer needed, just as the work of a pedagogue terminated when his youthful charge came of age.

Coleman suggests that possibly Timothy had the tutelage of a pedagogue, and later studied under a *grammaticus* and possibly a *rhetor*.[57]

A possible synonym of the Greek *paidagōgus* is *epitropos*, used by Paul in Galatians 4:2 of the guardian of a young child *(nēpios)*.[58] Also, Jesus used the word *epitropos* in referring to a foreman over vineyard workers (Matt. 20:8).

In the ancient world of Bible times, the education of children in the home was of paramount importance. Relatively little is known about the attitude of Christian parents in New Testament times toward the Greco-Roman educational system, but it is noteworthy that many of the early Christian apologists were "skilled and trained in all Greek knowledge before they became Christians."[59] These apologists often quoted the Greek poets and philosophers.[60] Tertullian believed that no Christian should become a schoolmaster, but he said it was permissible for Christian children to attend pagan schools because there was no other way for them to receive the basics of a school education.[61] Barclay observes that Christian parents in the early church continued to be committed to the primacy of the home in teaching children.

> The Church was not intensely concerned with schools as such; it was willing to use such schools as there were for the purposes of ordinary education. But the Church was intensely concerned with the home. The Church saw that in the last analysis the only true teachers of any child are the parents of that child. . . . The school is at best only an adjunct to the home. It is the parent who is responsible for bringing the child into the world; and it is the parent who is responsible for bringing the child to God.[62]

John Chrysostom (A.D. 345?–407), well trained by his mother Anthusa, wrote an essay, "An Address on Vainglory and the Right Way for Parents to

57. Lucien Coleman, "A First-Century Education," *Biblical Illustrator* 13 (Summer 1987): 70.
58. On the *nēpios,* a preschooler, see chapter 9.
59. Barclay, *Educational Ideals in the Ancient World,* 209.
60. Barclay discusses many apologists who were well schooled in pagan learning, including Justin Martyr, Lactantius, Hippolytus, Tatian, Aristides, Tertullian, Cyprian, Jerome, Augustine, Clement of Alexandria, Origen, Basil, Gregory of Nazianzus, and Gregory of Nyssa (ibid., 205–26).
61. Tertullian *De Idololatria* 10.
62. Barclay, *Educational Ideals in the Ancient World,* 261–62.

Bring Up Their Children."[63] Impressing on Christian parents the importance of teaching their children properly, he wrote, "What will become of boys when from earliest youth they are without teachers? . . . In our own day every man takes the greatest pains to train his boy in the arts and in literature and speech. But to exercise this child's soul in virtue, to that no man any longer pays heed."[64] He urged Christian parents to discipline their sons,[65] to teach them by stories (the "ear gate"), and to teach by means of the smell, eye, tongue, and touch "gates."[66]

The family, then, was extremely important in the education of children in Bible times and in the early church. This duty could not be delegated. "The early Church would have had sharp words to say about 'Christian' parents of today who think they have done all that is required of them when they have passed their children over to a teacher or an institution."[67] Parents today, who turn over the spiritual training and biblical nurturing of their children entirely to others, do so at the high risk of their boys and girls missing out on the most fundamental goal of life: to know and love the Lord Jesus Christ.

Do you want your children to turn out right? Then start them on the right path, in the way they should go!

---

63. Translated by and printed in M. L. W. Laistner, *Christianity and Pagan Culture in the Later Roman Empire* (Ithaca, N.Y.: Cornell University Press, 1951), 85–112.
64. Ibid., 94–95 (*An Address on Vainglory* 18).
65. Ibid., 95 (*An Address on Vainglory* 19).
66. Ibid., 98–110 (*An Address on Vainglory* 26–63).
67. Marrou, *A History of Education in Antiquity,* 419.

9

"And the Child Grew"

Growth Stages of Children in the Bible

All animals and humans start out small and develop through various stages of growth. In the animal world we call young sheep "lambs," young cows "calves," baby chickens "chicks," and young horses "foals." Baby dogs are puppies, baby cats are kittens, baby pigs are piglets. Usually one word suffices to designate the just-born, young, and growing animal, as distinct from the fully-grown, adult animal.

However, for humans we have a number of words to depict growth stages. The newborn is a "baby." While children are still quite young and before they are talking or walking, we call them "infants." "Toddlers" designate those who are walking, perhaps one- and two-year-olds. "Preschoolers" generally refer to children from two to five years old. Elementary school-age boys and girls are those in grades one through six, or roughly ages six through eleven. "Junior highs" are twelve through fourteen-year-olds. "Teenagers" usually denote young people fourteen or fifteen through eighteen years old. College-age youth specify, roughly, those eighteen or nineteen through twenty-two.

Does the Bible have similar terms in Hebrew and Greek for these stages of growth? While the biblical terms do not correspond precisely with these words in English, the Old and New Testaments do have a number of picturesque words to depict children's growth stages.

Hebrew Words for "Children"

The Hebrew word *yeled* is a general term for a child, boy, son, or young person. It comes from the verb *yālad*, "to bear, give birth to," or "to become

149

a parent." A related word *môledeth* means "offspring" or "relatives." The feminine form *yaldāh* means "girl." *Yeled* suggests the idea of offspring more than the thought of a particular age range. It refers to the young boy Ishmael (Gen. 21:8), three-month-old Moses (Exod. 2:3, 6, 8), young people who served Rehoboam (1 Kings 12:8, 10, 14), and teenage Daniel and his three friends (Dan. 1:4, 10, 13, 15, 17). *Yal^edûth*, used only three times (Ps. 110:3; Eccles. 11:9–10), probably means "youth."[1]

A young nursing infant is called a "suckling" (*yônēq*, a participial form of the verb *yānaq*, "to suck, nurse"). The New International Version renders it "infants" in its occurrences in Numbers 11:12; Deuteronomy 32:25; 1 Samuel 15:3; 22:19; Psalm 8:2; Isaiah 11:8; Jeremiah 44:7; and Lamentations 2:11; 4:4.

Another Hebrew word for baby is *ᶜôlēl*. It occurs with its synonym *yônēq*, "infant," in 1 Samuel 15:3; 22:19; Psalm 8:2; Jeremiah 44:7; and Lamentations 2:11; 4:4. The word *ᶜôlēl* is used of children praising the Lord (Ps. 8:2), being out in the street (Jer. 6:11), begging (Lam. 4:4), and of an unborn baby (Job 3:16b). Scholars debate whether this noun stems from the verb *ālal*, "to be mischievous," or *ᶜûl*, "to suck, give milk." The related word *ᶜăyîl*, "young boy," occurs only twice, both times in Job (19:18; 21:11).

A similar noun *ᶜûl* refers to a nursing baby (used only twice, in Isa. 49:15 and 65:20), and is from the verb "to suck."

When a child was weaned, perhaps at age two or three, he was called a *gāmûl*, a "weaned child." The verb *gāmal* means "to be complete, to recompense, to ripen," so the participial nominal form refers to a child whose nursing is completed; he is like ripened grapes. Isaiah 11:8 uses this word ("young child," NIV), along with the *yônēq*, "infant." In Psalm 131:2 "weaned child" is used twice.

A word that occurs forty-two times in the Old Testament, meaning "little children," is *ṭap*. While its origin is disrupted, the word probably derives from the verb *ṭāpap*, "to take quick little steps, to trip along."[2] The noun seems to convey young children, perhaps comparable to our preschoolers or young school-age children, who often skip along or walk briskly.[3] Numerous verses refer to "women and children," thereby suggesting little ones who are not old enough to be on their own and must therefore accompany their mothers. In Ezekiel 9:6 the *ṭap* are distinguished from young men and young women.

1. For more on *yeled* and related words, see *Theological Wordbook of the Old Testament*, 1:378–80; and J. Schreiner and G. Johannes Botterweck, "*yālad*," in *Theological Dictionary of the Old Testament*, 6 (1990): 76–81.
2. *Theological Wordbook of the Old Testament*, 1:352. The verb is used only in Isaiah 3:16, which refers to haughty women "tripping along [*ṭāpāp*] with mincing steps."
3. The New International Version translates this word in various ways, including "little ones," "little children," "children" (and even "families" in Judg. 15:22).

Women and their little ones were the unfortunate objects of warfare, by being taken captive or put to death (Gen. 34:29; Num. 31:9; Deut. 20:14; Judg. 21:10; Esther 3:13; 8:11; Jer. 41:16; Ezek. 9:6). Young children often accompanied their mothers in traveling by foot, either in an extended family (Gen. 45:19; 46:5; cf. 43:8) or with the entire nation Israel (Exod. 10:10; 12:37; Ezra 8:21). Sometimes flocks and herds are mentioned with the traveling women and children (Gen. 50:8; Num. 32:26; Josh. 1:14; Judg. 18:21).

Occasionally the word *ṭap* refers to all children as distinguished from men and women (Deut. 2:34; 3:6; 31:12; 2 Chron. 20:13; 31:18; Jer. 40:7; 43:6).[4]

The concept of "little [few] in years" is denoted by *qāṭān*, from *qāṭōn*, "to be small or insignificant." This adjective is used of Benjamin (Gen. 42:15), David (1 Sam. 17:14), and Naaman's young (little) servant girl (2 Kings 5:2). Second Kings 2:23 records the jeering of young (*qᵉṭannîm*) lads. Also, in the millennium a little (*qāṭōn*) child will lead animals (Isa. 11:6). The word does not specify a particular age range; it contrasts with one who is fully developed.[5]

The young man is the *bāḥûr*, a word that comes from *bāḥar*, "to choose," and which means "in the prime or choice time of young manhood." Such a person is marriageable (Ruth 3:10; Isa. 62:5), strong ("The glory of young men is their strength," Prov. 20:29), and handsome (Ezek. 23:6, 12, 23). Saul was such a young man (1 Sam. 9:2). Because of their vigor and strength, they are usually enlisted as soldiers. Therefore, for young men to die in battle (Deut. 32:25; 2 Kings 8:12; 2 Chron. 36:17; Jer. 11:22; 18:21; 48:15; 49:26; 51:3, 22; Lam. 1:15; Ezek. 30:17; Amos 4:10) or to be taken captive (Lam. 1:18; 5:13–14) signaled God's judgment. Besides being happy in his youth (Eccles. 11:9), the young person is to fear God ("Remember your Creator in the days of your youth," Eccles. 12:1).

A number of verses refer to young women or maidens along with young men (Pss. 78:63; 148:12; Isa. 23:4; Jer. 31:13; Lam. 1:18; 2:21; Amos 8:13; Zech. 9:17).

A young person of marriageable age was an *ʿelem*, a word used of David when he killed Goliath (1 Sam. 17:56) and of the boy who retrieved arrows for Jonathan (1 Sam. 20:22). The feminine form is *ʿalmāh*, a young woman

---

4. In Numbers 32:16 and 24 the New International Version translates *ṭap* "women and children," as if the word included both groups. However, this is inconsistent with the other forty occurrences of the word, where it is plainly limited to young children, which is clearly the case in verse 26 in the same context. The idea that the word includes women, as well as children, is based on Locher's suggestion that the word means "household" or "dependents" (C. Locher, "*ṭap*," in *Theological Dictionary of the Old Testament*, 5 (1986):348–49). It is preferable, however, to take the word to mean "little ones" or "young children."

5. Another word meaning "younger" or "youngest" is *ṣāʿîr*, a relative term referring not to children, but to adults who are younger than others, such as one of Lot's daughters (Gen. 19:31, 34–35, 38); Rachel, a daughter of Laban (29:26); Benjamin (43:33); Ephraim (48:14); Hiel's youngest son, Segub (1 Kings 16:34; cf. Josh. 6:26); and Elihu (Job 32:6).

of the age of puberty, who was characterized by virginity. Young women described by this word include Rebekah[6] (Gen. 24:43), Moses' sister Miriam (Exod. 2:8), and Mary (Isa. 7:14; Matt. 1:23).[7]

The words *na^{c}ar*, "boy or youth," and *na^{c}ărāh*, "girl or youth," have a wide range of meaning. The masculine form refers to the newborn Ichabod (1 Sam. 4:21), Moses, an infant a few months old (Exod. 2:6), David and Bathsheba's baby (2 Sam. 12:16), Samuel when he was unweaned (1 Sam. 1:22), and when he was three years old (1:24). The lad who returned Jonathan's arrows, a *na^{c}ar*, was also an *^{c}elem* (1 Sam. 20:21–22). Joseph was a *na^{c}ar* at age seventeen (Gen. 37:2), and at age thirty (41:12, 46), and David was a *na^{c}ar* when he slew Goliath (1 Sam. 17:33, 42). The boys who mocked Elisha (2 Kings 2:23) were small (*q^{e}tannîm*) boys (*n^{ec}ārîm*). Young Shechem, a *na^{c}ar*, was of marriageable age (Gen. 34:19), and when Josiah, young king of Judah, was sixteen, he was a *na^{c}ar* (2 Chron. 34:3). David called his grown son Absalom a *na^{c}ar* (2 Sam. 14:21; 18:5) and his grown son Solomon a *na^{c}ar* (1 Chron. 22:5; 29:1). The *na^{c}ar* was used of spies with Joshua (Josh. 6:23). Even forty-one-year-old Rehoboam (1 Kings 14:21) was a *na^{c}ar* (2 Chron. 13:7). But the *n^{ec}ārîm* are contrasted to old age (Ps. 148:12; Jer. 51:22). The *n^{ec}ārîm* in Proverbs are young men (1:4; 7:7) or children (20:11; 22:6, 15; 23:13; 29:15).

Occasionally the New International Version renders this Hebrew word as "steward" (Ziba was Mephibosheth's steward, 2 Sam. 16:1), "young officers" (of Ahab, 1 Kings 20:15, 17, 19), "young aide" (Joshua was Moses' aide, Exod. 33:11), "servant" (Abraham's servant, Gen. 18:7; Purah, Gideon's servant, Judg. 7:10–11; Amnon's servant, 2 Sam. 13:17; Gehazi, Elisha's "servant," 2 Kings 4:12; 5:20; 8:4), and "underlings" (of the Assyrian king, 2 Kings 19:6). Hildebrandt suggests that *na^{c}ar*, therefore, means a squire.[8] While this may point to the status of the individual as a "personal attendant" or "military cadet,"[9] the word "squire" seems too limiting for a word that denotes a newborn infant as well as young adults.

Perhaps the synonym "inexperienced," used with *na^{c}ar* of Solomon (1 Chron. 22:5; 29:1) and Rehoboam (2 Chron. 13:7), suggests that *na^{c}ar*

---

6. *B^{e}tûlāh*, "maiden," does not convey the idea of virginity as clearly as does *^{c}almāh*. For instance *b^{e}tûlāh* was inadequate in itself to describe Rebekah; she was a *b^{e}tûlāh* who had not had sexual relations with a man (Gen. 24:16). And in Joel 1:8 *b^{e}tûlāh* is used of a young married woman. However, *^{c}almāh* by itself always seems to designate a virgin (Allan A. MacRae, "*^{c}lm*," in *Theological Wordbook of the Old Testament*, 2:672).

7. The word *^{c}almāh* is also used in Psalm 68:25; Proverbs 30:19; and Song of Songs 1:3; 6:18. The fact that Matthew 1:23, in quoting Isaiah 7:14, used *^{c}almāh* to refer to Mary, Jesus' virgin mother, confirms the meaning of virginity for that word.

8. Ted Hildebrandt, "Proverbs 22:6a: Train Up a Child?" *Grace Theological Journal* 9 (1988): 11–12, 14.

9. Ibid., 11. Cf. John McDonald, "The Status and Role of the *Na^{c}ar* in Israelite Society," *Journal of the Near Eastern Society* 35 (1976): 147–70.

carries the idea of a person who is not accepted in the community as a leader. Jeremiah's words that he is a *na͑ar* (incorrectly rendered "child" in the NIV) reveal that he was one whose authority was not yet accepted in the community (Jer. 1:6–7).

Usually the feminine *na͑ărāh* refers to a marriageable girl (2 Kings 5:2), though, like *na͑ar*, it too has a wide range of meaning. The young widow Ruth is called a *na͑ărāh* (Ruth 4:12), as well as maids (Gen. 24:61) and attendants of Pharaoh's daughter (Exod. 2:5).

A synonym of *yeled*, "child," is *bēn*, occurring in the Old Testament almost five thousand times and referring usually to a male son or boy. Figuratively, it is used for children generally, for descendants such as grandchildren and for people belonging to a category or group as in "sons of prophets" or "sons of Ammon" (i.e., Ammonites).[10] In Isaiah 7:14 the prophet said an *͑almāh*, "virgin," would become pregnant and would bear "a son," and therefore 9:6 states, "For to us a child [*yeled*] is born, to us a son [*bēn*] is given." The corresponding feminine is *bat*, meaning either the female child in a family or the female members of a group, as in "daughters of the Philistines," which means Philistine women.[11]

Greek Words for "Children"

As in Hebrew, the Greek language has several words for children, suggestive of various stages of growth or relationships. Aristophanes of Byzantium (257–180? B.C.) wrote of the *brephos*, the newborn; *paidion*, the nursing child; *paidarion*, the child who can walk and speak; *paidiskos*, a child servant; *pais*, the child who can be educated; and others.[12] Hippocrates (460–377? B.C.) identified seven stages of life, with the first four being *paidion* (until age 7), *pais* (ages 7–14), *meirakion* (ages 14–21), and *neaniskos* (ages 21–28).[13] Other classical Greek writers, however, did not use these and other terms consistently to refer to the same age levels. *Pais*, for example, has a broad range of meaning.

Classical Greek words referring to very young children include *brephos*, "newborn"; *nēpios*, "baby"; and *mikros*, "little one."[14] In later Greek prose *teknon*, the general word for child (from *tiktō*, "to give birth"), may describe a child as old as six.

10. Elmer A. Martens, "*bēn*," in *Theological Wordbook of the Old Testament*, 1:114. Also see H. Haag, "*bēn*," in *Theological Dictionary of the Old Testament*, 2 (1975):145–59.

11. Martens, "*bēn*," 1:115.

12. Hippocrates *De Hebdomadibus* 5; Mark Golden, *Children and Childhood in Classical Athens* (Baltimore: Johns Hopkins University Press, 1990), 14.

13. Golden, *Children and Childhood in Classical Athens*, 14–15.

14. Outside its use in poetry, *brephos* occurs in only two passages in Xenophon, and *mikros* is attested only in a comedy by Menander (ibid., 15).

These same terms and others are used in the New Testament. *Brephos,* "a newborn infant," refers to the baby Jesus (Luke 2:12, 16), the Israelite babies who were threatened to die at the edict of the pharaoh (Acts 7:19), and very young Timothy (2 Tim. 3:15). The word also refers to unborn John the Baptist (Luke 1:41, 44), a usage that supports the pro-life view that the newborn are human beings (see chap. 5). Of interest is the fact that John the Baptist was "six months old" in the womb at the time this word *brephos* was used of him (cf. Luke 1:26 and 1:39). First Peter 2:2 includes the only metaphorical use of *brephos* (which occurs with "newborn"), a verse that challenges believers to crave the Word of God much as a newborn desires milk—a graphic presentation of strong, intense desire.

Five of the eight occurrences of *brephos* are in Luke and Acts, books written by the physician Luke. When Matthew and Mark wrote of people bringing "little children" to Jesus, they used the word *paidia* (Matt. 19:13; Mark 10:13). But Luke used the more precise term *brephos* (Luke 18:15). Jesus took them in his arms and put his hands on them and prayed for them. What a beautiful picture of his loving, intimate concern for infants and young children! (For more on this, see chap. 12.)

Nēpios denotes a baby, young child, or minor, in contrast to the mature adult.[15] Four of its eleven New Testament occurrences speak of little children literally, including Jesus' words that spiritual truths are revealed to them (Matt. 11:25; Luke 10:21); and his quotation of Psalm 8:2 in Matthew 21:16, where *nēpios* translates the Hebrew *'ôlēl,* "young children," and in which Jesus approved of children shouting "Hosanna" to him. An individual may be the legal heir to an estate, but while he is still a *nēpios,* a minor, "he is no different from a slave" (Gal. 4:1).

The figurative use of *nēpios* points to the contrast between children and adults (1 Cor. 13:11), between the unsaved and the saved ("when we were children, we were in slavery," Gal. 4:3), between the pupil and the teacher (Rom. 2:20), and between the spiritually immature and mature (1 Cor. 3:1; Eph. 4:14; 1 Thess. 2:7; Heb. 5:13). The related verb *nēpiazō,* "to be like a child," used only in 1 Corinthians 14:20, speaks metaphorically of being innocent or inexperienced regarding evil (*tē kakia*).[16]

In Matthew 21:16 the NIV renders the participial noun *thēlazantōn* as "infants." This word, a synonym of *nēpios,* translates the Hebrew *yônēq,* "a suckling or nursing child."

15. In an epitaph on a child's gravestone in ancient Greece, the *nēpios* is said to have lived four years, five months, and twenty days (James Hope Moulton and George Milligan, *The Vocabulary of the Greek New Testament* [1930; reprint, Grand Rapids: Wm. B. Eerdmans Publishing Co., 1974], 426).

16. For more on *nēpios,* see G. Bertram, "*nēpios, nēpiazō,*" in *Theological Dictionary of the New Testament,* 4 (1967):912–23.

Pais, "child" or "young person," may stem from a word meaning "small" or "insignificant," and may be related to *paizō,* "to play."[17] Used only in the Gospels and Acts, *pais* refers to two-year-old boys (Matt. 2:16), twelve-year-old Jesus (Luke 2:43), Jairus's twelve-year-old daughter (8:51, 54), the official's son (John 4:51), a demon-possessed boy (Luke 9:42), children shouting "Hosanna" (Matt. 21:15; as already seen, they are also called *nēpios*), and Eutychus (Acts 20:12), who was also called a *neanias,* "young person" (20:9).

Individuals in a lower social position, such as servants, are also referred to as *pais.* These include the centurion's servant (Matt. 8:6, 8, 13; Luke 7:7), Herod's attendants (Matt. 14:2), the servants in Jesus' parable of the wise manager (Luke 12:45), and a servant of the prodigal son's father (15:26).

Figuratively, *pais* is used of God's "servants," including the nation Israel (Luke 1:54), David (1:69; Acts 4:25), and five times of Jesus himself (Matt. 12:18; Acts 3:13, 26; 4:27, 30).

Paidion, a diminutive of *pais,* usually designates a small child, though again the age range varies. The word seems to convey a feeling of affection. The word specifies Jesus as a newborn (Matt. 2:8–9, 11, 13 [twice], 14, 20 [twice], 21; Luke 2:17), and is used of a newborn baby (John 16:21), of eight-day-old John the Baptist (Luke 1:59, 66, 76, 80), eight-day-old Jesus (2:27, 40), three-month-old Moses (Heb. 11:23), children playing (Matt. 11:16; Luke 7:32), children with their parents at the feeding of five thousand men (Matt. 14:21) and of four thousand men (15:38), a little child whom Jesus used as a visual illustration (18:2–5; Mark 9:36–37; Luke 9:47–48), little children whose parents brought them to Jesus (Matt. 19:13–14; Mark 10:13–15; Luke 18:16–17), Jairus's twelve-year-old daughter (Mark 5:39–40 [twice]), whom Jesus affectionately called "little girl" (5:41), the son of the official who called his boy *paidion* (John 4:49), a demon-possessed boy (Mark 9:24),[18] a demon-possessed daughter (7:30), children eating bread at a table (7:28), and children in bed (Luke 11:7).

Interestingly, after his resurrection Jesus called his eleven disciples *paidia* (John 21:5), which the NIV renders "friends." Urging the Corinthians to become spiritually mature, Paul wrote, "Stop thinking like children [*paidia*]" (1 Cor. 14:20). In Jesus' incarnation he shared the nature of children *(paidia)* who "have flesh and blood," that is, he became human (Heb. 2:14). Three times John addressed his readers with the affectionate title "Dear children" *(paidia,* 1 John 2:13, 18; 3:7).[19]

17. Golden, *Children and Childhood in Classical Athens,* 12–13, 53.
18. As already seen, Jairus's daughter, the official's son, and the demon-possessed boy also are each called *pais.*
19. The fact that *paidion* is common in greetings in ancient Greek helps explain Jesus' use of the word in John 21:5 and John's use in 1 John (Moulton and Milligan, *The Vocabulary of the Greek New Testament,* 474).

Another diminutive of *pais* is *paidarion*, found in extrabiblical Greek sources, meaning "little boy" or "youngster."[20] The New Testament uses the word only once (John 6:9), which records Andrew's words in introducing to Jesus a little boy who had some barley loaves and fish. Matthew, Mark, and Luke, who also record Jesus' miracle of feeding the five thousand, make no mention of this lad.

Five times Jesus used *mikron*, "small in amount, size, or significance," in reference to children. He spoke of giving a cup of cold water to "one of these little ones" (Matt. 10:42), he denounced anyone who would cause "these little ones who believe in me to sin" (18:6; Mark 9:42; Luke 17:2), that is, any who would entice children away from following him. Just as a shepherd hunts for one lost sheep, so God the Father does not want "any of these little ones" to perish (Matt. 18:14). Therefore, it is wrong to "look down on" (*kataphroneō*, "to despise, scorn, disregard") any child (18:10).

Teknon, from *tiktō*, "to give birth," points to the child's origin and his relationship to his parents. While *teknon* suggests a child's kinship to his parents, *paidion* emphasizes the child's subordinate, minority position under discipline (the verb *paideuō* means "to train or chastise").[21] *Teknon* occurs ninety-three times in the Greek New Testament, with thirty-eight of those occurrences in the Gospels. Natural parent-child relationships are mentioned in a number of verses (Matt. 7:11; 10:21; 15:26; 18:25; 19:29; 22:24; 27:25; Mark 7:27; 10:29–30; 12:19; 13:12; Luke 1:7, 17; 11:13; 14:26; 18:29; 19:44; 20:31; 23:28; Acts 7:5; 21:5, 21; 1 Cor. 7:14; Gal. 4:25, 27; Eph. 6:1, 4; Col. 3:20–21; 1 Thess. 2:7, 11; 1 Tim. 3:4, 12; 5:4; Titus 1:6; 2 John 1, 13; Rev. 12:4–5).

Other times *teknon* refers to one's descendants (Matt. 3:9; Luke 3:8; John 8:39; Acts 2:39; 13:32; 1 Peter 3:6), disciples (Mark 10:24), converts (1 Cor. 4:14; 2 Cor. 6:13; Gal. 4:19; Philem. 10), or followers (Rev. 2:23). Jesus addressed the inhabitants of Jerusalem as the city's "children" (Matt. 23:37; Luke 13:34). Jesus likened the consequences of wisdom to wisdom's "children" (Matt. 11:19; Luke 7:35).

Teknon is also a kind address[22] to certain individuals and is often translated "son," as in Mary's words to twelve-year-old Jesus (Luke 2:48), the prodigal's father to the older son (15:31), Abraham to the rich man (16:25), Jesus' words to the paralytic (Matt. 9:2; Mark 2:5), and the father's words to his older son about working in the vineyard (Matt. 21:28).

Because of his close association with Timothy and Titus in the ministry, and his having led Timothy to the Lord, Paul considered his relationship to

20. Albrecht Oepke, "*pais*," in *Theological Dictionary of the New Testament*, 5 (1967): 638.
21. Brooke Foss Westcott, *The Epistles of St John: The Greek Text with Notes and Essays* (London: Macmillan & Co., 1883), 58.
22. Moulton and Milligan, *The Vocabulary of the Greek New Testament*, 628.

them as a father-child relationship, calling each of them his *teknon* "in the faith" (Phil. 2:22; 1 Tim. 1:2, 18; 2 Tim. 1:2; 2:1; Titus 1:4).

In the believers' spiritual relationship to the Lord, they are viewed as his children (Rom. 8:16–17, 21; 9:7–8 [twice]; Gal. 4:28, 31; Eph. 5:1, 8; Phil. 2:15; 1 Peter 1:14; 1 John 3:1–2, 10; 5:2; 2 John 4, 13). The unsaved are called "the children of wrath" (Eph. 2:3), that is, those over whom God's wrath hangs; and false teachers are "an accursed brood" (2 Peter 2:14), literally, "children of [God's] curse," that is, those who stand under God's curse.

John used seven of the nine occurrences of the diminutive *teknion*, "small child," to refer to his adult Christian readers affectionately (1 John 2:1, 12, 28; 3:7, 18; 4:4; 5:21; "dear children" in the NIV). Jesus addressed his disciples this way one time in the upper room (John 13:33), and Paul called his Galatian converts by this term (Gal. 4:19).

Words for a young person are *neanias* and *neaniskos*. *Neanias*, occurring four times and only in the Book of Acts, refers to Saul, who witnessed Stephen's martyrdom (7:58), Eutychus (20:9; he was also called a *pais*, 20:12), and Paul's nephew (23:17). The ten occurrences of *neaniskos* speak of the son of the widow of Nain (Luke 7:14), the rich young man who asked Jesus about eternal life (Matt. 19:20, 22), a young, unnamed man who followed Jesus when he was arrested but ran when officials grabbed him (Mark 14:51), one of the angels at Jesus' empty tomb (16:5), young men who, as Peter quoted Joel's prophecy, will see visions (Acts 2:17), young men who carried out dead Sapphira and buried her (5:10), and Paul's nephew (23:18, also called a *neanias* in v. 17). In addition, John addressed his readers as "young men" (*neaniskoi*, 1 John 2:13–14).[23]

From these four occurrences of *neanias* and ten uses of *neaniskos* it is difficult to determine the age range intended by these two words,[24] but apparently they refer to young adult men. They conversed with Jesus, Paul, and a Roman commander, were able to run, and were strong enough to carry out a corpse and bury it.[25]

The Greek *hyios*, usually translated "son," like the Hebrew *bēn*, refers to a son or boy, but also designates physical descendants, membership of a cate-

23. When John addressed believers as "dear children" (*teknia*, 1 John 2:12, and *paidia*, 2:14), "young men" (*neaniskoi*, 2:13–14), and "fathers" (*pateres*, 2:13–14), he may have been referring not to age differentiations, or stages of spiritual growth (Augustine's view), but to spiritual experiences of all his readers. That is, as spiritual "children" of God, they were forgiven; as spiritual "fathers," they knew the Father; and as spiritual "young men" they had spiritual victory over Satan (Zane C. Hodges, "1 John," in *The Bible Knowledge Commentary, New Testament*, ed. John F. Walvoord and Roy B. Zuck [Wheaton, Ill.: Victor Books, 1983]; and Westcott, *The Epistles of St. John*, 60).

24. Moulton and Milligan mention a papyrus that refers to a *neanias* of seventeen years of age (*The Vocabulary of the Greek New Testament*, 423).

25. *Neōteros* is a comparative adjective meaning "younger" and is used of the prodigal son as the younger of his father's two boys (Luke 15:12–13). The word also occurs in Luke 22:26; 1 Timothy 5:1–2, 11, 14; Titus 2:4; and 1 Peter 5:5 in reference to younger men, women, and widows.

gory or a group, a group of people, or a characteristic of an individual (as in "sons of disobedience," Eph. 5:6). "Son of God" points up Jesus' deity; he stands in a Father-Son relationship in the Trinity, and he is characterized by deity. The New Testament uses *hyios* 359 times, with 70 percent of the occurrences in the Gospels. Whereas in family contexts *teknon* and *teknia* point to one's origin as a "born one," *hyios* refers more to the status and privilege of the familial relationship between a son and his father.[26]

26. For more on *hyios* see W. von Martitz, "*hyios,*" in *Theological Dictionary of the New Testament,* 8 (1972): 335–40, and Edward Schwiezer, "*hyios,*" ibid., 8:363–92. For a summary of the New Testament terms for children, see Hans-Ruedi Weber, *Jesus and the Children* (Atlanta: John Knox Press, 1979), 52–60.

10

"HONOR YOUR FATHER AND YOUR MOTHER"

The Role of Children in Bible Families

Recreational Activities of Children in the Bible

We naturally associate children with play. Play is a child's response to the world around him, in which he enjoys playing with toys by himself, and then playing with others, and later developing various motor skills (e.g., bicycling, skating, or swimming), intellectual skills (e.g., checkers or chess), and sports. Though the Bible says little about children's play, the few references give brief insights into the subject, and verify the fact that even in biblical times childhood was a time of fun and leisure, as well as work. In describing wealthy, wicked people, Job commented that "they send forth their children as a flock—their little ones dance about" (Job 21:11). Isaiah predicted that in the Messiah's millennial reign children's natural curiosity about snake's holes will not result in their being harmed (Isa. 11:8). Speaking of the same time period, Zechariah noted that boys and girls will play in the "city streets" (Zech. 8:5).

Jesus remarked on children's games of imitation in the marketplaces in which they first playacted a wedding and then quickly changed (because of their short attention span?) to playact a funeral (Matt. 11:16–17; Luke 7:32). He suggested by this that his contemporaries were fickle and vacillating, not pleased with anything. They were not satisfied with John the Baptist's asceticism or with Jesus' indulgence.[1]

Because of the agricultural milieu in which they lived in Israel, most children, no doubt, soon developed skills relating to outdoor life, including hunting, fishing, and using the slingshot and bow and arrows. David illustrates the

---

1. Craig L. Blomberg, *Matthew,* New American Commentary (Nashville: Broadman Press, 1992), 189; William Hendriksen, *Exposition of the Gospel According to Matthew* (Grand Rapids: Baker Book House, 1973), 492–93.

effectiveness of an adolescent's use of the sling (1 Sam. 17:40, 48–49), and Jonathan was good at archery (1 Sam. 20:20). The fact that David's skillful warriors could shoot arrows or toss stones from a sling with either the right hand or the left (1 Chron. 12:2) possibly meant they had developed those skills earlier in life, perhaps as young boys.

Some children and young people also developed musical skills. Children who Jesus said acted out weddings in their playtime "played the flute" (Matt. 11:17). David's skill on the harp enabled him to have access to Saul's palace (1 Sam. 16:23; 18:10; 19:9; cf. Amos 6:5). Other musical instruments mentioned in the Bible include lyres, tambourines, cymbals, trumpets, horns, pipes, and zithers—string, wind, and percussion instruments—but we are not told at what ages individuals learned to play them. That young people (*bāḥûr*) played musical instruments is clear from Lamentations 5:14, which speaks of the young men stopping their music.[2]

Some animals make excellent pets for children. In a parable told to David, Nathan spoke of a poor man who bought a little ewe lamb that "grew up with him and his children" (2 Sam. 12:3). Dogs were normally scavengers (1 Kings 14:11; 21:19; 2 Kings 9:10), but a Canaanite woman talking with Jesus referred to dogs eating crumbs from a table (Matt. 15:27). God told Job that a crocodile would be inappropriate as a pet, though a girl might have a pet bird (Job 41:5).

Toys used by young children in the ancient Near East (e.g., Mesopotamia and Egypt) and in the Greco-Roman Empire may also have been played with by Israelite children.

Rattles, whistles, toys, teeter-totters, hoops, clay animals, dolls, toy dishes, knucklebones (a game something like jacks), kites, pull toys, a form of checkers, chess (played in Babylon before 2000 B.C.), swings, marbles, dice, yo-yos, balls, a stick with two small wheels, and even small chariots drawn by a donkey or a goat—many of these toys and games known in the ancient world are surprisingly similar to today's toys.[3] "In the rubble of biblical cities, archaeolo-

2. For a helpful discussion of musical instruments in the ancient Near East, with eleven pictorials, see D. E. Stradling and K. A. Kitchen, "Music and Musical Instruments," in *The Illustrated Bible Dictionary*, 3 vols. (Wheaton, Ill.: Tyndale House Publishers, 1980), 2:1031–40.

3. For discussion, sketches, and photographs of many of these toys, see Hugo Blümner, *The Home Life of the Ancient Greeks*, trans. Alice Zimmern, rev. ed. (New York: Cooper Square Publishers, 1966), 87–98; Mark Golden, *Children and Childhood in Classical Athens* (Baltimore: Johns Hopkins University Press, 1990), 19–20, 34, 54, 56, 69, 74; Barbara Kaye Greenleaf, *Children through the Ages* (New York: McGraw-Hill Book Co., 1978), 8–10; Ian Jenkins, *Greek and Roman Life* (London: Trustees of the British Museum, 1986), 31, 35; W. K. Lacey, *The Family in Classical Greece* (Ithaca, N.Y.: Cornell University Press, 1968), 134–35; *The Lion Encyclopedia of the Bible*, rev. ed. (Batavia, Ill.: Lion Publishing Corp., 1986), 189–92; Paul MacKendrick, "The World of Pericles," in *Greece and Rome: Builders of Our World*, ed. Merle Severy (Washington, D.C.: National Geographic Society, 1968), 139–40; Beryl Rawson, "Adult-Child Relationships in Roman Society," in *Marriage Divorce, and Children in Ancient Rome*, ed. Beryl Rawson (Oxford: Clarendon Press, 1991), 19–20; William H. Stephens, *The New Testament World in Pictures* (Nashville: Broadman Press, 1987), 331–32; and D. J. Wiseman, "Games," in *The Illustrated Bible Dictionary*, 1:540–42.

gists have found such durable children's toys as whistles, balls, dolls, animals, and models of furniture used perhaps in ancient dollhouses."[4]

In ancient Athens, children played "hide-and-seek, tug-of-war, blindman's bluff, trick or treat, ducks and drakes, and jackstones."[5] Boys learned archery, horseback riding, swimming, boating, disc throwing, javelin throwing, boxing, wrestling, and fencing.[6]

The Greek games formed the basis for special New Testament metaphors about the Christian life, including races (1 Cor. 9:24–26a; Gal. 2:2; 5:7; Phil. 2:16; Heb. 12:1–2) and boxing (1 Cor. 9:26b). People living in Israel in New Testament times would have been familiar with chariot racing in the Jerusalem amphitheater built by Herod, and the stadiums at Tiberias, Jericho, and Tarichaea.[7]

Responsibilities of Children

If someone were to ask you, "What does the Bible tell children to do?" what answer would you give? Probably many people would respond with two things: boys and girls are to trust the Lord and to obey their parents. But in addition to these two obligations, the Bible assigns a number of other responsibilities to children—nine altogether.

Honor and Respect Their Parents

The fifth commandment, "Honor your father and your mother" (Exod. 20:12; Deut. 5:16), is the only one of the ten addressed specifically to children and the only one with a promise. That promise ("so that you may live long in the land the LORD your God is giving you") probably refers not to a long life for each obedient individual, but to the duration of the nation Israel as God's covenant people. Through Malachi, the Lord reminded his people that just as "a son honors his father" they should honor him (Mal. 1:6).

In responding to a question by the Pharisees, Jesus quoted the words "Honor your father and mother" (Matt. 15:4; Mark 7:10) and then pointed out that they were hypocritical in failing to help their parents while appearing spiritual (Matt. 15:5–6; Mark 7:11–13). Again Jesus quoted these words about honoring one's parents when conversing with the rich young man (Matt. 19:19; Mark 10:19; Luke 18:20). Paul cited this command in Ephesians 6:2–3. His motivation—"that it may go well with you and that you may enjoy long life on the earth"—differs slightly from the promise in the Old Testament. This New Testament promise of prosperity and longevity for the

4. Edith Deen, *Family Living in the Bible* (New York: Harper & Row, Publishers, 1963), 92.
5. MacKendrick, "The World of Pericles," 140.
6. Blümner, *The Home Life of the Ancient Greeks*, 124–26, 265–305.
7. George Farmer, "Boyhood," in *A Dictionary of Christ and the Gospels*, ed. James Hastings, 2 vols. (New York: Charles Scribner's Sons, 1907), 1:222.

individual believer "states a general principle that obedience fosters self-discipline, which, in turn, brings stability and longevity in one's life."[8]

Leviticus 19:3 records the same command, worded in a slightly different way: "Each of you must respect his mother and father." One of the ways men become qualified for serving as an elder in the local church is by having children who regard him "with proper respect" (1 Tim. 3:4).

One way children honor their parents is by being proud of them ("parents are the pride of their children," Prov. 17:6b). Another way is by expressing love to them. The Bible records only three examples of men who kissed their parents: Jacob, who kissed his father Isaac (Gen. 27:27); Joseph, who wept over and kissed his father Jacob when he died (50:1); and Elisha, who kissed his parents good-by when he left them to join with Elijah (1 Kings 19:20). Rahab told Joshua and Caleb of her concern for the welfare of her family (Josh. 2:12–13); and David, out of concern for his parents' safety, sent them to Moab away from Saul's fury (1 Sam. 22:3–4). Jesus' care for his mother Mary is seen in his words from the cross when he committed her to John (John 19:26–27).

Under the Mosaic law, to dishonor one's parents resulted in a person being cursed (Deut. 27:16) by God, that is, subject to punishment by the Lord and his favor withdrawn. Cursing one's parents was so despicable that the Law viewed it as a crime deserving of capital punishment (Exod. 21:17; Lev. 20:9; Prov. 20:20). In Matthew 19:19 (cf. Mark 7:10) Jesus quoted the fifth commandment and also the penalty of death for cursing one's parents, as written in Exodus 21:17 and Leviticus 20:9. No record of such a sin and its consequent punishment are recorded in the Scriptures, so possibly it was never carried out; the threatened punishment may have served as a strong deterrent.

Robbing one's parents brings shame and disgrace to the robber (Prov. 19:26) and indicates that he is a destructive person (28:24), meaning perhaps that he destroys their reputation and peace. To curse one's father or to refuse to bless one's mother are associated with sins of pride, violence, and neglect of the poor (30:11–14), and results in death ("his lamp will be snuffed out," 20:20).

To mock a father with even a contemptuous glance or to make fun of obeying one's mother leads to an untimely and contemptible death: "The eye that mocks a father, that scorns obedience to a mother, will be pecked out by the ravens of the valley, will be eaten by the vultures" (30:17). In the southern kingdom of Judah, Micah accused the sons of dishonoring their fathers and the daughters of opposing their mothers (Micah 7:6). One of the reasons God judged Jerusalem by having it conquered by the Babylonians was the inhabitants' disdain for their fathers and mothers (Ezek. 22:7). In fact, slighting

8. Harold W. Hoehner, "Ephesians," in *The Bible Knowledge Commentary, New Testament*, ed. John F. Walvoord and Roy B. Zuck (Wheaton, Ill.: Victor Books, 1983), 642.

one's parents was one of the very first of more than a dozen sins Ezekiel mentioned in 22:7–12. Parental disrespect was a serious offense![9]

The ultimate act of disregard of one's parents was to murder them, which Paul mentioned in 1 Timothy 1:9. By contrast, mothers who are wise and diligent deserve their children's respect and blessing (Prov. 31:28). Even when mothers are old, they are not to be despised (23:22b), even if because of age they are unattractive physically, have medical problems, or are in need of constant care.

Respect for one's parents was to extend to respect for all elders. Moses wrote, "Rise in the presence of the aged, show respect for the elderly and revere your God. I am the Lord" (Lev. 19:32). Failure to do so was cause for alarm, as Job noted (Job 19:18; 30:1, 9–10).

Obey Their Parents

One of the saddest commentaries on the degeneration of any society is the disobedience of children toward their parents. In strong, specific language Paul wrote that disobeying one's parents ranks with other sins such as envy, murder, slander, deceit, and pride (Rom. 1:28–31), and that it is characteristic of the last days (2 Tim. 3:1–5). Disobedience to one's father or mother is no small matter; God considers it a serious transgression.

This is also evident in the Mosaic law, which states that a son who was persistently rebellious even after parental warnings was to be taken to the elders and, if judged guilty, was to be stoned to death (Deut. 21:18–21). Such a son was ultimately rebelling against the Lord. However, this legislation "was not cruel nor did it give parents a right to abuse their children."[10] "Contrary to its apparent severity, this law was designed to protect children and it marks a significant restraint upon the father's authority over his family. . . . We see here the beginnings of a recognition of social responsibility towards children. . . ."[11]

By refusing to live in sin, believers today please the Lord just as obedient children please their parents (1 Peter 1:14). Writing directly to children, Paul

---

9. In other cultures, too, children were expected to honor and respect their parents. For example, "The Instruction of Onchsheshonqy," an Egyptian writing, includes these exhortations: "Do not belittle an old man in your heart" and "May the son do honor to his father!" (Miriam Lichtheim, *Ancient Egyptian Literature: A Book of Readings*, 3 vols. [Berkeley, Calif.: University of California Press, 1980], 3:165 [7.22], 3:167 [10.21]). For similar instructions in pagan classical Athens, see Golden, *Children and Childhood in Classical Athens*, 102. Pempelus, a Greek moralist, wrote in his treatise "On Parents" that honoring one's parents is demanded by nature because they have given their offspring life and benefits (O. Larry Yarbrough, "Parents and Children in the Jewish Family of Antiquity," in *The Jewish Family in Antiquity*, ed. Shaye J. D. Cohen (Atlanta: Scholars Press, 1993), 53.

10. Jack S. Deere, "Deuteronomy," in *The Bible Knowledge Commentary, Old Testament*, ed. John F. Walvoord and Roy B. Zuck (Wheaton, Ill.: Victor Books, 1985), 301.

11. R. E. Clements, "The Relation of Children to the People of God in the Old Testament," *Baptist Quarterly* 21 (January 1986): 196.

urged them to follow their parents' commands because it is the right thing to do (Eph. 6:1) and it pleases the Lord (Col. 3:20).

An elder's qualifications include his managing his family well and seeing that his children obey him (1 Tim. 3:4), that they are believers, and that they are not charged by others as being "wild and disobedient" (Titus 1:6). "Wild" translates *asōtia,* meaning one who squanders his money extravagantly[12] or lives an unrestrained life, and "disobedient" renders the word *anypotaktos,* "unruly or insubordinate" (also used in 1 Tim. 1:9 and Titus 1:10, where it means rebellious).

By learning to respond to the authority of their parents, children learn to respect and respond to other authorities, an important lesson in life. To heed correction is a sign of wisdom (Prov. 15:32b). Learning to do what others tell them to do is not easy for children. They are naturally inclined to go their own way, to be disobedient, to be nonsubmissive and obstinate. No parent needs to teach his children to disobey; they do it naturally! In the proverb, "Folly is bound up in the heart of a child" (Prov. 22:15a), the word "folly" (*'ĕwîl*) means arrogant obstinance. This kind of person is "quick to quarrel" (20:3b) and "spurns his father's discipline" (15:5a). Because of this bent toward disobeying, wise parents begin correcting and disciplining their children at an early age. Left to themselves without learning obedience, children soon learn they can "get away" with whatever they want and that disobedience has no serious consequences. No wonder Paul wrote that it is "right" for children to obey their parents (Eph. 6:1). It is right because it helps direct children into proper conduct, it helps children avoid serious mistakes, it helps them avoid physical and spiritual harm now and in the future, and it brings honor to themselves (Prov. 13:18b).

Examples of disobedient offspring include Hophni and Phinehas, Eli's sons who were "wicked men,"[13] and "had no regard for God" (1 Sam. 2:12). Samuel's sons did not follow his godly example; as judges they acquired money dishonestly, accepted bribes, and perverted justice (1 Sam. 8:1–3). These adult sons were, no doubt, ungodly because their fathers had failed to teach them obedience as they were growing up. David's son Adonijah tried to usurp the throne by asserting himself (1 Kings 1:5). This act of defiance, as an adult, stemmed directly from the fact that David "had never interfered with him by asking, 'Why do you behave as you do?'" (1 Kings 1:6). Children need parental interference! Without it they grow up to disrespect their parents and others.

12. Fritz Rienecker and Cleon L. Rogers, Jr., *A Linguistic Key to the Greek New Testament* (Grand Rapids: Zondervan Publishing House, 1980), 651.
13. "Wicked men" is literally "sons of Belial." In Hebrew "Belial" combines two words meaning "without worth," and is used in Deuteronomy 13:13; 1 Samuel 1:16; 2:12; 10:27; 25:17; 30:22 ("troublemakers"); and 1 Kings 21:10, 13 ("scoundrels").

The boys who jeered at the prophet Elisha (2 Kings 2:23–24) revealed their innate sin nature, which apparently had not been curbed by their parents.

Bible examples of obedient children or teens include Isaac, who willingly went with his father Abraham on a three-day trip (Gen. 22:7); Jacob, who "obeyed his father and mother" who told him to go to Paddan Aram to find a wife (28:6–7); Saul, who went to look for his father's donkeys (1 Sam. 9:3–5); David, who obeyed his father by taking food to his brothers at a military camp (1 Sam. 17:17–20); the widow's son, who brought jars to his mother (2 Kings 4:5–6); and Jesus, who "was obedient" to Mary and Joseph when growing up in Nazareth (Luke 2:51).

Accept Discipline

Related to the command addressed to children to obey their parents is the call for the young to accept the discipline their fathers or mothers give them. Children naturally resist discipline because it is unpleasant and even painful (Heb. 12:11), but it is necessary ("what son is not disciplined by his father?" 12:7). To be effective, discipline is two-sided; it must be given by parents, and it must be received by children. Because of youngsters' innate dislike of being disciplined for wrongdoing and because they need correcting, the Book of Proverbs repeatedly summons boys and girls to accept parental discipline and correction.[14]

To spurn such discipline shows a person's folly (Prov. 1:7b; 15:5a) and stupidity (12:1b). The word "stupid" in 12:1 is *ba'ar*, "to be brutish or dull-minded," like an animal. Ignoring discipline even leads others astray (10:17b), perhaps by peer influence, and results in poverty and shame (13:18a), ignorance (19:27), and even death (15:10b). No wonder an undisciplined child actually despises himself (15:32a) and is a mocker (13:1b; 15:12a).

On the other hand, heeding discipline and accepting corrections or rebukes provides rewards (13:13b), knowledge (12:1a; 15:5b, 31, 32b; 29:15a), a full, meaningful life (6:23b; 10:17a), and honor (13:18b). Because of these lasting results, many people look back on their childhood with respect for their parents for disciplining them ("we have all had human fathers who disciplined us and we respected them for it," Heb. 12:9).

When parents discipline their boys and girls, they picture the Lord's spiritual discipline of believers, his own people (Deut. 8:5; Prov. 3:11–12; Heb. 12:7, 10). This discipline from the Lord—punishment for sin or correction of wrong conduct by God's Word and his Holy Spirit—demonstrates his love and their relationship to him as his sons, and leads to deeper holiness, and

---

14. *Mûsār*, the Hebrew word for discipline, means moral discipline whether given verbally or by spankings or other forms of correction. "Correction" translates *tokaḥat*, from *yākaḥ*, "to reprove, rebuke, chide, or correct verbally."

righteousness and peace (12:10–11). No wonder his discipline is "for our good" (12:10).

Learn from Parental Instruction

Parents, and especially fathers, are to instruct their own in the ways of God (Deut. 6:6–9), and children are to respond to that instruction. Twenty-seven verses in Proverbs challenge sons to heed parental teaching: 1:8; 3:1; 4:1–5, 10a, 13, 20–21; 5:1; 6:20–21; 7:1–3, 24; 8:32–33; 13:1, 13; 19:20; 22:17; 23:19, 22, 26.

In these verses parents admonish their sons to listen, pay attention, lay hold of, not forsake, not forget, keep, keep in their heart, bind, store up, guard, and apply their parents' teachings to their hearts. (For more on this, see Table 3 in chap. 8.)

Interestingly, Proverbs 1:8 and 6:20 mention the mother's teaching, and 31:1–9 record the instructions of a mother to her son Lemuel, a king. The "wife of noble character" also teaches her children: "faithful instruction is on her tongue" (31:26). Both parents are to be involved in teaching their children.

Results of receiving parental instruction are numerous: understanding the fear of the Lord (2:5) and upright living (2:9), having good companions (2:20), long life (3:2; 4:10), prosperity (3:2; 16:20), guidance (4:11–12; 6:23–24), life (4:22; 7:2), health (4:22), discretion and knowledge (5:2), self-preservation (19:16), wisdom (19:20), and ability to give sound (i.e., reliable) answers (22:21).

Listening to advice, whether from parents or others, is always wise (12:15; 13:10; 19:20).

Ask Their Parents about Spiritual Things

Spiritual activities in the home can provide wonderful teaching opportunities for parents. Rightly done, they can arouse boys' and girls' curiosity, so they ask questions about their meaning. In Israel, the Passover (Exod. 12:26–27), the consecration of the firstborn (13:13–16), and the setting up of twelve stones at Gilgal (Josh. 4:20–24), served to stimulate children's interest, causing them to inquire about their significance. "Ask your father," the Israelites were told, and "he will tell you" (Deut. 32:7). Today parents should be alert to similar teachable moments when their children ask about God and the Bible.

Fear the Lord

The father, possibly Solomon, who addressed his son in Proverbs 3, urged him to trust in the Lord, fear the Lord, and honor the Lord (Prov. 3:5, 7, 9). Children and young people are to heed the words of the wise "so that your trust may be in the Lord" (22:19). This includes hearing God's Word and worshiping him with their parents. Moses told the Israelites that every seven years the priests were to read the Law to the assembled men, women, and children so they could "learn to fear the LORD your God. . . . Their children, who do not know this law, must hear it and learn to fear the LORD your God" (Deut. 31:12–13). Joshua followed this command when the nation dedicated itself to the Lord at Mount Ebal. He read all the Law "to the whole assembly of Israel, including the women and the children" (Josh. 8:34–35). When Jehoshaphat, in the presence of the people of Judah, prayed for the Lord's deliverance from the Moabites and Ammonites, "all the men of Judah, with their wives and children [*bēnîm*, 'sons'] and little ones [*ṭap*] stood before the Lord" (2 Chron. 20:13). When the rebuilt walls of Jerusalem were dedicated to the LORD, the people, including women and children, rejoiced (Neh. 12:43).

Parents were told to "command your children to obey carefully all the words of this law" (Deut. 32:46). Obviously, then, children were to listen to God's Word and to respond to their parents' instruction by fearing the Lord. To fear the Lord means "to acknowledge his superiority over man, to recognize his deity and thus respond in awe, humility, worship, love, trust, and obedience."[15] Children are expected to join others in praising the Lord (Ps. 148:12), and young people are to "remember" their Creator (Eccles. 12:1), that is, to trust him, obey his commands, and serve him.[16] Youth are admonished to maintain personal purity by obeying God's Word (Ps. 119:9), to be exemplary in their speech, life, love, faith, and purity (1 Tim. 4:12), to pursue godly virtues (2 Tim. 2:22), and to be self-controlled (Titus 2:6). Children's actions reveal their character, showing whether they are pure and upright (Prov. 20:11).

As stated earlier, children were to ask questions of their parents about religious ceremonies (Exod. 12:26–27; 13:14–15). What a challenge this is to Christian parents today to live and worship in such a way that their children's curiosity and interest in spiritual things is aroused. This should be the goal toward which all parental instruction, discipline, and guidance is aimed: to encourage our children to trust the Lord. Apart from this goal, little else in life has meaning.

Imitate Their Parents

Young children tend to imitate what their parents and other caring adults do or say, whether good or bad. As fathers and mothers lead godly lives, they can be encouraged to know their children will imitate them. This fact was the basis of Paul's appeal to the believers at Ephesus to imitate the Lord, just as children who are loved imitate their parents (Eph. 5:1).

15. Roy B. Zuck, "A Theology of the Wisdom Books and the Song of Songs," in *A Biblical Theology of the Old Testament,* ed. Roy B. Zuck (Chicago: Moody Press, 1991), 215.
16. In Psalms 63:6 and 119:55 "remembering" the Lord parallels meditating on him and keeping the Law.

Care for Their Parents

As parents care for their children as they are growing up, so children should care for their elderly parents. This is especially important for elderly grandmothers who are widowed (1 Tim. 5:4–5, 16), an Old Testament example being Naomi, who was cared for by her grandson Obed (Ruth 4:15). Respect for one's elderly mother pleases the Lord (Prov. 23:22).

Burying one's parents was a responsibility of grown children, as seen in Esau and Jacob, both 120 years old, burying their 180-year-old father Isaac (Gen. 35:29), and 56-year-old Joseph and his brothers burying their 147-year-old father Jacob (50:7, 13–14).

Even pagans in the Roman Empire recognized the importance of caring for one's parents in their older years. Statesman and orator Cicero (106–43 B.C.) wrote, "To refuse to maintain one's parents is wicked."[17]

Work with and for Their Parents

In Bible times children shared in the work of the family. Cain worked in the fields, and Abel looked after flocks (Gen. 4:2). Rachel brought sheep to the well for water (29:6), and Jethro's seven daughters also got water for his flocks (Exod. 2:16). David, as an adolescent, looked after sheep (1 Sam. 16:11). The son of the Shunamite helped his father in the field (2 Kings 4:18). Jeremiah referred to children gathering wood for a fire (Jer. 7:18).

Children's Problems

Being a child is not easy. Besides being unable to do everything adults can do, and being the uncomfortable "object" of parental discipline, many children face other problems. Some of the problems boys and girls experience today were also known to children in Bible times.

Parental Partiality

Sometimes a parent favors one child over another, giving him or her more attention, love, or gifts than his or her siblings. Children notice this, and those who are slighted are hurt, and the favored ones may tend to develop a false sense of superiority.

A clear case of parental favoritism is Isaac who loved Esau, and Rebekah who loved Jacob (Gen. 25:28). This tension in the family resulted in elderly Isaac being tricked to give his blessing to his younger son Jacob, whose mother thought up the scheme, rather than to the elder son Esau (Gen. 27:1–40). Though this was God's plan, from the human standpoint it led to problems

---

17. *Letters to Atticus* 176.2 (see Garth R. Lambert, *Rhetoric Rampant: The Family under Siege in the Early Western Tradition* [London, Ont.: University of Western Ontario, 1982], 21).

between the siblings, with Jacob having to leave town (27:41–28:5) for twenty years (31:38).

Jacob himself became another case of parental partiality. He loved Joseph more than his other eleven sons because he was born in Jacob's old age (he was ninety-one years old, 37:3) and was born to his favorite wife Rachel. This, no doubt, contributed to the ten half brothers' jealousy and malice toward Joseph.

In-law Problems

Adjusting to one's in-laws can be difficult. This is illustrated in Isaac and Rebekah who were disappointed with their son Esau's two foreign wives, who were Hittites (Gen. 26:34–35; 28:8). In fact, Rebekah was so disgusted with them that she urged Isaac to send their twin son Jacob away to Paddan Aram to find an Israelite wife there (27:46–28:2).

In Micah's day Judah was so corrupt spiritually that daughters-in-law opposed their mothers-in-law (Micah 7:6). Jesus cited this verse in describing the results of his own ministry (Matt. 10:35; Luke 12:53): some family members would believe in him and some would not, resulting in family discord.

Children away from Home

Leaving home for the first time to go to camp or some other activity can be difficult for children. The Bible speaks of several children and young people who were away from home, most of whom were taken away unwillingly. These include 17-year-old Joseph, who was sold by his brothers to Egypt (Gen. 37:12–36) and lived there for 93 years, when he died at the age of 110 (50:26); Moses, who was raised as a boy in Pharaoh's palace in Egypt (Exod. 2:8–10); Naaman's servant girl, who was taken captive from Israel to Aram (2 Kings 5:1–3); and Daniel and his three companions, who were taken captive from Judah to Babylon (Dan. 1:3–7). Each of these seven children or young people trusted in the Lord and were faithful to him, even though they were many miles from their parents and their home country. This speaks well of the training they had received at home. Today godly parents can take courage in the fact that giving their children a strong spiritual upbringing can result in their offspring being faithful to the Lord, even when they are no longer under their parents' tutelage.

Sibling Rivalry

Every parent who has more than one child faces the problem of sibling conflict. Brothers and sisters argue and even fight, each wanting his or her own way. This problem is also seen in the Bible. Amazingly, Cain, the first child born into the human race, became a murderer by taking the life of his younger brother (Gen. 4:8). This cruel act stemmed from anger because the Lord did not favor Cain's offering (4:4–5), and the anger led to depression (4:6). This demonstrates the dire results that can eventuate from sibling jealousy, anger, and rivalry, which in Cain's case revealed his evil character (1 John 3:12).

Taking things into her own hands rather than trusting the Lord's timing, Sarah had Abraham bear a child by her Egyptian maidservant Hagar. Later, after Sarah gave birth to Isaac in her old age, Ishmael, then a teenager, made fun of Isaac (Gen. 21:9), and even "persecuted" him (Gal. 4:29). At Sarah's prodding, Abraham sent Hagar and Ishmael away (Gen. 21:10–21). Apparently, these half brothers never got together again until decades later when they together (when Isaac was seventy-five years old) buried their father Abraham (25:9). Since the Arabs have descended from Ishmael, the Arab-Israeli struggle today continues the sibling conflict begun more than four thousand years ago!

When Jacob fooled his father Isaac, thereby as the younger son receiving the blessing due the elder son (27:1–40), Esau "held a grudge against" his twin brother Jacob and was determined to kill him (27:41). It comes as no surprise, then, that when Jacob arranged to meet Esau twenty years later, Jacob was "in great fear and distress" (32:7). Later (as Isaac and Ishmael did with Abraham), Jacob and Esau together buried their 180-year-old father Isaac (35:28–29).

When Joseph was seventeen, his rivalry with his four half brothers born to Jacob's two maidservants Bilhah and Zilpah (30:3–13) was revealed by his giving a bad report about them to their father Jacob (37:2). All ten half brothers of Joseph, knowing he was their dad's favorite, "hated him and could not speak a kind word to him" (37:4). And his dreams about his superiority over them only inflamed their jealousy that much more (37:8, 11). Amazed at his dream, they asked, "Will you actually rule us?" (37:8). Rivalry among siblings was underway!

Miriam and Aaron expressed the feelings of many siblings when they complained, "Has the Lord spoken only through Moses? . . . Hasn't he also spoken through us?" (Num. 12:2). Centuries later Gideon bore seventy sons by his wives, and one son Abimelech by a concubine (Judg. 8:29–31). Rivalry between those legitimate sons and one illegitimate half brother led to Abimelech's murdering all but one of the seventy in an effort to quell any attempt on their part to assume leadership over the people (9:1–21).

Jephthah, also illegitimately born because his mother was a prostitute (11:1), experienced conflict with his half brothers, who drove him out of town (11:2–3). Typical of an older brother making fun of a younger brother is Eliab, who chided David for visiting their battle site. Eliab, Jesse's oldest son, even accused teenage David of being conceited and wicked (1 Sam. 17:28–29). Two other instances of sibling rivalry were between Amnon, David's eldest son, and his half sister Tamar, whom he raped (2 Sam. 13:1–19), and between Amnon and Absalom, who was Tamar's full brother and who killed Amnon (13:23–29) for his sin in clearly violating the Law (Lev. 18:9).

Reading the Old Testament narratives, one is readily struck by the preeminence of younger siblings over the older in several families: Abel rather than Cain was accepted by God; Adam's line was reckoned through Seth, not Cain; Isaac, not Ishmael, became the heir of Abraham; Jacob, not Esau, received his father Isaac's blessing; Rachel, the younger of two sisters, was Jacob's favored wife; Joseph, the eleventh son born to Jacob, was esteemed by Jacob higher than his half brothers; though Zerah's hand came out of his mother Tamar's womb first (Gen. 38:27–30), his twin brother Perez was in David's and Jesus' genealogical line (Ruth 4:18–21; Matt. 1:3); Ephraim, Joseph's younger son rather than Manasseh, was blessed by Joseph. Moses, the youngest of three, was leader of Israel, not Miriam or Aaron;[18] David, Jesse's youngest, was selected by God to be Israel's second king (1 Sam. 16:10–13), and Solomon, not David's oldest son, became the third king. Though "the older will serve the younger," as God said to Rebekah (Gen. 25:23), the "rejected" siblings were often blessed along with the chosen. "Both Leah and Rachel married Jacob, just as both Isaac and Ishmael founded nations; both Jacob and Esau were given dominion and fertility, and both Ephraim and Manasseh were promised future greatness."[19] These examples show that God often does the unexpected and that his actions are gratuitous.

Even Plutarch (A.D. 46?–120?), Greek moralist, wrote about the problem of sibling conflict in Greek history. He wrote that enmity between brothers may arise "from rivalry for parents' affection, differences in ability or achievement, competition for honors or office, the instigation of wives and other intimates, the roles of younger and older, or childhood squabbles."[20] These reasons correspond with some of the cases of sibling rivalry recorded in the Bible. Several of these factors seem to have been part of the rivalry between the prodigal son and his brother, and between the brother and their father (Luke 15:25–31).

However, we should not think that all siblings in the Bible were rivals. Full brothers generally had strong relationships, as seen in Joseph's concern for his younger brother Benjamin (Gen. 43:34). Brothers can help each other in difficult times: "A brother is born for adversity" (Prov. 17:17b). A brother (as well as a father) was responsible to protect the honor of his sister; "thus the sons of Jacob spoke of Dinah as 'our daughter' (Gen. 34:17), and Absalom

18. Aaron was three years older than Moses (Exod. 7:7).
19. Frederick E. Greenspahn, *When Brothers Dwell Together: The Preeminence of Younger Siblings in the Hebrew Bible* (New York: Oxford University Press, 1994), 133.
20. Plutarch *On Brotherly Love* (*Moralia* 478A–492D), cited in Golden, *Children and Childhood in Classical Athens,* 118.

felt more deeply aggrieved over the crime against Tamar than did David himself" (2 Sam. 13:21).[21]

Illnesses of Children

Parents hate to see their offspring suffer from injury, illness, or disease, or to be maimed in some way. Naturally, loving parents are anxious for them to enjoy full health.

The Bible records this concern of parents for children who were sick or maimed. Mephibosheth, Jonathan's son, became crippled at the age of five (2 Sam. 4:4). David and Bathsheba's illegitimate baby died after a seven-day illness (12:15, 18). Abijah, son of Jeroboam, king of Israel's northern tribes, died of an illness (1 Kings 14:1, 12), as Ahijah the prophet predicted. The son of the widow of Zarephath became ill and "grew worse and worse" and died (1 Kings 17:17), but God used Elijah to bring the boy back to life (17:18–24). Elisha too was used by the Lord to restore to life a boy who died of a sunstroke (2 Kings 4:18–21, 32–39).

Jesus' healing ministry touched the lives of a number of children. He healed an official's son (John 4:43–53) "who was close to death" with a fever (4:47, 52), he delivered a girl of Syrophoenicia from demon possession (Matt. 15:21–28; Mark 7:24–30), and he healed a demon-possessed boy who was an epileptic and was speechless, an only child of his parents (Matt. 17:14–18; Mark 9:14–29; Luke 9:37–43a).

Two children who died were raised back to life by Jesus. One was the son of a widow of Nain, as they were in the funeral procession to the gravesite (Luke 7:11–17). The other was Jairus's twelve-year-old daughter (Matt. 9:18–26; Mark 5:22–43; Luke 8:41–56).

Sometimes children are born with physical maladies. This was true of a man who had been born blind and whom Jesus healed (John 9:1–7), and of two men who were crippled from birth, one of whom was healed by Peter and John in Jerusalem (Acts 3:1–10), and the other who was healed by Paul in Lystra (14:8–10).

Jesus' love for children means that he feels compassion toward children when they are sick, physically or intellectually disabled, or emotionally handicapped.

Children Born out of Wedlock

As noted in chapter 2, approximately 1 million children in the United States were born illegitimately in 1993. That is 26 percent of the 4 million births in 1993, which compares with 11 percent in 1970.[22] Add to the figure

21. Ella Davis Issacs and Nathan Isaacs, "Relationships, Family," in *International Standard Bible Encyclopedia*, 4 (1988): 76.

22. The most recent figures indicate that in 1994 more than 30 percent of all births in America were nonmarital births, compared with 5.3 percent in 1960 (*Marriage in America: A Report to the Nation* [New York: Institute for American Values, 1995], 7).

of 1 million the many others who were born out of wedlock in years before 1993, and the number of illicit children in this nation is staggering.

This flies directly in the face of God's clear prohibition against premarital and extramarital relations. And yet a number of children referred to in the Bible were born illegitimately. These included Moab and Ben-Ammi, sons born by the incestuous relationship of Lot's two daughters (Gen. 19:30–38), from whom descended the Moabites and Ammonites, perpetual enemies of Israel. Tamar's two sons, Perez and Zerah, were born by her incestuous relationship with her father-in-law Judah (38:1–30). David and Bathsheba gave birth to an illegitimate boy who died in infancy (2 Sam. 12:15–23), and Gomer, the prophet Hosea's estranged wife, gave birth to three children by illicit relations (Hosea 1:2–9).

Incest, illicit sexual involvement with one's relatives, was clearly forbidden in the Scriptures. Incest was usually with adolescent or adult relatives, but even relations with a daughter or granddaughter (Lev. 18:17; 20:14) or daughter-in-law (Ezek. 22:11) were forbidden. The emotional scars resulting from such a deplorable sin make this offense against children a diabolically reprehensible act.

Orphans

To have a close family member, such as a sibling, half sibling, or stepsibling, as a constant rival in one's childhood would be disturbing. To have a parent who displays favoritism toward one of his or her children would be a problem for the neglected child. To be ill as a child, unable to treat oneself, would also be disquieting. But to be without a father would be most frightening.

Historically, many children have become fatherless as a result of war, accidents, or illness. By the time children in America born in 1870 turned fifteen, about 15 percent of them had experienced the death of their fathers.[23] But because of medical advances, only about 3 percent of all children born in 1950 lost their fathers through death before reaching age fifteen.[24]

Today, however, the principal cause of fatherlessness in America is paternal choice. Through divorce or through fathering a child apart from marriage and then leaving the mother and child, "millions of men today are voluntarily abdicating their fatherhood."[25] In 1900 three out of every four single parents were widowed, but by contrast, in 1992 "only about 5 percent of all female-headed households with children had experienced the death of the father."[26] Stated another way, in 1970, 11 percent of America's children were living

23. Peter Uhlenberg, "Changing Configurations of the Life Course," in *Transactions: The Family and the Life Course in Historical Perspective,* ed. Tamara K. Hareven (New York: Academic Press, 1978), 78.

24. Ibid., 78–79.

25. David Blankenhorn, *Fatherless America* (New York: Basic Books, 1995), 23.

26. Ibid., 22–23.

with their mothers only, but in 1993 that group climbed to 23 percent.[27] And that represents one out of four of all the nation's children! In 1970, 3 percent of the children who were living with only their mothers had mothers who were divorced, but in 1993 that group tripled to 9 percent.[28]

While a child grieves over the loss of a father by death, he still has the memories of that father-child relationship. But being abandoned voluntarily by one's father leaves deep, almost unerasable, emotional scars on a child. "The primary consequences of fatherlessness are rising male violence and declining child well-being."[29] Paternal abandonment of children is "the underlying source of our most important social problems, especially those rooted in violence."[30]

The Bible speaks often of orphans or the fatherless—forty-three times in the Old Testament and only twice in the New. In Bible times being fatherless normally resulted from paternal death, often by war and not by divorce. In the Old Testament "fatherless" and "orphans" translate the same Hebrew word. We think of an orphan as a child without either parent and the fatherless as one living with his or her mother. But the Bible makes no such distinction. If a child was without a father, he was considered an orphan, even though he was living with his mother. This is because "in most cases a father was the family's sole source of material security. If he no longer was alive, the family unit faced financial difficulties."[31]

Therefore, Israelites were strongly encouraged to aid orphans or to take them into their families (Job 29:12; 31:17). Because of their helplessness, they were easy prey to oppression—being robbed (Job 24:3; Isa. 10:2), kidnapped (Job 24:9), acquired by gambling (Job 6:27), or even murdered (Ps. 94:6). To oppress orphans was a sign of wickedness (Job 22:9). No wonder the fatherless often lived in fear (Ps. 10:18). Therefore, a terrible curse to pronounce on the wicked was to wish that their children be fatherless (Ps. 109:9, 12).

God champions the cause of the fatherless (Deut. 10:18; Pss. 10:14, 18; 68:5; 146:9; Jer. 49:11; Hosea 14:3), evidenced by the fact that in the Mosaic law God stipulated certain provisions for them. Their rights of inheritance were to be protected (Num. 27:7–11), their property was to be safeguarded (Prov. 23:10), they were to be free to glean the fields and vineyards (Deut. 24:19–21), to be allowed

27. U.S. Bureau of the Census, *Statistical Abstract of the United States 1994* (Washington, D.C.: U.S. Department of Commerce, 1994), 66.

28. Ibid.

29. Blankenhorn, *Fatherless America*, 26, 240–41, n. 3.

30. Ibid. Blankenhorn states that having a father enriches children in four ways: it provides physical protection for the child, it gives children material resources, it provides paternal cultural transmission, and it gives children the day-to-day nurturing they want and need from both parents (ibid., 25).

31. William L. Coleman, *Today's Handbook of Bible Times and Customs* (Minneapolis: Bethany House Publishers, 1984), 141.

to participate in the annual feasts (Deut. 16:11, 14), and to receive a portion of tithe crops collected every three years (Deut. 14:29; 26:12). The Israelites were to treat the fatherless with justice (Deut. 24:17; Ps. 82:3); failure to do so meant being judged by God (Deut. 27:19; Mal. 3:5). Those who took advantage of helpless orphans would themselves be killed, with the result that their own children would become childless (Exod. 22:22–24). God will "take up their case" against the oppressors of orphans (Prov. 23:11). While defending the city of Jerusalem against the Babylonian invasion in 586 B.C., many Jewish fathers were killed in battle, resulting in their boys and girls becoming orphans (Lam. 5:3). The prophets frequently spoke out against oppression of the fatherless (Isa. 1:17, 23; Jer. 5:28; 7:6; 22:3; Ezek. 22:7; Zech. 7:10).

The word for orphans occurs only twice in the New Testament. In John 14:18 Jesus promised he would not leave his followers as orphans, that is, desolate; he added, "I will come to you," possibly referring to his resurrection.[32] His death would not conceal his promises, for in three days he would be with them again.

The concern in the Old Testament for widows and orphans is echoed in James 1:27, in which James said a genuine relationship to the Lord is expressed in outward acts, including "looking after orphans and widows in their distress."[33]

Believers today do well to follow both the Old Testament example of caring for the fatherless and the New Testament admonition of James 1:27. Christians can help single-parenting mothers in a variety of ways: babysitting their children without pay, running errands for them, helping in housecleaning or house repairs, taking their children to activities such as playgrounds, sports events, circus performances, and camps. Boys without fathers welcome Christian men who befriend them and spend time with them. To neglect today's fatherless children—of which there are many—is to overlook one of the greatest needs in our nation and to fail to express our trust in the Lord in a tangible way. Being "a helper of the fatherless" (Ps. 10:14) can offset, to some degree, the dolorous condition of children living without their fathers or either parent.

32. That these words of Jesus referred to his return to his disciples by means of his resurrection (rather than the Holy Spirit's coming on the day of Pentecost or Jesus' yet future second coming) is suggested by his words in the next verse: "You will see me; Because I live, you also will live" (John 14:19). See Edwin A. Blum, "John," in *The Bible Knowledge Commentary, New Commentary*, 323–24.

33. *Thlipsis*, "distress," is the general word for trouble, difficulty, or tribulation.

11

"UNTO US A CHILD IS BORN"

Jesus' Birth and Boyhood

Night and day. Light and dark. Cold and heat. Sunshine and rain. Desert and forest.

These striking contrasts in nature pale into insignificance when you consider the contrasts between the circumstances surrounding Jesus' birth and the circumstances relating to childbirth today in most Western countries.

Pregnancy tests. Sonograms. Regular medical checkups. Prenatal classes for wives and husbands. Hospital sessions for siblings of the yet-to-be-born. Nearby hospitals with specially equipped obstetric units. Immaculately clean hospital labor and delivery rooms, with technological medical equipment. Epidural injections to ease labor pains. Highly trained obstetricians. Experienced nurses. Separate nurseries for bathing and monitoring the baby for hours following birth. Food delivered to the mother from the hospital kitchen.

None of these helps was available when Jesus was born! Think of how frightening it would be to a mother today to deliver her baby in a barn.[1] No

---

1. Kenneth E. Bailey has championed the view that "the inn" of Luke 2:7 refers to a guest room in a peasant's house; that Joseph, being a descendant of David, would have had relatives in Bethlehem who would have welcomed him to their home; that Jesus was born in the living quarters of such a house because the guest room (the "inn") was occupied; that the mangers (animal feeding troughs) were inside the house but on a lower level; that the house may have been built into the side of a cave; and that Jesus, therefore, was born in the living quarters of a peasant home and placed in a manger inside the home ("The Manger and the Inn: The Cultural Background of Luke 2:7," *Theological Review* 11 [1979]: 33–44; cf. B. Witherington III, "Birth of Jesus," in *Dictionary of Jesus and the Gospels,* ed. Joel B. Green, Scot McKnight, and I. Howard Marshall [Downers Grove: InterVarsity Press, 1992], 69–70). Though the other two occurrences of the word for "inn" *(katalyma)* are in Mark 14:14 and Luke 22:11, where it does mean a guest room (the "upper room"), it must be recognized that Luke 2:7 refers to "*a katalyma* of a house." Could *katalyma* not refer, as traditionally understood, to a lodging place (a great house) for travelers? Even if Jesus were born in a house and not a barn, the manger in which he was placed at birth bespeaks his modest, humble beginnings. Early tradition—Justin Martyr (ca. A.D. 100–165) *Dialogue with Trypho* 78, and Origen (ca. 185–254) *Against Celsus* 1.52—asserts that he was born in a cave, used for both a dwelling place and a shelter for cattle (James Orr, "Jesus Christ," in *International Standard Bible Encyclopedia,* 3 (1939):1632.

accompanying physician. No nurse. Not even a midwife. Alone, seventy-five miles away from one's hometown, relatives, and friends. The high possibility of infection to the baby or mother from the surrounding unsanitary conditions. No way to ease her excruciating labor pains. No way to adjust the temperature.

Truly these were extraordinarily despicable circumstances for Jesus' birth! And yet the physical surroundings of his birth were only one of the several unlikely, surprising aspects of his entry into the world. Consider the following facts.

Facts about Jesus' Birth

He Was Born of a Virgin

From the human viewpoint, Jesus' virgin birth seemed a biological impossibility. Starting with Cain, every baby born into the world has been conceived by the sperm of a man uniting with the ovum of a woman. In Jesus' case, however, no male was involved. His mother Mary became pregnant by a miraculous work of God, the Holy Spirit.[2] As the angel Gabriel told Joseph, to whom Mary was pledged to be married, "What is conceived in her is from the Holy Spirit" (Matt. 1:20). Gabriel also assured Mary, "The Holy Spirit will come upon you, and the power of the Most High will overshadow you" (Luke 1:35).

Imagine! A virgin—a young, unmarried woman who had had no sexual relations with a man—becoming pregnant and giving birth to a boy! The profound uniqueness of Jesus' birth is seen in the fact that he is the only one of whom it can be said, he was "born of a woman" (Gal. 4:4), that is, he was not conceived by a man and a woman.

Some people object to Jesus' virgin birth (actually virginal conception) by pointing out that the female ovum contains half the forty-six chromosomes that are in every cell of the human body, and that the other twenty-three chromosomes come from the male sperm. How could Jesus be fully human, it is asked, if he had no human father? The answer is that "the Holy Spirit fashioned the necessary genes and chromosomes" normally supplied by the male sperm.[3] The sperm cell which united with Mary's ovum was of divine, not human, origin.[4]

---

2. As Bernard Ramm wrote, "The virgin birth of Jesus Christ is a biological miracle" (*The Christian View of Science and Scripture* [Grand Rapids: Wm B. Eerdmans Publishing Co., 1954], 205).

3. J. Stafford Wright, "Virgin Birth," in *The Illustrated Bible Dictionary*, 3 vols. (Wheaton, Ill.: Tyndale House Publishers, 1980), 3:1626.

4. Ibid. Cf. idem, "The Virgin Birth as a Biological Necessity," *Faith and Thought* 95 (1966–67): 19–29.

His Birth Was Predicted Hundreds of Years in Advance

Think of the time of the Crusades in Europe, starting shortly before A.D. 1100 and ending about two hundred years later, just before A.D. 1300. Christians traveled to Jerusalem in large groups in several unsuccessful attempts to free the city from the Muslims. Suppose someone around A.D. 1200, the time of the Fourth Crusade, predicted the unusual birth of a certain individual in a specifically named town in the year 1900—seven hundred years in advance! From a human standpoint, such a prediction would be impossible. And yet that is what happened with regard to Jesus' birth. Two individuals, not just one, predicted Jesus' birth seven hundred years in advance. Isaiah wrote that Jesus would be born of a virgin (Isa. 7:14), and Isaiah's contemporary, Micah, prophesied the exact place—the small village of Bethlehem—where he would be born (Micah 5:2). Only God could have enabled those prophets to pronounce such facts so far ahead. Jesus' virgin birth and his village birth fulfilled these prophecies with precision!

When Isaiah recorded the prophecy of Isaiah 7:14, "The virgin will be with child and will give birth to a son, and will call him Immanuel," he used the word *ʿalmāh*, rendered "virgin." Some say this word should be translated "young woman," suggesting that *beṭûlāh* is more properly understood as virgin. They propose that *ʿalmāh*, "young woman," refers not only to Mary, but also to a historical person in Isaiah's day, such as the wife of King Ahaz, the wife of Isaiah, or some other unnamed Israelite woman. However, several factors argue against this double reference view. First, in its eight occurrences in the Old Testament,[5] *ʿalmāh* never refers to a married woman. It always refers to a sexually mature, marriageable woman. Second, the Septuagint, the Greek translation of the Old Testament, has the word *parthenos*, which clearly means a virgin. Third, in Matthew's quotation of this verse in Matthew 1:23 he too used the word *parthenos*. Fourth, while *beṭûlāh* sometimes means a virgin, other times it refers to a young married woman, as in Joel 1:8. Rebekah was called a *beṭûlāh*, but to clarify that she was a virgin the explanation was added that "no man had ever lain with her" (Gen. 24:16). In other words, *beṭûlāh* by itself does not clearly specify virginity as does *ʿalmāh*. Fifth, Isaiah wrote of "*the* virgin." (Also, the Greek has the definite article in Matthew 1:23.) What other woman other than Mary, Jesus' mother, could qualify as *the* virgin who was pregnant? Any other woman, such as Ahaz's or Isaiah's wife, would no longer be a virgin when she became pregnant. Mary was the world's only "pregnant virgin."

In addition, the Hebrew *hārāh*, rendered in the NIV "will be with child," is not a verb or participle, but is an adjective meaning "pregnant."[6] "Literally,

---

5. Genesis 24:43; Exodus 2:8; 1 Chronicles 15:20; Psalm 68:25; Proverbs 30:19; Song of Songs 1:3; 6:8; Isaiah 7:14.

6. J. A. Alexander, *Commentary on the Prophecies of Isaiah* (reprint, Grand Rapids: Zondervan Publishing House, 1953), 172.

the verse reads, 'Behold the pregnant virgin is bearing [or 'will bear'] a son and she calls [or 'will call'] his name Immanuel.'"[7] The "sign" of which Isaiah spoke is that the virgin was still a virgin during her pregnancy. Sixth, among Jews today ʿalmāh clearly means a virgin.

Another indication of the virgin birth is Mary's question in Luke 1:34: "How will this be since I am a virgin?" She would hardly be puzzled over a natural conception. "The thing that puzzled her was the fact that this child was to be conceived in her before she began living with Joseph."[8]

How could Micah's prediction of Jesus' birthplace in Bethlehem be fulfilled when Mary was living in Nazareth (Luke 2:4–5), seventy-five miles north? God handled that problem by simply having the Roman emperor Caesar Augustus, residing in Rome 1,400 miles away, decree that a census be taken throughout the entire Roman world (2:1). Since this decree required everyone to register in his ancestral hometown, Joseph, a descendant of David, had to register in David's birthplace, Bethlehem (2:11; cf. 1 Sam. 16:1, 13).

According to common belief, Mary was nine months pregnant when she and Joseph made the trip, and she delivered the baby as soon as they arrived in Bethlehem. However, Luke 2:6 seems to allow for a few days or possibly weeks after their arrival in Bethlehem before the baby Jesus arrived: "While they were there, the time came for the baby to be born." And yet, Caesar's decree was providentially timed so that Mary was sure to be in Bethlehem, in accord with Micah's prophecy. Probably riding on a donkey for several days, Mary would have been extremely uncomfortable. And the jouncing of the donkey ride could have induced her delivery en route over the steep hills of Ephraim before they reached their destination. But again God overrode those risks, and Jesus was born exactly where the prophecy had specified.

His Birth Was Announced by Angels

No postman delivered clever birth announcement cards to Joseph and Mary's friends and relatives. No local newspaper listed Jesus as a new arrival. No hospital marquee publicized his coming.

Instead, an angel brought the news to shepherds who were watching their sheep at night (Luke 2:8–14). These lowly laborers, who remain anonymous to us, spread the news of the arrival of this one whom the angel said was the "Savior . . . Christ the Lord" (2:11). They were "the first believers [in Jesus], the first worshippers [sic], the first preachers" of his birth.[9] As with any birth, the people who heard the news were happy and grateful to the Lord (2:17–18, 20).

7. Robert G. Gromacki, *The Virgin Birth* (reprint, Grand Rapids: Baker Book House, 1981), 148.

8. S. Lewis Johnson, Jr., "Whose Son Is He?" *Eternity,* December 1954, 7.

9. Orr, "Jesus Christ," 3:1633.

His Birth Was Timed Perfectly

Some babies are born "full term," exactly forty weeks after conception. Others, however, "choose" to come days or weeks earlier or a few days later. No expectant mother knows exactly when she will give birth to her baby (except those prescheduled by their doctors for labor inducement or a Caesarean section).

Some babies arrive at convenient times, when the father is off work or is otherwise available. But most babies come at inconvenient times—in the middle of the night, or in the middle of the week, for example. Some babies are born quickly, soon after the mother's labor pains begin, whereas others seem to stall their arrival. New arrivals have come in odd places—in taxis, cars, motels, even airplanes.

Jesus' birth, though inconvenient to Joseph and Mary because of their travels to Bethlehem, was timed perfectly, in accord with God's schedule. The Lord Jesus was born "in the fullness of time" (Gal. 4:4, KJV), that is, at the most appropriate time. Several factors demonstrate that Jesus' incarnation was perfectly timed.

One such factor was the *Pax Romana* ("Roman peace"). Caesar Augustus, born as Gaius Octavius, ended over one hundred years of civil war by his victory over Mark Antony and Cleopatra in 31 B.C. He became Rome's first emperor, ruling from 31 B.C. to A.D. 14. He introduced a number of reforms resulting in extensive peace and increased prosperity. Augustus's reign began a two-hundred-year period of peace, in which other countries were unable to wage a major war against Rome. In writing of his accomplishments, he alluded to his having established peace.[10] The well-trained Roman army helped maintain this peace. In Augustus's day, in about 20 B.C., the army consisted of 350,000 soldiers. Each Roman legion included about 6,000 infantrymen and 120 cavalrymen. Centurians, mentioned twenty-one times in the Synoptic Gospels and Acts, each commanded about 100 soldiers. Jesus was born into this world of relative peace from military conflict. This facilitated his ministry and made it relatively easy for Christianity to spread across the empire. Peace and order in the Roman province of Judea had been established by Herod the Great in 37 B.C., several years before Jesus' birth. A factor in Herod's peaceful and prosperous rule in Judea was his personal friendship with Augustus.

A second factor was the construction of Roman roads and bridges, many of them built by soldiers. This road system linked the entire empire from Britain to the Persian Gulf with a network of 50,000 miles of highway and 200,000 miles of secondary roads.[11] "The Romans traveled about more easi-

---

10. Augustus *Rex Gestae* ("Acts of Augustus") 13.25.34.
11. John J. Putnam, "Conqueror's Path to Mighty Empire," in *Greece and Rome: Builders of Our World,* ed. Merle Severy (Washington, D.C.: National Geographic Society, 1968), 421.

ly, quickly, and safely than any other people before them or after them until the 1700s."[12] In addition, commercial and military ships sailed the Mediterranean Sea, further facilitating travel. Clearly, Roman roads and ships aided the spread of Christianity.

A third element marking Jesus' incarnation as coming at an ideal time was the Greek language, spoken almost universally from 300 B.C. In his conquests from 334 to 323 B.C. Alexander the Great spread Greek culture and the Greek language throughout the then-known civilized world. Koine, a simplified form of Attic Greek, became the language of commerce, politics, government, and education. Many people were bilingual, speaking their own local language but also using Greek. Jesus' mother tongue was Aramaic, the native language of Palestine in the first century. But he, no doubt, also spoke Hebrew and Greek.[13] The widespread use of Greek aided the communication of the gospel by Jesus and his followers. Since Koine was dominant from the Tiber River in Italy to the Tigris River in Persia and beyond, it is no accident that the New Testament was written in that language and did not need to be translated until about A.D. 200.[14]

A fourth factor pointing to the timeliness of the Lord's incarnation is the development of Jewish synagogues. Possibly having been started during the Babylonian captivity five hundred years before Christ, synagogues in the time of Jesus had been established wherever Jews had settled. Since Jewish male adults were given opportunity in the synagogues to read and comment on the Old Testament Scriptures,[15] Jesus often taught in the synagogues of Galilee (Matt. 4:23; 9:35; Mark 1:39; Luke 4:15), and more specifically, in Capernaum (Mark 1:21; Luke 4:31–33; John 6:59) and Nazareth (Matt. 13:54; Mark 6:2; Luke 4:16). He also taught in the synagogues of Judea (Luke 4:44). When questioned by Annas the high priest about his teaching, Jesus said he taught openly "in synagogues or at the temple, where all the Jews come together" (John 18:20). He also healed three individuals in synagogues: a demon-possessed man (Mark 1:23; Luke 4:33), a man with a withered hand (Matt. 12:9; Mark 3:1; Luke 6:6), and a woman crippled for eighteen years (Luke 13:10).

The presence of synagogues in many cities in the Roman world would have enabled many Jews to hear the gospel through the ministry of Jesus' followers. Without the practice of assembling regularly in the synagogues, the Savior's message might not have spread so rapidly to a good number of Jews.

12. William F. McDonald, "Roman Empire," in *The World Book Encyclopedia*, 1964 ed., 16:386.

13. For evidence of his having spoken all three languages, see Roy B. Zuck, *Teaching as Jesus Taught* (Grand Rapids: Baker Book House, 1995), 64–65.

14. Bo Riecke, *The New Testament Era*, trans. David E. Green (Philadelphia: Fortress Press, 1968), 40.

15. Usually the synagogue sermon was given "by one who had already devoted some study and thought to the text or by a visiting rabbi" (William S. LaSor and Tamara C. Eskenazi, "Synagogue," in *International Standard Bible Encyclopedia*, 4 (1988): 683.

Paul frequently taught and preached in synagogues outside Judea and Galilee, thus helping spread the gospel quickly to Jews living abroad (Acts 22:19; 26:11). He communicated in synagogues in Damascus (Acts 9:20), Salamis (13:5), Pisidian Antioch (13:14), Iconium (14:1), Thessalonica (17:1–2), Berea (17:10), Athens (17:17), Corinth (18:4), and Ephesus (18:19, 26; 19:8).

A fifth element that suggests the well-timed appearance of the Savior is the Roman and Jewish anticipation that a great ruler would come from Judea. The Roman historians, Tacitus (ca. A.D. 55–120) and Suetonius (A.D. 69?–140), both attested to this expectation.[16] How appropriate that the Savior of the world was born at the very time some people were looking for the coming of a Savior!

Jesus' first coming was providentially timed—when the world was enjoying a relative degree of freedom from military aggression, when roads helped facilitate the travels of the messengers of the gospel, when a common language and Jewish places of worship and teaching helped advance the extension of Christianity, and when some people were anticipating the coming of a world ruler from Judea.

Questions about Jesus' Birth

When Was Jesus Born?

Several questions about Jesus' birth puzzle readers of the Gospels. One pertains to the year he was born. Because B.C. marks the years before Jesus' birth and A.D. (Anno Domini, "After the Lord") refers to years following his birth, many people assume his birth year was A.D. 1. However, in A.D. 525 Pope John I asked Dionysius Exiguus, a monk in Rome, to standardize the calendar in relation to the birthdate of Christ. But Dionysius miscalculated that date by four years. Following a statement by Clement of Alexandria that Christ was born in the twenty-eighth year of Caesar Augustus's reign, Dionysius said Augustus began reigning in 27 B.C. Actually, though, Augustus had assumed the throne four years earlier in 31 B.C.

Also, Jesus was born when Herod the Great was king of Judea (Matt. 2:1). Since Herod died in 4 B.C., Jesus was born in or before that year.[17]

According to Luke 2:1–3, Jesus' birth occurred after a census was ordered by Caesar Augustus, at which time Quirinius was governor of Syria. A census

---

16. Tacitus *Annals* 5.13 and Suetonius *Vespasian* 4.5. Suetonius wrote, "There had spread over all the Orient an old and established belief that it was fated at that time for men coming from Judaea [*sic*] to rule the world." Brown points out that Virgil (70–19 B.C.), a Roman poet, bore witness "to wide expectation of a world ruler who would bring peace" (Raymond E. Brown, *The Birth of the Messiah*, rev. ed. [New York: Doubleday & Co., 1993], 189, n. 29; see Virgil *Fourth Eclogue*).

17. While scholars debate the year of Herod's death, it is noteworthy that Josephus mentioned that an eclipse of the moon occurred just before Herod died (*The Antiquities of the Jews* 17.167). That eclipse occurred on March 12/13, 4 B.C. The Jews celebrated the Passover after Herod's death (ibid., 17.213), and the feast that year was on April 11, 4 B.C. Therefore, Herod died between March 12 and April 11. Jesus, then, was born sometime before March 12, 4 B.C. (Witherington, "Birth of Jesus," 66–67).

under Quirinius (who served from A.D. 6 to A.D. 9) occurred in A.D. 6,[18] which seems to contradict the proposal that Jesus was born in or before 4 B.C. Ramsay, however, pointed out years ago that Quirinius was governor of Syria twice, from 11–10 to 8–7 B.C. and from A.D. 6 to A.D. 9.[19] Another perhaps preferable explanation is to understand the Greek word *prōtē* to mean not "first" but "before," which is its meaning in John 15:18. Just as the world hated Christ *before* it hated his disciples, so the census took place *before* Quirinius was governor of Syria, that is before A.D. 6.[20] The exact date of that census cannot be determined but it may have been when Herod was seriously ill, for Augustus may have wanted to assess the situation in Judea before Herod died. This would place the census shortly before 4 B.C.[21]

Another factor in determining the year of Jesus' birth is Luke's designation that Jesus was "about thirty years old when he began his ministry" (Luke 3:23) and that he began "in the fifteenth year of the reign of Tiberius Caesar" (3:1), which was around A.D. 27–29. This would place Jesus' birth around 4 B.C.

As for the day of Jesus' birth, church fathers Tertullian (ca. A.D. 160–230), Hippolytus (A.D. 165–235), and Chrysostom (A.D. 345?–407) said the date was December 25. Some object to a midwinter date since shepherds were tending their flocks outside, which, it is argued, would have been more com-

---

W. E. Filmer has suggested Herod died in January 1 B.C. ("The Chronology of the Reign of Herod the Great," *Journal of Theological Studies* 17 [1966]: 283–98; cf. Ernest L. Martin, "The Nativity and Herod's Death," in *Chronos, Kairos, Christos*, ed. Jerry Vardaman and Edwin W. Yamauchi [Winona Lake, Ind.: Eisenbrauns, 1989], 85–92). For responses to this view, see Timothy D. Barnes, "The Date of Herod's Death," *Journal of Theological Studies* 19 (1968): 204–9; Douglas Johnson, "And They Went Eight Stades toward Herodeion," in *Chronos, Kairos, Christos*, 93–99; and Harold W. Hoehner, "The Date of the Death of Herod the Great," in *Chronos, Kairos, Christos*, 101–11.

18. Josephus *The Antiquities of the Jews* 18.1–10; cf. Reicke, *The New Testament Era*, 135–37.

19. W. M. Ramsay, *The Bearing of Recent Discoveries on the Trustworthiness of the New Testament*, 4th ed. (London: Hodder & Stoughton, 1920), 255–74. Also, see J. Gresham Machen, *The Virgin Birth of Christ* (New York: Harper & Brothers Publishers, 1930), 240–41.

Or Quirinius's "governorship" may have meant he served Augustus as a special representative in the region of Syria when Saturinus and Varus were governors there (D. J. Hayles, "The Roman Census and Jesus' Birth: Was Luke Correct? Part 2: Quirinius's Career and a Census in Herod's Day," *Buried History* 10 [1974]: 28–29; and Stephen Douglas Wilson, *In the Fullness of Time* [Nashville: Broadman Press, 1991], 34–35). It is disheartening to read Brown's observation that Luke was in error in associating the birth of Jesus with a census conducted under Quirinius (Brown, *The Birth of the Messiah*, 554).

20. A. B. J. Higgins, "Sidelights on Christian Beginnings in the Graeco-Roman World," *Evangelical Quarterly* 41 (October 1969): 200–201; Harold W. Hoehner, *Chronological Aspects of the Life of Christ* (Grand Rapids: Zondervan Publishing House, 1977), 18–22; and John Nolland, *Luke 1–9:20* (Dallas, Tex.: Word Books, Publishers, 1989), 101–2. For an evaluation of these and other views related to the census under Augustus and Quirinius, see Darrell L. Bock, *Luke 1:1–9:50* (Grand Rapids: Baker Book House, 1994), 901–9.

21. Hoehner, *Chronological Aspects of the Life of Christ*, 26; Alfred Edersheim, *The Life and Times of Jesus the Messiah*, 2 vols., 3d ed. (1886; reprint, Grand Rapids: Wm. B. Eerdmans Publishing Co., 1962), 1:186–87. Humphreys has argued for a spring, 5 B.C. date for Jesus' birth, based on the appearance of a comet in that year (Colin J. Humphreys, "The Star of Bethlehem, a Comet in 5 B.C. and the Date of Christ's Birth," *Tyndale Bulletin* 43 (1992), 31–56.

mon in the spring and summer. However, the Mishnah (*M. Šekalim* 7.4) suggests that sheep around Bethlehem were kept outside year round.[22]

Who Were the Magi?

Tradition says the Magi were kings from the Far East, but more likely they were priestly astronomers from Parthia or Persia, though some suggest Arabia.[23] Matthew 2:1 simply states they came from "the east," that is, east of Judea. Their bringing three gifts to Jesus—gold, frankincense, and myrrh—has led to the tradition that three men came. But this has no biblical or secular support. The names of Balthasar, Caspar, and Melkon stem from an Armenian Infancy Gospel written about A.D. 500. Later the spelling of Melkon became Melchior, as seen in a sixth-century mosaic in a church at Ravenna, Italy.[24]

The Magi apparently believed that the movement of stars announced the birth of important people.[25] And yet in spite of this tendency toward astrology[26] God used the movement of a "star" to cause them to find and worship Jesus. This highlights the irony that whereas Gentile religious leaders sought Jesus out, the ruling king of the Jews (Herod) sought to kill him, not worship him (Matt. 2:3–12). "It is a striking picture—Herod the king, and Christ the King; Christ a power even in his cradle, and inspiring terror [and] attracting homage!"[27]

The Magi visited Jesus in a "house" in Bethlehem (Matt. 2:11) "after Jesus was born" (2:1). This fact and the fact that Herod wanted to kill all baby boys in Bethlehem two years of age and under (2:16) suggest that days, months, or perhaps nearly two years lapsed between his birth and the time the Magi saw "his star" and arrived in Bethlehem.

What Was the "Star" the Magi Saw?

When the Magi arrived in Jerusalem, they explained, "We have seen his star in the east and have come to worship him" (Matt. 2:2).[28] After Herod or-

22. A. B. J. Higgins, "Sidelights on Christian Beginnings in the Graeco-Roman World," *Evangelical Quarterly* 41 (October 1969): 200–201; Harold W. Hoehner, *Chronological Aspects of the Life of Christ* (Grand Rapids: Zondervan Publishing House, 1977), 18–22; and John Nolland, *Luke 1–9:20* (Dallas, Tex.: Word Books, Publishers, 1989), 101–2. For an evaluation of these and other views related to the census under Augustus and Quirinius, see Darrell L. Bock, *Luke 1:1–9:50* (Grand Rapids: Baker Book House, 1994), 901–9.

23. Herodotus 1.101, 132 used the term "magi" of some Medians who served as priests in Persia. Three early church fathers—Justin Martyr (*Dialogue with Trypho* 78.1), Tertullian (*Against Marcion* 3.13), and Clement of Rome (*1 Corinthians* 25:1–2)—said the Magi came from Arabia. Others — Clement of Alexandria (*Stromata* 1.15), Origen, Chrysostom, and Augustine—favored Persia.

24. David Hughes, *The Star of Bethlehem Mystery* (London: J. M. Dent & Sons, 1979), 26–27.

25. "It is important to remember that there are many references in ancient literature to Magi visiting kings and emperors in other countries. For example, Tiridates, the King of Armenia, led a procession of Magi to pay homage to Nero in Rome in A.D. 66" (Humphreys, "The Star of Bethlehem," 33). In a footnote Humphreys supports this observation by references to Suetonius *Nero* 13, 30; Tacitus *Annals* 16.23; and Dio Cassius *Roman History* 63.1 (ibid.).

26. Astronomers in ancient Persia combined their study of the movement of heavenly bodies with interest in astrology, the attempt to show that planets affect human affairs.

27. Orr, "Jesus Christ," 3:1633.

28. "In the east" does not necessarily mean the star was located in the east and seen by the Magi west of the star's location. The Greek *en tē anatolē* may mean "in its rising" (NIV note has "when it rose"). That is, the wise men residing east of Judea saw the "star" *west* of them when it rose.

dered them to look for the child in Bethlehem (based on the chief priests and the teachers of the Law who called Herod's attention to the Bethlehem prediction in Micah 5:2), the star "went ahead of them until it stopped over the place where the child was" (Matt. 2:9). Apparently, only the Magi saw this star, which somehow enabled them to pinpoint Jesus' exact location. But what was the star?

A number of suggestions have been proposed. Some say it was a supernova, a "new star" that suddenly burst into brilliant light.[29] However, this view does not explain how the star seen by the Magi could have directed them to Bethlehem, there is no record of such a supernova at the time of Jesus' birth, and supernovae are usually not seen by the naked eye.

Another view is that the Magi saw and followed a comet. Haley's comet appeared in 11 B.C., but that is too early for Jesus' birthdate. Also, a comet could hardly have "stopped over the place where the child was" (Matt. 2:9). And comets usually were viewed as portends of calamity, not of significant births. However, Humphreys holds that a comet was recorded by the Chinese (who kept careful astronomical records of comets) as having appeared in 5 B.C. and was visible for seventy days. He says Origen identified the Bethlehem star as a comet.[30] Humphreys suggests the Magi saw the comet in the east in the morning sky, and that they traveled to Jerusalem, a journey of one to two months, in which time the comet moved to the south in the morning sky.[31]

A third suggestion is that the "star" was a planetary conjunction, that is, an apparent lineup of two or more planets near each other. In the early seventeenth century the German astronomer Johannes Kepler calculated that a "triple conjunction" of the planets Jupiter and Saturn occurred in 7 B.C. in the Pisces constellation. They were seen together on May 29, September 29, and December 4. In the first conjunction Jupiter, moving eastward, appeared to come near Saturn. This, some believe, caused the wise men to sense that an important event was occurring in Judea. Then, because of the motion of the earth, the two planets would seem to stop and then move westward in their second conjunction, thus "guiding" the Magi to the west. Then the planets would seem again to stand still, about when the Magi arrived in Jerusalem. The wise men's travel from Jerusalem to Bethlehem would then have been "guided" by the third conjunction of Jupiter and Saturn. Though Kepler later rejected the conjunction theory in favor of a supernova, others have continued to propose this planetary conjunction view.[32]

---

29. Arthur C. Clarke, *Report on Planet Three and Other Speculations* (New York: Harper & Row, 1972); and idem, "Does the Star of Bethlehem Still Shine?" *Reader's Digest*, January 1955, 121–23.

30. Humphreys, "The Star of Bethlehem," 38 (Origen *Contra Celsum* 1.58).

31. Ibid., 55.

32. For example, Konradin Ferrari-D'Occhieppo, "The Star of the Magi and Babylonian Astronomy," in *Chronos, Kairos, Christos*, 41–53; and Hughes, *The Star of Bethlehem Mystery*, 189–94.

This view faces several problems. First, the two planets in 7 B.C. came no closer to each other than about one degree, or double the moon's diameter. "Some conjunctions can actually make [two] planets like one star, but that wasn't the case with those that occurred in 7 B.C."[33] Second, the date of 7 B.C. does not match with the observations noted earlier in this chapter regarding Jesus' birthdate in 4 B.C. Third, the word for "star" in Matthew 2 is singular, whereas the planetary conjunction theory calls for a grouping of planets.[34] Fourth, if the conjunction were so significant, it seems strange that Herod knew nothing about it.[35]

Since each of these (and similar) theories falls short of satisfying the facts revealed in Matthew 2, astral phenomena probably do not provide an explanation for the "star" seen by the Magi.[36] An unusual idea is that the star was an angel.[37] While it is true that angels are sometimes called stars, as in Revelation 1:20, the "angels" of the seven churches in Revelation 2–3 may be leaders of those churches. (In Matt. 11:10 the word *angelos* was used of John the Baptist as a human messenger.) It would seem strange for Jesus to address those church letters to angelic beings.

The appearing and reappearing of the star, its stopping over Jesus' residence, and the fact that no one other than the Magi seem to have seen it suggest a distinct phenomenon. Perhaps the best explanation is that this unique shining was the glory of God, often seen in the Old Testament as a visible manifestation of God's presence, something like the pillar of fire and cloud that led Israel through the wilderness for forty years.[38] Jesus called this the Shekinah glory, for "shekinah" in Hebrew *(šekînāh)* means "radiance." This view seems to fit all the facts recorded in Matthew 2 about the "star."

How Can Jesus' Two Genealogies in Matthew and Luke Be Reconciled?

The genealogies of Jesus in Matthew 1:1–17 and Luke 3:23–38 have similarities and differences. Both list the same fourteen names from Abraham to David. Both mention Joseph, who was engaged to Mary, but both purposefully avoid any suggestion that Joseph was Jesus' physical father. Matthew

---

33. Kenneth Boa and William Proctor, *The Return of the Star of Bethlehem* (Garden City, N.Y.: Doubleday & Co., 1980), 66.

34. Ibid., 68.

35. Ibid.

36. Even Chrysostom said natural phenomena do not explain Matthew's record of the star (*Homilies on Matthew* 6.2).

37. Gerardus D. Bouw, "On the Star of Bethlehem," *Creation Research Society Quarterly* 17 (December 1980): 174–81.

38. Louis A. Barbieri, "Matthew," in *The Bible Knowledge Commentary, New Testament,* ed. John F. Walvoord and Roy B. Zuck (Wheaton, Ill.: Victor Books, 1983), 22; Kenneth D. Boa, "The Star of Bethlehem" (Th.M. thesis, Dallas Theological Seminary, 1972), 73–91; Boa and Proctor, *The Return of the Star of Bethlehem*, 105–24; Kent R. Hughes, "The Magi's Worship," *Christianity Today*, December 13, 1985, 27; Machen, *The Virgin Birth of Christ*, 227–28; and William Varner, "The Mythology of the Magi," *Voice*, November/December 1988, 8–10.

1:16 refers to "Joseph, the husband of Mary, of whom was born Jesus." The pronoun "whom" is feminine, thus pointing to the fact that Jesus was born only to Mary and not to Joseph—a clear indication of Jesus' virgin birth. Luke 3:23 reads, "He was the son, so it was thought, of Joseph." This too upholds the virgin birth, for Jesus, being raised by Joseph and Mary, was referred to as their son, whereas he was actually the son of Mary only and descended from Heli, Mary's father.

As for differences, Matthew's genealogy has three sets of fourteen names each (Matt. 1:17), whereas Luke has seventy-six names, including twenty names before Abraham which Matthew did not include. Matthew began his listing with Abraham; this would have been fitting for his Gospel which emphasized Jesus as the Messiah and was addressed to Jews. Luke's record, however, begins with Jesus and moves back to Adam, an appropriate approach because of Luke's emphasis on Jesus' humanity and Luke's message to Gentiles about Jesus as the Son of Man.

From Abraham to Jesus, Matthew has forty-two names (counting David twice), and Luke has fifty-six. Obviously, then, Matthew intentionally omitted some. Also Matthew 1:16 says Jacob was the father of Joseph, and thus Jesus' grandfather, whereas Luke 3:23 says Heli was Joseph's father and thus Jesus' grandfather. Both lists refer to a Zerubbabel whose son was Shealtiel (Matt. 1:13; Luke 3:27), but they were probably not the same individuals. In Luke, Shealtiel's father was Neri, but in Matthew, Shealtiel's father was Jeconiah.

One explanation of the alleged disparities in the two records is that both Gospels give Joseph's genealogy: Matthew traced it through Joseph's *actual* father Jacob (Matt. 1:16) and Luke developed it through Heli (Luke 3:23), Joseph's *legal* father. Heli died without having children and so his brother Jacob carried out a levirate marriage (see discussion of the levirate marriage custom in chap. 4), marrying Heli's widow and giving birth to Joseph. Jacob then was the actual father of Joseph (Matthew's genealogy), and Heli was the legal father of Joseph (the Lucan genealogy). This view was first proposed by Julius Africanus around A.D. 220, as cited in Eusebius *Ecclesiastical History* 1.7.4–5. However, this view assumes a levirate marriage with no proof, and it causes one to wonder why Joseph's physical *and* legal lines were traced when Jesus did not descend physically from Joseph.[39]

A second, perhaps preferable, view is that Matthew recorded Jesus' *legal* line through Joseph, and that Luke presented the Savior's *physical* line through Mary. Matthew's record traces Jesus' line to David through David's son Solomon, of whom Joseph was the legal descendant (Matt. 1:6, 16). Luke, on the other hand, mentioned David's son Nathan, not Solomon, of

---

39. It would seem strange for Luke to present Joseph's genealogy after having stated that Jesus was only thought to be Joseph's son (Norval Geldenhuys, *Commentary on the Gospel of Luke* [Grand Rapids: Wm. B. Eerdmans Publishing Co., 1951], 151).

whom Mary was a physical descendant. Though Mary is not mentioned in Luke 3, Luke had already shown that physically Jesus is the son of Mary (1:28, 31; 2:5–7). This view assumes that Mary's father was Heli, a view held by the Talmud.[40] Martin Luther set forth this more acceptable view, and it is held by a number of conservative scholars.[41]

Jesus as an Infant

Matthew and Luke recorded a number of incidents pertaining not only to Mary's pregnancy and Jesus' birth, but also to his infancy and boyhood. One of the best-known events relating to his earliest days is an angel's announcement of his birth to shepherds: "Today in the town of David a Savior has been born to you; he is Christ the Lord" (Luke 2:11). These words reveal his mission ("a Savior") and his deity ("Christ the Lord"). While these words are an astounding revelation about a baby, they stand in full accord with Old Testament prophecies about his person and mission. He was to be named Immanuel, "God with us" (Isa. 7:14; cf. Matt. 1:23); he is the "Mighty God" who will reign on David's throne (Isa. 9:6) as the "ruler over Israel" (Micah 5:2); he is the eternal one (Micah 5:2; cf. "Everlasting Father," lit. "Father of eternity" in Isa. 9:6); and the purpose of his coming was to take on himself the sins of the human race as a sacrificial substitute (53:4–12).

Immediately after the angelic proclamation, the shepherds hurried to town and found the baby lying in a manger and wrapped in strips of cloth (Luke 2:12, "swaddling clothes," KJV).[42] Spreading the word to others, all of whom were amazed (2:17–18), the shepherds returned to their sheep-tending with praise to God on their lips (2:20).

Other interesting events followed the shepherds' visit. In keeping with Mosaic stipulations (Lev. 12:1–3), Mary had Jesus circumcised on his eighth day. Also, at that time she named him Jesus, following an angel's instructions given to her even before she had conceived (Luke 1:31; 2:21). After Mary's conception an angel also told Joseph to name him Jesus "because he will save his people from their sins" (Matt. 1:21). Being God manifest in the flesh

40. If Jesus were physically a son of Joseph and not virgin born, then he would have been a direct descendant of Jeconiah (Matt. 1:12). In that case, he could not rule in the future millennium as Israel's King because God had said to Jehoiakim, the father of Jeconiah (also called Jehoiachin) that no physical descendant of his would sit on David's throne. Jesus was Jeconiah's legal descendant, but if Joseph were his *physical* father, he would be disqualified from being the King of Israel. So he had to be virgin born!

41. For example, Gleason L. Archer, *Encyclopedia of Bible Difficulties* (Grand Rapids: Zondervan Publishing House, 1982), 316; John Albert Bengel, *Gnomon of the New Testament*, 5 vols. (1762; reprint, Edinburgh: T. & T. Clark, 1857), 2:46–47; Frederick Godet, *A Commentary on the Gospel of St Luke*, 2d ed. (1887; reprint, Grand Rapids: Kregel Publications, 1981), 128–32; and Gromacki, *The Virgin Birth*, 150–57. For a presentation and evaluation of these and other proposed solutions, see Bock, *Luke 1:1–9:50*, 918-23.

42. On this practice of wrapping a newborn in cloth strips, see chapter 4.

(John 1:14; Col. 2:9; 1 Tim. 3:16), Jesus had no spiritual need of the rite of circumcision, which depicted the Hebrews being separated or "cut off" from sin. And yet Mary and Joseph obediently followed the Old Testament requirement, thereby in a sense numbering Jesus "with transgressors" (Isa. 53:12) even as a baby.[43]

Joseph and Mary also followed the Israelite practice of consecrating the firstborn child to the Lord (Exod. 13:2, 12). The Mosaic law stipulated that forty days after giving birth to a boy a mother was to present an offering to the Lord in connection with her ritual purification (Lev. 12:4, 6–7). Being relatively poor, they brought two birds as an offering (Lev. 12:8; Luke 2:22–24). This firstborn consecration and purification sacrifice meant Joseph and Mary traveled with baby Jesus from Bethlehem to Jerusalem, a short distance of about five miles, when he was less than six weeks old. No doubt they returned to Bethlehem, where the Magi found them in a house (Matt. 2:7–11).

When the parents took Jesus to Jerusalem, a righteous man who went into the temple courts "was waiting for the consolation of Israel," that is, for the Messiah who would bring comfort (*paraklēsis*) to the nation (Luke 2:25). Simeon, probably an old man (2:26, 29), took the baby Jesus in his arms (2:28).[44] Knowing from the Holy Spirit (2:25–27) that this infant was the long-awaited Messiah, Simeon praised God for seeing the Lord's "salvation" in the person of Jesus, who became a source of blessing to both Gentiles (a frequent emphasis in the Gospel of Luke and the Book of Isaiah[45]) and Israel (Luke 2:30–31; cf. Isa. 46:13; 52:9–10). Mary and Joseph marveled at these prophecies about Jesus' forthcoming ministry (Luke 2:33). Frequently Luke wrote of people's amazement at the Messiah (*thaumazō*, "to be amazed or astonished," occurs in 1:21, 63; 2:18, 33; 4:22; 8:25; 9:43; 11:14, 38; 20:26; 24:12, 41). After Simeon gave praise to the Lord, he gave a blessing to Joseph and Mary and made a prediction: Jews who trusted Jesus would "rise" in spiritual blessing and those who did not would "fall," their response to him revealing their hearts (2:34–35). When Simeon added that a sword would pierce Mary's soul, he was pointing ahead to the agony she would experience in seeing her son die on the cross.[46]

Another elderly person, a widowed prophetess named Anna, lived in the temple precincts where she worshiped the Lord daily (2:36–37). She too was delighted to see the newborn Jesus; perhaps she saw him in Simeon's arms.[47]

---

43. Herbert Lockyer, *All the Children of the Bible* (Grand Rapids: Zondervan Publishing House, 1970), 193.

44. Interestingly, later Jesus in his adult ministry took children in his arms (Mark 9:36; 10:16).

45. Isaiah 42:6; 49:10, 22.

46. For a summary of eight other views on the meaning of her soul being pierced, see Brown, *The Birth of the Messiah*, 462–63.

47. William Hendriksen, *Exposition of the Gospel According to Luke*, New Testament Commentary (Grand Rapids: Baker Book House, 1978), 173.

She thanked the Lord for the child and then spoke about him to people who were anticipating "the redemption of Jerusalem" (2:38), that is, the release of Jerusalem from foreign oppression by means of the awaited Messiah. Here was a forty-day-old baby being admired by two elderly people—not an uncommon sight even today. And yet they were doing more than adoring a beautiful infant. They delighted in the fact that they had seen the Messiah, the one they and other devout Jews longed for.

Luke 2:39 states that having fulfilled their obligations at the temple, Joseph and Mary moved with Jesus to Nazareth. However, Matthew's account of the Magi belongs chronologically between Luke 2:38 and 39. (Matthew's statement in 2:22–23 that the three returned to Nazareth coincides with Luke 2:39.)

After the Magi worshiped the baby Jesus in his house (Matt. 2:1–11), they returned to their country, presumably Parthia. Then, because of Herod's determination to kill this newly announced "king of the Jews" (2:2), whom he feared as a potential rival, an angel told Joseph to escape with "the child and his mother" (2:13)[48] to Egypt. Since Jesus was born shortly before Herod the Great died in April, 4 B.C. (as discussed earlier in this chapter), this family of three may have been in Egypt only a few weeks or months. Possibly they stayed with some Jewish family since a number of Jews resided in Egypt (Jer. 43:7; 44:1; Acts 2:10). This would have been a safe place for the three because Egypt was outside Herod's area of rule. Herod angrily ordered that all baby boys in and around Bethlehem be slaughtered (Matt. 2:16), a gruesome, heartless act typical of his slaughters of close family members in his closing days, including three of his sons, Alexander, Aristobulus, and Antipater. Though no one knows how many babies were needlessly killed, Maier suggests that the number may be based on the assumption that Bethlehem had about two thousand inhabitants.[49] If each family consisted of two adults and six children, that would be about 250 families,[50] each with perhaps one male child under two years old.

Matthew 2:15 states that the return of the three to the land of Israel fulfilled the prophecy of Hosea 11:1, "When Israel was a child, I loved him, and out of Egypt I called my son." But since Hosea clearly spoke of God's "son" as Israel, how could Matthew say that Hosea 11:1 refers to Christ? Some say Israel was a type of Christ, and others say Christ existed potentially in Israel.[51] However, when Matthew wrote that Jesus' return from Egypt fulfilled Hosea 11:1, he may have used "fulfilled" in the sense of Jesus "heightening" or en-

48. "The child and his mother" occurs five times in chapter 2 (vv. 11, 13, 14, 20, 21). "Child" renders the diminutive *paidion* (see chap. 9).

49. Paul L. Maier, *First Christmas* (New York: Harper & Row, 1971), 84.

50. However, Maier suggests the number of babies slaughtered was only twenty-five.

51. For example, William Hendriksen, *Exposition of the Gospel According to Matthew*, New Testament Commentary (Grand Rapids: Baker Book House, 1973), 178–79.

larging the original meaning. In other words, the event was fulfilled in Jesus not in the sense of a prophecy being realized but in the sense of it being filled with more meaning or a higher meaning.[52]

After Herod died, an angel told Joseph that it was safe to return to Israel. On the way he heard that Herod's son Archelaus was reigning over Judea (as well as over Samaria and Idumea). Afraid because of Archelaus's tyranny—he had killed three thousand Jews in a Passover massacre—Joseph was directed by an angel to go to his hometown of Nazareth.[53] Antipas, another son of Herod the Great, was reigning over Galilee, but he was less tyrannical.

This angelic directive is the sixth of numerous appearances of angels in relation to Jesus' birth and infancy, as seen in this list.

> *The angel Gabriel told Zechariah about the birth of John the Baptist (Luke 1:11–20).*
> *The angel Gabriel told Mary she would give birth to Jesus (1:26–37).*
> *An angel told Joseph about Mary's virginal conception (Matt. 1:20–21).*
> *An angel announced Jesus' birth to shepherds (Luke 2:8–12).*
> *An angel told Joseph to escape to Egypt (Matt. 2:13–14).*
> *An angel told Joseph to return to Israel (2:19–20).*

Of interest is the fact that Jesus spent the first few years of his life in several locations: Bethlehem, Jerusalem, Bethlehem again, Egypt, and Nazareth.

Jesus as a Boy

His Growth

The Gospels are not intended as a full biography of all the years of Jesus' life on earth. Instead, the Gospels focus on the theological purpose of his coming, emphasizing, as Luke put it, "all that Jesus began to do and to teach" (Acts 1:1). Therefore, little is said about Jesus' boyhood. However, Luke gave four glimpses of his childhood: two verses that summarize his growth as a child (Luke 2:40, 52), a passage that reports an incident in his life as a twelve-year-old (2:41–51), and a verse that briefly mentions his hometown where he was brought up (4:16). Interestingly, the two verses summarizing his growth in various aspects of his life surround the incident when he was in the temple at Jerusalem. Apparently, that event in which Jesus conversed with teachers in the temple serves as an example of his wisdom, which is mentioned in both verses 40 and 52.

According to Luke 2:40, Jesus grew like a normal child: physically ("the child grew [in height] and became strong"), intellectually and morally ("he

52. Roy B. Zuck, *Basic Bible Interpretation* (Wheaton, Ill.: Victor Books, 1991), 267.
53. For discussion of the clause "He will be called a Nazarene" (Matt. 2:23), see Barbieri, "Matthew," 23.

was filled with wisdom"), and spiritually ("the grace of God was upon him"). The first two parts are similar to what Luke wrote about John the Baptist ("And the child grew and became strong"), except that Luke added that John became strong "in spirit," that is, he excelled in moral and spiritual matters.[54]

Luke 2:52 provides the second summary statement about Jesus' boyhood growth. Here, however, four areas are mentioned, whereas verse 40 speaks of three. The word "grew" translates the verb *proekopten,* "He was advancing or progressing" (lit., "cutting his way forward"). He increased intellectually and morally ("in wisdom"), physically (in "stature"), spiritually ("in favor with God"), and socially ("in favor with . . . men"). Being "without sin" (Heb. 4:15), Jesus developed perfectly. "From beginning to end progress was unimpaired and unimpeded by sin. . . ."[55] As he advanced from one stage of growth to another, he was perfect at each stage.[56]

When Jesus was twelve years of age, Mary and Joseph took him with them to Jerusalem for the Passover Feast. This festival was followed by the seven-day Feast of Unleavened Bread (Exod. 23:15; Lev. 23:4–8; Deut. 16:1–8). The entire eight-day occasion was sometimes called simply the Passover (Luke 22:1, 7; John 19:14; Acts 12:3–4). Mary and Joseph journeyed each spring to Jerusalem from Nazareth for this celebration of worship (Luke 2:41), but on this occasion they took Jesus with them, perhaps to help prepare him for assuming "manhood" at age thirteen.[57] Was this his first Passover visit? Or had Mary and Joseph taken him with them on previous occasions, with this being reported as a special event? While Luke did not clarify that point, some commentators suggest this was the first time he went along.[58] But if that were the case, who took care of him at home while Mary and Joseph went to Jerusalem in the previous years? As Hendrickx observed, "The rabbinical interpretation of the law was that a boy was not obliged to make the journey before he had completed his twelfth year and so had reached the age of thirteen, but pious parents used to take their sons with them at an earlier age."[59]

---

54. Brown suggests that "spirit" should be capitalized to refer to his growth in the Holy Spirit, because of the Spirit's frequent association with John the Baptist in Luke 1:15, 41, 67 (Brown, *The Birth of the Messiah,* 374). However, if the third Person of the Trinity is intended, one might expect spirit (*pneumati*) to be preceded by a definite article.

55. Hendriksen, *Exposition of the Gospel According to Luke,* 180.

56. Alfred Plummer, *A Critical and Exegetical Commentary on the Gospel According to St. Luke,* International Critical Commentary (Edinburgh: T. & T. Clark, 1896), 79.

57. Jewish boys were viewed as reaching manhood legally at age thirteen. "At five years old [one comes] to the study of Scripture; at ten years to the Mishnah; at thirteen years to the fulfillment of the commandments; at fifteen years to the Talmud; at eighteen years to the bride-chamber . . ." (*Aboth m Ab.* 5.21, cited in Emil Schürer, *The Jewish People in the Age of Jesus Christ (175 B.C.–A.D. 135),* rev. and ed. Geza Vermes, Fergus Millar, and Matthew Black, 3 vols. [Edinburgh: T. & T. Clark, 1979], 2:421).

58. For example, Hendriksen says this is "a reasonable inference" (*Exposition of the Gospel According to Luke,* 183).

59. Herman Hendrickx, *The Infancy Narratives,* rev. ed. (London: Geoffrey Chapman, 1984), 113–14.

After the feast, when the pilgrims were journeying home, Mary and Joseph assumed Jesus was in the crowd, possibly with relatives or friends. Or Joseph may have assumed he was with the women and children who traveled ahead of the men, while Mary may have assumed he was with Joseph.[60] At the end of the day (after traveling about fifteen miles), they were alarmed that he was not with the crowd. Any parent whose child has been missing for even a few minutes can appreciate Mary and Joseph's concern. Returning to Jerusalem, they found him on the third day.[61]

He was in the temple precincts, listening to the teachers and asking them questions (2:46), two actions of a student learning from his instructors. But there was more: he also answered their questions (2:47)! The significance of his questions and the depth of his answers caused everyone who heard him— the teachers and possibly others—to be amazed (*existanto*, "to be beside themselves in astonishment," a word Luke used eleven times in Luke and Acts) at his perception or insight *(synesis)*. Did they discuss the Passover? Or did they discuss other aspects of the Law and the Prophets?[62] Whatever the subjects, those who heard him were impressed. "The fact that [the rabbis] would even discuss these deep religious topics with a mere boy underscores their astonishment at this very gifted young savant."[63]

When Mary and Joseph found Jesus they were "astonished" (*exeplagēsan*, from *ekplēssō*, "to be knocked out, to be overwhelmed"). They were, no doubt, relieved while also surprised to find him there conversing with his elders, seemingly unconcerned that they would be anxiously searching for him.[64] In Jesus' response, he answered Mary with two questions: "Why were you [plural] searching for me? Didn't you [plural] know I had to be in my Father's house?" (2:49).[65] In contrast to Mary's reference to "your father and I" (Joseph, of course, was his legal father, but not his biological father), Jesus spoke of his *heavenly* Father. At twelve, Jesus knew of his messianic vocation and the obligation this placed on him. The temple—the place of the nation's religious learning and worship—was fittingly "his place."[66] Surprisingly, Jo-

60. Ibid., 114.
61. The first day Mary and Joseph had traveled without Jesus, they returned on the second day, and found him the next day.
62. Other questions about this incident not answered in the Lucan account are these: Where did he stay those two nights his parents were away? Where and what did he eat? How many hours did he spend each day with the teachers? How did they learn of him? Did he introduce himself? What specific questions were asked and what answers were given?
63. Wilson, *In the Fullness of Time*, 95.
64. "Anxiously" translates the participle *odynōmenoi*, "to be suffering intense pain or sadness," a word used only by Luke (Luke 2:48; 16:24–25; Acts 20:38).
65. Answering a question with another question was typical of Jesus' teaching style in his adult ministry (Zuck, *Teaching as Jesus Taught*, 285–86).
66. The phrase "in my Father's house" is rendered "about My Father's business" in the King James Version and the New King James Version. The Greek *en tois tou patros mou* is literally "in the [plural] . . . of my Father," that is, in the activities pertaining to his Father or in the places (temple precincts) of his Father.

seph, to whom an angel had explained that Jesus would "save his people from their sins" (Matt. 1:21), and Mary, to whom the angel Gabriel had announced Jesus' deity (he "will be called the Son of the Most High," Luke 1:32, and "the Son of God," 1:35) and his coming messianic rule (1:32–33), did not understand his words (2:50). Though he was fully aware of his relationship to his heavenly Father, he obeyed his "parents" by going with them to Nazareth (2:51).

Two contrasts are evident: While Jesus' insight into spiritual matters was amazing (2:47), Mary and Joseph lacked insight into this statement about his mission. And although he was God's Son, he exercised obedience to his mother and Joseph.

His Training

As discussed in chapter 8, Jewish children were taught the Scriptures by their parents, beginning at an early age. As "home-school" teachers, parents instructed their children formally and informally (Deut. 6:6–7), encouraging them to know the Old Testament, to participate in and understand the meaning of the annual Jewish feasts, to appreciate how God worked on behalf of the nation in past generations. Much was learned by repetition and memorization. Parental instruction also included guidance in proper conduct and proper attitudes toward others.

Jesus' frequent references to the Old Testament in his public ministry reflect his early home training in knowing the Scriptures. Table 5 shows how extensive was his knowledge of the Old Testament. In these thirty-nine passages from Luke, he referred to passages from sixteen books, with the predominant ones being Deuteronomy, Psalms, and Isaiah. These books are also prominent in his sayings recorded in Matthew, Mark, and John.[67]

The Bible says nothing about Jesus having attended school, but, no doubt, he followed the custom of children going to a synagogue school beginning at age six.[68]

Table 5

Jesus' Quotations from
and References to Old Testament Passages,
Recorded in the Gospel of Luke

Passages in Luke	Old Testament Passages
4:4	Deuteronomy 8:3
4:8	Deuteronomy 6:13
4:12	Deuteronomy 6:16
4:18–19	Isaiah 61:1–2

67. Henry M. Shires, *Finding the Old Testament in the New* (Philadelphia: Westminster Press, 1974), 88, 190–96.
68. Alfred Edersheim, *Sketches of Jewish Social Life in the Days of Christ* (1876; reprint, Grand Rapids: Wm. B. Eerdmans Publishing Co., 1976), 133.

4:25	1 Kings 17:1
4:26	1 Kings 17:8–16
4:27	2 Kings 5:1–14
5:14	Leviticus 14:2–32
6:3–4	1 Samuel 21:6; Leviticus 24:5, 9
6:25	Isaiah 65:13
6:30	Deuteronomy 15:7–8, 10
7:22	Isaiah 61:1–2
7:27	Malachi 3:1
7:46a	Psalm 23:5
8:10	Isaiah 6:9
11:30	Jonah 1:17
11:32	Jonah 3:5
11:51	Genesis 4:8; 2 Chronicles 24:20–21
12:24	Job 38:41
12:28	1 Kings 10:4–7
13:35	Psalm 118:26
17:14	Leviticus 14:2
17:26	Genesis 6:5–8; 7:6–24
17:28–29	Genesis 19:1–28
17:32	Genesis 19:26
18:7	Psalm 88:1
18:20	Exodus 20:12–16; Deuteronomy 5:16–20
19:40	Habakkuk 2:11
19:46	Isaiah 56:7; Jeremiah 7:11
20:17	Psalm 118:22
20:37	Exodus 3:6
20:42–43	Psalm 110:1
21:24	Isaiah 63:18
22:20	Jeremiah 31:31–34
22:21	Psalm 41:9
22:37	Isaiah 53:12
23:30	Isaiah 2:19; Hosea 10:8
23:34	Psalm 22:18
23:46	Psalm 31:5a

Since Joshua ben Gamala, high priest from A.D. 63 to 65, referred to schools having been established in every province and town in Judea, "it is reasonable to envisage them as operating in the age of Jesus."[69] Also, Jesus regularly attended the Sabbath services in the synagogue. "On the Sabbath day he went into the synagogue, as was his custom" (Luke 4:16). There in his childhood, youth, and adult years he heard the Law read in Hebrew, paraphrased in Aramaic, and interpreted.

Along with other schoolchildren Jesus learned to read and write. This is evident from his reading from Isaiah in a synagogue service (4:16–20), and his writing on the ground (John 8:6, 8). Undoubtedly, he knew and could read and converse in Hebrew, Aramaic, and Greek.

69. Schürer, *The Jewish People in the Age of Jesus Christ (175 B.C.–A.D. 135)*, 2:419.

However, if he went to school as a child, why did the Jews ask, "How did this man get such learning without having studied?" (John 7:15). The verse literally reads "How does this man know letters (*grammata*), not having learned?" *Grammata* refers to literature or writings in general, but here it probably designates the Old Testament.[70] The words "not having learned" do not suggest he lacked schooling as a child. Instead they mean he had never been a disciple of another rabbi in a rabbinical school, a Jewish school of higher education.

At home Jesus learned carpentry, no doubt from Joseph. When Jesus began teaching in the synagogue in his hometown of Nazareth, people were amazed for they knew him in his growing up years as "the carpenter" (Mark 6:3) and "the carpenter's son" (Matt. 13:55).

His upbringing in a small Galilean town and his skill at carpentry acquainted him with many aspects of everyday village and country life, which were later utilized in his teaching ministry. He knew about the problem of getting a speck of sawdust in one's eye (Matt. 7:3–5), the wisdom of building a house on a rock rather than on sand (7:24–27), the corroding effect of moths and rust (6:19–20), the sewing of patches of cloth and the pouring of wine into wineskins (9:16–17),[71] the use of storerooms in a house (13:52), the need for oil in oil lamps (5:15; 25:3–4, 8–10), the value of coins (20:2, 9–10, 13; 22:19–21), the value of a capstone (21:42, 44), the payment of taxes (22:15–21), and the use of flat roofs on houses (24:17).

Jesus referred to kitchen items including salt (5:13), yeast (13:33; 16:6, 11), flour (13:33), bread (15:26), spices (23:23), and the washing of dishes (23:25–26). His acquaintance with outdoor life showed itself in his references to birds (6:26; 13:4) and vultures (24:28), and numerous animals including dogs (7:6; 15:26), pigs (7:6), wolves (7:15; 10:16), sheep (9:36; 10:16; 12:12; 15:24; 18:12–13; 25:33; 26:31), snakes (10:16; 12:34; 23:33), doves (10:16), fish (7:10; 13:47–50; 17:27), gnats (23:24), camels (23:24), hens (23:37), chicks (23:37), and goats (25:33).

He was also familiar with horticultural items, as noted in the Gospel of Matthew, including lilies (6:28), grass (6:30), trees with good and bad fruit (7:17–20; 12:33), thornbushes and thistles (7:16; 13:7, 22), figs and fig trees (7:16; 21:18–22; 24:32–33), reeds (11:7), seeds (13:3–9, 18–23; 25:24, 26), weeds (13:24, 30), wheat (13:25–26, 29–30), mustard seed (13:31–32), harvesting (9:37–38; 21:34, 41; 25:24, 26), and grapes and vineyards (7:16; 20:1–16; 21:28, 33, 39–41; 26:29). He also spoke of farming and farmers (13:3; 21:33; 24:40), sackcloth and ashes (11:21), yokes (11:29–30), pearls (7:6; 13:45–46), millstones (18:6; 24:41), a watchtower (21:33), and tombs

70. F. Godet, *Commentary on the Gospel of John*, trans. M. D. Cusin and S. Taylor, 3d ed., 2 vols. (Edinburgh: T. & T. Clark, 1892), 2:275.

71. For a brief explanation of this passage, see Zuck, *Teaching as Jesus Taught*, 205.

(23:27, 29). Surely his childhood home training, schooling, play, and observations of life around him contributed strongly to his colorful teaching—with its numerous references to home life, flora, fauna, and horticulture.

Apocryphal Stories of Jesus' Childhood

While Jesus grew physically, intellectually, morally, socially, and spiritually, there is no indication that his parents or neighbors considered him a prodigy. Except for the account of his conversing with the rabbis in the temple at twelve years of age, the Gospels are silent about any events in his childhood, youth, and early manhood. They focus instead on his three-and-a-half-year ministry, beginning when he was "about thirty years old" (Luke 3:23).

And yet strange stories developed in the second century A.D. about Jesus' miraculous knowledge and power in his infancy and boyhood. For example, according to the *Protoevangeluim of James*, a great light appeared in the cave where Mary and Joseph were at the time of Jesus' birth. When he was born, the light withdrew.[72] The *Latin Infancy Gospel* records that Joseph supposedly said at Jesus' birth, "While I held him, looking into his face, he laughed at me with a most joyful laugh, and, opening his eyes, he looked intently at me, and suddenly a great light came forth from his eyes like a great flash of lightning."[73] The *Arabic Gospel of Jesus' Childhood* begins by recording Jesus' words spoken to Mary while he was an infant lying in a cradle: "I am Jesus, the Son of God, the Logos, whom thou hast brought forth."[74]

As Mary, Joseph, and Jesus traveled to Egypt, the infant Jesus ordered dragons not to harm anyone; lions, leopards, and wolves worshiped him; and he told a palm tree to bend down so Mary could eat its dates. When they entered a temple in Hermopolis, Egypt, all the idols fell to the ground and were shattered.[75]

According to the *Infancy Gospel of Thomas*, Jesus, at five years of age, formed twelve sparrows from clay and when he clapped his hands, they flew off. Later when a boy fell off the roof of a house and died, Jesus leaped down from the roof and healed the boy. The child raised several others from the

---

72. *Protoevangeluim of James* 19.3–5 (David L. Dungan and David R. Cartlidge, *Sourcebook of Texts for the Comparative Study of the Gospels*, 3d ed. [Missoula, Mont.: Society of Biblical Literature, 1971], 23).

73. *Latin Infancy Gospel* 74 (Dungan and Cartlidge, *Sourcebook of Texts for the Comparative Study of the Gospels*, 29). Cullman translates the clause about Jesus' laughing in this way: "He smiled at me with the most sweet smile" (Oscar Cullmann, "Infancy Gospels," in *New Testament Apocrypha*, ed. Wilhelm Schneemelcher, trans. and ed. R. McL. Wilson, rev. ed., 2 vols. (Louisville: Westminster/John Knox Press, 1991), 1:466.

74. Cited in J. G. Tasker, "Apocryphal Gospels," in *A Dictionary of the Bible*, ed. James Hastings (New York: Charles Scribner's Sons, 1919), extra volume, 433.

75. *The Gospel of Pseudo-Matthew* 18.1–2; 19.1–2; 20.1–2, 23 (Dungan and Cartlidge, *Sourcebook of Tests for the Comparative Study of the Gospels*, 37, 38, 40; Cullmann, "Infancy Gospels," 462–64).

dead. At the age of six, a water jug he was carrying broke, so he put water in his garment and carried it home that way. On one occasion in Joseph's carpenter shop, one piece of wood was shorter than the other, so he stretched it to equal the other in length.[76]

Several acts of vengeance by the child Jesus are also recorded in the *Infancy Gospel of Thomas*. When a boy scattered some water, Jesus caused the boy's body to be withered; when a child accidentally bumped into Jesus' shoulder, Jesus became angry and caused the boy to fall down dead; some people who cursed him were immediately blinded; and when a teacher got angry with Jesus and hit him on the head, the child cursed the teacher, who then fainted.[77]

How should we evaluate these stories? Should they be accepted as authentic events in Jesus' boyhood? In contrast to Luke's portrayal of Jesus' normally developing childhood (Luke 2:40, 52), these apocryphal writings read like fairy tales. The quixotic nature of these stories is unlike the sober Gospel accounts of his divine power in his adult ministry. In their effort to fill in "the silent years" of Jesus' growth, these apocryphal tales present a wonder child who is "unreal, mythical, [and] impossible."[78]

Several factors point to their lack of veracity. First, they contradict John 2:11, which clearly states that the changing of water to wine was the Lord's first miracle. Second, a number of these legendary accounts would have been needless in Jesus' childhood. Why would he need to command dragons not to harm him and others? What purpose would have been served in his causing clay sparrows to come to life and fly away? Third, the several so-called miracles of revenge are totally out of character for the Lord. The four Gospels record Jesus performing thirty-five miracles in his public ministry, twenty-six of which were miracles of healing or restoration to life. These acts demonstrated his compassion, not his vengeance (Matt. 14:14; 20:34; Mark 1:41), and they encouraged faith in him (Luke 7:1–10; John 4:53). The other nine miracles involved nature, such as turning water to wine, stilling a storm, walking on the water, feeding five thousand men, feeding four thousand men, and finding money in a fish's mouth.[79] These helped people recognize his deity and place their faith in him (e.g., Matt. 14:25–33; John 2:11).

The only miracle some might say was an act of revenge is his cursing the fig tree (Matt. 21:18–19; Mark 11:12–14). However, this was not done out of personal anger or in revenge for personal harm done to him. Since no figs

---

76. *The Infancy Gospel of Thomas* 2.1–5; 9.1–3; 11.2; 13.1–2 (Dungan and Cartlidge, *Sourcebook of Texts for the Comparative Study of the Gospels*, 41, 44, 45, 47; Cullmann, "Infancy Gospels," 444–47).

77. Ibid., 3.1–3; 4.1–2; 5.1–2; 14.2 (Dungan and Cartlidge, *Sourcebook of Texts for the Comparative Study of the Gospels*, 41–42, 46; Cullmann, "Infancy Gospels," 444–45, 447).

78. Herman Harrell Horne, *Jesus—Our Standard* (New York: Abingdon Press, 1918), 54.

79. For a list of the thirty-five miracles, see *The Bible Knowledge Commentary, New Testament*, 277.

were on the tree when they should have been, the tree symbolized that generation of the nation Israel, which was fruitless spiritually. Since they rejected him as their Messiah, Jesus rejected them. Unlike the apocryphal stories of his childhood, this denouncing of the fruit tree, a symbolic act, did not involve physical harm to other people borne out of personal wrath.

Fourth, some of the tales are fanciful, such as his speaking as an infant, commanding a palm tree to bend down, enabling clay sparrows to fly, and lengthening a piece of wood.

Fifth, these whimsical stories resemble legends in pagan religions. "If the name of Jesus did not stand alongside the description 'child' or 'boy,' one could not possibly hit upon the idea that these stories of the capricious divine boy were intended to supplement the tradition about him. Parallels from the legends of Krishna and Buddha, as well as all kinds of fables, can here be adduced in particular quantity."[80]

The Gospel writers left Jesus' boyhood and adolescent years silent (except for his few days at the temple at age twelve) in order to focus our attention on his adult ministry in which he came "to give his life a ransom for many" (Matt. 20:28; Mark 10:45). We do well to concentrate on what the Gospels emphasize: his miraculous virgin birth; his ministry of preaching, teaching, and healing; and his sacrificial death on the cross and his miraculous resurrection from the dead. As a centurion said when he observed Jesus' death, "Surely this man was the Son of God!" (Mark 15:39).

---

80. Cullmann, "Infancy Gospels," 442.

12

"He Took the Children in His Arms"

Jesus and Children

Some of the most touching scenes in all the Bible are those that depict Jesus with children around him. His words about children and his actions with them reveal his tender affection for the young.

On one occasion he took a little child to himself and said that welcoming little children was tantamount to welcoming him, the Lord. On another occasion, when parents were bringing their little children to him, he took the little ones in his arms and blessed them, saying that the kingdom of God belongs to individuals like them.

To us these scenes are moving. But to Jesus' close followers, his actions were disturbing, his words were stunning.

How could their Master, busy in teaching, preaching, and healing, have time for children? Their chatter would disturb him, their restless activity bother him. They would get in his way, and hinder his work. They would keep him from getting needed rest, or from engaging in more important ministry-related matters. How could children possibly contribute in any way to his work? How could they possibly exemplify or model his followers?

While few of the world's great religious leaders have had little regard for children,[1] Jesus was different. Not only did he welcome them; he even used them to teach adults some essential spiritual lessons! He never talked to children about what they could learn from adults, but he did tell adults some things to learn from children!

How contrary to the thinking of that day, which held that adults were wise and children lacked wisdom. Since children were to learn from adults, how could adults learn from children? How shocking, then, that Jesus reversed this view!

---

1. Leon Morris, *The Gospel According to St. Luke: An Introduction and Commentary* (Grand Rapids: Wm. B. Eerdmans Publishing Co., 1974), 266.

Want to enter God's kingdom? Then become like little children.

Want to be great in God's eyes? Then become like little children.

Want to let Jesus know you welcome and receive him? Then welcome little children.

Want to avoid judgment at God's hands? Then don't lead little children astray.

Want to identify with God's plans? Then don't belittle or despise little children.

Want to avoid rebuke from Jesus? Then don't prevent children from coming to him.

Want to follow Jesus' example of love? Then love, pray for, accept, be with, and bless little children.

These suggestions are clearly seen in Jesus' words and actions regarding children, recorded in the verses in the following table.

Table 6

Jesus' Words and Actions Regarding Children, Recorded in the Synoptic Gospels

Matthew 18:1–5	*Mark 9:33–37*	*Luke 9:46–48*
v. 1 At that time the disciples came to Jesus and asked, "Who is the greatest in the kingdom of heaven?"	*v. 33* They came to Capernaum. When he was in the house, he asked them, "What were you arguing about on the road?"	*v. 46* An argument started among the disciples as to which of them would be the greatest.
	v. 34 But they kept quiet because on the way they had argued about who was the greatest.	
	v. 35 Sitting down, Jesus called the Twelve and said, "If anyone wants to be first, he must be the very last, and the servant of all."	
v. 2 He called a little child and had him stand among them.	*v. 36a* He took a little child and had him stand among them. Taking him in his arms, he said to them,	*v. 47* Jesus, knowing their thoughts, took a little child and had him stand beside him.
v. 3 And he said, "I tell you the truth, unless you change and become like little children, you will never enter the kingdom of heaven."		

v. 4 "Therefore, whoever humbles himself like this child is the greatest in the kingdom of heaven."

v. 5 "And whoever welcomes a little child like this in my name welcomes me."

Matthew 18:6–7
v. 6 "But if anyone causes one of these little ones who believe in me to sin, it would be better for him to have a large millstone hung around his neck and to be drowned in the depths of the sea."

v. 7 "Woe to the world because of the things that cause people to sin! Such things must come, but woe to the man through whom they come."

Matthew 18:10, 14
v. 10 "See that you do not look down on one of these little ones. For I tell you that their angels in heaven always see the face of my Father in heaven."

v. 14 "In the same way your Father in heaven is not willing that any of these little ones should be lost."

v. 37 "Whoever welcomes one of these little children in my name welcomes me, and whoever welcomes me does not welcome me but the one who sent me."

Mark 9:42
v. 42 "And if anyone causes one of these little ones who believe in me to sin, it would be better for him to be thrown into the sea with a large millstone tied around his neck."

v. 48a Then he said to them, "Whoever welcomes this little child in my name welcomes me; and whoever welcomes me welcomes the one who sent me."

v. 48b "For he who is least among you all—he is the greatest."

Luke 17:1–2
v. 1 Jesus said to his disciples, "Things that cause people to sin are bound to come, but woe to that person through whom they come. It would be better for him to be thrown into the sea with a millstone tied around his neck than for him to cause one of these little ones to sin."

Matthew 19:13–15	*Mark 10:13–16*	*Luke 18:15–17*
v. 13 Then little children were brought to Jesus for him to place his hands on them and pray for them. But the disciples rebuked those who brought them.	*v. 13* People were bringing little children to Jesus to have him touch them, but the disciples rebuked them.	*v. 15* People were also bringing babies to Jesus to have him touch them. When the disciples saw this, they rebuked them.
v. 14 Jesus said, "Let the little children come to me, and do not hinder them, for the kingdom of heaven belongs to such as these."	*v. 14* When Jesus saw this, he was indignant. He said to them, "Let the little children come to me, and do not hinder them, for the kingdom of God belongs to such as these."	*v. 16* But Jesus called the children to him, and said, "Let the little children come to me, and do not hinder them, for the kingdom of God belongs to such as these."
v. 15 When he had placed his hands on them, he went on from there.	*v. 15* "I tell you the truth, anyone who will not receive the kingdom of God like a little child will never enter it."	*v. 17* "I tell you the truth, anyone who will not receive the kingdom of God like a little child will never enter it."
	v. 16 And he took the children in his arms, put his hands on them and blessed them.	

Matthew 18:1–14; Mark 9:33–37, 42; Luke 9:46–48; 17:1–2

These passages bear both similarities and differences. In all three Synoptics Jesus responded to the disciples' argument about who is the greatest in God's kingdom by a visual action (setting a child before them) and a verbal explanation (welcoming a child in his name is equal to welcoming him).

Mark wrote that Jesus asked the disciples what they were arguing about along the way (Luke added that Jesus knew their thoughts), and so, though at first they kept quiet (Mark 9:34) perhaps out of embarrassment, Matthew recorded that then they reported their question to him (Matt. 18:1). Mark placed Jesus' statement about being a servant at the beginning of his response (Mark 9:35), whereas Luke placed a similar statement (about the least being the greatest) at the end of the conversation (Luke 9:48b).

Matthew said Jesus "called" a little child *(paidion)* to him, and Mark and Luke wrote that Jesus "took" a little child. Matthew and Mark wrote that Jesus had the child "stand among them," and Luke wrote that the child stood beside Jesus. Since Mark added that Jesus took the child in his arms, presumably he called the child, had him stand beside him facing the disciples, and then set him on his lap (since Jesus was sitting down, Mark 9:35). The house in Capernaum was probably Peter and Andrew's (1:29).

Matthew included in this incident Jesus' statement about becoming like little children in order to enter the kingdom of heaven (Matt. 18:3), whereas Mark and Luke both included that statement with a later occasion when Jesus rebuked the disciples for preventing children from coming to him (Mark 10:15; Luke 18:17).

Only Matthew included Jesus' words that the person who humbles himself "like this child" is the greatest in God's eyes (Matt. 18:4).

Jesus' words about a millstone being thrown around the neck of one who causes "one of these little ones to sin" are recorded in all three Synoptics. However, Matthew placed those words immediately after the Lord's comments about welcoming a little child (Matt. 18:6–7), whereas Mark and Luke positioned them later (Mark 9:42; Luke 17:1–2) and Mark's record is briefer.

Only Matthew included Jesus' instruction not to look down on little ones, whose angels are in heaven (Matt. 18:10, 14).

Of interest is the way the passages on children function in their contexts. Jesus revealed his messiahship by his transfiguration, which was followed by a demonstration of his kingly power by healing a demon-possessed boy (Matt. 17:1–23; Mark 9:1–32; Luke 9:28–45). Perhaps the disciples' growing awareness of Jesus' coming kingdom led them to ponder who would have positions of honor in the kingdom. Would Peter, James, and John, who had been privileged to be with the Lord on the Mount of Transfiguration, receive the highest places? Would Peter, a prominent disciple, be in the top place of honor?[2] On the other hand, Peter had been sharply rebuked by Jesus (Matt. 16:23) and Jesus did not even respond to Peter's suggestion that three shelters be built on the mount. So, perhaps, Peter would not receive the highest position. But if he would not, who would?[3]

Jesus responded to their question about rank by pointing out that God's kingdom does not include people with high, self-focused ambitions. They needed to reverse (*strephō*, "to turn around") their thinking and become like little children (18:3). He had already given an example of humility in his submitting to paying the temple tax (17:24–27). Now he gave another example by calling a child to him, perhaps a child who already knew him and was, therefore, comfortable responding to and being with him.

Using a little child as a visual object lesson and with one brief sentence the Lord demonstrated that their question about prominence was highly inappropriate. With that kind of selfishness, they could not even get into the kingdom, let alone have a distinguished place in it!

---

2. Peter was frequently in the forefront in the Gospel of Matthew (4:18; 14:28–29; 15:15; 16:18, 22–23; 17:1, 4, 24–26; 18:21; 19:27; 26:33, 35, 37, 40, 58, 69, 73, 75).

3. William Hendriksen, *Exposition of the Gospel According to Matthew,* New Testament Commentary (Grand Rapids: Baker Book House, 1973), 685.

What did Jesus mean by the words, "become like little children"? Answers vary from children being receptive,[4] responsive to Jesus' call (like the little one Jesus called to him),[5] amenable and simple,[6] teachable,[7] modest and unspoiled,[8] trusting,[9] in need of instruction,[10] or sinless.

Preferable is the view that becoming like little children means two things: recognizing one's low estate and acknowledging one's helplessness and dependence. Just as children in the ancient world were viewed as insignificant, unimportant, and lacking in status,[11] and just as young children everywhere are totally dependent on adults to meet their needs, so Jesus' followers are to acknowledge their insignificance and weakness, and their dependence on him.[12]

Warfield commented on this idea this way: "The children of the kingdom enter it as children enter the world, stripped and naked—infants, for whom all must be done. . . ."[13] Lenski wrote that being childlike spiritually is like being children "who possess nothing but need everything; who are able to do nothing but receive everything. . . ."[14] Obviously, the disciples' aspiring to

4. I. Howard Marshall, *The Gospel of Luke*, New International Greek Testament Commentary (Grand Rapids: Wm. B. Eerdmans Publishing Co., 1978), 682.

5. George R. Beasley-Murray, *Baptism in the New Testament* (New York: St. Martin's Press, 1962), 326; and Lawrence O. Richards, *Expository Dictionary of Bible Words* (Grand Rapids: Zondervan Publishing House, 1985), 158.

6. Clement of Alexandria *Christ the Educator*, trans. Simon D. Wood (New York: Fathers of the Church, 1954), 20; S.E.L.O., *Children of Scripture* (London: G. Moorish, n.d.), 301; and Herbert Lockyer, *Everything Jesus Taught*, 5 vols. (New York: Harper & Row, 1976), 5:120.

7. B. A. Hinsdale, *Jesus as a Teacher* (St. Louis: Christian Publishing Co., 1895), 220; and Albert Barnes, *Barnes' Notes on the New Testament* (reprint, Grand Rapids: Kregel Publications, 1962), 82.

8. William L. Lane, *The Gospel According to Mark* (Grand Rapids: Wm. B. Eerdmans Publishing Co., 1974), 360.

9. Ernest Best, *Disciples and Discipleship: Studies in the Gospel According to Mark* (Edinburgh: T. & T. Clark, 1986), 96; and F. W. Farrar, *The Gospel According to St. Luke* (Cambridge: University Press, 1884), 333.

10. A follower of Jesus must admit, like a child, "that he is unwise in matters of the Kingdom [*sic*]" (Aloysius M. Ambrozic, *The Hidden Kingdom* [Washington, D.C.: Catholic Biblical Association of America, 1972], 152).

11. Leon Morris, *The Gospel According to Matthew* (Grand Rapids: Wm. B. Eerdmans Publishing Co., 1992), 459; idem, *The Gospel According to St. Luke: An Introduction and Commentary*, Tyndale New Testament Commentaries (Grand Rapids: Wm. B. Eerdmans Publishing Co., 1974), 176; Savas Agourides, "'Little Ones' in Matthew," *Bible Translator* 35 (July 1984): 330; Walter L. Liefeld, "Luke," in *The Expositor's Bible Commentary*, 12 vols. (Grand Rapids: Zondervan Publishing House, 1979–1992), 8 (1984): 931; and David Rhoades and Donald Michie, *Mark as Story: Introduction to the Narrative of a Gospel* (Philadelphia: Fortress Press, 1982), 132.

12. Hugh Anderson, *The Gospel of Mark*, New Century Bible Commentary (Grand Rapids: Wm. B. Eerdmans Publishing Co., 1976), 246; Craig L. Blomberg, *Matthew*, New American Commentary (Nashville: Broadman Press, 1992), 273; C. E. B. Cranfield, *The Gospel According to Saint Mark* (Cambridge: University Press, 1966), 324; Joseph A. Fitzmyer, *The Gospel According to Luke (X–XXIV)*, Anchor Bible (Garden City, N.Y.: Doubleday & Co., 1985), 1194; David Gooding, *According to Luke* (Grand Rapids: Wm. B. Eerdmans Publishing Co., 1987), 295; Jerome Kodell, "Luke and the Children: The Beginning and End of the Great Interpolation," *Catholic Biblical Quarterly* 49 (1987): 425, 428–29; David L. McKenna, *Mark*, Communicator's Commentary (Waco, Tex.: Word Books, Publisher, 1982), 206; Albrecht Oepke, "*pais*," in *Theological Dictionary of the New Testament*, 5 (1967):649; Alfred Plummer, *An Exegetical Commentary on the Gospel According to St. Matthew* (1915; reprint, Grand Rapids: Baker Book House, 1982), 249; and Hans-Ruedi Weber, *Jesus and the Children* (Atlanta: John Knox Press, 1979), 29.

greatness stood "far from the disposition which belongs to children of the kingdom."[15] Simply stated, entry into the kingdom requires recognizing one's childlike low estate and sensing one's helplessness. A person must acknowledge his sinful condition and his inability to save himself.[16]

Jesus then discussed the matter of rank in the kingdom, in direct response to the disciples' question in verse 1. In a striking paradox, he said that greatness in the kingdom results from humility (Matt. 18:4). The least is the greatest; the lowest is the highest. What is great before God is not a clamoring for prestige, but a humbling of oneself "like this child." In verse 3 he referred to children in general; now in verse 4 he referred to the child he had called to come stand beside him. Entry comes to those who are lowly and helpless; status comes to those who have a humble spirit like children. "A little child has no idea that he is great, and so in the kingdom of heaven the greatest is he who is least conscious of being great."[17] "True humility does not hanker after greatness, does not even think of it."[18]

The parallel passages in Mark 9:33–37 and Luke 9:46–48 do not include a statement corresponding to Matthew 18:4, which links childlike humility with greatness in the kingdom. However, Mark's report of Jesus taking a little child in his arms (Mark 9:36) is preceded by the Lord's words to the disciples, "If anyone wants to be first, he must be the very last, and the servant of all" (9:35). Luke, however, concluded Jesus' remarks to the disciples about children and greatness by the Lord's words, "For he who is least among you all— he is the greatest" (Luke 9:48). These two affirmations present the same truth but in reverse order: to be first, be the last; the least is the greatest.[19]

13. Benjamin B. Warfield, "Children," in *A Dictionary of Christ and the Gospels*, ed. James Hastings, 2 vols. (New York: Charles Scribner's Sons, 1907), 1:304 (reprinted in John E. Meeter, ed., *Selected Shorter Writings of Benjamin B. Warfield—I* [Nutley, N.J.: Presbyterian Reformed Publishing Co., 1970], 230).

14. R. C. H. Lenski, *The Interpretation of St. Matthew's Gospel* (Minneapolis: Augsburg Publishing House, 1964), 681.

15. Warfield, "Children," 1:304.

16. Another view is that becoming like a child means learning to say ʾabbāʾ ("father") again (Joachim Jeremias, *New Testament Theology* [New York: Scribner, 1971], 155–56) in the sense of placing one's trust in the Lord (Robert N. Brown, "Jesus and the Child as a Model of Spirituality," *Irish Biblical Studies* 4 [October 1982]: 187–89). Another suggestion is that becoming like a little child means to begin one's religious life afresh, seeing one's need for a new beginning, which requires humility (W. D. Davies and Dale C. Allison, Jr., *A Critical and Exegetical Commentary on the Gospel According to St. Matthew*, International Critical Commentary, 2 vols. (Edinburgh: T. & T. Clark, 1991), 2:758.

17. R. V. G. Tasker, *The Gospel According to St. Matthew: An Introduction and Commentary*, Tyndale New Testament Commentaries (Grand Rapids: Wm. B. Eerdmans Publishing Co., 1961), 175.

18. Lenski, *The Interpretation of St. Matthew's Gospel*, 683.

19. Robert Leaney suggests that in speaking of the "least among you," Jesus was referring to himself, with the child in their midst also being a symbol of himself ("Jesus and the Symbol of the Child [Luke ix. 46–48]," *Expository Times* 66 [1954]: 91–92). However, this seems unlikely, for this suggestion ignores the fact that the disciples were disputing about greatness. Also Jesus was not identifying himself with the child for he distinguished himself from the child ("Whoever welcomes this little child in my name welcomes me").

This debate among the disciples about which of them would be the greatest (Mark 9:33–34; Luke 9:46) stands as one of many spiritual inadequacies of the disciples, as seen in Mark's Gospel.[20] They misunderstood his teaching about the leaven (Mark 8:15–21), Peter rebuked Jesus about his death (8:31–32), they were powerless in dealing with a demon-possessed boy (9:18, 28–29), and they lacked understanding and were afraid (9:32).

Luke's second passage on Jesus and the children (Luke 18:15–17) is introduced by Jesus' similar words in 18:14: "For everyone who exalts himself will be humbled, and he who humbles himself will be exalted." (The fact that Jesus made this same remark in Luke 14:11 and Matthew 23:12 shows that some of his proverbial comments were made on more than one occasion.) Paradoxically, being elevated in God's eyes results not, as some suppose, from self-exaltation but from self-depreciation.

Matthew 18:5–6 relates Jesus' promise about receiving a child (v. 5)[21] and his warning against those who cause "little ones" to sin (v. 6). A number of writers say that the wording "welcomes a little child like this" refers not to literal children but to disciples who are like children. This view is based on the "children" who are defined in verses 3–4, as those believing adults who sense their lowly and hopeless condition and are humble.[22] However, since the little child was still on Jesus' lap, it seems preferable to see his words, "a little child like this," as meaning *both* children literally, and his adult followers.[23] As Bethune wrote years ago, "What right has one to say that the Master did not mean the little children themselves, whom he directly pointed to them? Besides, if it be true that all who become as little children are saved, is not the inference irresistible that those whom they become like, are saved also, when they go as little children before God?"[24]

20. McKenna, *Mark*, 195.

21. Matthew wrote "a little child such as this," Mark 9:37 has "one of these little children," and Luke 9:48 has "this little child."

22. Agourides, "'Little Ones' in Matthew," 330, 332; Barnes, *Barnes' Notes on the New Testament*, 82; Blomberg, *Matthew*, 273–74; D. A. Carson, "Matthew," in *Expositor's Bible Commentary*, 8:398; Hendriksen, *Exposition of the Gospel According to Matthew*, 689; Benjamin B. Warfield, "Little Ones," in *Dictionary of Christ and the Gospels*, 2:36–39 (reprinted in *Selected Shorter Writings of Benjamin B. Warfield—I*, 234–52).

23. Lenski says *both* literal children and believers with childlike humility are involved (*The Interpretation of St. Matthew's Gospel*, 686; and idem, *The Interpretation of St. Luke's Gospel* [Minneapolis: Augsburg Publishing House, 1961], 545–46). This is also the view of Beasley-Murray, *Baptism in the New Testament*, 327; R. T. France, *The Gospel According to Matthew: An Introduction and Commentary*, Tyndale New Testament Commentaries (Grand Rapids: Wm. B. Eerdmans Publishing Co., 1985), 284; Ezra P. Gould, *A Critical and Exegetical Commentary on the Gospel of St. Mark*, International Critical Commentary (Edinburgh: T. & T. Clark, 1896), 188; Robert P. Lightner, *Heaven for Those Who Can't Believe* (Schaumburg, Ill.: Regular Baptist Press, 1977), 37; and Alan H. McNeile, *The Gospel According to St. Matthew* (London: Macmillan & Co., 1955), 277.

24. George W. Bethune, "The Favour of God in Christ to Little Children," in *Children in Heaven*, ed. William E. Schenck (Philadelphia: Presbyterian Board of Publication, 1865), 140.

Rather than catering to important and popular people or being concerned about themselves, Jesus' followers are to treat favorably those who are viewed as unimportant and needy ("the world's little people"[25]). And by receiving them in Jesus' name, that is, on his behalf or for his sake, they would be receiving Christ himself, and God the Father who sent him. In other words, children are like his representatives, for they, like him, are humble. The Jews believed that a messenger of a king was to be treated like the king himself.[26] Therefore, the child was to be received as if he were Jesus. But this idea that Jesus' envoy was a child would have been shocking to his disciples.[27] To be true disciples of his, Jesus' followers must not only become like children; they must also forget about their own status and welcome children in the sense of loving them, helping them, caring for them, accepting them, and showing kindness to them. Believers must treat children just as they would their Lord. In fact, by welcoming a child of lowly estate, one welcomes Jesus and the Father, thus "playing host to God himself."[28]

Jesus' teaching shows that since greatness is found in the least, then all are great, and there is no place for wrangling over rank. "All people count, while comparison counts for nothing."[29] Servants rank "as high as their masters" for "there is no seniority in the Kingdom [sic]."[30]

The Lord's reference to "one of these little ones who believe in me" (18:6) suggests that young children can and do believe in him and receive him as their Savior.

The opposite of welcoming, helping, and loving children is to cause them to sin (18:6). Thirteen times Matthew used the verb *skandalizō*, "to offend, cause to fall, ensnare in a trap." Harming a child—by deceiving him, leading him into false teaching or sin, or setting a bad example by proudly striving for selfish interests—was a serious offense, so serious that physical death by drowning should be preferred. That is, before carrying out such a deed, it would be better for such a person to be put out of the way by an awful death, namely, drowning by having a large millstone tied around his neck and his being thrown into the sea. Placing grain between two circular stone slabs, each about four inches thick

25. Morris, *The Gospel According to Matthew*, 461. There seems to be little basis for saying the little ones are a special category of believers, those who are particularly vulnerable or persecuted (Weber, *Jesus and the Children*, 48–49), or recent converts, or materially or spiritually poor believers. The context of Matthew 10:42 shows, however, that "little ones" there probably refers to insignificant disciples. But that need not determine the meaning of "little ones" in another context, namely, 18:6, 10, 14.

26. "A man's messenger is like the man himself" (*m. Berakot* 5.5).

27. Weber, *Jesus and the Children* , 50.

28. John Nolland, *Luke 9:21–18:34*, Word Biblical Commentary (Dallas, Tex.: Word Books, Publisher, 1993), 521.

29. Darrell L. Bock, *Luke 1:1–9:50* (Grand Rapids: Baker Book House, 1994), 897.

30. J. Duncan M. Derrett, "Why Jesus Blessed the Children (Mark 10:13–16 par.)," *Novum Testamentum* 25 (1983): 17.

and seventeen to twenty inches in diameter, women turned the top stone with an upright pin near the rim to grind the grain. Occasionally, larger round stones were used, with a donkey connected to the upper stone to turn it as the animal walked in circles. Such an animal-driven millstone was so heavy that tying it around a person's neck would make escape from drowning impossible.[31] In these remarkable strong words, Jesus revealed two things: the danger of leading astray small children who love the Lord, and his own deep love for and valuing of "little ones." His followers should set aside boastful, self-centered ambition for kingdom positions and focus on serving and helping others, including vulnerable, dependent young children.

Verses 7–9 of Matthew 18 report the Lord's affirmation that stumbling blocks or entrapments (*skandalon*, from *skandalizō*, "to cause to sin, entrap"), though inevitable, will be judged by God. Even his disciples must not let themselves be ensnared by sin. Here, too, drastic action is necessary to avoid succumbing to temptation. In fact, one of the best ways to avoid causing little ones to be ensnared by sin is to avoid sin in one's own life.

Returning in verse 10 to the subject of "the little ones,"[32] Jesus firmly urged his listeners not to "look down on one of these little ones." By thinking themselves deserving of high rank in God's kingdom, they readily would scorn others, especially young children. Besides not damaging (*skandalizō*, v. 6) children, adult believers must not even *think* badly about them (*kataphroneō* means "to despise, disregard, or treat with contempt"), as if they amount to nothing. Again Jesus emphasized that children are to be viewed as highly important.

One reason for esteeming children and not disparaging them is that "their angels" are concerned about and are in constant communication with the heavenly Father about those children. Based on this verse, some writers say each believing child has his own guardian angel. True, angels do minister to believers (Heb. 1:14), and one way they do this is by guarding them (Ps. 91:11; cf. 34:7) and possibly mediating for them (Job 33:23). But these verses and Matthew 18:10 do not specify that *each* believer or child has a different angel guarding him. Warfield presents the idea that the angels of the "little ones" are their spirits after death.[33] However, nowhere does Scripture refer to believers in heaven as angels. Jesus did not refer to children who became angels or angels who had been children; instead he distinguished the two groups by the words "their children." As "their" (the children's) angels, these angelic beings have a special relationship to them, and carry out a special ministry on

---

31. Drowning was a common punishment in Greek and Roman society. Though rare in Jewish circles, Josephus referred to it being done at least once in Galilee (*The Antiquities of the Jews* 14.15.10).

32. "Little ones" *(mikroi)* occurs three times in this passage: in verses 6, 10, and 14.

33. Benjamin B. Warfield, "The Angels of Christ's 'Little Ones,'" *Bible Student* 6 (1902): 241–50 (reprinted in *Selected Shorter Writings of Benjamin B. Warfield—I*, 253–66). Carson also holds this view ("Matthew," 8:465).

their behalf (constantly beholding God the Father's face). How then can adults dare look down on young believing children?

To demonstrate God's loving care for children, Jesus stated that a shepherd with one hundred sheep will leave all ninety-nine and hunt for the lost one that "wandered off" (18:12). Here is another reason to regard children highly: God prizes them just as a shepherd rejoices over finding one sheep (18:13). "With a God like that, how dare anyone cause even one of the sheep to go astray?"[34]

Also, since God loves them, not wanting even one of them to perish (18:14),[35] should not Christians have the same loving concern for children's salvation and for protecting them from harmful influences?

Matthew 19:13–15; Mark 10:13–16; Luke 18:15–17

These verses about people bringing children to Jesus for him to bless them is the last of three similar passages in each of the Synoptic Gospels on Jesus and children.

Matthew 18:1–5	A child in their midst
Matthew 18:6–7	A millstone around the neck
Matthew 18:10, 14	Little ones' angels
Matthew 19:13–15	Children brought to Jesus
Mark 9:33–37	A child in their midst
Mark 9:42	A millstone around the neck
Mark 10:13–16	Children brought to Jesus
Luke 9:46–48	A child in their midst
Luke 17:1–2	A millstone around the neck
Luke 18:15–17	Children brought to Jesus

In all three Synoptics the pericope about children is followed by the account of the rich young man, who failed to acknowledge his own helplessness as a child. Also, the records in Matthew and Mark about children being brought to Jesus are preceded by his instructions about marriage and divorce.

Luke 18:15–17 appropriately follows and illustrates Jesus' words about the tax collector who humbled himself like a child before God (18:9–14).[36] In fact, several examples of humility "surround" the incident of Jesus and the children in order to demonstrate childlike dependence or faith in God, including the blind beggar (18:35–43) and Zacchaeus, another tax collector (19:1–9).

34. Carson, "Matthew," 8:401.
35. Lenski points out that the neuter for "one" in verses 6, 10, and 14 connects these verses to the neuter *paidion* in verse 2 ("a little child"), in verse 4 ("this little child"), and in verse 5 ("one such little child"), thereby showing that Jesus was still speaking of little children in verses 6, 10, 14.

Luke's two accounts about Jesus and children in 9:46–50 and 18:15–17 form a kind of *inclusio* to the "travel section" of Luke 9:51–19:44. The Lord's loving attitude toward children was, no doubt, known by the populace, for people (presumably parents) brought them to him for him to place his hands on them (Matt. 19:13) and touch them (Mark 10:13; Luke 18:15), and to pray for them (Matt. 19:13). He did place his hands on them (Matt. 19:15; Mark 10:16), and Mark added that Jesus took them in his arms (which Jesus also did when he set a child before the disciples, 9:36) and blessed them (10:16). Luke simply stated that he called them to him (Luke 18:16).

These were "little children" (*paidia,* Matt. 19:13; Mark 10:13), whereas Luke 18:15 has *brephoi* (infants or toddlers), which suggests that children of various young ages were included.[37] Possibly when the youngest ones were "brought," they were being carried.

Since Jesus frequently placed his hands on those he healed, some say the parents wanted their children to be healed.[38] However, nothing in these passages suggests the young ones were sick. According to the Babylonian Talmud, Jewish children were brought by their parents on the Day of Atonement for the scribes to bless them and pray for them.[39] To lay one's hands on another person and to pray for him or her was a form of blessing, asking God for his favor to rest on that person. Even today Jewish children are taken to the rabbi, who places his hand on the heads of children in the synagogue on Friday nights and blesses them.[40] The tense of the verb *kateulogeō,* "to bless fervently" (a word occurring only here in the New Testament), points to a repeated action. Jesus had urged the Twelve to receive little children (Matt. 18:5); here he put into action what he had commanded.

How quickly the disciples forgot what Jesus had said about welcoming children and not harming them (Matt. 18:4–6; Mark 9:37; Luke 9:48). Thinking young children would be a nuisance to the Lord, the disciples rebuked (*epitimaō,* "to reprove, censure, or threaten") those who brought their youngsters. The disciples wanted to stop them from disturbing Jesus, possibly

36. Stephen Fowl suggests that 18:15–17 does not expound 18:9–14 ("Receiving the Kingdom of God as a Child: Children and Riches in Luke 18:15ff.," *New Testament Studies* 39 [January 1993]: 153–58). However, John F. Hart defends the relationship of 18:15–17 to 18:9–14, seeing verse 14 as the link ("Review of 'Receiving the Kingdom of God as a Child: Children and Riches in Luke 18:15ff.,' by Stephen Fowl," *Journal of the Grace Evangelical Society* [Spring 1995]: 90–91).

37. Of interest is the fact that Luke used *brephos* six times in his Gospel (1:41, 44; 2:12, 16; 18:15; Acts 7:19), whereas the other Gospel writers did not use it at all.

38. Hugh K. Wagner, "Suffer Little Children and Forbid Them Not, to Come unto Me," *Bibliotheca Sacra* 65 (April 1908): 214–48.

39. *Sopherim* 18.5; cited by Joachim Jeremias, *Infant Baptism in the First Four Centuries,* trans. David Cairns (Philadelphia: Westminster Press, 1962), 49. Also see Weber, *Jesus and the Children,* 15.

40. I. Abrahams, *Studies in Pharisaism and the Gospels* (1917; reprint, New York: KTAV Publishing House, 1967), 119–20.

because they thought he was too busy, too tired, or unconcerned. The disciples reproved the parents because they believed their actions were improper, and because Jewish adults considered it a waste to spend time with children.[41] (Other examples of the disciples' lack of openness to others coming to Jesus are recorded in Matthew 15:23 and Luke 9:49–50.)

Only Mark wrote that Jesus was indignant at their action (Mark 10:14).[42] This is typical of Mark's frequent mention of Jesus' emotions (cf. 1:25, 41, 43; 3:5; 7:34; 8:12; 9:19), and Matthew's frequent omission of Jesus' human emotions. Following a positive, to-the-point command ("Let the little children come to me") and a terse negative command ("Do not hinder [lit., 'stop hindering'] them" Matt. 19:14; Mark 10:14; Luke 18:16),[43] Jesus gave the reason: "The kingdom of God [or heaven] belongs to such as these." These children who longingly came to Jesus and all who are like them belong to the Lord and his kingdom. "How shocking, therefore, to try to prevent them from approaching the King!"[44] How important, then, to give priority to children and ministries on their behalf.

Luke 9:51–19:44 is known as Luke's "travel narrative," from the time Jesus resolutely set out for Jerusalem (9:51) to his entering the temple (19:45) near the beginning of the week when he was crucified.[45] This lengthy section portrays Jesus' reversal of status from what would normally be expected. Rather than shunning despicable sinners or lowly individuals, God accepts them. And rather than accepting those who view themselves as spiritually superior, God rejects them. This is seen, as Talbert observes, in the good Samaritan and the bad priest and Levite (10:25–37), good inactive Mary and bad active Martha (10:38–42), the good unclean and the bad clean (11:37–41), the good poor and the bad rich (12:13–21), the good humble and the bad exalted (14:7–11), the good prodigal and the bad older brother (15:11–32), good Lazarus and the bad rich man (16:19–31), the good tax collector and the bad Pharisee (18:9–14), the good parents and children and the bad disciples (18:15–17), and the good poor and the bad rich ruler (18:18–30).[46] This frequent reversal of values helps underscore the contrast between the disci-

41. Oepke, "*pais*," 5:646–47.
42. This word "to be indignant" is used of the disciples who were disturbed by James' and John's request to have prominent positions next to Jesus (Matt. 20:24; Mark 10:41); of the Twelve in their disgust with a woman who lovingly poured perfume on Jesus' head (Matt. 26:8; Mark 14:4); and of the chief priests and teachers of the Law, who were angry that children were praising Jesus in the temple area (Matt. 21:15). But only once did a Gospel writer refer to Jesus being indignant (Mark 10:14).
43. This is the third prohibition he gave regarding children: Do not cause them to sin, do not despise them, do not detain them.
44. Alfred Plummer, *An Exegetical Commentary on the Gospel According to St. Matthew* (reprint, Grand Rapids: Baker Book House, 1982), 262.
45. Most of the material in this section is found only in Luke's Gospel (viz., 9:51–18:14 and 19:2–27).
46. Charles H. Talbert, *Reading Luke* (New York: Crossroad Publishing Co., 1982), 171–72.

ples' poor attitude toward children, which Jesus denounced, and the childlike attitude needed by those who would enter the kingdom of God.

Mark and Luke then recorded Jesus' words that a person who "will not receive the kingdom like a little child will never enter it" (Mark 10:15; Luke 18:17). This is similar to Jesus' words in Matthew, "Unless you change and become like little children, you will never enter the kingdom of heaven" (Matt. 18:3). Not only are children to be welcomed or received (Matt. 18:5; Mark 9:37); also the kingdom is to be received. To "receive" the kingdom, an unusual expression, suggests receiving or responding to the message of the kingdom. To "enter" the kingdom is equivalent to receiving salvation, as Jesus explained to the rich young man (Luke 18:24–25) and to Nicodemus (John 3:5).

Some writers contend that receiving the kingdom like a child means receiving it just as one would receive a child, that is, eagerly and affectionately.[47] However, it is preferable to understand the phrase to mean "receiving the kingdom as a child receives it." But what constitutes a childlike attitude? As stated earlier, a child recognizes his lowly, helpless condition, he knows he is insignificant, small, and totally dependent. God's kingdom is not achieved by human effort; "it must be received as God's gift through simple trust by those who acknowledge their inability to gain it any other way."[48]

Several points become evident in this incident. First, parents today, like parents then, should be concerned about bringing their young ones to the Lord Jesus. Second, Jesus is never too busy for children. Third, Jesus loves young children. As Major wrote, "Jesus may be justly acclaimed as the lover of little children."[49] Fourth, to obstruct children's ministries is to oppose what Jesus desires. Fifth, members of God's kingdom include children and adults who come to the Lord with a childlike sense of helplessness and dependence. Sixth, children are the model of how to receive God's kingdom, that is, how to enjoy the blessings that come from being under God's rule.

Other Incidents Involving Children

Healing and Restoring to Life

Jesus' concern and love for children is also seen in his willingness to heal sick children. As stated in chapter 1, the Gospels record his restoring three

47. W. K. L. Clarke, *New Testament Problems* (London: SPCK, 1929), 36–38; C. J. Cadoux, *The Historic Mission of Jesus* (New York: Harper, 1941), 230–31; Frederick Schilling, "What Means the Saying about Receiving the Kingdom of God as a Little Child?" *Expository Times* 77 (1965–66): 56–58; and Vernon K. Robbins, "Pronouncement Stories and Jesus' Blessing of the Children: A Rhetorical Approach," *Semeia* 29 (1983): 59. Also see J. I. H. McDonald, "Receiving and Entering the Kingdom. A Study of Mark 10:15," *Studia Evangelica*, ed. Elizabeth A. Livingstone, 6 (1973): 329–30.

48. John G. Grassmick, "Mark," in *The Bible Knowledge Commentary, New Testament,* ed. John F. Walvoord and Roy B. Zuck (Wheaton, Ill.: Victor Books, 1983), 150.

49. H. D. A. Major, *The Mission and Message of Jesus* (New York: E. P. Dutton & Co., 1938), 128.

children back to health. One was the royal official's little boy who was close to death in Capernaum (John 4:43–54). (The child is called "son" [*hyios,* vv. 46–47, 50, 52–53], "little child" [*paidion,* v. 49], and "child" or "boy" [*pais,* v. 51].) Another was an epileptic, deaf and dumb demon-possessed boy, the only child of his parents, whom Jesus healed when he descended from the Mount of Transfiguration (Matt. 17:14–18; Mark 9:17–27; Luke 9:37–43). In both cases the father sought out Jesus for help. In fact, the official even traveled about twenty miles from his hometown of Capernaum to Cana, where Jesus was.

Two of the three people Jesus raised from the dead were children: the twelve-year-old daughter of Jairus, a synagogue ruler (Matt. 9:18–19, 23–26; Mark 5:21–24, 35–43), and the son of a widow from Nain, a Galilean town about twenty miles southwest of Capernaum (Luke 7:11–17). In the girl's case, Jesus affectionately called her "Talitha" (Mark 5:41), an Aramaic word meaning "little girl." And in the case of the widow's son (an incident reported only by Luke), Jesus was moved with compassion toward the grieving mother. The words "his heart went out to her" translate *esplanchnisthē,* a verb related to the plural noun *splanchna,* "inner parts of the body." That is, he felt sympathy for her. In raising the widow's son from the dead, Jesus then addressed the corpse in the funeral procession as "young man" (*neaniske,* 7:14).

Receiving Children's Praise

After Jesus chided the disciples for interfering with parents bringing their children to him (Matt. 19:13–15), a rich young man who came to Jesus showed that he failed to have a childlike attitude (19:16–22). Though "first" or prominent in wealth, the man would discover that he was "last." Conversely, Jesus' followers who become "last" by giving up everything including family and possessions (19:28–29) to follow the Lord (as Peter said he had done, 19:27), would be "first." The same thought of the lowly and faithful being blessed was then illustrated by Jesus' parable of the vineyard workers, all of whom received the same wages even though some worked fewer hours than others (20:1–15). Again, as with small children who are honored by the Lord, Jesus said, "The last will be first, and the first will be last" (20:16).

Yet two of the disciples, James and John, still clamored for high positions in the kingdom (20:20–21)! Again they failed to grasp their Lord's words about the kingdom of heaven belonging to people who are like children with humble, dependent attitudes. So once again the Lord affirmed the paradoxical principle that greatness comes from humility: "Whoever wants to become great among you must be your servant, and whoever wants to be first must be your slave" (20:26–27). He set the example of servanthood by coming "not to be served, but to serve" (20:28).

Then at Jesus' triumphal entry, the crowds praised him with shouts of "Hosanna!" (21:9). But when he drove merchants out from the temple area

(21:12–13) and healed blind and lame people there (21:14), the religious leaders became angry. They were also infuriated that children in the temple were shouting "Hosanna to the Son of David," just as their parents had done (21:15).

Jesus had reason to be indignant when the disciples sought to prevent his being disturbed by children (Mark 10:14). But the priests and teachers were wrong in being indignant (Matt. 21:15) that children were shouting and that he did not stop them. Whereas Jesus was vexed because the disciples stopped children, the leaders were vexed because Jesus would not stop children!

When the priests and teachers asked, "Do you hear what these children are saying?" (21:16), they were challenging him to stop the children's echoing of the crowd's praise. However, his response in the form of a question turned their rebuke back on them. Beginning with the words, "Have you never read. . . ." (a question he asked several times, 12:3, 5; 19:4; 21:42; 22:31), he then quoted Psalm 8:2, "From the lips of children and infants you have ordained praise" (21:16). In other words, rather than the children's praise being impertinent, it was entirely fitting—far more appropriate, in fact, than the squabbles of the religious elite! Interestingly, "of children" translates *nēpiōn* ("preschoolers") and "of infants" renders the participle of the verb *thēlazō*, "to suck." Here is still another indication of the Lord's appreciation of and love for the very young.

If the Lord receives praise from infants, who cannot even talk, certainly the praise of preschoolers and older children, who shouted "Hosanna" to Jesus, is acceptable.

Here again, those who are "first" or who are in prominent places, namely, the Jewish leaders, are actually "last" in God's eyes. And those who are "last" or least, namely, young children, are actually "first" in the Lord's kingdom. By rejecting Jesus, the spiritual rulers "did not even have the insights of children, who were receiving him (cf. Matt. 18:3–4)."[50]

These several encounters of our Savior with children, even very young children, demonstrate that the young, being precious in God's sight, are to be loved, appreciated, blessed, prayed for, welcomed, and protected. Adults are to become like children and are to learn from them. Heaven will be populated with children—and with adults who have become childlike in their loving response to the Savior.

---

50. Louis A. Barbieri, "Matthew," in *The Bible Knowledge Commentary, New Testament*, 69.

13

"OF SUCH IS THE KINGDOM OF GOD"

Children, Baptism, and Salvation

Anyone interested in the spiritual welfare of children confronts a number of serious theological and practical questions.

Are children born with a sin nature? If so, what is their eternal destiny if they die as infants? Will they be condemned to an eternity in hell, or will they in some way make it to heaven? If they are doomed to eternal punishment, is God fair? If they go to heaven, how is their sin covered?

Are unregenerate infants in heaven? And if so, does this mean that heaven is attainable by some means other than faith in Christ? And how can anyone who is not regenerate be in heaven?

Is it important for young children to be led to receive Christ as Savior at the earliest possible age in order for their sin nature to be atoned for before they die? Or is the answer for infants to be baptized? If infant baptism is the answer, what effect does it actually have? Does it bring salvation, thus enabling an infant who dies to go to heaven? If it provides entry into the church, the body of Christ, as some teach, how does that differ from baptismal regeneration? If a child dies without being baptized, will he be eternally lost? If so, why, and if not, why not?

If children are not born with a sin nature, is infant baptism necessary? And if children are born "innocent," at what age do they become sinners accountable to God? Is there an "age of accountability"? How do the doctrines of Adam's imputed sin nature and of original sin relate to the question of children's "lostness" or innocence?

If infants are incapable of exercising personal faith in Christ, how can they be lost? If they can neither consciously accept or reject Christ, will they be lost forever if they die in infancy? Are they doomed to hell even though they did not have the ability to believe?

217

If a child is baptized as an infant, is conversion later as an adolescent or adult necessary, or is the individual already in God's family? What scriptural basis do some churches give in support of this practice of infant baptism? Why do other churches refuse to baptize infants? On what Scripture do they base their view? Does their view mean children do not need salvation? What is the purpose of baptism, according to the New Testament?

Do children of Christian parents stand in some special relationship to God? If so, what effect does that have on their children's spiritual condition? If they are not in a special relationship to God by virtue of their being born to believing parents, what does this say about the evangelism of children? Is there such a thing as "household salvation," in which young children are saved because they are in a Christian family? What is the eternal destiny of children of unsaved parents?

If children are not baptized as infants, at what age should they be baptized and why? At what age are they capable of understanding the gospel and coming to Christ for salvation? Are children saved up to the time they sense an accountability before God? If so, does this mean they are saved at birth and then later become lost and in need of salvation again? If this is not what the Bible teaches, then if infants who die go to heaven, on what basis do they do so?

Are young children who may not fully comprehend all aspects of sin and salvation genuinely converted, or are they being encouraged to "go through the motions," with the result that they are not genuinely regenerated and then have doubts about salvation in later childhood or early adolescence? How can parents and workers with children be sure these youngsters adequately comprehend what is involved in salvation?

This chapter seeks to address these thorny questions—questions of deep importance and on which churches have differed for centuries. More than mere theoretical issues, these questions impinge on the very heart of the gospel and relate pointedly to children and their salvation, and how we should minister to them.

Will Infants Who Die Go to Heaven?

As discussed in chapter 12, Jesus made some interesting, even startling, statements about children. Included in those comments were his words to the disciples, "The kingdom of heaven [or 'of God'] belongs to such as these" (Matt. 19:14; Mark 10:14; Luke 18:16); or as the New American Standard Bible puts it, "Of such is the kingdom of heaven [or 'of God']." This indicates that adults who are like children in acknowledging their lowly and helpless condition will enter God's kingdom. But the Greek *toiautē* ("of such as these") also indicates that children too are in God's kingdom. And as Luke wrote, this includes infants (Luke 18:15–17). But how do those young children get into the kingdom? Undoubtedly, many infants get there by death.

The high infant mortality in many countries of the world now and in past centuries suggests that numerous young children are in heaven. Jesus' statement, however, should not be understood as meaning that all children, regardless of their age, are members of God's kingdom.[1] Other children, who live several years beyond infancy and then receive Christ as their Savior (receiving the kingdom as a child; Mark 10:15; Luke 18:17), go to heaven when they die. Having been regenerated by their faith in Christ, they obviously belong to the kingdom of God (John 3:3). They are among those "little ones who believe in me," as Jesus said (Matt. 18:6).

When the baby boy born illegitimately to David and Bathsheba became ill, David prayed and fasted for his healing, lying in anguish on the ground each night. But a week after the baby became sick, he died (2 Sam. 12:15–18). Then David told his servants, "I will go to him, but he will not return to me" (12:23). This speaks of the finality of death, but it also speaks of David's intense desire to be with his son. Some say David was referring only to his own death but not to his being in conscious fellowship with his son after death.[2] However, there would hardly be any comfort in David's saying he would die too. Instead, this verse suggests that his son was experiencing after death a conscious existence in God's presence, and that David anticipated some day joining him. This fact has been a source of great comfort to many Christian parents whose infants have died. "The idea of meeting his child in the unconscious grave could not have rationally comforted him; nor could the thought of meeting him in hell have cheered his spirit; but the thought of meeting him in heaven had in itself the power of turning his weeping into joy."[3]

Though the Bible does not explicitly state that deceased infants of *unsaved* parents go to heaven, Jesus' words to the disciples and David's words to his servants may well imply that this is the case. For this reason a number of authors assert that heaven is occupied with many children, perhaps with even more children than adults. In the nineteenth century John Newton wrote that the number of infants in heaven "so greatly exceeds the aggregate of adult believers that, comparatively speaking, the kingdom may be said to consist of little children."[4] Charles Spurgeon wrote, "I rejoice to know that the souls of all infants, as soon as they die, speed their way to paradise. Think what a multitude there is of them!"[5]

1. Perry G. Downs, "Child Evangelization," *Journal of Christian Education* 3 (1983): 10.
2. John Sanders, *No Other Name* (Grand Rapids: Wm. B. Eerdmans Publishing Co., 1992), 289.
3. R. A. Webb, *The Theology of Infant Salvation* (Clarksville, Tenn.: Presbyterian Committee of Publication, 1907), 20–21.
4. John Newton, *The Works of John Newton*, 3d ed., 6 vols. (1820; reprint, Edinburgh: Banner of Truth Trust, 1985), 4:552.
5. Charles H. Spurgeon, *Spurgeon at His Best* (Grand Rapids: Baker Book House, 1988), 95.

How can there be in heaven a countless number of people "from every nation, tribe, people and language" (Rev. 7:9)? Surely not every tribe of people around the world has adult believers. Is it not possible, therefore, that a number of tribes will be represented by children who die in infancy? And if this is the case, this would point to the probability that infants of even unbelieving parents go to heaven.

Another argument in support of infants being in heaven is Jesus' words that "Your Father in heaven is not willing that any of these little ones should be lost" (Matt. 18:14). In view of that fact, "how can it be that little children, who are set before [the disciples] as . . . patterns for imitation . . . should perish?"[6] Since it is the Lord's will that these little ones not perish, it is clear that at death they "go to be among the blessed in that heaven, to the kingdom [to] which . . . they belong. . . ."[7]

Almost half a century ago Linton advocated the idea that there will be no babies in heaven. He argued for this view by saying that since everyone in heaven will have a resurrected body, no one will be resurrected to "the weakness of infancy, or the unwisdom of childhood, but into a full grown man."[8] However, this wrongly assumes that an infant in heaven "still needs to grow to maturity," and that his resurrection would "not be a work of perfection."[9] Is it not possible that infants can be resurrected with perfect bodies and still be infants?

By What Means Will Deceased Infants Go to Heaven?

Numerous answers have been given to this question. First, some say all children who die as infants are taken to heaven because of the doctrine of universalism. That is, since everyone will ultimately be saved and no one will be in hell, infants too will naturally be in heaven, even though they had no opportunity to believe.

However, the teaching that all will ultimately be saved runs counter to Bible verses that affirm the eternal damnation of the unsaved (e.g., Matt. 25:46; John 3:16, 18; 3:36; Rev. 20:15). And yet this is not to deny the heavenly home of dead infants. It simply means that universalism is not the basis of their salvation.

Second, some affirm a heavenly destiny for infants because they are born innocent, without sin. Ingle, a Southern Baptist seminary professor, writes

6. George W. Bethune, "The Favour of God in Christ to Little Children," in *Children in Heaven,* ed. William E. Schenck (Philadelphia: Presbyterian Board of Publication, 1865), 144.
7. Ibid., 145.
8. John Linton, *Concerning Infants in Heaven* (Grand Rapids: Wm. B. Eerdmans Publishing Co., 1949), 68.
9. Ibid., 69.

that a child "does not inherit lostness [from Adam]; he chooses it."[10] All persons, Ingle says,

are born with a tendency toward sin; all are destined to sin. However, the individual is not responsible for the sins of the [human] race or his inherited nature. He becomes an actual sinner in the eyes of God when, as a morally responsible person, he chooses sin and rebels against God. Thus there is a time between birth and moral accountability when the child is not guilty for sin.[11]

Inchley believes that children are not "in a state of being lost from God," and that until they deliberately refuse Christ, they belong to him.[12] "We must resist the temptation," Jeschke writes, "to place the human race into only two classes, the saved and the lost. We are required to recognize also a third class, the innocent. . . ."[13] However, this view that children are born innocent and without an inherited sin nature conflicts with Scriptures that teach that everyone enters the world as a sinner. "Even though innocent compared to adults who consciously sin, infants and all who can't believe are under the curse of Adam's sin."[14] "In Adam all die" (1 Cor. 15:22). God told Noah after the flood that he would not bring about another flood of that magnitude "even though every inclination of [man's] heart is evil from childhood" (Gen. 8:21). Solomon wrote, "Folly is bound up in the heart of a child" (Prov. 22:15). And David said he was born "sinful at birth" (Ps. 51:5), and that "even from birth the wicked go astray" (58:3). As Paul affirmed, "There is no one righteous, not even one" (Rom. 3:10). All are "under sin" (3:9) and under God's wrath (John 3:36), and that includes children.

Everyone is born with a sin nature, inherited from Adam, because all mankind was somehow in Adam when he sinned (Rom. 5:12). His sin plunged the entire human race into a stance of guilt before God, because all sinned "in Adam." Therefore, people sin because they are sinners; it is not that they become sinners by sinning.[15] This means that because all infants come with a sin nature, they are all lost and condemned. To say infants are neutral or innocent with respect to sin, and that they are not sinners until they knowingly commit acts of sin, overlooks these significant Scripture verses about the universality of sin. "A theology of childhood salvation must begin with the point that all people, including children,

10. Clifford Ingle, "Children and Conversion," *Sunday School Builder*, March 1989, 9.

11. Clifford Ingle, "Moving in the Right Direction," in *Children and Conversion*, ed. Clifford Ingle (Nashville: Broadman Press, 1970), 153–54.

12. John Inchley, *Kids and the Kingdom* (Wheaton, Ill.: Tyndale House Publishers, 1976), 14, 33.

13. Marlin Jeschke, *Believers Baptism for Children of the Church* (Scottdale, Penn.: Herald Press, 1983), 104.

14. Robert P. Lightner, *Heaven for Those Who Can't Believe* (Schaumburg, Ill.: Regular Baptist Press, 1977), 7–8.

15. Ibid., 8.

are sinful and in need of redemption."[16] Therefore, there must be some reason other than sinlessness that accounts for infants being in heaven.

A third explanation is that when infants die they immediately mature and are then given opportunity to place their faith in Christ for salvation. This view, first proposed by Gregory of Nyssa of the fourth century, builds on the conviction that faith is necessary for salvation.[17] Buswell has suggested the unlikely view that immediately before death the intelligence of the infant is enlarged so that the child can accept Christ as Savior.[18]

This view, however, is only conjecture; it has no biblical support. If infants immediately before or after death are given the opportunity to be saved, this suggests that some will go to heaven and others will not. And if this enablement to believe occurs after death, where is the child while he is confronted with the claims of Christ? This view wrongly suggests a neutral state after death, before one's final destiny in heaven or hell.

Fourth, infants who die will be in heaven because they are elected by God. Ulrich Zwingli, the Swiss Reformer, asserted that all children of believing parents are among the elect and, therefore, will be saved, and that probably dying infants of non-Christian parents are also among the elect. Many Reformed theologians hold this view. Charles Hodge based the belief that "all who die in infancy are saved" on Romans 5:18–19, "Consequently, just as the result of one trespass was condemnation for all men, so also the result of one act of righteousness was justification that brings life for all men. For just as through the disobedience of the one man the many were made sinners, so also through the obedience of the one man the many will be made righteous." He also referred to Romans 5:20, "But where sin increased, grace increased all the more." Warfield also defended the view that all infants who die go to heaven by pointing out that for infants God's electing grace supersedes their inborn sin nature because God has chosen them.[19] The Westminster Confession says, "Elect infants, dying in infancy, are regenerated and saved by Christ through the Spirit."[20] While this statement does not explicitly affirm that all dying infants are elect (the words "elect infants" leave the question open), most Presbyterians would, no doubt, affirm that all infants who die are in fact included among the elect.[21]

---

16. Downs, "Child Evangelization," 11.

17. George J. Dyer, "The Unbaptized Infant in Eternity," *Chicago Studies* 2 (1963): 147. Sanders points out that a number of Roman Catholics affirm this view (*No Other Name*, 298; see Ladislaus Boros, *The Mystery of Death*, trans. Gregory Bainbridge [New York: Herder & Herder, 1965], 109–11).

18. J. Oliver Buswell, Jr., *A Systematic Theology of the Christian Religion*, 2 vols. (Grand Rapids: Zondervan Publishing House, 1963), 2:162.

19. Benjamin B. Warfield, "The Development of the Doctrine of Infant Salvation," in *Studies in Theology* (New York: Oxford University Press, 1932), 438.

20. Westminster Confession, chap. 10, sec. 3.

21. For example, Thomas Smyth, "Opinions on Infant Salvation," in *Children in Heaven*, 34; and Roger Nicole, cited by Ronald H. Nash, in *What about Those Who Have Never Heard?* ed. John Sanders (Downers Grove, Ill.: InterVarsity Press, 1995), 119–20.

Fifth, infants can be saved by the "baptism of desire," that is, if they desired baptism but were unable to obtain it before they died, they would go to heaven. This view was held in the ninth century by Hincmar of Rheims (d. 882).[22] Martin Luther applied the idea of the baptism of desire to Christian parents, saying that their desire for their children's baptism, even if not carried out, guarantees their offspring's salvation. However, how can an infant desire baptism? And how does a parent's mere desire substitute for a child's salvation? Also, this view does not adequately address the question of infants of unsaved parents, who may not desire salvation for their young or may know nothing of salvation and baptism. This suggests that salvation for those infants is not available and that they are lost forever.

A sixth view maintains that all infants who die will be regenerated because they have not willfully rejected Christ.[23] This view follows this line of reasoning: (1) Only those who consciously reject Christ are condemned to hell. (2) Infants cannot knowingly turn from Christ. (3) Therefore, all dying infants will be in heaven, even though they are born sinners and do not exercise faith. The problem with this view is that it makes eternal damnation dependent on a willful refusal to believe in Jesus Christ. If this is the basis of judgment in hell, how can those who never heard of Christ be condemned? Therefore, the basis of the condemnation is not rejection of Christ, but the commitment of sins based on one's inherited sin nature. "In Adam all die" (1 Cor. 15:22; cf. Rom. 5:12). Paul reasoned in Romans 1 that all are under the guilt of sin and the wrath of God because of their sin. Therefore, only God's grace can atone for the sin of infants. This leads to the seventh view, which I prefer over the other views.

A seventh view is that all infants enjoy heavenly bliss not because they are born sinless or because they mature immediately after death so they can exercise faith or because they are elect or had a desire for baptism or salvation or because they did not willingly reject Christ, but because of the redemptive work of Christ on the cross. Like everyone, infants need salvation. And salvation is only through Christ. Therefore, even though infants cannot exercise faith in him, he can remove their depravity. "If they be saved, it must be entirely by the sovereign mercy and positive operation of God. . . . All redeemed sinners owe their salvation to sovereign grace . . . but the salvation of infants is with peculiar circumstances of [God's] favour."[24] In July 1525, the Anabaptist theologian Balthasar Hübmaier, writing against the Swiss Reformers' practice of infant baptism, stated that while we cannot know for sure on what basis unbaptized infants go to heaven, God no doubt saves them because of his grace.[25] Also, Spurgeon said infants enter heaven "as a matter of free grace

---

22. Warfield, *Studies in Theology*, 415.
23. Neal Punt, *What's Good about the Good News?* (Chicago: Northland, 1988), chap. 11.
24. David McConoughy, "Are Infants Saved?" in *Children in Heaven*, 60.
25. Balthasar Hübmaier, *On the Christian Baptism of Believers*, in William R. Estep, ed. *Anabaptist Beginnings (1523–1533): A Source Book* (Nieuwkoop: D. De Graaf, 1976), 93.

with no reference to anything they have done."[26] Downs, Lightner, and Lockyer all concur.[27]

Sanders thinks it inconsistent to say God saves some (adults) by faith but others (infants) without faith.[28] This objection is answerable by noting that in all cases God's grace provides salvation. Even though infants cannot hear the Word and, therefore, cannot exercise faith (Rom. 10:17), God need not be limited, as Calvin noted, because he works in ways we cannot always perceive, and he can still bestow his grace.[29]

An eighth view is that infants qualify for entrance to heaven by virtue of their having been baptized. Roman Catholicism maintains that infant baptism removes the stain of original sin. "Baptism . . . signifies that by the power of the Holy Ghost all stain and defilement of sin is inwardly washed away, and that the soul is enriched and adorned with the admirable gift of heavenly justification. . . ."[30] The recently published new *Catechism of the Catholic Church* states, "Through Baptism we are freed from sin and reborn as sons of God; we become members of Christ, are incorporated into the Church and made sharers in her mission: Baptism is the sacrament of regeneration through water in the word."[31] Since the sacrament of infant baptism is necessary for salvation, according to Catholicism, infants must be baptized in order for them to qualify for heaven. The logical corollary of this position is that unbaptized infants do not enter heaven. In fact, according to Augustine (A.D. 354–430), "the wrath of God abides on them," they "remain in darkness," and they are eternally doomed, though their punishment is less severe than that of others.[32] As Sanders points out, Augustine's position was the dominant view of the Western church throughout the Middle Ages.[33] Even today

---

26. Charles H. Spurgeon, *Come Ye Children* (reprint, Warrenton, Mo.: Child Evangelism Fellowship, n.d.), 39.

27. Downs, "Child Evangelization," 11; Lightner, *Heaven for Those Who Can't Believe*, 14–15; Herbert Lockyer, *All the Children of the Bible* (Grand Rapids: Zondervan Publishing House, 1970), 97.

28. Sanders, *No Other Name*, 304.

29. John Calvin, *Institutes of the Christian Religion*, trans. John T. McNeill, 2 vols. (Philadelphia: Westminster Press, 1960), 4.16.17; 4.16.19.

30. *Catechism of the Council of Trent*, 144, cited by J. C. Macaulay, *The Bible and the Roman Church* (Chicago: Moody Press, 1949), 81. Also see Günter Koch, "Baptism," in *Handbook of Catholic Theology*, ed. Wolfgang Beinert and Francis Schüsler Florenza (New York: Crossroad Publishing Co., 1995), 43.

31. *Cateshism of the Catholic Church* (New Hope, N.Y.: St. Martin de Porres Community, 1994), 1213.

32. Augustine *On the Merits and Forgiveness of Sins and on the Baptism of Infants* 1.21, 28, 33–35, in Philip Schaff, ed., *A Select Library of the Nicene and Post-Nicene Fathers of the Christian Church* (New York: Charles Scribner's Sons, 1908), 5:22–23, 25, 28–29. A more harsh view on the woe of infants was held by Fulgenticus (d. 533), Alcimis Avitus (d. 525), and Gregory the Great (d. 604), according to Warfield ("The Polemics of Infant Baptism," in *Studies in Theology*, 413).

33. Sanders, *No Other Name*, 292. According to the Roman Catholic Catechism of the Council of Trent, "Infants, unless regenerated unto God through the grace of baptism, whether their parents be Christian or infidel, are born to eternal misery and perdition."

this harsh view is held by some Reformed theologians. After more than one hundred people, including a number of young children, died in the bombing of a federal building in Oklahoma City in 1995, Sproul chided Billy Graham for saying in the memorial service that innocent children who died in the bombing are in God's arms in heaven. Sproul wrote that all those who died without having received Christ as Savior, *whether adults or children,* "are experiencing . . . anguish and torment in hell."[34] A number of church leaders and theologians, however, believed that unbaptized infants do go to heaven, including Victor, John Wycliffe, the Lollards, and John Calvin.[35]

To soften the severity of the Augustinian position, the Roman Catholic Church developed the idea of Limbo (*limbus infantum*), a neutral place for infants who die unbaptized. In this place between heaven and hell, children experience neither bliss or torment.[36] While this is not an official dogma of the Catholic Church, it is not denied either. But, as McCarthy explains, "In discussing the fate of unbaptized infants, modern Catholicism usually entrusts their souls to the mercy of God, making no mention of limbo. . . . Nonetheless, even today, when a Catholic persists in asking where unbaptized infants go when they die, the answer usually comes back, 'Limbo.'"[37] No scriptural support can be given for this position, however. As Beasley-Murray wrote, "only an evil doctrine of God and man sets them [children dying before the age of responsibility] among the lost or in limbo. . . ."[38]

Obviously, if baptism is essential for salvation, many infants will not be in heaven. The Roman Catholic position limits salvation unduly, makes salvation obtainable not by faith but by a sacrament or work,[39] and in condemning many infants to limbo obliterates the view that Christ's atoning work removes, by his grace, the guilt of original sin for all infants and others who cannot believe.[40]

---

34. R. C. Sproul, Jr., "Comfort Ye My People," *World,* May 6, 1995, 26. He did admit, though, that "we cannot say for sure what happens to young children who die" (ibid.).
35. Calvin wrote that "infants are not excluded from the kingdom of heaven, who happen to die before they have had the privilege of baptism" (*Institutes of the Christian Religion,* 4.15.22).
36. Josef Finkenzeller, "Limbo," in *Handbook of Catholic Theology,* 433–35; Zachary Hayes, "Limbo," in *The Modern Catholic Encyclopedia* (Collegeville, Minn.: Liturgical Press, 1994), 511; and P. J. Hill, "Limbo," in *New Catholic Encyclopedia,* 18 vols. (New York: McGraw-Hill Book Co., 1967), 8:762–63, 765.
37. James G. McCarthy, *The Gospel According to Rome* (Eugene, Oreg.: Harvest House Publishers, 1995), 27.
38. George R. Beasley-Murray, *Baptism in the New Testament* (New York: St. Martin's Press, 1962), 343.
39. The Fifth Session of the Roman Catholic Council of Trent (1545–1565) states, "If anyone denies that by the grace of our Lord Jesus Christ, which is through Baptism [*sic*], the guilt of original sin is remitted . . . let him be anathema." Sue T. M. DeFerrari, "Baptism (Theology of)," in *New Catholic Encyclopedia,* 2:63.
40. After examining this problem of unbaptized infants, the Roman Catholic author, George Dyer, wonders if they might possibly be in heaven instead of limbo. "Is there any possibility, they [the unbaptized infants' parents] will ask, that the child is in heaven? We must say that the evidence to the contrary is not clear or so compelling that it would force us to deny them all hope of the child's salvation" ("The Unbaptized Infant in Eternity," 153).

This raises the question of whether infant baptism is taught in the Bible.

Should Infants Be Baptized?

Many Protestant and Roman Catholic churches baptize infants. But they do so for different reasons. Churches in the Reformed tradition baptize infants (a) to mark an individual's entrance into the church, and (b) to serve as a sign and seal of the child's participation in the covenant of grace.

On the other hand, many Protestants do not believe infant baptism is biblical because baptism, they assert, is to depict salvation that has already been received through faith in Christ. Since infants cannot believe, it is inappropriate to baptize them. Only those children, youth, or adults who have knowingly turned to Christ for salvation from sin should be baptized.

The following four arguments are the major ones used to support infant baptism, with responses by those who oppose it.

Did the Early Church Practice Infant Baptism?

Small writes, "There is no evidence anywhere in the early church to suggest that infant baptism was not apostolic practice from the early start."[41] Cullmann and Jeremias make much of the point that the first Christians baptized their infants.[42] Aland and Beasley-Murray, however, disagree just as strongly,[43] pointing to evidence that the early church did not baptize babies. Origen (ca. 185–254) is often quoted as saying, "The Church has received a tradition from the apostles to give baptism even to little children."[44] But as Aland argues, if this was the universal practice of the church, why did Origen write a strong polemic for it? This suggests that some pockets of Christians believed differently.[45] As Wamble observes, "Early Christians baptized neither infants nor young children. Literature predating A.D. 200 contains no reference to infant baptism. The evidence in the literature suggests adult baptism as the normal practice."[46]

For example, the earliest Christian manual, the *Didache*, written in the second century, "called for converts to learn Christianity's moral teaching before undergoing baptism,"[47] which obviously would eliminate the baptizing of in-

41. Dwight Hervey Small, *The Biblical Basis for Infant Baptism* (Westwood, N.J.: Fleming H. Revell Co., 1969), 106–7.

42. Oscar Cullmann, *Baptism in the New Testament* (London: SCM Press, 1950); and Joachim Jeremias, *Infant Baptism in the First Four Centuries*, trans. David Cairns (London: SCM Press, 1960).

43. Kurt Aland, *Did the Early Church Baptize Infants?* trans. G. R. Beasley-Murray (Philadelphia: Westminster Press, 1963); and Beasley-Murray, *Baptism in the New Testament*.

44. *Commentary on Romans*, 519 (Patrologia Graeca [Migne], 14, 1047).

45. Aland, *Did the Early Church Baptize Infants?* 47.

46. Hugh Wamble, "Historic Practices Regarding Children," in *Children and Conversion*, 71.

47. Ibid., 71–72.

fants. Aristides referred to baptizing children only after they are old enough to understand instruction about its meaning.[48] Irenaeus (ca. 130–202), rather than advocating infant baptism as Jeremias has suggested,[49] wrote that baptism is for those who have faith in Christ.[50] Writing about baptism, neither Justin Martyr (ca. 100–165) nor Clement of Alexandria (ca. 150–ca. 220) make mention of infant baptism.[51] Tertullian (ca. 160–ca. 215), of Carthage, felt that baptism should follow instruction and that repentance is a requirement for baptism.[52] Hippolytus (d. ca. 236) wrote that baptism was for adults and normally required a probationary period of three years.[53] On the other hand, Cyprian (ca. 200–258), bishop of Carthage, favored baptizing infants. Gregory of Nazianzus (ca. 325–390) "defended the baptism of children, but he nevertheless set the age of three as a lower limit for the reason, he says, that people should have some memory of the experience."[54] Also Chrysostom (ca. 345–370) favored the practice.[55] Augustine (354–430) advocated infant baptism as the means of removing original sin, which all mankind has inherited by their participation in Adam's sin. Roman Catholicism extended this view to propound the teaching that baptism is necessary for salvation or spiritual birth. The first clear testimonies for infant baptism emerged then, "about the first half of the third century."[56] While infant baptism was the most frequent practice of the church after A.D. 400, for more than twelve centuries, believers' baptism was the normal procedure in the earliest years of the church.

Did Household Baptism Include Infants?

While an examination of the history of the practice of infant baptism is helpful in studying this issue, of greater importance is what the New Testament says on the matter. Those who favor baptizing infants refer to household baptisms in the New Testament. When an adult believed in Christ and was baptized with his "household," it is argued that infants were, no doubt, present in those families and, therefore, they too would have been baptized.

48. Aristides *Apology* 15.6.

49. Jeremias, *Infant Baptism in the First Four Centuries,* 73.

50. Irenaeus *Against Heresies* 4.23.2. See Argyle, in A. Gilmore, ed., *Christian Baptism* (Valley Forge, Penn.: Judson Press, 1959), 198.

51. Arthur S. Yates, *Why Baptize Infants?* (Norwich: Canterbury Press, 1993), 39, 46–47.

52. Children should be baptized, Tertullian said, not as infants, but "when they are growing up, when they are learning, when they are being taught what they are coming to, when they have become competent to know Christ" (*De Baptismo* 18.4; cf. *De Paenitentia* 6.3.24). For a full discussion of Tertullian's comments on baptism in these tracts and also in his *De Anima,* see Aland, *Did the Early Church Baptize Infants?* 61–69, and Yates, *Why Baptize Infants?* 41–44.

53. Yates, *Why Baptize Infants?* 40.

54. Jeschke, *Believers' Baptism for Children of the Church,* 82. Also see Yates, *Why Baptize Infants?* 61.

55. Aland, *Did the Early Church Baptize Infants?* 79.

56. Ibid., 61.

These heads of households include Cornelius, Lydia, the Philippian jailer, Crispus, and Stephanas. When Peter told the apostles his experience in leading Cornelius to Christ, he reported that an angel who appeared to Cornelius said, "He will bring you a message through which you and all your household will be saved" (Acts 11:14). When Paul led Lydia to Christ, Luke wrote that after "the Lord opened her heart to respond to Paul's message . . . she and the members of her household were baptized" (16:14–15). Paul told the Philippian jailer, "Believe in the Lord Jesus and you will be saved—you and your household" (16:31). When Paul spoke to him "and to all the others in his house . . . he and all his family were baptized . . . he was filled with joy because they had come to believe in God" (16:32–34). In Corinth a synagogue ruler named Crispus heard Paul teaching and he "and his entire household believed in the Lord" (18:8). Writing to the Corinthians, Paul reminded them that he baptized only a few people, including Crispus, Gaius, and "the household of Stephanas" (1 Cor. 1:14–16).

Do these passages support the view that infants were included in these families and that they were, therefore, baptized as babies, and that the faith of the father (or mother, in the case of Lydia) substituted for the faith of the infants? Since no one of these passages explicitly mentions infants, it is an assumption that babies were present (nor admittedly, do the passages specify that infants were not present). Advocates of pedobaptism (baptism of infants) say it is reasonable to expect infants to have been present and then baptized. However, this is clearly an argument from silence, which, therefore, has relatively little weight. Berkhof, a covenant theologian and pedobaptist, admits there is no explicit instance in the New Testament that refers to children being baptized.[57] And Bromiley, a strong advocate of infant baptism, admits that "the accounts of household baptisms do not expressly state that small children were included," and "there is no specific command either to baptize or not to baptize infants."[58] Marcel, a French Reformed pastor, admits, "It is naturally possible, though not probable, that none of these 'houses' contained little children."[59]

In addition to the absence of references to infants, other factors in the household baptisms speak strongly *against* infants being baptized. In Cornelius's household, which included not only his family but also other relatives and close friends (Acts 10:24), "the Holy Spirit came on all who heard the

57. Louis Berkhof, *Systematic Theology* (Grand Rapids: Wm. B. Eerdmans Publishing Co., 1968), 632. Years ago H. R. Mackintosh, a Presbyterian theologian, wrote that we must "admit it frankly" that the New Testament is silent on the practice of infant baptism ("Thoughts on Infant Baptism," *Expositor* 13 [1917]: 195).

58. Geoffrey W. Bromiley, *Children of Promise: The Case for Baptizing Infants* (Grand Rapids: Wm. B. Eerdmans Publishing Co., 1979), 3, 11.

59. Pierre Ch. Marcel, *The Biblical Doctrine of Infant Baptism*, trans. Philip Edgcumbe Hughes (Cambridge: James Clarke & Co., 1953), 196.

message" and they spoke in tongues and then were baptized with water (10:44, 46–47; 11:15–17). Since *all* his household heard the gospel (11:14) and the Holy Spirit came on all of them, it is preposterous to conclude that the Holy Spirit came on infants, that infants spoke in tongues, and that infants were baptized![60]

Similarly, in the Philippian jailer's household, all who heard the word of the Lord were baptized, and ate, and rejoiced in their salvation (16:32–34). Are we to assume that in the early hours of the morning (after midnight, 16:25) the babies were brought out of their beds and listened to the message and were baptized and then "rejoiced with the servants at their father's faith in God as they joined the meal with Paul and Silas"?[61] This hardly seems probable.

Some respond by pointing to Paul's words in Acts 16:31, "Believe in the Lord Jesus, and you will be saved—you and your household." They suggest that the jailer exercised faith on behalf of others in his family. However, this verse, as Greek authority Alford observes, does not mean the jailer's faith would save his family, but that they could be saved the same way he was.[62]

Nor does the case of Crispus support the notion that his faith alone sufficed for the faith of others. The fact that "his entire household believed in the Lord" (Acts 18:8) clearly states that the numbers of his family each individually believed in Jesus. Since they and other Corinthians who believed were baptized, how could infants have been included since they are not old enough to exercise faith? To suggest that infants were included among those believers who were baptized is to read into the passage something that is not there.

If Stephanas's household included infants who were baptized with him, then one must also conclude that those infants were serving the saints, as part of his household (1 Cor. 16:15), and were to be respected and obeyed by the congregation (16:16). Therefore, "it is difficult to see how any consistency can be maintained between these two statements [1 Cor. 1:16 and 16:15] without assuming that the household of Stephanas was a group of adults."[63]

One of the reasons infant baptism proponents say babies were involved in these cases of household salvation is their emphasis on the solidarity of the family in Bible times. While it is true that the father was considered the head of the family, and while it is true that children in Israelite families were born into the nation with whom God had a special covenant relationship, it does not follow that the faith of a father served as a surrogate for the faith of his

60. Beasley-Murray, *Baptism in the New Testament*, 315; and George R. Beasley-Murray, *Baptism Today and Tomorrow* (New York: St. Martin's Press, 1966), 118.

61. Beasley-Murray, *Baptism in the New Testament*, 315.

62. Henry Alford, *The Greek Testament* (reprint [4 vols. in 2], Chicago: Moody Press, 1958), 2:184. Cf. R. J. Knowling, "The Acts of the Apostles," in *The Expositor's Greek Testament*, ed. W. Robertson Nicole, 5 vols. (Grand Rapids: Wm. B. Eerdmans Publishing Co., 1951), 2:352.

63. William B. Coble, "Problems Related to New Testament Teachings," in *Children and Conversion*, 66.

children. Furthermore, their view of this kind of spiritual family solidarity has led some advocates of infant baptism to challenge the concept of individual salvation. Marcel, for example, wrote, "A careful study of the idea of conversion would show that it is not a typically individual phenomenon."[64] However, in view of individual responsibility before God and the need for personal faith to be exercised in order to receive salvation, it seems strange that such a view should be suggested. Again this shows the weakness of the system of pedobaptism.

Acts 2:39 is used by infant baptism supporters to buttress their view. Following verse 38, which affirms that those who repent will have their sins forgiven and will receive the gift of the Holy Spirit, Peter said in verse 39, "The promise is for you and your children and for all who are far off—for all whom the Lord our God will call." The promise refers to the Holy Spirit, who will be given to those who turn to the Lord and are baptized. Advocates of the infant baptism rite say that "you and your children" implies that infants, as well as adults, should be baptized. However, verse 39 means that the children of Peter's adult hearers may be saved (and receive forgiveness of sins and the Holy Spirit) the same way the parents were saved, that is, by repentance. This implies a knowledge of the way of salvation and the exercise of faith. Acts 2:38–39, then, is similar to Acts 16:31: Adults and children can be regenerated only by turning to Christ in faith. Those "who are far off" (Acts 2:39) are Gentiles (Eph. 2:13, 17, 19), who also may receive the gift of salvation and the blessing of the Holy Spirit by faith in Christ.

First Corinthians 7:14 is another verse often referred to by those favoring infant baptism. "For the unbelieving husband has been sanctified through his wife, and the unbelieving wife has been sanctified through her believing husband. Otherwise your children would be unclean, but as it is, they are holy." They suggest that since a child of at least one believing parent is already "sanctified," the child is already saved and that, therefore, children of Christian parents should be baptized in anticipation of their holy or sanctified position. Calvin wrote, "In view of the fact that children of believers are exempt from the common condition of mankind, in order to be set apart for the Lord, why should we keep them back from the sign [of infant baptism]?"[65] However, the point of the verse is that in some homes one spouse became a believer while one remained unsaved, and that, therefore, the children were under the helpful spiritual influence of at least one Christian parent. Only in this sense of a favorable family environment were they "set apart" (the meaning of "sanctified") to the Lord. Rather than feeling any obligation to break up the marriage, the Christian partner should maintain the marriage for the sake of the

---

64. Marcel, *The Biblical Doctrine of Infant Baptism,* 119.
65. John Calvin, *The First Epistle of Paul the Apostle to the Corinthians,* trans. John W. Fraser (Grand Rapids: Wm. B. Eerdmans Publishing Co., 1960), 149–50.

children. It should be evident that 1 Corinthians 7:14 says nothing about baptism. As Jeremias admitted, we must "be content with the conclusion that 1 Corinthians 7:14 bears no reference to baptism."[66]

Does the Covenant of Grace Suggest Infant Baptism?

Another reason given in support of baptizing infants is that they are born into God's covenant of grace. The reasoning given in support of this view may be summarized as follows:

1. The Old and New Testaments speak of one covenant of grace, God's plan by which he has willed to give man justification.
2. In the Old Testament, circumcision was the sign and seal of being a participant in the covenant of grace.
3. A continuity exists in the people of God, a continuity in which the nation Israel was the church of the Old Testament and the New Testament church is the new Israel.
4. Therefore, infant baptism in this age has the same significance as and replaces circumcision of the Old Testament, and is the seal of one's being in the covenant people of God.

Regarding point 2, Marcel wrote that circumcision was given to Abraham "as a sign and seal of the remission of sins" and was "the sacrament of admission into the covenant of grace."[67]

Regarding point 3, covenant theologians say, as Marcel put it, that *"the church has been and remains one: the nation of Israel was the Church...."*[68] Bromiley states forthrightly, "The church is the Israel of God,"[69] and Murray asserts that "the church is generally one in both Testaments."[70]

Regarding point 4, Marcel writes that "baptism is the sacrament of entry into the covenant of grace" because "in the New Testament dispensation baptism has taken the place of circumcision."[71] The foundation for infant baptism, he asserts repeatedly, is the covenant of grace.[72] The basic premise for infant baptism, according to Murray, is that the New Testament economy is the unfolding and fulfillment of the covenant made with Abraham.[73]

Several points of criticism are in order. First, the covenant of grace, emphasized repeatedly by covenant theologians, is nowhere mentioned in the Bible. Of course, the Bible does not mention other theological terms that express

66. Jeremias, *Infant Baptism in the First Four Centuries,* 48.
67. Marcel, *The Biblical Doctrine of Infant Baptism,* 155–56.
68. Ibid., 95 (italics his).
69. Bromiley, *Children of Promise,* 107.
70. John Murray, *Christian Baptism* (Nutley, N.J.: Reformed Publishing Co., 1977), 48.
71. Marcel, *The Biblical Doctrine of Infant Baptism,* 154–155.
72. Ibid., 86, 151, 196.
73. Murray, *Christian Baptism,* 48.

sound doctrine such as the Trinity. But if the covenant of grace is so central to the continuity of the Old and New Testaments, is it not surprising that the Bible never refers even once to that covenant? True, God's covenant with Abraham (Gen. 12; 15; 17) stemmed totally from his grace. But so did other Old Testament covenants, including the Davidic Covenant in 2 Samuel 7 (which covenant theologians seldom discuss) and the New Covenant (Jer. 31; Ezek. 36).

Second, circumcision did, in fact, serve as the sign that Old Testament believers who descended from Abraham were recipients of the blessings of the Abrahamic Covenant. But some questions need to be asked in this connection. In what sense could circumcision be called the "seal" of that covenant, a term covenant theology proponents often use?[74] Does this mean that circumcision guaranteed an individual's continuance as a member of the covenant people? If so, what about circumcised Israelites who were cut off or banished from the nation because of disobedience, or were punished by God for abandoning his Law? How did circumcision "seal" them? Did not Paul write that "not all who descended from Israel are Israel" (Rom. 9:6), that is, not all those who were born as Israelites and were circumcised placed their faith in Yahweh?

Third, while individuals in every age are saved in the same way, namely, through faith in God's grace, the Bible nowhere refers to Old Testament believers as the "church" or to New Testament believers as the "new Israel."[75]

Fourth, equating Israel with the church overlooks the distinctive nature of the church, the body of Christ, which began on the day of Pentecost (cf. Matt. 16:18 with Acts 1:6) and will continue until Christ returns to rapture the church to heaven. The equal standing of believing Jews and Gentiles into a unique body as Christ's members was a mystery unknown in the Old Testament (Rom. 16:25; Eph. 3:4–6; Col. 1:26). First Corinthians 10:32 distinguishes between the nation Israel, the church, and unbelieving Gentiles.

Fifth, covenant theology emphasizes spiritual blessings in the covenant made with Abraham and overlooks the fact that God also made promises to Abraham that his physical descendants will someday as a nation possess a land area described in Genesis 15:18–21 in which specific boundaries are designated. To say the church is a continuation of the nation Israel and that the church inherits these land promises in some spiritual way defies the clear, natural language of Scripture. These land promises, yet to be fulfilled by Israel, point to a clear distinction between Israel and the church, a distinction

---

74. For example, "Circumcision was the sign and seal of the covenant administered to Abraham" (ibid.).

75. The term "Israel of God" in Galatians 6:16 does not equate church-age believers with Old Testament Israel. Instead it refers to Jews in the present Church Age who become Christians, members of the body of Christ, through faith in him. For a defense of this view see John Eadie, *Commentary on the Epistle of Paul to the Galatians* (1884; reprint, Minneapolis: James and Klock Christian Publishing Co., 1977), 470–71.

that is obliterated if the church is the new Israel and if baptism has the same significance as circumcision.

Sixth, nowhere does the Bible state that baptism and circumcision signify the same thing, or that the one replaces or supersedes the other. To say they do is to argue totally from silence. They cannot signify the same (viz., membership in the covenant people) in light of numerous differences: *(a)* Children of believing parents today are not born as Israelites. *(b)* Children of believing parents today are not promised a future inheritance in the land of Israel. *(c)* Circumcision was applied only to males, whereas today baptism of believers is for both males and females.[76] *(d)* Baptism in the New Testament followed salvation, whereas circumcision was performed on males eight days old.

Early Jewish Christians who had circumcised their male children also baptized converts. Therefore, since the two rites continued to exist among Jewish believers in the early years of the apostolic church, "there was little likelihood of baptism being seen as the fulfillment of the Jewish rite; nor would the two rites be given the same meaning."[77]

Seventh, Colossians 2:11 does not support the covenant theologians' position that Paul said baptism "replaced circumcision,"[78] and that "it is very probable" that this baptism includes infants.[79] Instead Paul argued that spiritual baptism—being placed into the body of Christ by the Holy Spirit at salvation (1 Cor. 12:13)—identifies the believer with Christ, and that a physical rite such as circumcision has no avail for salvation. "Paul did not have in mind the setting aside of circumcision by baptism,"[80] as if one replaced and continued the other.[81] In fact Colossians 2:11 says nothing about infants! He was

76. Calvin's response to this objection is quite weak, stating that women, though unable to receive circumcision, "yet shared in a certain sense in the circumcision of the male" (*Institutes of the Christian Religion*, 4.16.16). Strangely, Murray tries to get around this objection by simply asserting, "this difference in no way affects the fact that . . . baptism takes the place of circumcision as the sign and seal of the covenant" (Murray, *Christian Baptism*, 76). But this does not answer the objection; it simply reasserts his position without any defense of it.

Yates wisely asks, "If the baptism of infant boys necessarily relates back to circumcision in the old covenant, to what does the baptism of infant girls relate back?" (*Why Baptize Infants?* 96).

77. Yates, *Why Baptize Infants?* 93.

78. Jeremias, *Infant Baptism in the First Four Centuries*, 47.

79. Ibid., 48.

80. Aland, *Did the Early Church Baptize Infants?* 84.

81. Hunt points out that the analogy between circumcision and baptism in Colossians 2:11–12 was not used as an argument for infant baptism until *after* the mid-third century when the practice was already established. Tertullian's *De Baptismo* (ca. 200), which argues against infant baptism, makes no mention of these verses being used to support the baptism of infants as superseding circumcision. The same is true, Hunt observes, regarding Origen's and Cyprian's discussions on baptism. Hunt correctly observes that the circumcision mentioned in Colossians 2:11–12 refers not to water baptism but to the believer's union with Christ in his death (J. P. T. Hunt, "Colossians 2:11–12, The Circumcision/Baptism Analogy, and Infant Baptism," *Tyndale Bulletin* 41 [1990]: 227–44).

emphasizing, instead, that salvation is a kind of circumcision in which the believer has put off his old way of life and has a new life with Christ.

Another verse covenant theologians use to support the baptism of infants is Matthew 19:14 (cf. Mark 10:14; Luke 18:16), which records Jesus' words, "Let the little children come to me, and do not hinder them, for the kingdom of heaven belongs to such as these." Marcel argues that if children are in the kingdom of heaven, this proves they are in the covenant and, therefore, should be baptized.[82] Problems with this reasoning are that (a) Jesus was not saying *all* children are in the kingdom (many come to an age of accountability and do not turn to Jesus for salvation), and (b) the verse says nothing about baptism or the covenant of grace.

Some infant baptism advocates say this verse supports that practice because the command "do not hinder these" suggests a baptismal formula used in other verses on baptism (Acts 8:36; 10:47; 11:17).[83] But this thought is foreign to the context.[84]

Eighth, infant baptism fails to distinguish clearly between a ritual and the reality of salvation. Perhaps covenant theologians do not intend to convey that infant baptism regenerates, but their language often seems to indicate just that. Some of their statements come alarmingly close to baptismal regeneration. The following quotations illustrate this confusion and lack of clarity.

"The sign [of infant baptism] . . . opens to them a door into the church, that, adopted into it, they may be enrolled among the heirs of the Kingdom of heaven."[85]

Baptism of infants means they are "being engrafted into the body of the church," and are "rightly considered a part of the church, since they have been called heirs of the Kingdom of Heaven."[86]

"Because by the blessing of the promise they already belonged to the body of Christ, they are received into the church with this solemn sign [of infant baptism]."[87]

"Baptized infants are to be received as the children of God and treated accordingly."[88]

---

82. Marcel, *The Biblical Doctrine of Infant Baptism*, 122.

83. Oscar Cullmann, *Baptism in the New Testament*, trans. J. K. S. Reid (London: SCM Press, 1950), 73–80; J. Duncan M. Derrett, "Why Jesus Blessed the Children (Mark 10:13–16 par.)," *Novum Testamentum* 25 (1983): 7; Michael Green, *Baptism: Its Purpose, Practice and Power* (Downers Grove, Ill.: InterVarsity Press, 1987), 72; and Jeremias, *Infant Baptism in the First Four Centuries*, 53–54.

84. John Nolland, *Luke 9:21–18:34*, Word Biblical Commentary (Dallas, Tex.: Word Books, Publisher, 1993), 87.

85. Calvin, *Institutes of the Christian Religion*, 4.16.7.

86. Ibid., 4.16.9; 4.16.22.

87. Ibid., 4.15.22.

88. Murray, *Christian Baptism*, 59.

"Children by baptism . . . are Christians, and federally before baptism, and therefore they are baptized."[89]

"Baptism signifies and seals what lies at the basis and inception of a state of salvation, to wit, union with Christ, cleansing from the pollution of sin, and cleansing from the guilt of sin."[90]

Baptism "signifies union with Christ, purifying from the pollution of sin by regeneration of the Spirit, and purifying from the guilt of sin by the blood of Christ."[91]

"Baptism signifies union with Christ and membership in his body . . . baptism is for infants . . . the divine testimony of their union with Christ . . . [infants] are susceptible to God's efficacious grace in uniting them to Christ, in regenerating them by His Spirit, and in sprinkling them with the blood of his Son."[92]

"Baptism declares the inward regenerative operation of the Holy Spirit which makes us conformable to Jesus Christ."[93]

"Every reason exists to believe that the Holy Spirit has begun his work within" baptized children of confessing parents.[94]

"The baptism of infants . . . signifies the regenerative ministry of the Holy Spirit by which infant faith is possible, and without it an entry into the vicarious reconciliation of the Son according to the election of the Father."[95]

"This . . . substantiates the principle that the infant children of believers are rightful heirs of the covenant promises."[96]

"Baptism given to little children is the witness and attestation of their salvation. . . ."[97]

"What happens in the actual administration of the sacrament is that the individual baptized is thereby set by God within the Body of Christ."[98]

"Baptism is the initiation of the Christian person. It is his inclusion in the salvation history of God. It is the incorporation into the church, the Body of Christ."[99]

Part of the confusion stems from the failure to distinguish between the visible, local church (which in some cases includes unbelievers) and the invisible, universal church (the body of Christ, which includes all believers in the

89. Directory for the Public Worship of God, prepared by the Westminster Assembly, cited in ibid., 59, n. 31.
90. Murray, *Christian Baptism*, 77.
91. Ibid., 89.
92. Ibid., 90.
93. Bromiley, *Children of Promise*, 77.
94. Ibid., 80.
95. Ibid., 100.
96. Small, *The Biblical Basis for Infant Baptism*, 99.
97. Marcel, *The Biblical Doctrine of Infant Baptism*, 213.
98. Donald M. Baillie, *The Theology of the Sacraments* (New York: Charles Scribner, 1957), 89.
99. Green, *Baptism: Its Purpose, Practice and Power*, 120.

present Church Age). Another reason for the confusion lies in the failure to differentiate clearly between being a member of a covenant people and being a true child of God.

As a result, this practice wrongly leads many people baptized in infancy "to presume that they have been regenerated, and thereby they fail to feel the urgency of their need to come to personal faith in Christ."[100] Also, if infant baptism symbolizes future regeneration, it does not always do so, because some who are baptized as infants never come to saving faith later.

Ninth, some covenant theologians assert that if unbaptized infants die they will be saved.[101] But if that is the case (which I believe to be true), then the baptism of any infants at all seems unnecessary.

Tenth, those who advocate the baptismal rite for infants say that faith need not precede baptism, and yet at other times they argue that the ordinance cannot mean anything apart from faith.[102]

Eleventh, covenant theology's view of infant baptism demolishes the biblical concept of individual faith in Christ. Nowhere does the Bible allow for parents or anyone else exercising faith vicariously for another individual. As Kümmel put it, "The New Testament knows in no form a 'vicarious faith,' when it has to do with the question of gaining *sōtēria,* salvation."[103]

Salvation is guaranteed not by baptism, but by personal faith in Christ. To say that baptizing an infant places him or her into the body of Christ comes dangerously close to baptismal regeneration.

In the Reformation era, the Anabaptists strongly opposed infant baptism. Their reasoning followed this syllogism: (1) Water baptism is to be administered to those who have placed their faith in Jesus Christ. (2) Infants cannot exercise personal faith in Christ. (3) Therefore, baptism should not be administered to infants.[104] January 21, 1525, officially marks the beginning of the Anabaptist movement in Zurich, Switzerland, when Conrad Grebel baptized George Blaurock, and Blaurock then baptized others gathered in Feliz Manz's mother's home. From the study of

100. Wayne Grudem, *Systematic Theology* (Grand Rapids: Zondervan Publishing House, 1994), 980.

101. For example, Bromiley, *Children of Promise,* 102.

102. Small, *The Biblical Basis for Infant Baptism,* 84, 88–89. Small's answer to this objection is that repentance and faith are required of adults who come to Christ for salvation and are then baptized. However, this means there are two kinds of water baptism: one requiring faith (for adults) and the other not requiring faith (for infants). But the Bible says absolutely nothing about two kinds of baptism, one without faith and one with faith.

103. W. G. Kümmel, in *Theologische Rundschau* 1 (1950), 37, cited by Beasley-Murray, *Baptism in the New Testament,* 350.

104. Marcel argues against adult baptism by saying that if faith is a necessary condition of salvation (he believes it is not necessary), and since children cannot believe, children dying in infancy are condemned forever (Marcel, *The Biblical Doctrine of Infant Baptism,* 215). However, this makes no provision for what Calvin taught, namely, that God can exercise his grace on infants who die, thereby taking them to heaven.

the Scriptures these Swiss brethren believed their own infant baptism was of no value and so they received baptism as adults. They also affirmed that the church consists not of every citizen baptized as an infant (many of whom were not loyal to Christ but nonetheless were members of the church[105]), but of only baptized adult believers determined to follow Christ as his obedient disciples. Therefore, the church was redefined as a fellowship of true believers, separate from the state.

The early Anabaptist confession known as the Schleitheim Confession was drawn up by Michael Sattler and accepted by a gathering of Anabaptists on February 24, 1527. Its first article reads in part, "Baptism shall be given to all who have learned repentance and amendment of life, and who believe truly that their sins are taken away by Christ. . . . This excludes all infant baptism, the highest and chief abomination of the pope."[106]

The opposition of the Reformers against this so-called "heresy" was so strong that many Anabaptists were executed by drowning, beheading, or burning at the stake and many more were severely persecuted and imprisoned.[107]

Twelfth, to baptize infants is to make the ordinance of water baptism into something far different from its intention in the New Testament. The purpose of baptism was not to anticipate possible future faith of infants, or to substitute adult faith in place of infants who cannot believe, or to place infants into a covenant relationship. Nowhere does the Bible specify any of these purposes. Instead, baptism pictures one's personal faith in Christ; portrays his spiritual identity with Christ's death, burial, and resurrection; and depicts his dedication and devotion to Christ as one who is committed to serve him as his loyal disciple.[108] As Balthasar Hübmaier, the leading Anabaptist theologian of the sixteenth century, wrote on July 11, 1525, in the first of his six books and pamphlets on baptism, this ordinance is "a public confession and testimony of an inward faith."[109]

---

105. Beasley-Murray, *Baptism in the New Testament*, 371, 374.

106. "The Schleitheim Confession," in *Anabaptist Beginnings (1523–1533): A Source Book* 101 (also cited in W. J. McGlothlin, *Baptist Confessions of Faith* [Philadelphia: American Baptist Publication Society, 1911], 3–4), and in John H. Yoder, trans. and ed., *The Legacy of Michael Sattler* [Scottdale, Penn.: Herald Press, 1973], 36).

107. Thieleman J. van Braught, *Martyrs Mirror*, 10th ed. (Scottdale, Penn.: Herald Press, 1975), reports numerous accounts of Anabaptists who suffered and died for their faith, refusing to relinquish their practice of believers' baptism and refusing to baptize infants. My own ancestor, Hans Zaugg (the Swiss spelling of Zuck, and my own seven–great grandfather), an Anabaptist preacher, was imprisoned by the Reformed Church in Bern, Switzerland from January 31, 1659 to September 10, 1660 because of his firm convictions on this subject.

108. For a helpful discussion of baptism in relation to discipleship see Richard E. Averbeck, "The Focus of Baptism in the New Testament," *Grace Theological Journal* 2 (Fall 1981):265–301.

After the converts on the day of Pentecost, the Samaritans, the Ethiopian eunuch, Paul, Cornelius, the Philippian jailer, Lydia, Crispus, and the Ephesian "disciples" each believed in the Lord, *then* they were baptized (Acts 2:41; 8:12, 35–38; 9:18; 10:44, 47–48; 16:31–34; 18:8; 19:4–5). Even Jesus' Great Commission suggests that disciples, not infants, are to be the recipients of water baptism (Matt. 28:19). The New Testament pattern, then, points clearly to baptism as a vital sign of regeneration *by* Christ, a visual symbol of union *with* Christ, and a veritable signal of dedication *to* Christ.

What Is the Age of Accountability?

If infants who die go to heaven, then what about children who grow beyond infancy? At what age do they become accountable for their sin and thus in need of placing personal faith in Christ for salvation?

As stated earlier in this chapter, a number of verses support the view that all individuals are born with a sin nature, inherited from Adam. David wrote that God viewed him as a sinner from the time of his birth—and even from his conception, which suggests that the sin nature is passed from generation to generation. "Surely I was sinful at birth, sinful from the time my mother conceived me" (Ps. 51:5). David also affirmed this truth in Psalm 58:3: "Even from birth the wicked go astray; from the womb they are wayward and speak lies." "By nature," Paul wrote, we are "children of wrath" (Eph. 2:3), that is, born with a corrupt sinful nature that places us under God's wrath.

As already noted, Augustine believed that infants who die are condemned to hell, but if they were baptized they will go to heaven. This view rules out any need for considering a so-called "age of accountability."

Many who oppose Augustine's view, however, maintain that children dying as infants go to heaven, whether baptized or not. Some hold that such babies will be in heaven because they are innocent of original sin (and thus not counted guilty before God), whereas others say dying infants go to heaven because Christ's atoning work covers their imputed sin nature.

To say that dying infants will be in heaven because they were born innocent runs counter to the verses already cited. It also means that children come to a time in their growth when they pass from innocence to sinful actions, to an age when they deliberately and knowingly sin and are, therefore, accountable to God.

Erickson maintains this view, stating that "children are not under God's condemnation for [Adam's] sin, at least not until attaining an age of responsibility in moral and spiritual matters."[110] Until they reach such an "age of un-

---

109. *Vom christlichen Tauf* ("Concerning Christian Baptism"), cited by William R. Estep, *The Anabaptist Story*, rev. ed. (Grand Rapids: Wm. B. Eerdmans Publishing Co., 1975), 155.

110. Millard J. Erickson, *Christian Theology* (Grand Rapids: Baker Book House, 1985), 638.

derstanding and responsibility,"[111] they have only a "conditional imputation of guilt," are innocent, and without condemnation.[112] The age of responsibility, he suggests, is when a child accepts the fact of his corrupt nature and becomes aware of his tendency to sin.[113] One reason he holds this view that young children are not "sinful, condemned, and lost"[114] is that Jesus spoke of them as exemplary individuals who will inherit the kingdom of God (Matt. 18:3; 19:14). Coleman and Goff's view is similar: "At some point in the child's development he becomes aware of his hostile attitudes and is no longer innocent in his relationship to the Father."[115]

This view, however, overlooks verses that affirm that the sin nature is inherited at birth, and that the human race is condemned before God because of that imputed sin. This view also means that some will be in heaven on the basis of their innocence, rather than on the basis of Christ's redemptive work. Since the Bible nowhere speaks of a "conditional" imputation of sin or of supposedly innocent children becoming sinful, this view seems less than preferable.

Another view is that people are responsible to God "when confronted by Christ," implying that up to that time they are not accountable for their sin. "If they should learn of Christ and reject him, they are brought to full responsibility and full condemnation."[116] Sin is not inherited from Adam; it is a personal choice.[117] Children are sinners not because they inherit a sin nature, but because they willfully sin.[118] However, this too overlooks verses in Scripture that attest that Adam's sin is imparted to the entire human race and that each one is born with a sinful nature. And because of that sin nature, individuals commit acts of sin. They are, therefore, guilty before God long before they are knowingly confronted with the message of Christ.

This sinful nature "manifests itself certainly within the first two years of a child's life, as anyone who has raised children can affirm."[119] But when is a child accountable to God for his sin? Or, stated differently, when is a child capable of believing in Christ? Most evangelicals agree that a specific age is impossible to identify,[120] since the rate of spiritual development differs from child to child and since the Bible does not designate such an age. The Bible

111. Ibid., 1103.
112. Ibid., 639.
113. Ibid.
114. Ibid., 638.
115. Robert E. Coleman and Lois Goff, "Winning the Children," *Asbury Seminarian* 26 (October 1972): 11.
116. William Hendricks, "The Age of Accountability," in *Children and Conversion*, 85, 87.
117. Ibid., 88.
118. Timothy Boyd, "Accountability, Age of," in *Holman Bible Dictionary* (Nashville: Holman Bible Publishers, 1991), 13.
119. Grudem, *Systematic Theology*, 500.
120. For example, Hendricks, "The Age of Accountability," 95; Inchley, *Kids and the Kingdom*, 159; and Lightner, *Heaven for Those Who Can't Believe*, 49.

points up the fact of accountability, not a specific age of accountability. "So then, each of us will give an account of himself to God" (Rom. 14:12). Some writers, however, have offered opinions on such an age: between seven and eleven,[121] age nine and above,[122] or adolescence.[123] Others place the age much earlier, such as three or four years of age,[124] or, as the theologian Strong suggests, five, seven, ten, or twelve.[125]

While the age varies from child to child, individual accountability seems to begin when the child "is old enough to sin consciously and deliberately,"[126] and old enough to comprehend the basic truths of the gospel. The age of accountability begins with "the first moment of [a child's] moral consciousness,"[127] and when he is old enough to understand that Christ died for him and that he can be saved by placing his trust in Christ. Deuteronomy 1:39 suggests that very young children have not yet reached a time of personal accountability for sin, for they "do not yet know good from bad." The Hebrew word rendered "little ones" in this verse is *ṭap*, which means, as discussed in chapter 9, preschoolers or young children who often skip along.

Children raised in Christian homes or who receive Christian instruction early in life often respond at younger ages than others. Parents whose children receive Christ as their Savior at the age of four or five may occasionally wonder if those youngsters' conversions are genuine. But the genuineness of that experience need not be doubted if the child clearly understood the awfulness of his sin and genuinely trusted in Jesus to forgive his sins and to take him to heaven. Jesus made it clear that young children can be saved, for he referred to "little ones who believe in me" (Matt. 18:6).[128] On the other hand, parents and teachers ought not pressure young children to receive Jesus Christ as their Savior; they should wait till the Holy Spirit has clearly spoken to their hearts, prompting them to turn to Jesus. An early childhood conversion can sometimes result in those children in later years, such as early adolescence, questioning their assurance. Parents and teachers can help prevent or lessen such a time of doubting by discussing with children the significance of their expe-

121. Inchley, *Kids and the Kingdom*, 163.
122. Hendricks, "The Age of Accountability," 95.
123. Jeschke, *Believers' Baptism for Children of the Church*, 112; and Robert H. Fischer, "The Proper Age for a Declaration of Faith," *Religious Education* 58 (September–October 1963):434. Tertullian wrote, "We maintain that the puberty of soul coincides with that of the body . . . at about the fourteenth year of life" (*De Anima* 38.1).
124. Coleman and Goff, "Winning the Children," 11. As discussed in chapter 1, many children have been saved in their preschool years.
125. Augustus H. Strong, "The Conversion of Children," *Watchman-Examiner*, September 23, 1965, 584. (This article is an abstract of a sermon Strong preached in 1865).
126. Ibid. "Anyone, then, who knows the good he ought to do and doesn't do it, sins" (James 4:17).
127. Ibid.
128. "*It is a mistake to set an arbitrary age for conversion. It is likewise a mistake to ignore the capacity of given age levels*" to believe in Jesus (Hendricks, "The Age of Accountability," 95 [italics his]).

rience in having come to Christ, and by nurturing them in spiritual truths.[129] Some boys or girls who were saved at an early age later are led by the Holy Spirit to rededicate their lives to Christ, thus affirming the sincerity of their desire to live for him.

Inviting children to be saved needs to be done carefully, and children who respond need to be nurtured.[130] Even in Christian homes conversion of children should be encouraged. One need not follow the reactionary view of Horace Bushnell, who insisted that a child of believing parents should "grow up a Christian, and never know himself as being otherwise."[131] Realization of sin must be present for salvation to occur.[132] Growing up to believe he or she has always been a Christian can be as troubling to those in later childhood or early adolescence as those who were converted at an early age. Bushnell's approach, while seeking to counter some extremes of revivalism in his day, neglects the importance of helping children recognize the fact of their sin and see their need of salvation. His emphasis can result in some children or teens questioning whether they are genuinely saved. In other words, salvation should be seen as more than merely "a culmination of an early, progressive response to the love of God."[133]

As parents and teachers lovingly and carefully seek to lead children to Christ and nurture them in their spiritual development, they share in Jesus' own deep and tender love for children—all of whom are "precious in his sight"!

---

129. Edward L. Hayes, "Evangelism of Children," in *Childhood Education in the Church*, 158–59.

130. Hayes gives five helpful pointers on giving evangelistic invitations to children: Ask children to respond "inside" before asking for outward response; make the invitation clear; use natural situations to talk to children about receiving Christ; avoid making the invitation too easy; and avoid group decisions with the young (ibid., 161).

131. Horace Bushnell, *Christian Nurture* (New Haven, Conn.: Yale University Press, 1916), 4. Bushnell added, "In other words, the aim, effort, and expectation should be, not, as is commonly assumed that the child is to grow up in sin, to be converted after he comes to a mature age, but that he is to open on the world as one that is spiritually renewed. . . ." (ibid.).

132. G. Temp Sparkman, "Implications of Conversion among Young Children," *Religious Education* 66 (July–August 1965): 300.

133. Inchley, *Kids and the Kingdom*, 131.

INDEX OF SUBJECTS

INDEX OF NAMES

INDEX OF BIBLICAL NAMES

Index of Scripture References

10:9 54, 75
10:10–11 54
10:12 55
10:18 77
15:33 46
15:34 50, 74
19:18 150, 163
21:10 77
21:11 150, 159
22:9 174
24:3 174
24:9 174
28:28 133
29:5 47, 113
29:7 46n3
29:12 174
30:1 163
30:9–10 163
31:13–15 95
31:15 54
31:17 174
31:31 95
32:16 151n5
33:6 54
42:13 94
42:13–15 100
42:14 64n56
42:14–15 65
42:16 103

Psalms
8:2 19, 150, 154, 216
10:14 174, 175
10:18 174
21:16 216
22:9 58
22:9–10 19
22:18 196
23:5 46, 196
28:9 102
31:5a 196
34:7 210
34:11 132
37:28 113
39:11 124n29
41:9 196
44:1 138
44:1–2 131
44:1–4 131
45:16–17 52
48:6 57

48:13 138
51:5 76, 221, 238
58:3 221, 238
58:8 56
63:6 167n16
68:5 174
68:25 152n7, 179n5
71:5–6 19, 132
71:6 49, 58
71:9 132
71:17 19
71:18 132
78:3–4 132, 138
78:4b 132
78:5 138
78:5–6 103, 131
78:7 132
78:56 138, 138n31
78:63 151
82:3 175
88:1 196
91:11 210
94:6 174
94:12 124
103:13 113
103:14 54
103:17 103
105:8–11 67
109:9 174
109:12 174
110:1 196
110:3 150
111:10 133
113:9 47
113–118 144
118:22 196
118:26 196
119:9 167
119:55 167n16
119:73 75
119:99 128
127:3 46
127:3–5 49
127:4–5 46
127:5 91
128:3 46
128:3–4 49
128:5–6 103
131:2 62, 150
137:9 82
139:13 54, 55

139:13–16 75
139:14 54, 55
139:14–15 54
139:15 54, 55
139:16 54
146:8 113
146:9 174
148:12 151, 152, 167

Proverbs
Book of 122, 133, 134
1:2 133
1:2–7 134
1:3 133n13
1:3–5 133
1:4 133n13, 152
1:7 133
1:7b 122, 123
1:8 128, 129, 136, 136n25, 137, 137n26, 141
1:9 141
1:10 129
1:15 129, 141
1:16 141
1:25 141
1:26 141
1:30 141
1:31 141
2:1 129, 137
2:1–4 141
2:5 141
2:9 133, 134
2:11 134
2:20 166
3:1 129, 137, 137n26, 141, 166
3:2 141
3:3 141
3:4 141
3:5 166
3:5–6a 141
3:6b 141
3:7 141, 166
3:8 141
3:9 141, 166
3:10 141
3:11 124, 129, 141
3:11–12 165
3:12 111, 113, 122, 123, 141
3:21 129, 134, 141